INTERTEMPORAL LINGUISTICS IN INTERNATIONAL LAW

Intertemporal Linguistics in International Law examines and offers an overdue solution to a specific problem central to the resolution of an ever-increasing number of international legal disputes: how to interpret a treaty with terms that change in meaning over time.

A wide-ranging review of the relevant international case law and scholarship reveals that no rule, principle or authority of international law – including even the oft-cited evolutionary interpretation doctrine – provides international adjudicators with the firm and practical guidance on this specific question that contemporary international litigants demand.

Using an analytical approach inspired by the comparative method and drawing on specific concepts from external fields including private law, legal theory and, principally, modern-day linguistics, Intertemporal Linguistics in International Law restructures the most relevant international case law around a new conceptual framework that offers fresh insight into the process of treaty interpretation. It demonstrates that by distinguishing between resolving ambiguity and resolving vagueness, and by identifying the temporal sense-intention with which a treaty term is used, international adjudicators can avail themselves of a more predictable and appropriate method for solving this complex and practically important problem of international law.

Volume 74 in the series Studies in International Law

Studies in International Law

Recent titles in this series

Security and International Law
Edited by Mary E Footer, Julia Schmidt and Nigel D White

Complicity and its Limits in the Law of International Responsibility
Vladyslav Lanovoy

Complicity in International Criminal Law
Marina Aksenova

Arctic Law and Governance: The Role of China and Finland
Edited by Timo Koivurova, Qin Tianbao, Tapio Nykänen and Sébastien Duyck

States, the Law and Access to Refugee Protection: Fortresses and Fairness
Edited by Maria O'Sullivan and Dallal Stevens

Revisiting the Concept of Defence in the Jus ad Bellum: The Dual Face of Defence
Johanna Friman

The International Legal Protection of Persons in Humanitarian Crises
Dug Cubie

The International Committee of the Red Cross and its Mandate to Protect and Assist: Law and Practice
Christy Shucksmith

The Impact of Investment Treaty Law on Host States: Enabling Good Governance
Mavluda Sattorova

Allocating International Responsibility Between Member States and International Organisations
Nikolaos Voulgaris

Predictability and Flexibility in the Law of Maritime Delimitation, 2nd edition
Yoshifumi Tanaka

Feminist Engagement with International Criminal Law: Norm Transfer, Complementarity, Rape and Consent
Eithne Dowds

Asylum Control and Access to Protection: Admission, Readmission and Human Rights
Mariagiulia Giuffré

For a complete list of titles in this series, see www.bloomsburyprofessional.com/uk/series/studies-in-international-law

Intertemporal Linguistics in International Law

Beyond Contemporaneous and Evolutionary Treaty Interpretation

Julian Wyatt

•HART•

OXFORD • LONDON • NEW YORK • NEW DELHI • SYDNEY

HART PUBLISHING

Bloomsbury Publishing Plc

Kemp House, Chawley Park, Cumnor Hill, Oxford, OX2 9PH, UK

1385 Broadway, New York, NY 10018, USA

First published in Great Britain 2019

A catalogue record for this book is available from the British Library.

Library of Congress Cataloging-in-Publication data

Names: Wyatt, Julian, author.

Title: Intertemporal linguistics in international law : beyond contemporaneous and evolutionary treaty interpretation / Julian Wyatt.

Description: Oxford ; New York : Hart, 2019. | Series: Studies in international law ; volume 74 | Includes bibliographical references and index.

Identifiers: LCCN 2019040300 (print) | LCCN 2019040301 (ebook) | ISBN 9781509929498 (hardback) | ISBN 9781509929504 (Epub)

Subjects: LCSH: Treaties—Interpretation and construction. | Treaties—Language. | Historical linguistics. | Forensic linguistics.

Classification: LCC KZ1304 .W93 2019 (print) | LCC KZ1304 (ebook) | DDC 341.01/4—dc23

LC record available at https://lccn.loc.gov/2019040300

LC ebook record available at https://lccn.loc.gov/2019040301

ISBN: HB: 978-1-50992-949-8
ePDF: 978-1-50992-951-1
ePub: 978-1-50992-950-4

Typeset by Compuscript Ltd, Shannon

To find out more about our authors and books visit www.hartpublishing.co.uk. Here you will find extracts, author information, details of forthcoming events and the option to sign up for our newsletters.

To my dear wife, Emmanuelle, who made this possible in so many ways

Preface

THIS WORK CONSTITUTES an attempt to provide practitioners and scholars of international law with a method for deciding whether to ignore or to acknowledge changes that impact on the meaning of a treaty term that needs to be interpreted. After finding that international law instruments, case law and scholarship all circle around but do not resolve the issue, it draws on recently developed notions of linguistics to propose a long-overdue solution to the problem labelled 'the problem of intertemporal linguistics' half a century ago.

The present book constitutes the first monograph to emerge from my comprehensive study of how international courts and tribunals do and should interpret treaty terms subject to a change in their meaning through time. Further particulars of that study – including many detailed case analyses – were presented in a PhD thesis defended at the University of Geneva's Faculty of Law in 2017. I would like to thank the esteemed members of my jury, Professors Boisson de Chazournes, Kolb, Marceau and DiStefano for their helpful comments, many of which contributed to refining the observations and conclusions that are now presented in this book.

I would also like to thank the many professors and legal scholars I was lucky enough to meet during an incredibly stimulating decade in Geneva, at the Graduate Institute, the University of Geneva's Faculty of Law and in private practice, as well as those at other institutions kind enough to give me an insight into the theory and practice of international law including the Max Planck Institute for Comparative Public Law and International Law, the Australian Attorney-General's International Law Office, and, most recently, the Australian National University's Centre for International & Public Law.

Contents

Table of Cases

Table of Figures

1

Introduction

IN JULY 1969, with the ink barely dry on the landmark Vienna Convention of the Law of Treaties ('VCLT') that he had helped draft as a member of the International Law Commission ('ILC'),[1] Shabtai Rosenne set about returning his correspondence. On his desk, he found a series of questions posed by Max Sørensen, the Danish jurist with the daunting task of producing a report for the Institute of International Law on the abstruse topic of '[t]he problem called the intertemporal law in the international order'.[2]

One of these questions explored the relationship between the intertemporal law problem and the interpretation of treaties. It asked whether the difficulty arising when a treaty needed to be interpreted and applied long after its text had been finalised could be conceived of as a simple problem of conflict and '*renvoi*', meaning that it would simply become a question of whether the treaty term should be taken to refer to earlier or later international law norms.[3] Rosenne wrote in reply:

> No. Leaving aside the question of development of language (intertemporal linguistics, a chapter in itself which cannot be ignored in the framework of 'interpretation'), surely what has to be elucidated is the solution to the peculiar conflict created by the intertemporal law in the combined processes of interpretation and application. This requires, first a careful analysis of what time-conflict really is, on the basis on which the decision on the choice of the rule can be made. The *US Nationals in Morocco Case* cited in paragraph 36 of the 'exposé préliminaire' has always seemed to me to exemplify the problem of intertemporel [*sic*] linguistics, ie the meaning of words at the time used and when interpreted. It is a problem of interpretation not one of conflict or choice of law.[4]

[1] Vienna Convention on the Law of Treaties 1969 (1155 UNTS 331). The VCLT was adopted on 22 May 1969 at the conclusion of the second session of the United Nations Conference on the Law of Treaties in Vienna ('Vienna Conference'). The Vienna Conference was set up upon the recommendation of the ILC and began with a consideration of the draft articles on the law of treaties that the ILC had adopted in 1966, see UN Conference on the Law of Treaties, 'Official Records, First Session, Vienna' (Vienna, United Nations, 1968) 11 (meeting of 28 March 1968, per T Elias [Chairman]).

[2] See Institut de droit international and Max Sørensen, 'Le problème dit du droit intertemporel dans l'ordre international – Rapport provisoire' (12 February 1973) *Annuaire* 1 (present author's translation of the French title).

[3] ibid 62, 68 (Sørensen's Question 9).

[4] ibid 80–81 (observations of Shabtai Rosenne dated 10 July 1969, § 9).

As a reply to a question about which era's international law norms should be applied, it is notable that Rosenne focused on the 'development of language' and changes in the meaning of *words* through time – rather than merely the development of international *law* through time. Rosenne's brief but important observation sought to move the debate beyond the narrow question of which era's rules should be considered 'relevant rules of international law' under what became VCLT Article 31(3)(c) to a concept that addresses all types of change that might affect the interpretation of a treaty through time – the broader issue he called 'the problem of intertemporal linguistics'.[5]

It seems likely that Rosenne's July 1969 insistence on this wider notion of the intertemporal interpretation problem was borne of frustration arising from the ILC's and then the VCLT's ultimately failure to take a position on both the narrower question of which era's law should apply and the separate and at least equally intriguing question of how to respond to mere changes in the meaning of a treaty's terms. Indeed, in comments made to the ILC in his capacity as a representative of his home State, he had, some four years earlier, already presented the concept of 'inter-temporal linguistics' to another rapporteur, the ILC's Special Rapporteur on the Law of Treaties, Humphrey Waldock, only to have Waldock dismiss it on the basis that the introduction of this concept into the law of treaties 'may unduly complicate matters'.[6]

For Rosenne, the problem of intertemporal linguistics could 'not be ignored in the framework of "interpretation"',[7] so he must have hoped for – and indeed expected – countless studies to turn their attention to solving it. Fifty years later, and despite a quantity of international case law and legal scholarship on treaty interpretation that would have surpassed even his most optimistic expectations, this problem has been effectively ignored. Rosenne has since passed, but the present study makes an effort to ensure that his interest in the problem of intertemporal linguistics moves on, striving not only to analyse, but also to propose a solution to this challenging problem of international law.

I. THE PROBLEM OF INTERTEMPORAL LINGUISTICS

This book examines, in the international law context, the interrelation of two of the most vexed concepts of legal science: interpretation and time. It does so by focusing on one specific type of situation: when an adjudicator is required to interpret a term appearing on the face of a legal instrument and the meaning of that term has changed since the instrument came into being. This situation inherently poses a question: which of the earlier or later meaning should be

[5] VCLT, art 31.

[6] International Law Commission, *Yearbook 1966, vol II* (New York, United Nations, 1967) 95–96 (§ 7).

[7] IDI and Sørensen (n 2) 80–81 (observations of Shabtai Rosenne dated 10 July 1969, § 9).

used by the interpreter? In international law circles, this is precisely Rosenne's problem of intertemporal linguistics (hereinafter also the 'Problem').

The issue raised by the problem of intertemporal linguistics occupies a space at the very core of legal decision-making processes and has been raised at different points in history in many different systems and branches of law. It has notably been examined by important schools of Western legal theory active around the turn of the twentieth century, including the French *école évolutionniste*, the German *Freirechtsschule* and the Anglo-American sociological school, with prominent authors of that era such as François Gény,[8] Rudolf von Jhering,[9] Eugen Ehrlich[10] and Roscoe Pound[11] devoting attention to the problem. Today, the issue is particularly prominent in its guise as part of the debate surrounding originalism in the constitutional law of the United States of America.[12] Since the mid-1980s, it has also attracted substantial attention in relation to statutory interpretation in the same domestic legal system.[13] There, as well as in various other legal systems, it has generated controversy for the interpretation of not only laws, but also instruments such as contracts.[14] The present author has even encountered the same issue at the core of an international commercial arbitration, where the changing meaning of a geographical

[8] See, eg François Gény, *Méthode d'interprétation et sources en droit privé positif: essai critique*, vol 2 (Paris, Librairie générale de droit et de jurisprudence (LGDJ), 1919) 253–75.

[9] See, eg Rudolf von Jhering, *Geist des römischen Rechts auf den verschiedenen Stufen seiner Entwicklung*, vol II, 2nd edn (Leipzig, Breitkopf und Härtel, 1869) 327.

[10] See, eg Eugen Ehrlich, 'Judicial Freedom of Decision, its Principles and Objects' in Ernest Bruncken (tr), *Science of Legal Method: Select Essays by Various Authors* (Boston MA, Boston Book Company, 1903) 61; see also Eugen Ehrlich, *Freie Rechtsfindung und freie Rechtswissenschaft* (Leipzig, CL Hirschfeld, 1903); Eugen Ehrlich, *Grundlegung der Soziologie des Rechts* (München, Duncker & Humblot, 1913).

[11] See, eg Roscoe Pound, 'Courts and Legislation' (1913) 7 *American Political Science Review* 361, 364–66, 379–83.

[12] Ronald Dworkin, 'The Arduous Virtue of Fidelity: Originalism, Scalia, Tribe, and Nerve' (1996) 65 *Fordham Law Review* 1249; see, eg Jack M Balkin, 'Framework Originalism and the Living Constitution' (2009) 103 *Northwestern University Law Review* 549; Antonin Scalia, *A Matter of Interpretation: Federal Courts and the Law* (Princeton NJ, Princeton University Press, 1997); Randy E Barnett, 'Originalism for Nonoriginalists, An' (1999) 45 *Loyola Law Review* 611. The same debate has also emerged in other systems of constitutional law, see, eg Jeffrey Goldsworthy, 'Originalism in Constitutional Interpretation' (1997) 25 *Federal Law Review* 1.

[13] See especially William N Eskridge, 'Dynamic Statutory Interpretation' (1986) 135 *University of Pennsylvania Law Review* 1479; and William N Eskridge, *Dynamic Statutory Interpretation* (Cambridge MA, Harvard University Press, 1994); see also Daniel A Farber, 'Statutory Interpretation and Legislative Supremacy' (1989) 78 *The Georgetown Law Journal* 281; Anthony D'Amato, 'The Injustice of Dynamic Statutory Interpretations' (1995) 64 *University of Cincinnati Law Review* 911; Stephen F Ross, 'The Location and Limits of Dynamic Statutory Interpretation in Modern Judicial Reasoning' (2002) 2 *Issues in Legal Scholarship*; Bernard W Bell, 'Hypnotized by Images of the Past: Dynamic Interpretation and the Flawed Majoritarianism of Statutory Law' (1 November 2002) 2 *Issues in Legal Scholarship*.

[14] See, eg Nancy S Kim, 'Evolving Business and Social Norms and Interpretation Rules: The Need for a Dynamic Approach to Contract Disputes' (2005) 84 *Nebraksa Law Review* 506; Alex M Johnson Jr and Ross D Taylor, 'Revolutionizing Judicial Interpretation of Charitable Trusts: Applying Relational Contracts and Dynamic Interpretation to Cy Pres and America's Cup Litigation' (1989) 74 *Iowa Law Review* 545.

designation in long-term contracts for the provision of natural resources was at issue. Wherever law takes a written form and subsequently needs to be interpreted and applied, the problem of intertemporal linguistics may arise.

There are, broadly-speaking, two possible ways of solving a problem of intertemporal linguistics: (a) what this study will call the 'static approach' (which selects the meaning that a treaty term had at the time the treaty was concluded); and (b) the 'dynamic approach' (which selects the meaning of a treaty term prevailing at the time the treaty was applied).[15]

As a book dedicated to how the problem of intertemporal linguistics most commonly presents itself in the field of international law, this study enquires into how international courts and tribunals do and should solve the Problem when it arises in the specific context of interpreting treaties. The ultimate objective of the book is to set out a conceptually well-founded and workable method for international courts and tribunals confronted with interpreting a treaty term that has undergone a change in meaning through time such that they can appropriately and predictably choose between using a treaty term's original meaning (the static approach) and later-emerging meaning (the dynamic approach).

However, the book is not intended merely to posit a solution to a practical problem arising at international courts and tribunals. It also seeks to generate insights into some of the most important cross-cutting questions of modern-day international law. By examining how an interpreter should choose between two distinct meanings of a treaty term and by assessing the doctrines regularly associated with this choice – including the much-discussed doctrine of evolutionary treaty interpretation, this book inherently explores the proper role of the contemporary international adjudicator at a time when that role has become both practically significant and increasingly controversial. Finally, by proposing the use of an analytical approach to framing practical legal problems and a linguistics-inspired solution to a problem ultimately left unresolved by the VCLT's general and flexible interpretative rules, *Intertemporal Linguistics in International Law* also probes whether the central and very widely-used

[15] The word 'dynamic' (drawn from the Greek word 'δύναμις', referring to power or force), does not describe the notion perfectly or even as well as the French expression that speaks of an interpretation that is 'actualisante', but it has the clear benefit of being understood in very clear opposition to 'static' (στατικός, meaning 'causing to stand'). This allows the problem of intertemporal linguistics to be understood as a contest between two competing and diametrically opposed approaches to solving it. It is noteworthy that several relevant texts, particularly those emanating from the German-speaking world, use the terms static and dynamic to describe similar dichotomies – see, eg Rudolf Bernhardt, 'Homogenität, Kontinuität und Dissonanzen in der Rechtsprechung des Internationalen Gerichtshofs – Eine Fall-Studie zum Südwestafrika/Namibia-Komplex' (1973) 33 *Zeitschrift für ausländisches öffentliches Recht und Völkerrecht* 1, 35; Kai Schollendorf, *Die Auslegung völkerrechtlicher Verträge in der Spruchpraxis des Appellate Body der Welthandelsorganisation (WTO)* (Berlin, Duncker & Humblot, 2005) 193, 196, 206; Oliver Dörr and Kirsten Schmalenbach, 'Article 31. General rule of interpretation' in Oliver Dörr and Kirsten Schmalenbach (eds), *Vienna Convention on the Law of Treaties: A Commentary* (Berlin, Springer, 2012) 533 (§ 23); Mehrdad Payandeh, *Internationales Gemeinschaftsrecht* (Heidelberg, Springer, 2010) 320–23.

interpretative provisions of the now 50-year-old landmark convention on treaties are still fit for the purposes of modern-day international law.

II. SCOPE

The scope of this book is simultaneously both wide and narrow.

It is wide in the sense that it addresses an issue of interpretation across a broad range of fields of international law. In doing so, and without neglecting to take into account the specificities of each of the various fields, it takes a horizontal, cross-cutting approach in response to what Abi-Saab has called the 'complexification' of international law,[16] rather than the vertical, specialised approach favoured by most contemporary studies of similar phenomena.[17] Indeed, the much-lauded creation of specific courts and tribunals in functionally, politically and conceptually very distinct branches of international law has itself been one of the main drivers of the specialisation among international lawyers that has in turn generated well-known fears regarding the 'fragmentation' of international law.[18] The examination of a truly cross-cutting issue of international law in the particular context of a *sui generis* field – such as international human rights law – runs the risk of concluding that a particular

[16] Georges Abi-Saab, 'Fragmentation or Unification: Some Concluding Remarks' (1998) 31 *NYU Journal of International Law and Politics* 919, 925–26.

[17] Studies dedicated to similar topics of international law most often focus on interpretative practice in the sub-field of international human rights law – see, eg Jochen Abr Frowein, 'Die evolutive Auslegung der EMRK' in Thilo Marauhn (ed), *Recht, Politik und Rechtspolitik in den internationalen Beziehungen* (Tübingen, Mohr Siebeck, 2005); Malgosia Fitzmaurice, 'Dynamic (Evolutive) Interpretation of Treaties and the European Court of Human Rights' in Alexander Orakhelashvili and Sarah Williams (eds), *40 Years of the Vienna Convention on the Law of Treaties* (London, British Institute of International and Comparative Law, 2010); Antoine Garapon, 'Les limites à l'interprétation évolutive de la Convention' (2011) 3 *Revista de Estudos Constitucionais, Hermenêutica e Teoria do Direito* 25; George Letsas, 'The ECHR as a Living Instrument: Its Meaning and Legitimacy' in Andreas Føllesdal, Birgit Peters and Geir Ulfstein (eds), *Constituting Europe: The European Court of Human Rights in a National, European and Global Context* (Cambridge, Cambridge University Press, 2013); or in the sub-field of GATT/WTO law – see, eg AM Feldman, 'Evolving Treaty Obligations: A Proposal for Analyzing Subsequent Practice Derived from WTO Dispute Settlement' (2009) 41 *NYU Journal of International Law and Politics* 655; Sondre Torp Helmersen, 'Evolutive Treaty Interpretation by the WTO Appellate Body' (Master's Thesis, University of Oslo, 2012); Eva Greschek, *Die evolutive Auslegung voelkerrechtlicher Vertraege am Beispiel des GATT* (Frankfurt, Peter Lang, 2012), but may also look at the interpretation of one instrument, such as the UN Sales Convention (CISG) – see, eg Michael P Van Alstine, 'Dynamic Treaty Interpretation' (1998) 146 *University of Pennsylvania Law Review* 687; or even at an associated doctrine in relation to one particular international case – see, eg Robin McCaig, 'The Further Evolution of the Evolutionary Approach to Treaty Interpretation' (2010) 69 *Cambridge Law Journal* 250, one of many articles looking at the evolutionary interpretation doctrine almost uniquely in relation to how it was putatively used in the *Related Rights* case. See *Dispute regarding Navigational and Related Rights (Costa Rica v Nicaragua)*, Judgment [2009] ICJ Reports 213.

[18] See International Law Commission and Martii Koskenniemi, 'Fragmentation of International Law: Difficulties arising from diversification and expansion of international law' A/CN.4/L.682 (Geneva, United Nations, 2006).

approach to that issue – here treaty interpretation – is *generally* justified, when it is in fact only justified by functional, political or conceptual features specific to that particular sub-field of international law. By examining the relevant practice of all major and truly international courts and tribunals, the present study avoids these potential pitfalls and opens a pathway toward a generally applicable approach as a sub-rule of the generally applicable rules of treaty interpretation. A welcome by-product of this broad-spectrum approach is that it allows the author to pursue his existing interest in comparative law within international law,[19] and, with luck, to bring greater attention to this new and increasingly important but still neglected area of international legal study. Indeed, modern-day international lawyers can learn so much about the rules and principles of the discipline from how differently positioned international courts and tribunals apply these same rules to different types of law in different contexts.

Yet the book's scope is, as a necessary corollary of its breadth in terms of the number of sub-fields of international law it engages with, also quite narrow in terms of how much of their practice it examines. Examining the treaty interpretation carried out by all these international courts and tribunals in general would now be a gargantuan task. This book accordingly restricts itself to the small sub-category of treaty interpretation that addresses the problem of intertemporal linguistics: that which occurs when the meaning of a contested treaty term has relevantly changed between the time of the treaty's conclusion and the time at which the treaty falls to be applied. In most interpretations of a treaty, no such change in meaning will have occurred and newer fields whose international case law is dominated by more recent treaties – such as international criminal law – may not even have encountered cases falling within the scope of this study.

The result is that, as mentioned above, this book examines the problem of intertemporal linguistics uniquely in the context of (i) the most relevant type of international legal text, namely treaties, and (ii) the most important interpreters of modern-day international law with something to say on this issue, namely international courts and tribunals ranging from the International Court of Justice ('ICJ'), the Permanent Court of International Justice ('PCIJ') and State-State arbitral bodies, to the European Court of Human Rights, the Inter-American Court of Human Rights, the WTO Appellate Body, WTO Panels and investment arbitration tribunals.

Of course, international law also involves the interpretation of other sources of norms including customary international law norms, unilateral declarations

[19] See, eg Julian Wyatt, 'Beyond Fragmentation: WTO Jurisprudence, Environmental Norms and Interactions Between Subsystems of International Law' (2008) *SSRN eLibrary*, papers.ssrn.com/sol3/papers.cfm?abstract_id=1777045; Julian Wyatt, 'Law-Making at the Intersection of International Environmental, Humanitarian and Criminal Law: The Issue of Damage to the Environment in International Armed Conflict' (2010) 92 (879) *International Review of the Red Cross* 593; Gabrielle Marceau and Julian Wyatt, 'Trade and the Environment: The WTO's Efforts to Balance Economic and Sustainable Development' in *Economie Environnement Ethique: De la responsabilité sociale et sociétale* (Zurich, Schulthess, 2009).

and the decisions of other courts and tribunals. In addition, international law is interpreted by actors other than international courts and tribunals, ranging from scholars to States and even the individuals bringing actions under international law against States in certain domestic and international courts and tribunals. However, it is only through an analysis of the combination of *treaty interpretation* by the above-named *international courts and tribunals* that this study can hope to identify practice capable of generating meaningful insights applicable across the whole spectrum of modern-day international law.

After all, sources of international law other than treaties are all more inherently positioned somewhere specific on the temporal continuum and thereby pre-judge the question posed by the problem of intertemporal linguistics. Customary international law, for example, is generally considered to be undergoing constant change, while the decisions of courts and tribunals occur at a particular moment in the past. Treaties, while plentiful and diverse, share common features and are governed by a set of fixed rules determining their operation and, crucially, interpretation. Focussing on treaties allows us to address the lion's share of modern-day interpretation of international law norms while leaning on the common base of the VCLT rules with an eye to their specific role and ongoing suitability.

Equally, national courts have disparate modi operandi and sit within long-established, non-international and sometimes widely diverging institutional structures that may influence their response to the Problem in ways that are irrelevant to the non-State-specific field of international law. By contrast, modern-day international courts and tribunals, as varied as they might be, all ultimately stem from a treaty in force between States, rather than laws forged within a State or State-like institution. In addition, these international courts and tribunals call on the agency of international adjudicators who, unlike many other interpreters of international law, sit outside the apparatus of a State. It is specifically their practice, therefore, that raises crucial questions as to the relationship between the traditional subjects of international law: States and the heavy de facto influencers of contemporary international law: international adjudicators.

III. METHODOLOGICAL FEATURES

A. Focus on a Neutrally Stated Practical Problem, not Doctrines

The thin, horizontal layer selected for this study in turn necessitates the use of a methodological approach inspired by the field of comparative law. This approach itself sets this study apart from the vast majority of international law texts in this area.

In relation to the loosely analogous field of contract law, the comparative lawyer Kadner pointed out that when a topic is characterised by 'great diversity', the 'starting point can no longer be the different … systems and their gaps and faults; it must be the legal issue under examination'.[20] Crucially, the legal issue examined cannot be a doctrine that exists in one system, but does not necessarily exist or take the same form in another. It must instead be a legal issue detached from any doctrines or principles used by any specific systems. It must, in addition, be stated broadly and neutrally enough to permit objective and truly comparative analysis. This is why Kadner's study of comparative contract law, like many studies guided by the comparative method, identifies 'specific legal questions' that can be tendered in a completely neutral way, Kadner offering them as fact-based case scenarios before analysing the 'solutions' to them.[21] Such an approach ensures that attention remains focused on the specific legal problems and solutions that can be compared across systems and not diverted off-course by analysis of doctrines used in one or more of the different systems; including for purposes going beyond the scope of providing a solution to the specific legal question.

Being wary of the confusion characterising the true meaning of many doctrines of international law, especially in the era of ever greater specialisation and complexification of the international legal order, the present book follows this functional aspect of the comparative method and poses a specific question in completely neutral terms: 'how do and should international courts and tribunals interpret treaties with terms whose meanings have changed through time?'. This question exactly mirrors the problem of intertemporal linguistics, a problem, not a doctrine, that asks how interpreters should choose between the original and later-emerging meaning of a treaty term without advocating any position one way or the other.

Recent years have witnessed the publication of several different studies on doctrines relating to this question and therefore raising many of the same issues as those explored by the present study. However, they take as the starting point an existing doctrine of international law – usually the doctrine referred to as evolutionary, evolutive or dynamic treaty interpretation – and analyse that doctrine and the case law referring to it. They accordingly produce works which constitute a *tour d'horizon* of how one specific doctrine related to the problem of intertemporal linguistics is invoked and applied. However, in so doing, they fail to provide an objective response to the (wider) question of how treaty terms subject to relevant semantic change through time are and should be interpreted.

The benefits of exploring the interface between the interpretation of treaties and the effluxion of time by posing a specific question – rather than by analysing a specific doctrine – are manifold.

First, a doctrine generally takes a position on an underlying question; it takes a side. By focussing on the doctrine, rather than the question upon which it takes a position, a doctrine-oriented analysis runs the risk of pre-judging the question from the outset. Moreover, where the counterpoint to the position taken by the

[20] Thomas Kadner Graziano, *Comparative Contract Law: Cases, Materials and Exercises* (Basingstoke, Palgrave Macmillan, 2009) 15.

[21] Kadner Graziano, ibid, 8–17.

analysed doctrine is contained within another doctrine not addressed by the study, a study of the doctrine in isolation – rather than the question – may fail to properly evaluate all the pros and cons of the position taken by the doctrine it analyses.

The doctrine of evolutionary treaty interpretation is clearly a doctrine that takes a particular position on a wider question, favouring the use of a treaty term's later-emerging meaning over the use of its original meaning. There are, however, other doctrines – such as the principle of contemporaneity – which take the opposite position on the same question, favouring a treaty term's original meaning. Almost all published studies of evolutionary treaty interpretation, by focusing on the doctrine rather than the underlying question, fail to adequately engage with the opposing static treaty interpretation doctrine.[22] They accordingly tender analyses that fall short of comprehensively evaluating not only the underlying question, but also the doctrine itself.

Second, when one evaluates a legal question using a doctrine, one is presuming that there is a precise overlap between how the doctrine is invoked and applied and how the question is answered. Yet this is rarely the case. Kadner's comparative study of contract law is again illuminating. His 'scenario 1' explores the specific question of whether the advertisement of a product at a specific price by a seller binds the seller to sell the product to a buyer at that price.[23] In many systems of domestic private law, treatment of this question would fall within the scope of the notion of an invitation to treat (*invitatio ad offerendum*). However, not all systems have this notion, while others which do have it would not consider the situation to be solely governed by the notion of an invitation to treat. Moreover, the notion of an invitation to treat plays an important role in very different situations – such as in relation to tenders for large projects – so much of the doctrine and case law on invitations to treat will be estranged from the question posed by Kadner's scenario 1. A study of invitations to treat in different systems of contract law therefore fails to reliably yield any meaningful insight into how the wider and essential question of private law posed by Kadner is dealt with by those systems, or how it should be dealt with in general. By contrast, a study focusing on Kadner's generally expressed 'scenario 1', detached from any related doctrines, ensures that the central question is properly analysed.

[22] See, eg Katharina Böth, *Evolutive Auslegung völkerrechtlicher Verträge: Eine Untersuchung zu Voraussetzungen und Grenzen in Anbetracht der Praxis internationaler Streitbeilegungsinstitutionen* (Berlin, Duncker & Humblot, 2013) 132 (who dedicates a mere two paragraphs of her 188-page book to the antithetical principle of contemporaneity and, even then, ends up discussing the distinct notion of the intertemporal law); Eirik Bjorge, *The Evolutionary Interpretation of Treaties* (Oxford, Oxford University Press, 2014) (whose book presents an eight-paragraph section on the principle of contemporaneity in which he largely, and somewhat spuriously, seeks to undermine the weight of the authorities endorsing this opposing position); and Sondre Torp Helmersen, 'Evolutive Treaty Interpretation: Legality, Semantics and Distinctions' (2013) 6 *European Journal of Legal Studies* 127, 132 (who justifies his decision to ignore the principle of contemporaneity by asserting that it has fallen out of favour).

[23] Kadner Graziano (n 20) 9–10.

The dangers inherent in the doctrine-focused approach are even more apparent when one concentrates on a review of case law for insight into the state of the applicable rules or principles. As will be seen, there is no precise overlap between the case law invoking evolutionary or dynamic treaty interpretation and the case law taking a dynamic approach to the problem of intertemporal linguistics. To the extent that previous studies have focused on the case law that invokes and applies – or at least purports to apply – evolutionary treaty interpretation, they therefore become estranged from the Problem. Indeed, one of the present study's most important contentions is that a rigorous study of how international adjudicators in fact respond to a precise issue is much more likely to yield insight into the adequacy of interpretative rules than a study of the multifarious instances in which they invoke a doctrine putatively linked to particular issue, but which, in reality, often has little to do with it.

Of course, a research project structured around a specific question cannot avoid the case law and literature invoking doctrines that are closely linked to that question and should not attempt to do so. However, if it wishes to provide a proper analysis of actual and potential responses to a question, it must remain focused on that question and not be drawn into the debates internal to – or at least specific to – the doctrines related to it. This 'question-focus' or 'problem-focus' is thus the defining methodological feature of the present study.

B. Directed Towards a Workable Solution, not a Restatement of the Problem

The most ambitious feature of this project is undoubtedly its single-minded quest to *solve* the problem of intertemporal linguistics. Whereas other projects touching on the Problem describe the case law and scholarship relating to the issue or at most reframe it, this book seeks to identify a set of guidelines for when international courts and tribunals should take the static or the dynamic approach. In the comprehensive study that comes closest to tackling the issue addressed by this book, Djeffal uses the *Denkbewegung* of 'functional reconstruction', 'reorganising and restating something that is already there in a faithful manner so that it can be better dealt with'.[24] He focuses on using the intertemporal interpretation issue to understand the functions of the interpretative method and the VCLT's rules on treaty interpretation, rather than to solve the intertemporal interpretation question. In the conclusion of his 2016 book, Djeffal states:

> This study resulted in the conclusion that the VCLT is intertemporally open and that, within this openness, interpreters can take a stance insofar as their jurisdiction is concerned. This might prove to be unsatisfactory to lawyers and legal scholars if they

[24] Christian Djeffal, *Static and Evolutive Treaty Interpretation: A Functional Reconstruction* (Cambridge, Cambridge University Press, 2016) 73.

> prefer guidance over discretion. With this mindset, intertemporal openness is a problem to be solved by a new scholarly doctrine or a solution deduced from a theoretical insight. This inquiry has taken another stance: Intertemporal openness has not been conceived as the problem but as part of the solution.[25]

The present author willingly confesses to falling, perhaps on account of his background as a legal practitioner, squarely in the camp of those who prefer guidance over discretion. But this is not just a personal or general preference applicable to all legal questions. International law has now reached a point of maturity as a legal system at which it must specifically demand more guidance and less discretion, especially as regards issues central to the ever more widespread and legally more important phenomenon of third-party dispute settlement. Issues do not come much more central to modern-day international cases than treaty interpretation and, as many treaties age with political deadlock over their amendment, the practical importance of the problem of intertemporal linguistics will only increase.

While he admits that the VCLT's interpretative rules are too broad and open to resolve a question such as the problem of intertemporal linguistics, Djeffal also asserts that they nonetheless 'enhance international legal discourse' and regards the ILC as having been the 'perfect mechanism' for codifying the approach to the interpretation of treaties.[26] As will be seen, this book takes a sharply different view. One cannot but value the quality of the work that went into developing the VCLT. However, the last 50 years have seen massive development, including in fields affecting treaty interpretation. Treaty-making, including multilateral treaty-making in novel forms, has flourished, third-party international dispute settlement has blossomed and related fields of endeavour, such as legal theory and various fields of linguistics, have come on in leaps and bounds. The result is that, in 2019, we now not only have a much better understanding of what the act of interpretation actually entails, but also deserve a conceptually stronger treaty interpretation system that can cope more easily with the diversity of the modern-day international legal system and meet the demands of the broad range of actors now depending on international courts and tribunals for an appropriate resolution of their disputes.

It is no longer a time to content oneself with interpretative rules and interpretative approaches that do not offend anyone, but do not help anyone either. Ideally, the ILC itself would have taken on the responsibility for fine-tuning the rules of treaty interpretation in order to cover the aspects left open by the now 50-year-old VCLT provisions. The recent conclusions on subsequent agreement and subsequent practice are a modest step in this direction. However, with its ill-fated *Treaties over Time* study, the ILC, like many scholars writing on associated notions, shunned the opportunity to provide general guidance for interpreters

[25] Ibid 357.
[26] ibid.

confronted with the problem of intertemporal linguistics, leaving it to be, as Djeffal, notes 'solved by a new scholarly doctrine or a solution deduced from a theoretical insight'.[27] The present piece of scholarship takes up that challenge, adducing theoretical insights – particularly from the field of linguistics – to propose a practical solution to the problem of intertemporal linguistics.

C. Open to Necessary Teachings from Fields External to International Law

The third major methodological feature of the present study arises directly from its insatiable appetite for a workable solution to the Problem. Recognising that a solution probably will not be found if we stay purely within the scope of international legal thinking, it resorts, where this appears to be absolutely necessary, to other fields of intellectual endeavour. In this book, this methodology is most readily apparent in the use of concepts from the fields of linguistics and legal theory to clarify the nature of the Problem (especially in chapter 4), to distinguish decisions claiming to take a position on the Problem from those that actually do (*passim*), and to formulate the method which international adjudicators might wish to use when interpreting a treaty raising the problem of intertemporal linguistics (chapters 7, 8 and 9). There are, in addition, hallmarks of an analytical philosophy-style approach to answering the question posed, including in the book's very structure – which sharply focuses on defining the problem and extracting it from the existing literature – and the heavier use of diagrams and formal notation than is customary in the field of international law.

However, it should not be forgotten that these unusual features are purely methodological. This study uses concepts and insights from fields outside of international law and a somewhat scientific approach solely to solve the legal problem it addresses where the law itself does not seem capable of solving it. The present book's focus remains squarely on examining and solving the legal problem through whatever means necessary, not on a sort of intellectual experimentation that simply wishes to see what might be revealed by viewing a known area of the law from a particular external perspective. The legal framework known to the users of the international legal system is always preferred and will only be departed from where it can be effectively improved by externally provided concepts and principles. As will be seen, in an area of definitional anarchy and conceptual deficiency, insights from linguistics on the nature of semantic change and the differences between intensional and extensional definitions are undoubtedly helpful, while the linguistic and legal theory distinction between ambiguity and vagueness and computational linguistic methods of word-sense disambiguation offer workable means for filling the gap left by the rules of treaty interpretation when it comes to treaty terms whose meanings have changed through time.

[27] ibid.

It is axiomatic that international law should never be placed solely within the framework of a domestic system of law, yet might be assisted by reference to the general principles that a domestic system uses for matters international law does not seem to address. By the same token, international law's development will be led astray by ill-conceived efforts to place it in the framework of other fields of intellectual endeavour, yet edified by filling its own gaps through the careful and specific selection of insights and notions from those external fields.

IV. STRUCTURE

This book has three substantive parts.

Part I is dedicated to clarifying the nature of the problem of intertemporal linguistics and ensuring that we focus uniquely on the question that it poses. It describes how the Problem has traditionally been addressed by two doctrines commonly associated with it, the principle of contemporaneity (chapter 2) and the evolutionary interpretation doctrine (chapter 3), finding that both have only served to distort and confuse examination of the Problem. Part I therefore seeks to detach the problem of intertemporal linguistics from these associated doctrines and, having returned attention to it, to offer (in chapter 4) a more rigorous, almost scientific definition of what the Problem entails as well as of the two opposing approaches that can be taken when it arises.

Part II of this book then addresses two popular views regularly stated in relation to the Problem. It ultimately casts aside as misconceptions the popular views (a) that the VCLT's interpretative provisions allow any interpreter faced with the Problem to solve it (chapter 5) and (b) that the case law of modern-day international courts and tribunals has now settled on using a dynamic approach and thus solved the Problem (chapter 6).

Having detached the problem of intertemporal linguistics from the doctrines that have traditionally prevented a proper treatment of it and dispensed with the conventional wisdom considering it to have already been solved, the book turns, in its Part III, to formulating a proposed solution to the Problem. Chapter 7 uses insight from the fields of linguistics and legal theory – as well as an analogous provision of the VCLT's interpretative rules – to import a distinction between ambiguity and vagueness into international law and propose a corollary two-step interpretative process fully suited to solving the Problem. Chapter 8 then identifies the element that defines the disambiguation process central to solving the Problem: the temporal sense-intention. Chapter 9 is dedicated to the key task of inferring that sense-intention, looking through the international case law and scholarship most relevant to the Problem for features of interpretative situations that may imply either a fixed or mobile sense-intention. Chapter 10 then leans on analogous private law methods for inferring party-intention to create an ordered series of indicia and presumptions that can be used as a rigorous and fail-safe method for identifying the temporal sense-intention attaching to a treaty term and thus to appropriately and predictably solve any problem of intertemporal linguistics that a treaty term may present.

The book then concludes, in chapter 11, with some brief remarks on the merits of using an analytical approach and proposing a scientific solution to a problem of treaty interpretation, a task that many international lawyers still prefer to see as an art rather than a science. In doing so it momentarily reflects on whether, in light of the enormous changes to international law since 1969, the interpretative rules set out in the Vienna Convention on the Law of Treaties remain fit for the purposes of modern-day international dispute settlement.

Part I

The Problem – Detaching it from the Doctrines

2

The Rise and Fall of the Principle of Contemporaneity

I. SURFACING AND CONSECRATION OF THE STATIC APPROACH AS THE PRINCIPLE OF CONTEMPORANEITY

SPECIFIC DISCUSSION OF the temporal aspects of treaty interpretation was, until the 1960s, extremely rare. However, this does not mean that a prevailing approach to the problem of intertemporal linguistics cannot be gleaned from the scholarship and practice of international law prior to that time.

A. In the Classical Period of International Law

Early international law scholarship was particularly critical to the development of post-World War II international legal thinking on the issue. As noted by Ludwik Ehrlich in his 1928 Hague Course, 'doctrine has played a very important role in the development of the principles of treaty interpretation'.[1] With little else to draw on, the first international adjudicators relied heavily on the earliest international law texts, with the result that many of today's key notions of treaty interpretation date from international law scholarship from this period.

The 1625 publication of the first dedicated chapter on interpretation in an international law monograph, chapter XVI of book II of Grotius' *De jure belli ac pacis libri tres*, already mentions a surprisingly large number of the interpretative rules and factors invoked by international lawyers today. In those pages, Grotius set out what have since become, for example, the ordinary meaning rule,[2] the principle of effective interpretation[3] and the teleological principle of interpretation,[4] as well as other principles of treaty law such as versions of the fundamental change of circumstances[5] and *lex specialis*[6] rules.

[1] Ludwik Ehrlich, 'L'interprétation des traités' (1928) 24 *Collected Courses of the Hague Academy of International Law* 1, 8 (present author's translation).
[2] Hugo Grotius, *The Rights of War and Peace* (Indianapolis IN, Liberty Fund, 2005) 849 (bk II, ch XVI, § II).
[3] ibid 853, 859, 875 (bk II, ch XVI, §§ VI, XII and XXII).
[4] ibid 854–55 (bk II, ch XVI, § VIII).
[5] ibid 877–79 (bk II, ch XVI, § XXVII).
[6] ibid 881 (bk II, ch XVI, § XXIX).

The problem of intertemporal linguistics, however, is quite specific and generally only presents itself in the context of adjudicators having to interpret a legal instrument whose meaning has changed between the time it was written and the time at which it falls to be interpreted and applied. Until the early twentieth century, of course, it was extremely rare for any courts and tribunals to be called upon to interpret treaties. It would accordingly not be surprising if early international legal scholars – including the so-called 'fathers of international law' – had never tackled the Problem. After all, if the Problem had never arisen in international law, one might wonder how they could purport to even know about, let alone resolve it.

Yet authors including Grotius, Pufendorf, Wolff and Vattel made a deliberate effort to cover not just the problems that had already arisen in international law at the times they were writing, but instead all the problems that they thought might one day arise. This meant that, even if they did so only briefly, these authors ultimately touched on more specific issues of treaty interpretation, including the problem of intertemporal linguistics.

Grotius himself did not directly address the issue posed by changes to the meaning of a treaty term,[7] but he indirectly pointed to it when, as part of his statement of the ordinary meaning rule, he quoted from and referred to classical texts focused on how different words are used across time.[8] The link he made between the ordinary meaning rule and changes in word use was then rendered even more explicit by Pufendorf's restatement of Grotius's rule,[9] but it was only with the remarkable international law text of Christian Wolff that the ordinary meaning rule was first given a clearly temporal qualification.

As part of his extremely detailed *Jus naturae and jus gentium* of the 1740s, Wolff wrote a 95-page chapter on interpretation, the extra detail affording him an opportunity to develop, within the frame of an international law text, certain ideas for interpretation that had not been discussed by Grotius.[10] One such idea was Wolff's static approach to the determination of the ordinary meaning – or *usus loquendi* – principle.[11] The most important words of Wolff's relevant

[7] But see Panos Merkouris, *Article 31(3)(c) VCLT and the Principle of Systemic Integration: Normative Shadows in Plato's Cave* (Leiden, Brill, 2015) 104, who claims that Grotius 'affirmed the principle of contemporaneity' when he discussed the issue of how to interpret the term 'Allies' in the provision of the League made between the Romans and Carthaginians after the Sicilian War (in bk II, ch XVI, § XIII), despite the fact that there was no meaning change in the word 'Allies' over the relevant period of time (see s 4.II.D below).

[8] Grotius (n 2) 849 (bk II, ch XVI, § II), Grotius quoting from a part of poem about meaning change by Horace ('Horace: Ars Poetica' 70–72 – www.thelatinlibrary.com/horace/arspoet.shtml; Horace, *The Epistles, Including the Ars Poetica* [WF Masom and AF Watt trs, London, University Tutorial Press, 1905] 51).

[9] Samuel Pufendorf, *Of the Law of Nature and Nations* (Basil Kennett tr, London, J Walthoe, R Wilkin, J and J Bonwicke, S Birt, T Ward, and T Osborne, 1729) 535 (bk V, ch XII, § III).

[10] Christian Wolff, *Jus naturae: methodo scientifica pertractatum*, vol 6 (Halle, Renger, 1746) 318–413 (Volume VI, Chapter III, 'De Interpretatione', §§ 459–560); Ehrlich (n 1) 24–25.

[11] Wolff (n 10) 328 (bk VI, ch III, § 471).

dictum, '*pacta interpretanda sunt secundum usum loquendi ejus temporis, quo condita fuerunt*' roughly translate as 'conventions should be interpreted according to the language in use at the time they were made', meaning that Wolff's addition of the words '*ejus temporis*' to the words '*usum loquendi*' clearly indicated his view that the meaning to be used by an interpreter – at least under the ordinary meaning rule – is that which was current at the time the treaty was written.

Irrespective of whether Wolff's temporal qualification of the *usus loquendi* rule was indeed as logically infallible as he appears to have imagined, it met with widespread approval among scholars and practitioners of both domestic and international law. On the domestic law side, an 1823 commentator on the French Civil Code, for example, invoked the above-mentioned ancient quotations about change in meaning and quoted Wolff's maxim when asserting in his domestic legal context that one must understand words according to the meaning they had when the instrument was made.[12] In international law circles, Wolff's static qualification of the ordinary meaning rule, like many of his other ideas, found greater prominence as a result of Emer de Vattel's famous 1758 French vulgarisation of Wolff's somewhat abstruse Latin work.

In section 258 of book II of his celebrated *Droit des gens*, Vattel stated as part of his fifth general principle of interpretation that every treaty must be given 'its meaning as naturally understood by the persons concerned when the treaty was drawn up and accepted'.[13] His preference for the static approach to the Problem was then confirmed in a subsequent section specifically addressing the problem of interpreting old treaties, where he notably restated the time for determining the ordinary meaning to be when the treaty was 'concluded and drawn-up' and openly stated: '[w]hen interpreting an old act [or treaty], it is therefore necessary to know the common usage of the [term at the] time when it was written'.[14]

Already in these formulations of the *usus loquendi* rule, we see that Vattel did not hesitate to add new nuances to existing principles stated by Wolff and others. He appears to have refined the *usus loquendi* principle from general usage to the particular usage of the parties and divided the moment at which the instrument was made, into the moments at which it was drawn-up and concluded. In an example of the pragmatism for which he was famous, the diplomat Vattel then also stated how interpreters can apply a static method of interpretation, directing them to look at and compare the instruments and literature from the

[12] Charles Bonaventure Marie Toullier, *Le droit civil français, suivant l'ordre du code*, vol 6 (Paris, Warée, 1823) 294.

[13] Emer de Vattel, *Le droit des gens, ou principes de la loi naturelle appliqués à la conduite et aux affaires des nations et des souverains*, vol I (Paris, J-P Aillaud, 1835) 464 (livre II, chapitre XVII, § 268, present author's translation).

[14] ibid 468 (livre II, chapitre XVII, § 272, present author's translations).

time when the relevant legal instrument was made[15] – a test still useful today for determining whether an international court or tribunal has adopted a static or dynamic approach to a problem of intertemporal linguistics.

Subsequent international law scholarship, to the extent that it adverted to the temporal aspects of the ordinary meaning rule, overwhelmingly accepted the position set out in Vattel's enormously influential work. It seems that Wolff and Vattel's rule, pursuant to which a term's ordinary meaning was that which the term had at the time it was drafted or concluded, was quickly established. It was apparently considered to be required by logic and common sense alone and, moreover, not to permit of any exceptions.[16]

B. In the Nineteenth Century

On the whole, the key figures of nineteenth-century international law remained faithful to the principles for treaty interpretation set out by the classical authors. In relation to the specific issue explored by this study, they were, however, often more measured than Wolff and those following him had been. For example, Phillimore's *Commentaries upon International Law* of 1854 – the first international law text addressing interpretation that places explicit reliance on Roman law, domestic law and legal theory – addresses the temporal issue directly, but does not state the static approach to resolving it as overtly as Wolff or Vattel, instead affirming simply that changes to the meaning of 'particular words employed' necessitates an interpretation which may exceptionally 'require a knowledge of the antiquated as well as of the present use of the words'.[17]

Yet where the authors of this period did take a clear position on the problem of intertemporal linguistics, the static approach was overwhelmingly preferred. Francis Lieber's *Legal and Political Hermeneutics* of 1837 specifically noted that the issue was bound up with the ordinary meaning rule,[18] before indicating that, for him, the ordinary meaning of a term is intrinsically related to how the drafter understood that term when he or she committed it to writing. Lieber clearly favoured the static approach to the Problem when he stated, for example,

[15] ibid.

[16] Note, however, that the qualification preventing the use of the ordinary meaning rule itself when there is evidence that a special meaning is intended – established at least since Grotius and possibly even since the time Marcellus's thoughts were collected in Justinian's *corpus juris civilis* – appears to have remained undisturbed by these temporal refinements. On the modern form of this qualification, see s 7.III.C below.

[17] Robert Phillimore, *Commentaries upon International Law*, vol 2 (Philadelphia PN, T & JW Johnson, 1854) 73.

[18] Francis Lieber, *Legal and Political Hermeneutics or Principles of Interpretation and Construction in Law and Politics with Remarks on Precedents and Authorities* (Boston MA, Charles C Little and James Brown, 1839) 101 (ch IV, § IX).

that 'we are to take the words in that meaning which we may faithfully believe their utterer attached to them', and, following Vattel, that

> [one of the] chief rules in ascertaining the meaning of doubtful words ... with regard to dead languages [is the use of sources] from contemporary writers in the same language, or other contemporaries, who have chanced to explain the doubtful word.[19]

C. In the Twentieth Century

In light of the relatively late development of the international dispute settlement system, it is unsurprising that international lawyers took a conservative approach to matters of judicial interpretation and did not consider its temporal issues in as much detail as their domestic law counterparts of that time. Following the course chartered by arbitrators throughout the nineteenth century, those charged with deciding disputes under the aegis of the burgeoning Permanent Court of Arbitration and judges at the newly established Permanent Court of International Justice focused on giving effect to the intention of parties who concluded the relevant treaty. With a focus on sub-issues such as the evidence from which the parties' intention could be ascertained,[20] and how the emerging category of multilateral treaties should be interpreted,[21] twentieth-century international law scholarship dedicated to treaty interpretation offered surprisingly little analysis of the problem of intertemporal linguistics.

There was, however, one notable exception in this regard. In 1928, Ludwik Ehrlich, Professor of International Law at the University of Lwów and judge at the Permanent Court of International Justice, delivered a course at the Hague Academy that was dedicated to the topic of treaty interpretation – an admirable enterprise when one considers the dearth of material available on the topic at that time.[22] Ehrlich's course expended substantial energy defending the position that international law does indeed have its own rules for treaty interpretation, even if they have been adapted from Roman law and domestic law rules regarding the interpretation of other legal instruments.[23] In the course of his statement of the principles of treaty interpretation, Ehrlich took a clear position on the

[19] ibid 102 (ch IV, § IX).

[20] See, eg Philip Marshall Brown, 'The Interpretation of the General Pact for the Renunciation of War' (1929) 23 *American Journal of International Law* 374. In addition to the texts cited just above, see, eg, the debate between Brown and Fachiri in the 1929 issues of the *American Journal of International Law*: Alexander P Fachiri, 'Interpretation of Treaties' (1929) 23 *American Journal of International Law* 745; Philip Marshall Brown, 'The Interpretation of Treaties' (1929) 23 *American Journal of International Law* 819; see also Charles Cheney Hyde, 'Judge Anzilotti on the Interpretation of Treaties' (1933) 27 *American Journal of International Law* 502.

[21] See, eg Quincy Wright, 'The Interpretation of Multilateral Treaties' (1929) 23 *American Journal of International Law* 94.

[22] Ehrlich (n 1).

[23] ibid 70–77.

Problem that may have been brief and borne more than a striking resemblance to Vattel's,[24] but went further than the latter in at least three respects.[25] The relative lack of attention subsequent doctrine and case law paid to Ehrlich's study of this issue is accordingly quite surprising, especially when one considers not only the sophistication of its analysis, but also the prestigious forum in which it was presented.

By the 1950s, the static approach to the problem of intertemporal linguistics had become so entrenched that it was declared as an indisputable principle of treaty interpretation by some of the most prominent international legal scholars of the time.

First published in 1953, the leading French-language international law textbook of the time, Charles Rousseau's *Droit international public*, stated the static position unequivocally: 'It goes without saying that the interpreter must take into consideration the meaning of the words at the time the treaty was concluded'.[26] Meanwhile, in the English-language stream of international law scholarship of the same decade, Sir Gerald Fitzmaurice was busy distilling principles of international law from the case law of the then newly founded International Court of Justice. In the first of his seminal series of *British Yearbook of International Law* articles focused on treaty interpretation, Fitzmaurice stated five principles of treaty interpretation that he considered supported by the practice of the Court prior to 31 March 1951.[27] When updating his analysis to take into account the Court's practice in the 1951–54 period, Fitzmaurice considered it necessary to add a sixth principle, arguing that it was sufficiently important to be considered one of the major principles of treaty interpretation.[28] He named it 'the principle of contemporaneity' and promulgated it as follows:

> VI. Principle of Contemporaneity. The terms of a treaty must be interpreted according to the meaning which they possessed, or which would have been attributed to

[24] ibid 109: '120. Whether it is the ordinary meaning or a technical meaning of an expression, the presumption militates in favour of the meaning that the expression had at the time of the conclusion of the treaty, because this is the meaning that is presumed to have been present in the minds of the authors of the text or those who consented to it.' (present author's translation).

[25] First, Ehrlich framed the static approach not as part of a rule of interpretation, but as a default presumption. Second, he extended the application of the static approach beyond the determination of a treaty term's ordinary meaning to the determination of its *special* meaning as well. Third, by emphasising what 'was present in the minds' of the parties, Ehrlich impliedly linked the proper resolution of the problem of intertemporal linguistics to the matter of the drafters' (presumed) knowledge and intention.

[26] Charles E Rousseau, *Droit international public* (Paris, Sirey, 1970) 282–83 (present author's translation).

[27] Gerald Fitzmaurice, 'The Law and Procedure of the International Court of Justice: Treaty Interpretation and Certain Other Treaty Points' (1951) 28 *British Year Book of International Law* 1, 9–25.

[28] Gerald Fitzmaurice, 'The Law and Procedure of the International Court of Justice 1951–4: Treaty Interpretation and Other Treaty Points' (1957) 33 *British Year Book of International Law* 203, 203.

> them, and in the light of current linguistic usage, at the time when the treaty was originally concluded.[29]

By 1957, the answer to the problem of intertemporal linguistics was so unequivocal, that it was not really a problem at all. The most important international legal scholars almost unanimously agreed that, where the meaning of a treaty term had changed after the time of the treaty's conclusion, it was the original meaning that had to be used. Moreover, this static position on the issue had even been authoritatively canonised as a principle of treaty interpretation by Gerald Fitzmaurice who, in 1957, was not only one of the leading authorities on post-war international law, but also the *Institut de droit international* ('IDI')'s Rapporteur on the topic of treaty interpretation and the International Law Commission's Special Rapporteur on the law of treaties. The future therefore looked bright for this past-oriented solution to the Problem.

However, as will now be seen, the principle of contemporaneity would only end up enjoying a moment in the sun. A mere 15 years later, confusion over the content and justifications of the principle of contemporaneity had rendered it both problematic and controversial and, as an apparent consequence, the static approach to the Problem no longer held sway.

II. THE DECLINE AND FALL OF THE PRINCIPLE OF CONTEMPORANEITY

There were two main events that led to the decline and fall of the principle of contemporaneity soon after Fitzmaurice had proclaimed it: (i) the ILC's decision not to include it in draft articles that would ultimately become the Vienna Convention on the Law of Treaties; and (ii) the ICJ's apparent disregard of the principle of contemporaneity and discernible desire to move beyond the static approach in its *Namibia* advisory opinion of 1971. The fact that these two events were the major contributors to how the principle fell from grace is relatively well known. What is less known is why exactly both the ILC and the ICJ were both suddenly so loath to adopt – or even refer to – what had just previously appeared to be a well-established principle of treaty interpretation.

A. During the ILC Codification of the Law of Treaties

At the first session of the United Nations International Law Commission in 1949, the law of treaties was not only included in the agreed list of 14 topics for

[29] ibid 212 and see also, 203–04, where Fitzmaurice effectively defined the principle as 'interpretation of texts and terms in the light of the meaning they possessed, or the sense in which they were normally used at the time when the treaty was concluded' and 225, where he described it as '[t]he principle that treaty terms must be interpreted according to the meaning they possessed, or the sense in which they were normally employed, at the date when the treaty was entered into'.

codification,[30] but also garnered the highest number of votes when the members of the Commission were asked to select the topic for codification which they considered the most deserving of special priority.[31] JL Brierly was appointed the first Special Rapporteur for what became a 20-year codification effort culminating in States negotiating and adopting the VCLT, on the basis of the ILC draft text, at the Vienna conference sessions of 1968 and 1969.

Against some opposition, the ILC study group decided to include draft provisions on the interpretation of treaties, but only began formulating them under significant time pressure some 15 years after the codification project had begun.[32] This meant that, while the Commission's members vigorously debated the law of treaties and the draft codifications thereof at a total of 10 sessions between 1950 and 1966,[33] they only had the time to discuss the *interpretation* of treaties and at *two* of these sessions, in 1964[34] and 1966.[35] Closer investigation of the draft and adopted articles in relation to the intertemporal law and the interpretation of treaties reveals that, at least in respect of these particular topics, there was none of the long and sometimes tortuous back-and-forth process of drafting, discussion, amending and voting that international lawyers tend to associate with the ILC's codification of the law of treaties. Indeed, discounting very minor amendments, there were effectively only three versions of the relevant articles: (i) those introduced at the start of the 1964 session by Waldock in his third report;[36] (ii) those agreed at the end of the 1964 session, sent to governments for comment for two years and returned to the floor of the ILC for discussion at the start of the 1966 session;[37] and (iii) those returned by the drafting committee after the discussions of the 1966 session, voted on and then adopted with

[30] International Law Commission, 'Yearbook 1949, vol I' (New York, United Nations, 1956) 53 (6th meeting – 20 April 1949).

[31] ibid 58–59 (7th meeting – 21 April 1949).

[32] The previous Special Rapporteur on the law of treaties, Sir Gerald Fitzmaurice, had set up drafting a detailed code of the law of treaties and brought such great meticulousness to his task that, by 1960 when he was appointed to the bench of the ICJ, he had not even arrived at considering the sub-topic of treaty interpretation. The Commission was concerned that a law of treaties codification project done in Fitzmaurice's manner would take too long to complete, so instructed his successor as Special Rapporteur, Sir Humphrey Waldock, to 'prepare draft articles on the law of treaties intended to serve as the basis for a convention', not a code, and to 'cover[] the whole subject in two years' – First Report of the Special Rapporteur, Sir Humphrey Waldock (A/CN.4/144) in: International Law Commission, 'Yearbook 1962, vol II' (New York, United Nations, 1964) 29–30.

[33] 'International Law Commission – Summaries: Law of Treaties' (19 January 2009) – untreaty.un.org/ilc/summaries/1_1.htm.

[34] International Law Commission, 'Yearbook 1964, vol I' (New York, United Nations, 1965) 33–39, 275–97 (meetings 728 and 729 of 21–22 May 1964 [intertemporal law] and meetings 765, 766 and 767 of 14–16 July 1964 [on the interpretation of treaties]).

[35] International Law Commission, 'Yearbook 1966, vol I, pt 1' (New York, United Nations, 1967) 183–211 (meetings 869 through 875 of 14–22 June 1966).

[36] International Law Commission, 'Yearbook 1964, vol II' (New York, United Nations, 1965) 6–7, 52–65.

[37] ibid 199–208; ILC Yearbook 1966, vol I, pt 1 (n 35) 183.

very minor amendments as the Vienna Convention of the Law of Treaties at the Vienna Conference in 1969.[38]

At the Vienna Conference sessions of 1968 and 1969, only three of the 105 meetings of the Committee of the Whole[39] and one of the 36 plenary meetings[40] addressed the issue of treaty interpretation. Even on those occasions, most attention fell on the traditionally controversial question of the role that the preparatory work of a treaty should play in its interpretation.[41] The temporal questions surrounding treaty interpretation did not even make the agenda for the Vienna Conference after the ILC's 1964 and 1966 deletions of the two draft articles touching upon them.[42]

In light of these oft-forgotten historical facts, it appears that the time pressure placed on the final Special Rapporteur for the Law of Treaties and the Commission in general prevented the ILC from engaging with the interpretative and temporal issues in sufficient detail for the precise and subtle issue at the core of this study to be adequately addressed. Some members of the Commission even made comments along these lines at the time, with Erik Castrén summing up the ILC's treatment of the problem of how to interpret treaties over time by saying that: 'The problem of the temporal element in regard to the interpretation of treaties was too complex to be dealt with satisfactorily in the last stages of the Commission's work'.[43] Time pressures may indeed have played a role in the ILC's – and ultimately VCLT's – failure to take any position on the problem of intertemporal linguistics, but was the issue really so complex that it could not have been addressed by the ILC in the short time it had available to work on the interpretation of treaties? After all, back in the 1960s, a clear position on the problem had been posited in a couple of sentences by authors from Wolff, Vattel and Lieber to Ehrlich, Rousseau and Fitzmaurice.

In the present author's view, the ILC's work on the law of treaties made the problem of intertemporal linguistics more difficult that it needed to be, principally as a result of how scholars had sought to justify the static approach and how Fitzmaurice had ultimately stated that approach to the problem when he proclaimed it as the principle of contemporaneity.

Two features of how the static approach was presented prior to the codification of the law of treaties were particularly consequential for its ultimate

[38] 'Yearbook 1966, vol II' (New York, United Nations, 1967) 217–26; UN Conference on the Law of Treaties, 'Official Records, Second Session, Vienna' (United Nations, 1969) 57–59; Vienna Convention on the Law of Treaties 1969 (1155 UNTS 331), arts 31–33.

[39] UN Conference on the Law of Treaties, 'Official Records, First Session, Vienna' (Vienna, United Nations, 1968) 166–84 (meetings 31, 32 and 33 of 19, 20 and 22 April 1968).

[40] Vienna Conference Records, 1969 Session (n 38) 57–58 (thirteenth plenary meeting of 6 May 1969).

[41] See Vienna Conference Records, 1968 Session (n 39) 167–85.

[42] Draft art 56 on the intertemporal law and para (1)(b) within the general rule of interpretation (then draft art 69) having been deleted after discussions carried out within the ILC in the Northern summers of 1964 and 1966.

[43] International Law Commission, 'Yearbook 1966, vol I, pt 2' (New York, United Nations, 1967) 189 (per Castrén, 870th meeting – 15 June 1966).

rejection by the ILC and, ultimately, the VCLT. First, scholars asserting the static approach had claimed that it was overwhelmingly supported by the interpretative practice of international courts and tribunals in the 1855–1954 period – when in fact it was not. Second, in the form proclaimed by Fitzmaurice as the principle of contemporaneity, the static approach to the problem of intertemporal linguistics was confusingly linked to the intertemporal law doctrine – when it is substantively and structurally very distinct from that doctrine and would have been much better presented as a mere qualification of the ordinary and special meaning rules for treaty interpretation.

i. Unstable Foundations in the Pre-VCLT International Case Law

Prior promulgations of the static approach, while forceful and unequivocal, ultimately rested on shaky foundations unable to resist the scrutiny of an erudite Law of Treaties Study Group. As noted above, authors in the classical period of international law relied on inter-State practice and statements of general legal principle that were drawn from antiquity and the glossators actively developing Western European domestic law in the Middle Ages, while nineteenth and early-twentieth century writers also drew heavily on domestic law principles when writing on the interpretation of treaties. However, such sources soon came to be considered not good enough; scholars also needing to demonstrate that the principles they were stating were in accordance with the relevant practice of nascent international courts and tribunals. With the creation of the Permanent Court of Arbitration at the very end of the nineteenth century, a first golden era of international third-party dispute settlement was ushered in. Then, after the First World War, the Permanent Court of International Justice, despite only being active for 19 years, produced 29 judgments and 27 advisory opinions.[44] These developments increased the pressure on scholars to invoke international decisions as the basis for their statements of principle.

Even if they were most likely in fact just stating a principle that they considered inherently logical or to be established as a general principle of all legal systems, the twentieth-century authors asserting the static approach to the problem of intertemporal linguistics all cited international case law in support of it. Ehrlich's 1928 Hague Course cited two PCA decisions for the position and an advisory opinion of the Permanent Court of International Justice as an exception to the rule,[45] while Charles Rousseau drew on two further arbitral decisions handed down in the period 1869–1910 to support his unequivocally static view

[44] See www.icj-cij.org/en/pcij.

[45] *Affaire des boutres de Mascate (France/Grande-Bretagne)*, Award (1905) XI RIAA/RSA 83; *The North Atlantic Coast Fisheries Case (Great Britain/United States)*, Award (1910) XI RIAA/RSA 167; *Competence of the ILO in regard to International Regulation of the Conditions of the Labour of Persons Employed in Agriculture*, Advisory Opinion [1922] PCIJ Reports (Series B) No 2; see Ehrlich (n 1) 109–10.

of the issue.[46] Of course, when Fitzmaurice proclaimed this approach as a principle of treaty interpretation in 1957, he did so in a series of articles distilling principles from the 1951–54 practice of the International Court of Justice and cited three new international decisions he believed confirmed it:[47] the *Rights of US Nationals in Morocco* judgment of 1952,[48] Judge Levi Carneiro's separate opinion to the *Minquiers and Ecrehos* judgment of 1953[49] and, somewhat incongruously, the 1956 award of the Arbitral Commission charged with deciding the merits of the *Ambatielos* claim.[50]

Through this process, a principle of treaty interpretation that actually originated in legal principles that predated international dispute settlement soon found itself propped up by a diverse selection of international decisions from the hundred-or-so known to international lawyers at the end of the 1950s. However, those decisions did not in fact lend the static approach as much support as the authors citing them suggested.

A thorough examination of the four cases Rousseau cites in support his claim that 'the interpreter must take into consideration the meaning of the words at the time the treaty was concluded', for example, reveals that not even one of them can be considered a strong authority for the static approach.

Only a somewhat forced reading of the *Puget Sound* case yields support for the static approach. To understand that decision in such a way, one would have to infer semantic change in the treaty term 'belonging to' from the massive legal, social and political changes occurring in the Western United States in the short period between the 1846 conclusion and the 1869 application of the Oregon Treaty.[51] Yet it is in fact more natural to read that award – on account of the express statements of both of the commissioners – as a decision which emphasises the specific intention and contemplations of the drafters in any process of treaty interpretation.[52] This consideration, which ultimately yielded the crucial finding that 'belonging to' was used as a referential shorthand to certain properties and not as a conceptual category, is tangentially relevant to the problem of

[46] *Affaire des Compagnies de la baie d'Hudson et du détroit de Puget*, Sentence (1869) II RIAA/RSA 498; *The Alaska Boundary Case (Great Britain/United States)*, Award (1903) XV RIAA/RSA 481; *Affaire des boutres de Mascate (France/Grande-Bretagne)*, Award (n 45); *North Atlantic Coast Fisheries*, Award (n 45), see Rousseau (n 26) 282–83.

[47] Fitzmaurice (n 28) 225–27.

[48] *Case concerning Rights of Nationals of the United States of America in Morocco (France v United States of America)*, Judgment [1952] ICJ Reports 176.

[49] *The Minquiers and Ecrehos case*, Individual Opinion of Judge Levi Carneiro [1953] ICJ Reports 85.

[50] *The Ambatielos Claim (Greece/United Kingdom of Great Britain and Northern Ireland)*, Award (1956) XII RIAA/RSA 83.

[51] There is a very slight reference to such changes in one part of the report of the award: *Claims of the Hudson's Bay and Puget's Sound Agricultural Companies*, Award (1869) I, ch VIII (Moore's) History and digest of the international arbitrations to which the United States has been a party 237, 264.

[52] See ibid 264–67, per the British Commissioner (264); and per the US Commissioner (266–67).

intertemporal linguistics, but does not take a specific stance on how to interpret treaty terms with meanings that change through time.[53]

Rousseau's citation of the *Alaska Boundary* case in this context is even more surprising. That case was ultimately decided by the fact that the majority of the arbitrators placed greater emphasis on the part of a relevant treaty provision that used the word '*côte*' than another part of it that used the word '*océan*' in relation to an area with geographical features meaning that the coast was not always at the point where the land met the ocean.[54] These critical treaty terms were themselves hardly even interpreted and certainly not subject to any change in meaning between 1825 (when the Treaty of Saint Petersburg was concluded) and 1903 (when the Tribunal was called upon to apply it). Moreover, the *Alaska Boundary* award itself does not contain any express statement of a static approach to the problem of intertemporal linguistics. Indeed, the only static element of this award appears to be its substantial reference to the negotiating history, intentions and even maps contemporaneous with the conclusion of the treaty, attention to interpretative indicia hardly rare at this point in international legal history and not necessarily indicative of a desire to adopt the original rather than later meaning of a treaty term where it changes through time.[55]

For its part, the *Boutres de Mascate* award, cited in support of the static approach by Ehrlich, Rousseau and others such as Yasseen after them,[56] at least contained a statement regarding the meaning of the word '*protégé*' that appears to offer unequivocal support to the static approach.[57] However, when that statement is read in the wider context of the case, it becomes clear that the tribunal was only advocating the use of the meaning of the treaty term *at* the time of a treaty's conclusion instead of the meaning the term had well *prior* to the treaty's conclusion.[58] The award in fact takes no position on how to deal with meanings that emerge *after* the conclusion of a treaty and therefore does not lend any support to the static, as opposed to dynamic, approach to the problem of intertemporal linguistics. Instead, it seems to take an early position on the separate temporal issue now linked to VCLT Article 31(3)(c), namely whether the relevant rules of international law to be considered in an interpretation are those of the time of the treaty's conclusion or afterwards. While it appears

[53] See further Julian Wyatt, 'An Original or Modern-Day Meaning for Treaty Terms? The Problem of Intertemporal Linguistics in the Case Law of International Courts and Tribunals' (Doctorat en droit, University of Geneva, 2017) 53–59 – archive-ouverte.unige.ch/unige:102376 (s 3.1.1).

[54] For the treaty provision see Traité de Saint Pétersbourg 1825 [1825] *Hertslet's Commercial Treaties* 366, 367–68; For how the interpretative issue was ultimately decided (by the English Baron Alverstone after the American and Canadian arbitrators followed the positions of the US and Canada respectively): *Alaska Boundary*, Award (n 46) 497–98.

[55] See further Wyatt (n 53) 62–66 (s 3.1.3).

[56] Ehrlich (n 1) 109–10; Rousseau (n 26) 283; Mustafa Kamil Yasseen, 'L'interprétation des traités d'après la Convention de Vienne sur le droit des traités' (1976) 151 *Collected Courses of the Hague Academy of International Law* 1, 31.

[57] *Affaire des boutres de Mascate (France/Grande-Bretagne)*, Award (n 45) 94.

[58] See further Wyatt (n 53) 67–71 (s 3.1.4).

static by preferring the international law *rules* in existence at the time of the treaty's conclusion, it does not evince any clear preference in relation to the particular problem of whether to assign a changing treaty term its original or later *meaning*.[59]

Even the fourth instance cited by Rousseau, the landmark *North Atlantic Coast Fisheries* case, does not give as much support to the static approach as is commonly thought.[60] The official award states a static approach to treaty interpretation and appears to rely on it, but, if readers accept the Court's claim that the word 'bays' should be understood in its geographical and not its legal sense, then the word interpreted does not seem to have undergone the meaning change that would require either a genuinely static or a genuinely dynamic approach to be taken.[61] Moreover, while the case's *award* itself favours instruments prior to and contemporary with the treaty's conclusion, the unofficial, but practically much more important *recommendation* of the tribunal betrays a tendency toward to the dynamic approach by invoking texts, rules and practice from well after the treaty's conclusion in order to illuminate the meaning of the treaty term.[62] Indeed, on the issue addressed by this study, the *North Atlantic Coast Fisheries* award and the recommendation impliedly take almost diametrically opposed positions, indicating that, for the Tribunal, a static approach to the problem of intertemporal linguistics might have been legally required, but, in some cases, only a dynamic approach will be useful to the parties. Then there is the oft-ignored but significant matter of Luis Drago's quite lengthy and well-reasoned dissenting opinion that not only criticises elements of the static approach taken in the majority's award, but itself can be deemed the first opinion of an international court or tribunal advocating a clearly dynamic approach to the problem of intertemporal linguistics – both through its express terms and the interpretative processes it undertakes.[63]

Like the pre-World War I decisions cited by several authors in support of the static approach that became the principle of contemporaneity, the inter-war and post-war 'authorities' make some notable explicit statements in support of the static approach to the Problem but, when carefully considered in their full context, turn out to be much less supportive of that approach than claimed.

Of the three authorities for the principle of contemporaneity that Fitzmaurice found in the practice of the 1950s, only one actually proceeded to interpret a treaty in a way which selected the original meaning of a treaty term over its later meanings.

[59] See s 5.I.B below.
[60] See generally Wyatt (n 53) 84–103 (s 3.1.6).
[61] See in particular *North Atlantic Coast Fisheries*, Award (n 45) 195–96.
[62] ibid 199.
[63] See in particular *The North Atlantic Coast Fisheries Case (Great Britain, United States), Grounds for the Dissent to the Award on Question V by Dr Luis M Drago* (1910) XI RIAA/RSA 203, 206–10.

By uttering the phrase 'an instrument must not be appraised in the light of concepts which are not contemporaneous with it',[64] Judge Levi Carneiro's separate but concurring opinion in the *Minquiers and Ecrehos* case of 1953 appears prima facie to offer clear support to the static approach. It was never going to be missed by Fitzmaurice, who was a member of the British team of counsel on that case and is understandably also quoted in support of the principle of contemporaneity by jurists ranging from Judge van Wyk in his dissenting opinion in the 1962 phase of the *South West Africa* case,[65] to Yasseen's Hague Course[66] and Sinclair's important monograph on treaty law.[67] However, when considered in its wider context, it is far from clear that Judge Levi Carneiro's dictum supports the full scope of the principle of contemporaneity for which it is so often adduced as an authority.[68]

First, the *Minquiers and Ecrehos* case was ultimately decided on the basis of the British manifestations of sovereignty over the islands throughout this period, not on the basis of a particular interpretation of any one or more treaties, the Court finding that none of the treaties cited by the parties to the dispute (the Treaty of Paris of 1259, Treaty of Calais of 1360 and the Treaty of Troyes of 1420) specified which islands belonged to which country's King.[69] Second, as the sentence immediately prior to his much-quoted dictum – 'I do not regard the Treaty of Paris as a treaty of frontiers'[70] – reveals, Judge Levi Carneiro only used this apparently static approach to characterise the treaty (as a whole) as not falling within a legal category, not to ascertain the meaning of a specific treaty term.[71] Third, Judge Levi Carneiro determined the *effects* of the 1259 treaty, not its *meaning*, this being revealed by his famous dictum's use of the verb 'to appraise' rather than the verb 'to interpret',[72] as well as the fact that the first element of the intertemporal law doctrine – relating to the appreciation of juridical facts rather than the interpretation of treaty provisions – had been the subject of considerable attention in the oral pleadings before the *Minquiers and Ecrehos* Court.[73] By insisting on the notion of vassalage, Judge Levi Carneiro was merely seeking to determine the legal

[64] *Minquiers and Ecrehos*, Levi Carneiro Individual Opinion (n 49) 91.

[65] *South West Africa Cases (Ethiopia v South Africa; Liberia v South Africa)* (Preliminary Objections), Dissenting Opinion of Judge van Wyk [1962] ICJ Reports 575, 584.

[66] Yasseen (n 56) 27, 31.

[67] Ian Sinclair, *The Vienna Convention on the Law of Treaties* (Manchester, Manchester University Press, 1984) 140.

[68] See further Wyatt (n 53) 122–25 (s 3.2.4).

[69] See *The Minquiers and Ecrehos case*, Judgment [1953] ICJ Reports 47, 54–55.

[70] *Minquiers and Ecrehos*, Levi Carneiro Individual Opinion (n 49) 91.

[71] ibid.

[72] ibid.

[73] See especially 'Pleadings, Oral Arguments, Documents', *The Minquiers and Ecrehos case*, vol II (International Court of Justice, 1953) 50–53, 59 (per Sir L. Heald) and 387 (per Prof Gros), on the distinction between the intertemporal law doctrine and the problem of intertemporal linguistics, see s 2.II.A.ii below.

effects of the treaty in its 1259 factual and legal context, rather than in the very different 1953 context of modern versions of such treaties focussed on the issue of territorial sovereignty.

In a similar fashion, while the substantive decision in the *Ambatielos* cases on the scope of the seventeenth-century treaty terms 'justice', 'right' and 'equity' made a general statement apparently favouring the static approach to the problem of intertemporal linguistics,[74] it did not apply this approach by restricting itself to the seventeenth-century meaning of those terms. The Commissioners' conclusion as to the meaning of the words 'justice', 'right' and 'equity' was not that they should be given their seventeenth-century meaning, but that their meaning was restricted to how those words are understood within the confines of each party's domestic legal system. The award clearly stated in a number of places that these words cannot have a meaning 'independent of the rules of English law' or 'different from that for which the municipal law of the State concerned provides',[75] yet reveals no effort to restrict the scope of these terms to English law of the seventeenth or even the eighteenth century. When the Commission fixed a meaning of the treaty terms in order to evaluate Greece's claims, it opted for a domestic meaning over an international meaning, not an original over a later meaning.[76]

Ultimately, while there were indeed several explicit statements in the case law of the pre-VCLT period that favoured the static approach to the problem of intertemporal linguistics, there were also several statements in favour of the dynamic approach that could and should have counterbalanced them. Like Luis Drago's *North Atlantic Coast Fisheries* dissent, the PCIJ's advisory opinion on *Nationality Decrees Issued in Tunis and Morocco* in fact offers more support to the dynamic than static approach, albeit in the very specific and uncontroversial context of interpreting a term that appears to expressly refer to evolving customary international law.[77] In addition, while Judge Levi Carneiro's individual *Minquiers and Ecrehos* opinion made a clear statement in favour of the static approach,[78] it is to some extent counter-balanced by the short, but potently progressive and dynamic approach contained in the individual declaration that Judge Alvarez appended to the judgment in the same case.[79]

In the end, among all the international decisions of the 1855–1954 period cited in support of the static approach to the problem of intertemporal linguistics, the ICJ's 1952 *Rights of US Nationals in Morocco* judgment stands alone as

[74] *The Ambatielos Claim (Greece/United Kingdom of Great Britain and Northern Ireland)*, Award (n 50) 108: 'Naturally, their wording was influenced by the customs of the period, and they must obviously be interpreted in the light of this fact.'

[75] ibid 109–10.

[76] See further Wyatt (n 53) 125–30 (s 3.2.5).

[77] *Nationality Decrees in Tunis and Morocco*, Advisory Opinion [1923] PCIJ Reports (Series B) No 4, 24, see also s 9.III below.

[78] *Minquiers and Ecrehos*, Levi Carneiro Individual Opinion (n 49) 91.

[79] *Minquiers and Ecrehos*, Judgment (n 69) 73.

a true authority for that approach.[80] There are aspects of the Court's important interpretation of the term 'dispute' in that judgment that are conceptually troublesome, but it cannot be denied that it used the original and not later meaning of this term.[81] Moreover, the Court's statement and use of the static approach in relation to the meaning of 'dispute' is further backed up by an oft-ignored purported use of the static approach in the Court's interpretation of the treaty expression 'economic liberty without any inequality'.[82] Even if it is far from certain that this expression underwent the semantic change capable of rendering the interpretation a clear application of the static approach to the Problem, the Court's focus on interpreting it 'against the background of the treaty provisions relating to trade and equality of treatment in economic matters existing at that time' further attests to its belief that treaty terms should be interpreted according to the meaning that they had at the time of the treaty's conclusion instead of the meaning they had at the time of the treaty's application.[83]

However, one strong case cannot support a principle on its own – and certainly not when there are other decisions and opinions from the same period advocating a contrary position on the same question. While the 1855–1954 practice clearly tended towards support for a static approach to the problem of intertemporal linguistics, it certainly did not conclusively establish it nor overwhelmingly apply it.[84] Moreover, by proclaiming the existence of principle of treaty interpretation on the basis of cases that ultimately arrived at their findings on the basis of other judicial approaches, authors such as Ehrlich, Rousseau and Fitzmaurice ran the risk of confusing readers and undermining the principle they were seeking to strengthen.

Inevitably, when the ILC's learned Law of Treaties Study Group turned its attention to the interpretation of treaties, attention fell on the case law that had been invoked in support of the various principles. Extensive reference to international decisions constitutes a feature of the Summary Records of the ILC's 1960s sessions formulating the law of treaties, especially when juxtaposed against the records of previous scholarly discussions of the law of treaties, including the IDI's 1956 Grenada session in which the case law of the PCA, PCIJ and ICJ is only very rarely mentioned.[85]

In the relevant parts of his third report introducing the topic of treaty interpretation, Special Rapporteur Waldock relied heavily on the *North Atlantic Fisheries* case cited by Ehrlich and Rousseau and also on the 1909 *Grisbadarna*

[80] *US Nationals in Morocco*, Judgment (n 48).
[81] ibid 189; see further Wyatt (n 53) 113–20 (ss 3.2.3.1 through 3.2.3.4).
[82] *US Nationals in Morocco*, Judgment (n 48) 183–84.
[83] ibid; see further Wyatt (n 53) 120–22 (s 3.2.3.5).
[84] Note that there was another international decision of this early period that appeared to constitute true authority for the static approach, but was not included among the case law invoked as authorities for the static approach in the pre-VCLT literature: *First award under the Convention between Costa Rica and Nicaragua of 8 April 1896 for the demarcation of the boundary between the two Republics*, Award (1897) XXVIII RIAA/RSA 215; see further Wyatt (n 53) 59–62 (s 3.1.2).
[85] Institut de droit international, 'De l'interprétation des traités' (1956) 46 *Annuaire*.

award, while also citing the *Rights of US Nationals in Morocco* judgment which Fitzmaurice had invoked to extend the scope of the principle of contemporaneity from rules of law to any linguistic usage.[86] This in turn provoked animated discussions within the ILC among international law experts who clearly knew these cases very well.

The fact that Waldock cited the *Grisbadarna* award among three '[i]nstances of the application of' the principle of contemporaneity was particularly problematic.[87] None of Ehrlich, Rousseau or Fitzmaurice had cited the 1909 *Grisbadarna* award among the decisions they understood as supporting the static approach, most likely because it did not.

The *Grisbadarna* case was a complex maritime boundary delimitation case.[88] The segment of the boundary closest to the shore had been agreed between the parties, so the Tribunal was required to delimit two segments of it: between the map-points XIX and XX and between the map-point XX and the beginning of the high seas. It was the outermost part of this boundary reaching out into the strait known as 'Skagerrak' that was the main matter of dispute, partly because of how its delimitation would affect rights to the lobster-filled shoals of the Grisbådarna banks.[89]

Three treaties were potentially applicable to this boundary: (i) the Peace Treaty of Roskilde of February–March 1658 by which Denmark ceded the province of Bohuslän to Sweden; (ii) the treaty of Copenhagen of 1660 by which the cession of Bohuslän in the Treaty of Roskilde was affirmed; and (iii) the boundary treaty of 26 October 1661 which is sometimes referred to as a 'regulation' carrying out the broader terms of the earlier peace treaties.

For present purposes, the Tribunal made two important findings. The first was that the 1661 Treaty did not fix the boundary beyond a point somewhere between map-points XIX and XX, and that this treaty could therefore not determine the boundary line for (the entirety of) either of the segments that the Tribunal was required to delimit. To the extent that this finding required an evaluation of the scope of the boundary that the 1661 Treaty delimited, it was an interpretative finding.[90] However, it certainly does not appear to have involved the interpretation of a treaty term, the Tribunal having apparently identified the point to which the 1661 Treaty may have delimited the boundary – 'point A' – on the basis of the map attached to that treaty rather than by interpreting any of its terms.

[86] ILC Yearbook 1964, vol II (n 36) 9–10, 57.

[87] ibid 57.

[88] *Affaire des Grisbadarna (Norvège/Suède)*, Award (1909) XI RIAA/RSA 147. For further analysis of the supposedly interpretative aspects of this case, see Wyatt (n 53) 105–11 (s 3.2.2).

[89] See 'Decision of the Permanent Court of Arbitration in the Matter of the Maritime Boundary Dispute between Norway and Sweden' (1 January 1910) 4 *The American Journal of International Law* 226, 234; Robert Kolb, *Case Law on Equitable Maritime Delimitation/ Jurisprudence sur les délimitations maritimes selon l'équité: Digest and Commentaries/ Répertoire et commentaries* (Alan Perry tr, The Hague, Martinus Nijhoff Publishers, 2003) 1–2, 8.

[90] *Affaire des Grisbadarna (Norvège/Suède)*, Award (n 88) 158.

The second finding, most important for the outcome of the case, was the Tribunal's decision to delimit the outermost segment of the border through neither the use of a method disclosed in any of the potentially applicable treaties, nor the use of either of the methods proposed for delimiting this segment by the two parties, but instead by drawing a line perpendicularly to the general direction of the coast of the land territory of which the maritime territory constituted an appurtenance.[91] The arbitrators considered this perpendicular-line rule to be 'much more in accord with the ideas of the seventeenth century and with the notion of law prevailing at that time' and capable of enabling them 'to arrive at a just and lawful determination of the boundary'.[92]

While sometimes considered supportive of the principle of contemporaneity, this second finding clearly did not result from the preference of an original meaning of a treaty term over the later meaning of a treaty term – or even from treaty interpretation at all. Indeed, the Tribunal simply filled a gap that the treaties did not cover; and chose to do it by using a principle that it considered – wrongly according to the analysis of Kolb[93] – to be more consistent with the legal principles applying at the time of those treaties. This deference to legal principles supposedly prevailing at the time that the treaties delimiting part of the border were concluded appears static but is certainly not a static approach to the *interpretative* problem at the core of this study. At most, the Tribunal's delimitation of the outermost segment of the maritime boundary constituted an attempt to follow the dictates of what would later be called the intertemporal law doctrine,[94] it did not take a position on the separate problem of intertemporal linguistics.

Waldock's reference to elements of this second finding of the *Grisbadarna* award as an instance of the application of the principle of contemporaneity must therefore have created great confusion about what that principle entailed. In the parts of the award where the Tribunal delimits the outermost segment of the boundary, it does not refer to interpreting any treaty or even to the act of interpretation itself, let alone different interpretative factors. Of course, Waldock also – and predominantly – referred to the *Grisbadarna* award as an instance of the application of the *intertemporal law*,[95] which it manifestly was. Indeed, by resorting to citing a case that is an authority for the intertemporal law doctrine as an instance of the principle of contemporaneity being applied, Waldock not only demonstrated the lack of international case law clearly applying the principle of contemporaneity at that time, but also revealed the conceptual confusion that would ultimately inflict mortal damage on the principle of contemporaneity.

[91] ibid 159–60; *The Grisbadarna Case (Norway/Sweden)*, Award (1909) XI The Hague Court Reports 121, 128–29.

[92] *Affaire des Grisbadarna (Norvège/Suède)*, Award (n 88) 160; *The Grisbadarna Case (Norway/Sweden)*, Award (n 91) 129.

[93] Kolb (n 89) 14.

[94] *Affaire des Grisbadarna (Norvège/Suède)*, Award (n 88) 159; *The Grisbadarna Case (Norway/Sweden)*, Award (n 91) 127.

[95] ILC Yearbook 1964, vol II (n 36) 9–10.

ii. Confusing Link to the Intertemporal Law Doctrine

In the present author's view, it was this linking of the principle of contemporaneity to the intertemporal law doctrine that most impaired not only the development of the principle of contemporaneity, but also many subsequent discussions of the problem of intertemporal linguistics. This unfortunate and conceptually erroneous linkage may have been due in large part to the work of Sir Humphrey Waldock in his role as the much hurried – and harried – final ILC Special Rapporteur on the Law of Treaties, but in fact has its origins in the 1957 *BYBIL* article in which Sir Gerald Fitzmaurice proclaimed the principle of contemporaneity.

After his first proper statement of the principle of contemporaneity on page 212 of his 1957 *BYBIL* article, Fitzmaurice began by explaining – quite correctly – that it 'could perhaps be regarded as constituting in a sense no more than a qualification to the principle (No II) of the natural and ordinary meaning'.[96] However, he then immediately moved on to comment on 'its affinities with the principle of the intertemporal law', before eventually going on to describe the principle of contemporaneity as 'really a particular application of the doctrine of the intertemporal law'.[97]

Waldock's reliance on the work of Fitzmaurice for the ILC's initial draft articles on treaty interpretation is palpable on the face of his third report of 1964, the first report in which an ILC Special Rapporteur tackled the question. For the first draft of those articles, he openly took 'inspiration from the 1956 resolution of the Institute of International Law' – which had been put together by Fitzmaurice as the IDI's rapporteur for that question – and 'from Sir G Fitzmaurice's formulation of the "major principles" of interpretation in' his 1957 *BYBIL* article,[98] before even quoting Fitzmaurice's *BYBIL* principles of treaty interpretation *in extenso*.[99]

Remarkably, Waldock was so influenced by Fitzmaurice's mention of affinities between the principle of contemporaneity and the intertemporal law doctrine that he immediately characterised it as but 'a reformulation of the first aspect of Judge Huber's "inter-temporal" law submitted to the Commission in article 56'.[100] Indeed, while Fitzmaurice had proclaimed the principle of contemporaneity as a principle of treaty *interpretation*, instead of including it in the interpretative section of part III of his draft, Waldock decided to put it in a section devoted to 'the *application* and *effects* of treaties' and as a paragraph of a provision entitled '[t]he intertemporal law'.[101] The first paragraph of draft article 56 was expressed as follows: '1. A treaty is to be interpreted in the

[96] Fitzmaurice (n 28) 212.
[97] ibid 212, 225.
[98] ILC Yearbook 1964, vol II (n 36) 55, paragraph 10.
[99] ibid 55–56 (Special Rapporteur's commentary on 'Article 70 – General rules', paragraph 12).
[100] ibid 56, paragraph 15.
[101] ibid 7–10 (Sir Humphrey Waldock's Third Report on the Law of Treaties).

light of the law in force at the time when the treaty was drawn up'.[102] Waldock's presentation of his draft article 56 to the members of the ILC in meetings on 21 and 22 May 1964 was met with confusion, apprehension and criticism. Several members of the commission understandably struggled with the placement of the rule outside the draft articles' section on the interpretation of treaties and suggested that it be moved to that section.[103] Others were concerned by this principle being stated under the title 'the intertemporal law' and therefore being linked to a notoriously difficult doctrine that could in turn raise conceptual difficulties that might prevent the Commission from making any progress on provisions said to be stating it.[104]

The intertemporal law doctrine is, after all, one of the most complex and misunderstood doctrines of general international law. As Judge Al-Khasawneh has noted, though '[a]t first sight it looks simple', 'the concept of the intertemporal law is an irretrievably elusive one'.[105] By linking the principle of contemporaneity to the intertemporal law, Waldock instantly made the principle of contemporaneity appear more complex and more controversial than it would have been had it been considered, for example, as a qualification on the interpretative rule insisting on the interpretation of treaty terms according to their ordinary meaning. Although a few members of the Commission specifically expressed their notional support for the principle that had been set out in Waldock's article 56(1),[106] most had reservations about taking such a clear position on a topic as difficult as the intersection between the intertemporal law and treaty interpretation.[107] This nervousness appears to have stemmed more obviously from unease over the meaning of the intertemporal law doctrine than from unease over the meaning of the principle of contemporaneity.

That the principle of contemporaneity should never have been linked to the intertemporal law doctrine is obvious upon closer consideration of what the intertemporal law doctrine entails. Fortunately, there is near-universal agreement

[102] ibid 8 (Sir Humphrey Waldock's Third Report on the Law of Treaties).

[103] ILC Yearbook 1964, vol I (n 34) 38 (per Amado, 729th meeting – 22 May 1964, § 47); ibid 37 (per de Luna, 729th meeting – 22 May 1964, § 32); ibid 36 (per Elias, 729th meeting – 22 May 1964, § 19); ibid 35 (per Castrén, 729th meeting – 22 May 1964, § 2); ibid 39 (per Ago, 729th meeting – 22 May 1964, § 50).

[104] ILC Yearbook 1964, vol I (n 34) 35 (per Reuter, 729th meeting – 22 May 1964, §§ 8–10); see, eg ibid 36 (per Bartos, 729th meeting – 22 May 1964, § 22).

[105] *Land and Maritime Boundary between Cameroon and Nigeria (Cameroon v Nigeria: Equatorial Guinea intervening)* (Merits), Separate Opinion of Judge Al-Khasawneh [2002] ICJ Reports 492, 500 (§ 11).

[106] ILC Yearbook 1964, vol I (n 34) 34 (per Paredes, 728th meeting – 21 May 1964, § 12); ibid 35 (per Reuter, 729th meeting – 22 May 1964, § 10); ibid 38–39 (per El-Erian, 729th meeting – 22 May 1964, § 48); ibid 39 (per Ago, 729th meeting – 22 May 1964, § 52).

[107] See, eg ILC Yearbook 1964, vol I (n 34) 34 (per Jiménez de Aréchaga, 728th meeting – 21 May 1964, § 10); ibid 35 (per Pal, 729th meeting – 22 May 1964, § 4); ibid 36–37 (per Tsuruoka, 729th meeting – 22 May 1964, § 24).

among international lawyers that the doctrine was stated in the following part of Judge Huber's *Island of Palmas* award:[108]

> Both Parties are also agreed that *a juridical fact must be appreciated* in the light of the law contemporary with it, and not of the law in force at the time when a dispute in regard to it arises or falls to be settled. *The effect of discovery by Spain* is therefore to be determined by the rules of international law in force in the first half of the 16th century – or (to take the earliest date) in the first quarter of it, i.e. at the time when the Portuguese or Spaniards made their appearance in the Sea of Celebes.[109]

Once one takes the perspective prompted by the problem of intertemporal linguistics, even a superficial review of this passage uncovers the differences between the principle of contemporaneity and the doctrine of the intertemporal law. The first limb of Huber's intertemporal law statement – the same passage as that quoted by Waldock in his third report[110] – speaks of the *appreciation* of acts, not the *interpretation* of terms or provisions. Huber speaks of *juridical facts* – not *treaty terms* or provisions – and of *effects* – not *meanings*. When Waldock said that 'treaties also are "juridical facts" to which the inter-temporal law applies',[111] he showed how the intertemporal law doctrine could be linked to the legal effects produced by treaties, but did not demonstrate that the doctrine has anything to do with ascertaining the meaning of a treaty's terms. The intertemporal law doctrine is dedicated to determining the legal effects of juridical facts or acts, not the meaning of legal norms. As explained by Reuter in his *Introduction au droit des traités*, one must distinguish between the juridical fact of making a law-making treaty and the treaty norm made law through that treaty-making act.[112]

With this act-versus-result distinction in mind, it is apparent that we should not apply the intertemporal law doctrine to the meaning of norms – or, indeed, to anything other than determining whether those norms came into existence. Of course, in sovereignty contexts, such as the *Island of Palmas* situation itself, the meaning of a treaty and its legal effects may coincide. It might then follow from this aspect of the intertemporal law doctrine that the provisions of treaties ceding or granting sovereignty should be understood on the basis of their

[108] See, eg 'Pleadings, Oral Arguments, Documents' (n 73) 50; Gerald Fitzmaurice, 'The Law and Procedure of the International Court of Justice, 1951–54: General Principles and Sources of Law' (1953) 30 *British Year Book of International Law* 1, 5; Shabtai Rosenne, 'The Temporal Application of the Vienna Convention on the Law of Treaties' (1970) 4 *Cornell International Law Journal* 1, 13; *The Right to Information on Consular Assistance in the Framework of the Guarantees of the Due Process of Law*, Concurring Opinion of Judge Cançado Trindade [1999] Inter-Am Ct HR (Ser A) No 16 (1999) 3 (§ 9, footnote 106).

[109] *Island of Palmas case (Netherlands/USA)*, Award (1928) XII RIAA/RSA 167, 845 (emphasis added).

[110] ILC Yearbook 1964, vol II (n 36) 9 (§ 1).

[111] ibid.

[112] Paul Reuter, *Introduction au droit des traités*, 3rd edn (Paris, Presses Universitaires de France, 1995) 21 (§ 50).

meaning contemporaneous with their conclusion, because the effects of such a treaty will frequently align exactly with the meaning of its terms.[113] However, it cannot have a wider application than this. In many non-territorial contexts, the specific effects intended to be produced by a treaty will be temporally distant from the moment of the treaty's conclusion. For example, in a constitutive treaty of an international organisation, States allow the organisation to make decisions on its behalf, but never know exactly what those decisions will be. To say that the specific effects produced by the State's ratification or acceptance of that treaty should be appreciated at the time of treaty's conclusion rests on the false assumption that they can be.

In any event, in the *Island of Palmas* case itself there was not even any such coincidence between the time used to determine the meaning of a treaty term and the time used to determine the treaty's effects, because the judicial fact whose effects needed to be determined was not a treaty-making act, but the act of discovery.[114] The dictum accordingly says absolutely nothing about treaty interpretation in particular and, as will be seen, it is even dangerous to apply to treaty interpretation by analogy.

Ultimately it appears that Waldock's effort to read a temporal rule of interpretation into the intertemporal law doctrine constitutes a further example of an often ill-advised over-reliance on the statement of the intertemporal law doctrine in the *Island of Palmas* award. As Judge Higgins has pointed out in her academic writing, 'the Huber *dictum* … has … been read in the most remarkably extensive fashion, as providing obligatory rules in circumstances that it never addressed, with consequences that it never intended'.[115] The interpretative aspect that Fitzmaurice – and with him Waldock – believed 'follows automatically' from that dictum and the doctrine of the intertemporal law in fact does not follow from it at all. Indeed, it is significant that many of the prominent scholars of international law who looked closely at the problem of the intertemporal law as part of the Institute of International Law's Eleventh Commission, including the rapporteur Max Sørensen himself, considered that the interpretative question posed by the problem of intertemporal linguistics was not part of the problem of the intertemporal law at all.[116]

When one considers the complexity already inherent in the intertemporal law doctrine and Waldock's somewhat tortured attempt to convert it into superficially incompatible yet supposedly complementary series of rules of treaty interpretation and treaty application, it is difficult to argue with do Nascimento

[113] See ss 9.V and 9.VIII below.

[114] *Island of Palmas*, Award (n 109) 843–46.

[115] Rosalyn Higgins, 'Time and the Law: International Perspectives on an Old Problem' (1997) 46 *International & Comparative Law Quarterly* 501, 516.

[116] Institut de droit international and Max Sørensen, 'Le problème dit du droit intertemporel dans l'ordre international – Rapport provisoire' (12 February 1973) *Annuaire* 1, 89 (Sørensen's rapport définitif); ibid 105 (per Guggenheim, 22 June 1972); see also ibid 107–08 (per Lachs, 14 November 1972).

e Silva's view that draft article 56 became the 'most difficult provision of those studied by the International Law Commission'.[117] As Al-Khasawneh has noted more recently,

> [t]he confusion was such that neither the International Law Commission ... nor the Vienna Conference itself, were able to resolve the issue, with the consequence that the concept of intertemporal law was dropped from the 1969 Vienna Convention on the Law of Treaties.[118]

The fact that draft article 56 was deleted had implications for the intertemporal law doctrine, the principle of contemporaneity and the wider problem of intertemporal linguistics. Yet the damage inflicted by the ill-advised linking of the principle to the doctrine in the first place was, from the perspective of the Problem, far more serious. Indeed, the removal of a principle of treaty interpretation from the application section of the draft where it appeared under the heading of a conceptually distinct doctrine was correct and beneficial. If the principle of contemporaneity had found a more faithful expression in the section of the draft articles under interpretation, international legal thinking on the problem of intertemporal linguistics would undoubtedly have been advanced. However, even the separate text that appeared in the name of the principle of contemporaneity in the draft provisions on treaty interpretation was still linked, through the commentary to it, to the intertemporal law doctrine. In particular, the understanding of the principle was undermined by the fact that one of the three international decisions postulated as an application of it – the *Grisbadarna* award – was, as we have seen, actually an intertemporal law case and not an interpretation case at all.

Moreover, Waldock's intertemporal law-influenced view of the principle of contemporaneity prompted him to state it in a watered-down form that caused it to diverge from what had initially encapsulated the static approach in two important respects.

First, the principle of contemporaneity – and the discussion of the problem of intertemporal linguistics – became estranged from the notions of ordinary and special meaning to which they had previously and quite correctly been linked. Fitzmaurice, when he promulgated the principle of contemporaneity, explicitly characterised it as 'no more than a qualification to' the natural and ordinary meaning rule and only stated it as a separate principle reluctantly on account of its especial importance.[119] Waldock preferred to understand the principle as an aspect of the (non-interpretative) doctrine of the intertemporal law, so steered it irretrievably away from the position it should have held as a mere qualification on how to determine the ordinary or special meaning of a contested treaty term.

[117] Geraldo Eulalio do Nascimento e Silva, 'Le facteur temps et les traités' (1977) 154 *Collected Courses of the Hague Academy of International Law* 215, 266.

[118] *Land and Maritime Boundary (Cameroon v Nigeria)*, Al-Khasawneh Separate Opinion (n 105) 502 (§ 14).

[119] Fitzmaurice (n 28) 212.

Second, Waldock – and, with him, most of the ILC's Law of Treaties Study Group – appeared to understand the principle of contemporaneity as relating purely to changes of a legal nature when it in fact extended beyond that to disavow all post-treaty changes that impacted on the meaning of a treaty term, including those of a mere linguistic and non-legal nature. Both of Waldock's draft provisions supposedly incorporating the principle of contemporaneity reflect this restriction: draft article 56(1) said that '[a] treaty is to be interpreted in the light of the *law* in force at the time when [it] was drawn up',[120] while his draft paragraph 1(b) of the general rule of interpretation spoke of interpreting a treaty '[i]n the light of the *rules of general international law* in force at the time of its conclusion'.[121] Even though Waldock once noted that the scope of the principle should, in accordance with the *Rights of US Nationals in Morocco* judgment, extend to 'linguistic usage' too,[122] his formulation of the principle of contemporaneity in treaty interpretation was effectively silent as to how a treaty term should be interpreted where its general and not necessarily legal meaning has undergone changes between the time of the treaty's conclusion and the time of its application.

The members of the Commission appeared to accept that the ILC was only going to deal with the temporal aspect of treaty interpretation solely insofar as a treaty's meaning was influenced by legal changes and started debating the issue solely in relation to which era's 'relevant rules of international law' should be taken into account under what ultimately became VCLT Article 31(3)(c).[123] This was a natural consequence of the fact that this was the only context in which Waldock had stated the principle of contemporaneity:

> Article 69. General rule of interpretation
>
> 1. A treaty shall be interpreted in good faith in accordance with the ordinary meaning to be given to each term:
>
> (a) In the context of the treaty and in the light of its objects and purposes; and
> (b) In the light of the rules of general international law in force at the time of its conclusion.[124]

Ultimately, and in part due to the confusion generated by how Waldock had presented the principle of contemporaneity, this temporal qualification on the 'relevant rules' was also removed from the draft, leaving temporal questions relating to the meaning of treaty terms unanswered by the drafts of the law of treaties that the ILC sent to the Vienna Conference.

120 ILC Yearbook 1964, vol II (n 36) 8 (Sir Humphrey Waldock's Third Report on the Law of Treaties) (emphasis added).

121 See ibid 199 (emphasis added).

122 ibid 57 (Sir Humphrey Waldock's Third Report on the Law of Treaties).

123 ILC Yearbook 1964, vol I (n 34) 278–81 (765th meeting – 14 July 1964, § 49 [per Tunkin], §§ 60–62 [per Verdross], § 93 [per Yasseen]).

124 ILC Yearbook 1964, vol II (n 36) 199.

The fact that the ILC's Law of Treaties study group – and the Vienna Convention that emerged from its work – chose not to take a position on whether treaty interpreters should use the original or later meaning of a treaty term whose meaning changed through time is not a problem in-and-of-itself. What is more disappointing from the perspective of the present study is that the principle of contemporaneity which, when originally stated, took a clear position on the problem of intertemporal linguistics and thereby focussed minds directly on the Problem, soon came to be understood in a sense that was only tangentially related to the Problem and therefore actually diverted attention away from it.

B. In the Relevant ICJ Case Law of the 1960s and 1970s

The second main blow to the principle of contemporaneity and the static approach that it originally represented was inflicted by the International Court of Justice. While the ILC and the VCLT may have left the principle of contemporaneity vulnerable by refusing to adopt it as a principle, it was the ICJ that essentially killed it off when, in its landmark *Namibia* advisory opinion, it did not mention the principle of contemporaneity, only paid lip service to the static approach and appeared to focus its attention on sowing the seeds for a counter-doctrine that favoured the later-emerging meaning of a treaty term.

It is often forgotten that the *Namibia* opinion's famous paragraph 53, so often regarded as the *fons et origo* of the evolutionary treaty interpretation doctrine, in fact began with an apparent reference to the static approach:

> *Mindful as it is of the primary necessity of interpreting an instrument in accordance with the intentions of the parties at the time of its conclusion*, the Court is bound to take into account the fact that the concepts embodied in Article 22 of the Covenant … were not static, but were by definition evolutionary …[125]

This has caused some distinguished international lawyers to insist that the Court was in fact declaring the principle of contemporaneity to be the primary rule and evolutionary treaty interpretation to be merely an occasional exception to it.[126] Ian Sinclair even took a similar view of the ICJ's next major dynamic treaty interpretation decision, the *Aegean Sea* judgment of 1978,[127] citing its 'variance with the principle of contemporaneity' and noting the 'special features of the *Aegean Continental Shelf* case' that were able to make it an exception to the rule.[128] Most authors, however, have instead drawn attention to the far

[125] *Legal Consequences for States of the Continued Presence of South Africa in Namibia (South West Africa) notwithstanding Security Council Resolution 276 (1970)*, Advisory Opinion [1971] ICJ Reports 16, 31–32 (§ 53) (emphasis added).

[126] *Gabčíkovo-Nagymaros Project (Hungary/Slovakia)*, Separate Opinion of Judge Bedjaoui [1997] ICJ Reports 120, 122 (§ 10).

[127] See *Aegean Sea Continental Shelf (Greece v Turkey)*, Judgment [1978] ICJ Reports 3.

[128] Sinclair (n 67) 125.

greater emphasis that the *Namibia* judges placed on developing the new, apparently dynamic doctrine and seize upon the *Aegean Sea* judgment as a further authoritative statement of the new doctrine favouring a dynamic approach to the problem of intertemporal linguistics.

Whether the ICJ's *Namibia* and *Aegean Sea* dicta were intended to set out exceptions to the principle of contemporaneity or to ground a new doctrine that ran counter to it was ultimately irrelevant to the levels of acceptance that the principle of contemporaneity would obtain. By having obstinately refused not only to apply, but even to name, the principle of contemporaneity in two important decisions raising intertemporal interpretation problems, the Court effectively ensured that it would never again be accepted as an axiomatic principle of treaty interpretation in the way that it had been up to and for a few years following Fitzmaurice's famous promulgation of it.

Modern-day readers of the *Namibia* advisory opinion may be surprised by the fact that the Court was able to establish a new doctrine for interpreting treaties through time without even referring directly to the principle of contemporaneity. Indeed, not only had the principle been proclaimed in an article that dominated scholarship on treaty interpretation at the time and received substantial attention at the ILC's Law of Treaties debates, but the man who proclaimed it, Sir Gerald Fitzmaurice, was even sitting as a judge at the *Namibia* proceedings.

Yet, as historians of international law will appreciate, the *Namibia* advisory opinion was no ordinary opinion and was handed down in an extraordinary political, social and legal context. Indeed, the 1971 *Namibia* advisory opinion was the Court's final act in the wider saga involving apartheid South Africa's administration of the former German colony of South West Africa – a dispute omnipresent at the United Nations throughout the 25 years following the conclusion of the Second World War that has been called 'the most explosive international issue of the post-war world'[129] and even 'the international *cause célèbre* of the century'.[130]

Among the complex of ICJ opinions and decisions running from the *International Status of South-West Africa* advisory opinion of July 1950[131] through to the *Namibia* advisory opinion of July 1971, the *South West Africa* judgments of 1962 and 1966 are undoubtedly the most famous and most controversial. The Court in those two cases was so finely-balanced that small changes to the composition of the bench through de facto disqualification, death and illness resulted in the 1962 judgment being effectively reversed amid drama the likes of

[129] *South West Africa Cases (Ethiopia v South Africa; Liberia v South Africa)* (Second Phase), Dissenting Opinion of Judge Padilla Nervo [1966] ICJ Reports 443, 452.

[130] John Dugard, *The South West Africa Namibia Dispute: Documents and Scholarly Writings on the Controversy Between South Africa and the United Nations* (Berkeley CA, University of California Press, 1973) xi.

[131] *International Status of South-West Africa*, Advisory Opinion [1950] ICJ Reports 128, 143–44.

which the august institution had never seen.[132] While many of those outraged by the Court's findings in favour of apartheid South Africa focused on the 'colonial' and 'European' nationalities of certain judges, a closer analysis of the voluminous opinions confirms that the renowned sociological jurist Wolfgang Friedmann was right to point out that 'national or other superficially political considerations' were actually not determining factors, with a 'stark division of jurisprudential approaches' being '[f]ar more significant'.[133] In a contemporaneous report on the 1966 case in *International Affairs*, Rosalyn Higgins spoke of the effect of 'the individual standpoints and philosophies of the individual Judges' in the part of the 'legal process [that …] involves interpreting whether the scope of certain rules … extends to the particular circumstances',[134] while one the *South West Africa* judges, Judge Tanaka, characterised 'the difference of opinions on the questions' as being 'in the final instance attributed to the difference between two methods of interpretation: teleological or sociological and conceptional or formalistic'.[135]

There will always be disagreement on the vexed issues of which jurisprudential school a particular judicial approach should be associated with,[136] but there can be no disagreement that the approaches of the 1962 and 1966 judgments differed in terms of judicial philosophy. For present purposes, it is significant that the principle of contemporaneity became associated with the formalist approach taken in this polemical complex of cases and, by extension, with the Court's tremendously unpopular 1966 *South West Africa* judgment.

The main interpretative issue addressed by the Court in the two *South West Africa* cases arose from Article 7(2) of the 1920 Mandate for South-West Africa, a provision through which the Mandatory agreed to have submitted to the PCIJ any unsettled 'between the Mandatory and another Member of the League of Nations relating to the interpretation or the application of the provisions of the Mandate' and which was invoked by Ethiopia and Liberia to justify the submission of their claims against South Africa to the International Court of Justice.[137]

[132] For details regarding the various events affecting the composition of the Court in each phase, see eg Rosalyn Higgins, 'The International Court and South West Africa: The Implications of the Judgment' (1966) 42 *International Affairs* 573, 585–90.

[133] Wolfgang G Friedmann, 'The Jurisprudential Implications of the South West Africa Case' (1967) 6 *Columbia Journal of Transnational Law* 1.

[134] Higgins (n 132) 586.

[135] *South West Africa Cases (Ethiopia v South Africa; Liberia v South Africa)* (Second Phase), Dissenting Opinion of Judge Tanaka [1966] ICJ Reports 250, 278.

[136] Note that Dugard considers the same conflict to be between legal positivists and teleologists (see John Dugard, 'The Opinion on South-West Africa (Namibia): The Teleologists Triumph' [1971] 88 *The South African Law Journal* 460, 471–75). In a 2019 English-language text, it seems most appropriate to follow the very similar concepts of American legal theory and to characterise this difference of approach as a conflict between legal formalism and legal instrumentalism – see, eg Lawrence Solum, 'Legal Theory Lexicon: Formalism & Instrumentalism' (*Legal Theory Blog*, 12 August 2012) – lsolum.typepad.com/legaltheory/2012/08/legal-theory-lexicon-formalism-instrumentalism.html.

[137] Mandate for South West Africa 1920 (in Dugard (n 130)) 72, art 7, para 2.

There was little doubt that, in combination with Article 37 of the ICJ Statute, any dispute that this provision would have required to be submitted to the PCIJ, would be referred to the ICJ. However, already at the preliminary objections stage, a dispute arose as to whether Ethiopia and Liberia, independent African States who had been members of the League of Nations, could avail themselves of a direct independent right to bring proceedings against South Africa, even after the dissolution of the League.

The conflict of views that emerged over the interpretation of Article 7(2) of the Mandate is actually much more appropriately characterised as a restrictive versus extensive interpretation conflict in a temporally-loaded context than as a problem of intertemporal linguistics.[138] Yet this detail did not dissuade a number of the opinions dissenting to the 1962 judgment and in support of the 1966 judgment from invoking the terms of the principle of contemporaneity – and the ICJ practice considered to support it – as part of their interpretation of this provision. In the 1962 phase, Judge Winiarski quoted the statement of the principle from the *Rights of US Nationals in Morocco* case,[139] while Judge ad hoc van Wyk cited not only Judge Carneiro's contemporaneity dictum in the *Minquiers* case, but also Fitzmaurice's 1957 *BYBIL* statement of the principle of contemporaneity itself.[140] Then, in paragraph 16 of its 1966 judgment, the controversial 'majority' of the Court cited the *Rights of Morocco* case approvingly as part of its argument that Article 7(2) of the Mandate did not confer on the Applicants any legal interest in South Africa's performance of its 'conduct' obligations.[141] Significantly, it was that passage of the notorious 1966 judgment that South Africa's memorial in the subsequent *Namibia* proceedings quoted in full in support of its claim that the 'principle of contemporaneity … is well established in international law'.[142]

When one digs a little deeper into the various formalist opinions handed down in the *South West Africa* cases, one sees that the judges – with the possible exception of the South African Judge ad hoc van Wyk – did not rely on the

[138] Indeed, the intensional content (see s 4.III.C below) of the expression 'another Member of the League of Nations' had most likely not changed between when the Mandate was concluded in 1920 and when the Court ruled on South Africa's preliminary objections in 1962. At both times, a 'Member of the League of Nations' meant a country that enjoyed the status of membership at the League of Nations.

[139] *South West Africa Cases (Ethiopia v South Africa; Liberia v South Africa)* (Preliminary Objections), Dissenting Opinion of Judge Winiarski [1962] ICJ Reports 449, 457.

[140] *South West Africa (Preliminary Objections)*, Van Wyk Dissenting Opinion (n 65) 587.

[141] *South West Africa Cases (Ethiopia v South Africa; Liberia v South Africa)* (Second Phase), Judgment [1966] ICJ Reports 6, 23 (§§ 16–17); see also *South West Africa Cases (Ethiopia v South Africa; Liberia v South Africa)* (Second Phase), Separate Opinion of Judge van Wyk [1966] ICJ Reports 67, 74–76.

[142] 'Pleadings, Oral Arguments, Documents', *Legal Consequences for States of the Continued Presence of South Africa in Namibia (South West Africa) notwithstanding Security Council Resolution 276 (1970), Advisory Opinion*, vol 1 (1970) 386 (§ 8).

principle of contemporaneity to advocate interpreting a treaty term according to its original rather than later-emerging meaning. Instead, they invoked it as a principle restricting the range of evidence in which an interpreter could justifiably seek evidence of the drafters' intentions – for them, the pole star of legal interpretation. In particular, the 1962 dissenters and 1966 majority criticised the 1962 judgment's substantial reference to events occurring at the League of Nations' final meeting in April 1946. For the more formalist judges, it was inadmissible to ascertain the intentions of the parties in 1920 on the basis of subsequent and temporally quite distant discussions.[143]

However, even if the principle of contemporaneity was not actually invoked as a static approach to the Problem, it was, through reference to how Fitzmaurice had stated the principle and the inherently static passage of the *Rights of US Nationals in Morocco* judgment, presented as the static approach to interpretation of treaties through time. The principle of contemporaneity – and the static approach – therefore became inextricably tied to the formalist opinions and decisions of the *South West Africa* cases.

In assessing how this contributed to the sudden decline of the principle of contemporaneity, we should not lose sight of the fact that the mid-1960s to early 1970s was possibly the most politically charged and fast-changing peacetime period in the life of the international community. The combined impact on international institutions of the wave of decolonisation that hit its zenith at this time, together with the civil rights movements and social upheaval of 1968, was substantial. The membership of the international community was greatly expanded, the traditional white and European majority being displaced by a group of newly independent States with different notions of international law and the particular goals to which it should be directed.

The *South West Africa* and *Namibia* complex of cases, which were themselves a product of the growing role and ambition of developing States, provided the flashpoint for the clash of traditional and modern – but really legally formalist and instrumentalist – approaches to international law and the international system. The Court had attracted virulent criticism from most quarters after its controversial 1966 decision to deny Ethiopia and Liberia the right to have their claims against South Africa heard. The judges who had insisted on a formalist application of the law in spite of the meta-legal reasons to hear the claim, especially the Australian President of the Court whose casting vote had ultimately decided the outcome of the 1966 judgment, were widely vilified.

The expanded General Assembly reacted by passing a resolution purporting to revoke South Africa's mandate over the territory.[144] Undeterred, South Africa

[143] *South West Africa (Preliminary Objections)*, Winiarski Dissenting Opinion (n 139) 452–53.

[144] UN General Assembly Resolution 2145 (XXI), was passed on 27 October 1966 with 114 votes in favour, only two against and only three abstentions.

continued to strengthen its grip[145] on the territory that had been re-named Namibia.[146] Increasingly frustrated by South Africa's intransigence, the General Assembly called on the Security Council,[147] who then, for the first time in its history, sought an advisory opinion from the International Court of Justice in an effort to solve the problem once and for all.[148] Yet the complex legal situation created by South Africa's mandate under the Mandates System of the since dissolved League of Nations raised doubts as to the legality and effect of the UN resolutions from the moment they were first drafted. By again involving the Court, the UN organs paved the way for a consideration of this legal question and a re-drawing of the ICJ's *South West Africa* battle-lines in a differently named epilogue to the earlier dispute.

Between 1966 and 1971, the composition and flavour of the Court had shifted substantially. By the time the *Namibia* arguments were heard, the majority of the ICJ bench clearly favoured the instrumentalist approach of the 1966 minority over the formalist approach of the 1966 majority. Moreover, South Africa had, in the intervening period, only served to entrench its status as the *bête noire* of the increasingly enlightened international community. This meant that, for the *Namibia* majority, not only the view of international law emerging from the 1966 judgment in South Africa's favour – but also the principles used in support of it, including the principle of contemporaneity and the static approach to the problem of intertemporal linguistics – were considered outdated, invalid and not deserving of any substantial attention. The fact that South Africa relied explicitly on the principle of contemporaneity in both its written and oral *Namibia* submissions served to enhance the damage done to the principle by mere association with an unpopular judgment and an even less popular cause.[149]

Against this backdrop, it is much easier to understand why the *Namibia* judges were so reluctant to refer to the principle of contemporaneity even when advocating an apparently dynamic approach to the very problem it takes a position on, namely the problem of intertemporal linguistics. Indeed, the only *Namibia* judge to explicitly mention the principle of contemporaneity, Judge de Castro, dismissed it very quickly while rejecting South Africa's interpretative

[145] In 1968–69, South Africa refused the United Nations Council for South West Africa landing rights in South Africa and South West Africa, replaced the old South West Africa Constitution Act of 1925 with a consolidating measure and transferred more powers to the central South African Government via the South-West Africa Affairs Act, see further Dugard (n 130) 435–36.

[146] See UN General Assembly Resolution 2372 (XXII): Question of South West Africa (12 June 1968), operative para 1.

[147] UN Security Council Resolution 264 (1969): The Situation in Namibia (20 March 1969), para 3; UN Security Council Resolution 269 (1969): Namibia (12 August 1969), para 5.

[148] UN Security Council Resolution 284 (1970): Namibia (29 July 1970).

[149] *South West Africa*, Pleadings, Oral Arguments, Documents, vol 1 (n 142) 386–87 (§§ 9–10); 'Pleadings, Oral Arguments, Documents', *Legal Consequences for States of the Continued Presence of South Africa in Namibia (South West Africa) notwithstanding Security Council Resolution 276*, vol II (International Court of Justice, 1970) 192.

approach as unduly conservative and restrictive.[150] At the time of the *Namibia* advisory opinion, the principle of contemporaneity – and with it the static approach to the problem of intertemporal linguistics – had fallen on the wrong side of history and thereby into disrepute.

This explanation of why the principle of contemporaneity was so stunningly neglected by the Court in *Namibia* is not adduced in support of any claim that the principle of contemporaneity should have been heeded by the *Namibia* judges, nor that the questions posed in that case should have been decided differently. It is rather adduced to show that the *Namibia* proceedings' neglect of the principle of contemporaneity is not necessarily a reflection on the cogency of the principle or on the static approach to the problem of intertemporal linguistics, but was instead largely – if not solely – attributable to contextual factors that had little to do with how treaties in general should be interpreted through time. Indeed, the opinions of the *Namibia* majority clearly indicate that the principle of contemporaneity was rejected out of hand without any examination of what it entailed, apparently on the basis of whose judicial philosophy it was considered a part of and the (regressive) outcomes it was understood to produce.

If there were indeed, as the conventional wisdom maintains, very strong positive correlations between, on the one hand, legal formalism and a preference for the original meaning of a treaty term and, on the other, legal instrumentalism and a preference for the later-emerging meaning of a treaty term, then this linkage would not be problematic. However, as will be explained below, one cannot safely conclude that the structurally distinct approaches of legal formalism and the static approach to the Problem are functionally linked.[151] In this light, the above observations regarding the way in which the principle of contemporaneity was ignored and rejected by the *Namibia* opinion become undeniably important to a study considering whether international adjudicators should adopt a static or a dynamic approach to problems of intertemporal linguistics.

III. TIME TO DETACH THE PRINCIPLE OF CONTEMPORANEITY FROM THE PROBLEM

Both the ILC and the ICJ are authoritative institutions of paramount importance to the development of international law. Their rejection of a principle or doctrine of international law would normally be fatal to any argument advocating it. However, as has now been made clear, in the 1960s and 1970s the ILC and ICJ did not reject the static approach to the problem of intertemporal linguistics. Instead it failed, in very particular contexts, to adopt a principle

[150] *Legal Consequences for States of the Continued Presence of South Africa in Namibia (South West Africa) notwithstanding Security Council Resolution 276 (1970)*, Separate Opinion of Judge de Castro [1971] ICJ Reports 170, 182.

[151] See s 5.II.B below.

going by the name of the principle of contemporaneity, but adduced in terms and contexts that made it only rarely reflective of the static approach. In light of all these circumstances, it would be foolhardy to rule out, on account of the ILC's codification of the Law of Treaties and ICJ's *Namibia* advisory opinion, the possibility that it might be more appropriate for an interpreter to prefer the original meaning of certain treaty terms over a different meaning that they later take on.

Ultimately, while the static approach to the problem of intertemporal linguistics escaped from these authoritative statements largely unscathed, the principle of contemporaneity did not. The ILC Law of Treaties Study Group was referred directly to the principle of contemporaneity on several occasions, but explicitly decided not to include any provision – or part of a provision – apparently reflecting it. Equally, the ICJ's *Namibia* judges were taken directly to passages declaring the principle of contemporaneity to be an established principle of international law, but decided not to mention it by name in a context in which it could clearly have been relevant.

This comparison of the relative fates of the static approach and the principle of contemporaneity itself points to the fact that the principle of contemporaneity took on connotations – and principally negative connotations – that caused it to diverge from the static approach. In particular, the principle of contemporaneity is now understood (i) as a mere application of the intertemporal law applicable solely to legal changes occurring after the conclusion of a treaty; and (ii) as a tenet of the formalist approach to interpretation preferred by, inter alia, ICJ judges supporting the deeply unpopular 1966 *South West Africa* judgment. In fact, both of these associations should never have been made, because the principle of contemporaneity is, at least as it was defined by Fitzmaurice, merely a position on the distinct problem of intertemporal linguistics.

The principle of contemporaneity is rarely cited today. Even studies devoted to the doctrine of evolutionary treaty interpretation, which supposedly takes a diametrically opposed position on the Problem, rarely mention it. Moreover, while it is very occasionally cited in the context of the Problem, the principle of contemporaneity remains too regularly associated with judicial processes other than the question of original or later-emerging meaning for it to be used as a reliable entry point into a study of that question.

Many prominent international lawyers continue to link the principle of contemporaneity to the intertemporal law doctrine. In WTO circles, adjudicators and scholars rely heavily, for all questions of treaty law, on Sinclair's 1984 monograph on the VCLT, a text which openly affirms the view that the 'principle of contemporaneity is really a particular application of the doctrine of the intertemporal law'.[152] Pauwelyn, for example, openly states that

[152] Sinclair (n 67) 125.

'the so-called "principle of contemporaneity" … is the first part of the intertemporal law according to which a juridical fact must be appreciated in the light of the law contemporary with it'.[153] Other prominent contemporary international lawyers have implied the link between the principle of contemporaneity and the intertemporal law doctrine by taking the view that the intertemporal law doctrine generally requires a static approach to the problems of intertemporal linguistics. For example, the *Iron Rhine* award handed down by judges Higgins, Simma and Tomka and Professors Schrans and Soons raised the question of intertemporal linguistics through reference to the main authorities for the dynamic approach, then stated its preference for 'an evolutive interpretation' over what it termed 'a strict application of the intertemporal rule'.[154] Equally, in his influential commentary to the celebrated State Responsibility articles of 2001, Special Rapporteur James Crawford characterised the 'evolutionary interpretation of treaty provisions' as '[o]ne possible qualification' on 'the general principle of intertemporal law' that he considered was set out in Article 13 of those articles.[155]

There are also strong indications that the principle of contemporaneity has likewise never managed to dissociate itself from the conservative, formalist judicial approach with which it became linked in the *South West Africa/Namibia* cases. Indeed, the principle is often opposed to a version of the evolutionary treaty interpretation doctrine that is in fact but an expression of a progressive, instrumentalist judicial approach,[156] particularly in more theoretical studies which place the evolutionary treaty debate in a wider, jurisprudential context. The recent study of Djeffal, for example, considers that 'the principle of contemporaneity and the principle of evolutive interpretation' are opposed to each other 'on a high level of abstraction' and 'describe the changeability of the law as a general feature of the international legal system which could be termed as paradigms'.[157] In the *Mount Fitzroy* case, the dissenting opinion of the eminent Salvadoran jurist, Reynaldo Galindo Pohl, even expressly stated that the principle of contemporaneity was 'not limited and cannot be limited to the interpretation of the terms in the meaning which they had at the time when

[153] Joost Pauwelyn, *Conflict of Norms in Public International Law: How WTO Law Relates to Other Rules of International Law* (Cambridge, Cambridge University Press, 2003) 264. Note that footnote 77 reads as follows: 'This was first expressed by Judge Huber in the *Island of Palmas* arbitration (*Netherlands v United States*) (1928) 2 RIAA 831 at 845.' He then goes on to refer to the *Rights of US Nationals in Morocco* case as an example.

[154] *Iron Rhine ('Ijzeren Rijn') Railway between the Kingdom of Belgium and the Kingdom of the Netherlands*, Award (2005) XXVII RIAA/RSA 35, 73 (§ 80).

[155] 'Articles on Responsibility of States for Internationally Wrongful Acts with commentaries' in International Law Commission, 'Yearbook 2001, vol II, pt 2' (New York, United Nations, 2001) 57–59 (art 13, paras 1 and 9).

[156] See further ch 3 below.

[157] Christian Djeffal, *Static and Evolutive Treaty Interpretation: A Functional Reconstruction* (Cambridge, Cambridge University Press, 2016) 179.

they were used'.[158] Echoing the wider manner in which it was used by some of the formalist judges in the *South West Africa* cases, Galindo Pohl argued that the principle of contemporaneity goes beyond the static approach and is in fact a general principle that even restricts evidentiary considerations to those contemporary with the intention of the author of the legal text, a manifestly formalist understanding of the principle.[159]

While its ongoing associations with the intertemporal law doctrine and a formalist judicial approach may be conceptually troublesome, it is a further feature of how the principle of contemporaneity is currently understood that most fatally undermines its usefulness for analysing the problem of intertemporal linguistics today.

Unfortunately, some prominent modern-day international lawyers have apparently understood the principle of contemporaneity as advocating not the static, but the *dynamic* approach to the problem of treaty terms with meanings that change through time. In his separate opinion to the well-known *Gabčíkovo* judgment of 1997, Judge Weeramantry advocates a strongly dynamic approach under the heading '(b) The Principle of Contemporaneity in the Application of Environmental Norms', asserting that it is '[a] recognition of the principle of contemporaneity' that would allow 1997 environmental standards to be used in the application of a 1977 treaty.[160] While Judge Weeramantry apparently corrected his misunderstanding of the principle of contemporaneity by citing it in support of an apparently static approach to an interpretative aspect of the *Kasikili/Sedudu* case decided two years later,[161] some damage to the principle was already done. Studies in the sub-field of international law most reliant on the *Gabčíkovo* case, international environmental law, continue to present the principle of contemporaneity as a principle favouring a dynamic approach. Afshin A-Khavari's 2003 article on 'The Passage of Time in International Environmental Disputes', for example, describes the principle of contemporaneity as a doctrine that allows 'modern developments in environmental law and science [to be] relevant to treaty relationships' and 'the basis upon which … contemporary circumstances' should be 'take[n] into account'.[162] Equally, section 6.3.5.3 of Jorge Viñuales' monograph on *Foreign Investment and the Environment in International Law* bears the title '[t]he principle of contemporaneity in the application of environmental norms', but goes on to

[158] *Boundary dispute between Argentina and Chile concerning the frontier line between boundary post 62 and Mount Fitzroy ('Laguna del Desierto')*, Dissenting Opinion of Reynaldo Galindo Pohl (1994) XXII RIAA/RSA 53, 56 (part I, paras 9–11).

[159] ibid (part I, paras 9–11).

[160] *Gabčíkovo-Nagymaros Project (Hungary/Slovakia)*, Separate Opinion of Vice-President Weeramantry [1997] ICJ Reports 88, 113–15.

[161] *Kasikili/Sedudu Island (Botswana/ Namibia)*, Dissenting Opinion of Vice-President Weeramantry [1999] ICJ Reports 1153, 1162 (§ 29).

[162] Afshin A-Khavari, 'The Passage of Time in International Environmental Disputes' (2003) 10 *Murdoch University Electronic Journal of Law* 43, paras 54–55.

describe the dynamic, not the static, approach to treaty interpretation.[163] It is salient that the section begins by quoting Judge Weeramantry's *Gabčíkovo* separate opinion, before moving seamlessly on to quote recent decisions of international courts and tribunals generally invoked in favour of the dynamic approach and against the principle of contemporaneity, such as the *Iron Rhine* award and the ICJ's key *Related Rights* paragraph 64 dictum.[164]

Clearly, the name that Fitzmaurice gave his statement of the static approach, by including a cognate of the ambiguous term 'contemporary', has confused international lawyers applying it half a century later. The word 'contemporaneity' is, of course, a nominalisation of the adjective 'contemporaneous', not of the related adjective with the same Latin roots, 'contemporary'. While something 'contemporaneous' with something else can only refer to things 'existing or occurring at the same time',[165] 'contemporary' is ambiguous between that meaning and a second meaning of '[m]odern ... or characteristic of the present period'.[166] Some later readers have simply misunderstood Fitzmaurice to have proclaimed a principle of *contemporary* interpretation rather than of a principle of *contemporaneous* interpretation.

Unfortunately, the potential for later readers to misunderstand Fitzmaurice's principle of contemporaneity as invoking the second sense of the word 'contemporary' is not obviated by the rest of his 1957 statement of that principle. Indeed, there is an equivalent and equally problematic ambiguity in the word 'current' that Fitzmaurice used when he described the principle of contemporaneity as giving treaty terms the 'meaning which ... would have been attributed to them ... in the light of *current* linguistic usage'.[167] Other parts of Fitzmaurice's article clearly reveal that he meant 'linguistic usage' current 'at the time when the treaty was originally concluded',[168] but modern readers taking his main statement of the principle of contemporaneity out of context could easily understand 'current' in its now most common sense of '[b]elonging the current week, month, or other period of time' or 'in progress' as in 'current events'.[169]

The words Fitzmaurice chose to proclaim the static approach to the problem of intertemporal linguistics – together with a modern-day tendency to invoke statements without considering them in their full context[170] – ultimately left

[163] Jorge E Viñuales, *Foreign Investment and the Environment in International Law* (Cambridge, Cambridge University Press, 2012) 156–57.

[164] ibid.

[165] 'contemporaneous, adj.', *OED Online* – www.oed.com/view/Entry/40108 (the meaning of the equivalent word in international law's other main language is equally clear, the TLFi defining something as 'contemporain de' something else when the two things 'existe ... en même temps' or 'pendant la même période' – see www.cnrtl.fr/definition/contemporain/adjectif).

[166] 'contemporary, adj. and n.', *OED Online* – www.oed.com/view/Entry/40115 (which notes that this sense of the word first appeared in usage in 1866).

[167] Fitzmaurice (n 28) 212 (emphasis added).

[168] ibid 225.

[169] 'current, adj.', *OED Online* – www.oed.com/view/Entry/46097.

[170] See s 6.II.A below.

the principle of contemporaneity open to misunderstandings that now only serve to add to the confusion that has always plagued it. Clearly, the principle of contemporaneity not only has a troubled history, but also a troubled present. Still today, it means too many different things to different international lawyers and regularly departs from a mere principle that the original meaning of a treaty term should be favoured over a meaning that term takes on after the treaty's conclusion.

If we are to objectively analyse and solve the problem of intertemporal linguistics, we need to evaluate both the static and the dynamic approaches to the question, but these approaches only. Since at least 1964, the principle of contemporaneity has not accurately encapsulated the static approach, becoming tied to considerations that are out-of-place in a focused consideration of the Problem. We must accordingly move beyond this doctrine, starting afresh with a notion of the static approach to the problem of intertemporal linguistics that is freed from its association with the principle of contemporaneity.

3

The Emergence and Splitting of the Evolutionary Treaty Interpretation Doctrine

OF ALL THE doctrines linked to the problem of intertemporal linguistics, none has been as often linked or as extensively written about as the doctrine of dynamic, evolutive or evolutionary treaty interpretation. Yet this does not mean that what this book will refer to as the evolutionary interpretation doctrine actually addresses or takes a position on the issue of whether treaty terms should be given their original or later-emerging meaning. Indeed, the doctrine emerged from a famous paragraph of the *Namibia* advisory opinion that appears to have been more concerned with laying the ground for the emergence of a more modern form of ICJ jurisprudence than with proclaiming a principle on the more minor and confined issue of how a treaty should be interpreted through time (section I). While initial statements of the evolutionary interpretation doctrine in the years following *Namibia* remained close to the problem of intertemporal linguistics, its scope was eventually so greatly expanded – chiefly through the decisions of international human rights courts – that what is effectively a new and separate doctrine emerged under its name (section II). With the emergence of this new form so structurally and functionally distinct from a dynamic position on the problem of intertemporal linguistics, the doctrine of evolutionary interpretation has begun creating great conceptual difficulty for adjudicators and scholars alike and has ultimately become of little use to a study focused squarely on the issue of original or later-emerging meaning (section III).

I. EMERGENCE AS AN AMALGAM OF INTERPRETATIVE AND PROGRESSIVE APPROACHES

A. A Doctrine Spawned by Paragraph 53 of the Namibia Advisory Opinion

While there were some prominent mentions of an apparently dynamic approach to the problem of intertemporal linguistics prior to 1971,[1] it is widely accepted

[1] See, eg *The North Atlantic Coast Fisheries Case (Great Britain, United States), Grounds for the Dissent to the Award on Question V by Dr Luis M Drago* (1910) XI RIAA/RSA 203; DW Bowett,

that the notion of evolutionary interpretation as a doctrine of international law first came to prominence in the International Court of Justice's *Namibia* advisory opinion.[2]

Indeed, the very first pieces of international law scholarship promulgating the existence of a doctrine of evolutionary interpretation were those that were dedicated to an analysis of the *Namibia* proceedings, with all these declarations of the existence of the new doctrine invoking the same paragraph 53 of the majority opinion.

In the same year that the advisory opinion was handed down, Brigitte Bollecker-Stern published a 53-page article on it in the *Annuaire français de droit international* in which she declared that the *Namibia* court had developed a 'new method of interpretation' comprising three rules, one of which she labelled '*l'interprétation évolutive*'.[3] For Stern, evolutive interpretation took the *contre-pied* of the traditional doctrine and was not a general principle of law common to civilised nations so must have been advanced by the Court as a 'new general principle of international law'.[4]

Rudolf Bernhardt's 1973 note on the entire *South West Africa-Namibia* complex of cases in the *Zeitschrift für ausländisches öffentliches Recht und Völkerrecht* runs along similar lines. It asserts that a 'dynamic interpretation' ultimately prevailed in these cases,[5] before quoting paragraph 53 of the *Namibia* dictum *in extenso* and then stating the existence of a new, temporal and interpretative principle pursuant to which an interpretation which takes into account the changes in the international order will often be preferable to an interpretation which is based only on the original will of the parties.[6]

United Nations Forces: A Legal Study of United Nations Practice (London, Stevens, 1964) 307–08; UN Conference on the Law of Treaties, 'Official Records, First Session, Vienna' (Vienna, United Nations, 1968) 182 (per Myslil [Czechoslovakia], Thirty-third meeting – 22 April 1968, § 54). *Certain Expenses of the United Nations (Article 17, paragraph 2, of the Charter)*, Separate Opinion of Judge Sir Percy Spender [1962] ICJ Reports 182, 186–87; *Nationality Decrees in Tunis and Morocco*, Advisory Opinion [1923] PCIJ Reports (Series B) No 4, 24.

[2] *Legal Consequences for States of the Continued Presence of South Africa in Namibia (South West Africa) notwithstanding Security Council Resolution 276 (1970)*, Advisory Opinion [1971] ICJ Reports 16, 31–32 (§ 53); see, eg Brigitte Stern, 'Interpretation in International Trade Law' in Malgosia Fitzmaurice, Olufemi Elias and Panos Merkouris (eds), *Treaty Interpretation and the Vienna Convention on the Law of Treaties: 30 Years On* (Leiden, Martinus Nijhoff Publishers, 2010) 120; *Dispute regarding Navigational and Related Rights (Costa Rica v Nicaragua)*, Declaration of Judge ad hoc Guillaume [2009] ICJ Reports 290, 295–96 (§ 12).

[3] Brigitte Bollecker(-Stern), 'L'avis consultatif en date du 21 juin 1971 de la Cour internationale de Justice dans l'affaire relative aux conséquences juridiques pour les Etats membres de la présence continue de l'Afrique du Sud en Namibie (Sud-Ouest africain)' (1971) 17 *Annuaire français de droit international* 281, 287–88, 290–93.

[4] ibid 292.

[5] Rudolf Bernhardt, 'Homogenität, Kontinuität und Dissonanzen in der Rechtsprechung des Internationalen Gerichtshofs – Eine Fall-Studie zum Südwestafrika/Namibia-Komplex' (1973) 33 *Zeitschrift für ausländisches öffentliches Recht und Völkerrecht* 1, 35.

[6] ibid 36.

Perhaps most significantly, the work of a group of esteemed international legal scholars working on 'the problem of the intertemporal law' at the Institute of International Law between 1968 and 1975 ascribed such importance to the *Namibia* dictum that they amended the interpretative paragraphs of their draft resolution to reflect it. Despite thinking, with other prominent members of the IDI's Eleventh Commission including Guggenheim and Lachs, that the *Namibia* dictum's interpretative statements were not sufficiently linked to the problem of the intertemporal law to merit a mention in the IDI's Resolution,[7] the conceptually astute rapporteur Max Sørensen still felt duty-bound to align the Institute with what he considered an important statement of principle by the Court.[8] He accordingly added to the draft 'interpretation' paragraph of the IDI resolution on the intertemporal law – that had previously been expressed in temporally neutral terms – a second sentence drawing heavily from the terms of paragraph 53 of the *Namibia* advisory opinion. That addition took an overtly dynamic position on the problem of intertemporal linguistics,[9] placing, even after the Commission's amendments, an explicitly temporal qualification on the rule in VCLT Article 31(3)(c) – a rule of interpretation that the ILC had left temporally open less than a decade earlier.[10]

Then, in his Hague course of 1978, Jiménez de Aréchaga also quoted extensively from the *Namibia* advisory opinion's paragraph 53 to confirm the establishment of the evolutionary interpretation doctrine, at least in the limited form that had found its way into the IDI's 1975 Wiesbaden resolution, namely of a qualification on the relevant rules principle in VCLT Article 31(3)(c).[11]

It can therefore be safely concluded that, by the end of the 1970s, international law had a new doctrine, and that this doctrine of evolutionary treaty interpretation emerged from paragraph 53 of the *Namibia* advisory opinion.

[7] Institut de droit international and Max Sørensen, 'Le problème dit du droit intertemporel dans l'ordre international – Rapport provisoire' (12 February 1973) *Annuaire* 1, 93–94, 105, 107.

[8] Sørensen had, according to the IDI's yearbook, earlier explained to the members of the Institut that he was particularly keen to maintain the relevant sentence as he would regret the Institute not following the ICJ on this topic – Institut de droit international, 'Le problème dit du droit intertemporel dans l'ordre international – Délibérations – Première séance plénière: jeudi 7 août 1975 (matin), Annuaire' (1975) *Annuaire* 339, 354 (Troisième séance plénière: vendredi 8 août 1975 [matin], per rapporteur Sørensen).

[9] IDI and Sørensen (n 7) 94, 99–100 ('Par ailleurs, toute interprétation et application d'un traité doit tenir compte de l'ensemble du système juridique international en vigueur au moment de l'interprétation et de l'application.').

[10] 'IDI (n 8) 368–69 (Septième séance plénière: lundi 11 août 1975 [après-midi], per Yasseen, Rosenne and Rapporteur Sørensen); Institut de droit international, 'The Intertemporal Problem in Public International Law – Resolution' (Wiesbaden, 1975), operative para 4.

[11] Eduardo Jiménez de Aréchaga, 'International Law in the Past Third of a Century' (1978) 159 *Collected Courses of the Hague Academy of International Law* 1, 48–50.

B. The Dual-purpose Behind the Foundational *Namibia* Dictum

The importance of paragraph 53 of the *Namibia* advisory opinion to the evolutionary interpretation doctrine is accordingly such that it merits being quoted in full:

> Mindful as it is of the primary necessity of interpreting an instrument in accordance with the intentions of the parties at the time of its conclusion, the Court is bound to take into account the fact that the concepts embodied in Article 22 of the Covenant – 'the strenuous conditions of the modern world' and 'the well-being and development' of the peoples concerned-were not static, but were by definition evolutionary, as also, therefore, was the concept of the 'sacred trust'. The parties to the Covenant must consequently be deemed to have accepted them as such. That is why, viewing the institutions of 1919, the Court must take into consideration the changes which have occurred in the supervening half-century, and its interpretation cannot remain unaffected by the subsequent development of law, through the Charter of the United Nations and by way of customary law. Moreover, an international instrument has to be interpreted and applied within the framework of the entire legal system prevailing at the time of the interpretation. In the domain to which the present proceedings relate, the last fifty years, as indicated above, have brought important developments. These developments leave little doubt that the ultimate objective of the sacred trust was the self-determination and independence of the peoples concerned. In this domain; as elsewhere, the *corpus iuris gentium* has been considerably enriched, and this the Court, if it is faithfully to discharge its functions, may not ignore.[12]

This much-quoted dictum is striking in several respects. However, for present purposes, its greatest significance lies in the fact that it presents, both on its face and when considered in its context, a hybrid of two different approaches: an interpretative approach and a judicial approach. The *interpretative* approach is *temporal* and takes a dynamic position on the problem of intertemporal linguistics, clearly proposing the use of the later-emerging – rather than original – meaning of a treaty term. The *judicial* approach is *progressive*, insisting on using advancements in the wider international social, political and legal order to develop existing legal institutions that now appear somewhat outmoded.

The hallmarks of the interpretative approach are clear on the face of paragraph 53 dictum – particularly its first half – and the paragraphs surrounding it. As the terms appearing within quotation marks reveal, the *Namibia* Court was staying close to the actual terms of the applicable treaty, placing particular emphasis on the meaning of the treaty term 'sacred trust'. Indeed, a few pages earlier, the Court had stated that it was 'necessary to refer to the actual text of Article 22 of the Covenant' and quoted the first paragraph of that provision in full.[13] Moreover, one of the most important steps towards the Court's ground-breaking statement of an apparently dynamic approach was its qualification of 'the concept of the "sacred trust"' in Article 22(1) of the Covenant

[12] *Namibia*, Advisory Opinion (n 2) 31–32 (§ 53).
[13] ibid 28 (§ 45).

as 'not static, but … by definition evolutionary'.[14] This shows that the *Namibia* Court not only focused on a specific term of a specific provision of the applicable treaty, but also moved towards its findings by qualifying that treaty term in a particular manner. By doing so, the Court brought its ultimate findings as to the nature of the obligations implied by a sacred trust – including the obligation to grant self-determination and independence – within the meaning of the term 'sacred trust', clearly making those important findings *interpretative*, even in the narrowest sense of interpretation.

Yet paragraph 53 of the *Namibia* advisory opinion also presents many aspects that suggest the Court was moving beyond mere interpretation – at least in its narrower sense – to a more general, progressive judicial approach.

This is most obvious in the second half of the paragraph and the much-quoted sentence that reads: '[m]oreover, an international instrument has to be interpreted and applied within the framework of the entire legal system prevailing at the time of the interpretation'.[15] The fact that the sentence begins with the word 'moreover' itself points to the hybrid nature of the dictum. It is as if the first half of the paragraph, which begins with a statement of the principle of contemporaneity before noting specific exceptions to it, is intended to stay broadly within the bounds of the conventional wisdom on treaty interpretation, while the second half of the paragraph seeks to break free of its constraints. Indeed, the second half of the paragraph is not only worded in extremely broad terms, but it deliberately goes beyond matters of interpretation by speaking of interpretation *and application*. This is significant because, whereas interpretation within the framework of the legal system prevailing at the time of interpretation relies on the treaty terms being sufficiently vague or ambiguous to channel external changes into the treaty, application within the framework of the later legal system does not. Mentioning 'application' therefore opens the door to forcibly adapting clear and unambiguous terms to the norms and values of a more modern legal order.

When reflecting extra-curially on the *Namibia* advisory opinion that he had co-authored as an ICJ judge, Manfred Lachs considered paragraph 53 to be stating that the Covenant 'cannot be *applied* as it might have been on the date of its making' and 'must [instead] be *applied* in the spirit of the law, as we live it today'.[16] He also considered paragraph 53 of the *Namibia* advisory opinion to have 'squarely raised the critical issue of intertemporal law',[17] when, as we have already seen, the intertemporal law doctrine is a doctrine applicable to application, not interpretation. Indeed, despite calling it a question of

[14] ibid 31 (§ 53).
[15] ibid (§ 53).
[16] Manfred Lachs, 'Some Reflections on the Contribution of the International Court of Justice to the Development of International Law' (1983) 10 *Syracuse Journal of International Law and Commerce* 239, 261 (emphasis added).
[17] ibid 239–41, 245.

'treaty interpretation',[18] Lachs even characterised the question that the relevant part of the *Namibia* opinion responded to as one which concerned the legal regime created by provision, namely whether the execution of the 'C' mandate regarding *South West Africa* in 1919 and 1920 gave South Africa rights over the territory that were tantamount to annexation,[19] not as one which concerned the meaning of any of the applicable treaty's terms.

Through his preparedness to refer to the ways in which *Namibia*'s paragraph 53 apparently sanctioned applying – not interpreting – a treaty in light of subsequently emerging law, Lachs acknowledged the overtly progressive nature of that advisory opinion. Indeed, it is significant that his 1983 article was dedicated to describing how the ICJ develops international law and takes a broad view that considers every exercise of the international judicial function to produce 'either a step forward or backward in the development of the law'.[20] Moreover, for Lachs, advisory proceedings, like the *Namibia* proceedings, offer 'a much greater potential to further develop the law than do judgments in contentious proceedings',[21] allowing the Court to go 'beyond the literal terms [of the questions posed] to facilitate … the appropriate development of the relevant legal issues'.[22] As Stern pointed out soon after the *Namibia* advisory opinion was handed down, paragraph 53 itself constitutes an example of such 'judicial opportunism', the *Namibia* Court ultimately not making any dispositive findings relying on the statements of principle contained in that famous paragraph.[23]

There is ample evidence both from the opinion itself and from the context in which it handed down to suggest that, when it made the trailblazing statements that appear in paragraph 53 of its advisory opinion, the *Namibia* Court was not simply aiming to resolve a specific and narrow point of treaty interpretation, but instead pursuing the much grander objective of breaking new ground for the emergence of a new and progressive kind of ICJ jurisprudence.

As part of our discussion of the decline of the principle of contemporaneity, we have already touched on the politically and morally charged context of the *South West Africa/Namibia* complex of cases of which this opinion constituted the Court's final act. We saw that this dispute provided a flashpoint in the development of the ICJ's jurisprudence, bringing the judges with a formalist and conservative judicial approach into irresolvable conflict with the judges favouring an instrumentalist and progressive approach. Of course, the *Namibia* advisory opinion gave this saga a decidedly progressive denouement, including very prominently in the parts of it that are cited as the foundations of the evolutionary interpretation doctrine.

[18] ibid 258, 259, 261.
[19] ibid 260.
[20] ibid 239–41, 245.
[21] ibid 249.
[22] ibid 251.
[23] Bollecker(-Stern) (n 3) 297.

While the relevant section of the *Namibia* advisory opinion is careful not to refer to any of the 1966 dissenting opinions, the paragraph 53 dictum very obviously alludes to – and builds on – Judge Jessup's unabashedly progressive 118-page *South West Africa* dissenting opinion. Indeed, the part of this dictum famously proclaiming that certain concepts in Article 22(1) of the Covenant 'were not static, but were by definition evolutionary',[24] develops Judge Jessup's claim that one of these same concepts '"the modern world" is not a static concept' on page 440 of his 1966 dissent, a section of that dissent focused on fleshing out the concept of '[t]he "sacred trust of civilization" referred to in Article 22 of the Covenant'.[25] Of course, that paragraph of Judge Jessup's opinion was not focused on how to interpret treaties through time, but instead on an overtly teleological reading of Article 22(1) of the Covenant, a fact demonstrated by the prominent references to its objectives in both its first and last sentences.[26]

It is also significant that the relevant section of the *Namibia* advisory opinion concludes pointedly with a block quotation from page 329 of the 1962 *South West Africa* judgment. While that judgment did not develop the progressive and teleological understanding of Article 22 in as much detail as the 1966 dissents, it was that particular section of the 1962 judgment that set out – in the more authoritative form of a judgment of the Court – the instrumentalist judges' objective-oriented conception of the issue. The relevant page spoke of the 'essential principles of the Mandates System', the 'features inherent in the Mandates system', declared that the 'system [was] dedicated to the avowed *object* of promoting the well-being and development of the peoples concerned' and concluded that 'each Mandate under the Mandates System constitutes a new international institution, the primary, overriding purpose of which is to promote "the well-being and development" of the people of the territory under Mandate'.[27]

The emphasis that the instrumentalist judges of the 1962 *South West Africa* majority and 1966 'minority' placed on the object and purpose of the first paragraph of Article 22 of the Covenant can be contrasted with the way in which the formalist 1966 'majority' – and the South African government – viewed the same provision. In a key part of the 1966 judgment, the Court did not take any issue with the principle that the instrumentalists had identified in the mandates system and the notion of the 'sacred trust', but argued that this principle had 'no residual juridical content which could, so far as any particular mandate is

[24] *Namibia*, Advisory Opinion (n 2) 31 (§ 53).

[25] *South West Africa Cases (Ethiopia v South Africa; Liberia v South Africa)* (Second Phase), Dissenting Opinion of Judge Jessup [1966] ICJ Reports 325, 440.

[26] ibid: 'The "sacred trust of civilization" referred to in Article 22 of the Covenant has as its purpose the development of certain specified peoples to "stand by themselves under the strenuous conditions of the modern world". … The objective is not fanciful nor illusory; States formerly under mandate are now members of the United Nations and are the sovereign equals of the States which formerly administered them as mandates.'

[27] *South West Africa Cases (Ethiopia v South Africa; Liberia v South Africa)* (Preliminary Objections), Judgment [1962] ICJ Reports 319, 329 (emphasis added).

concerned, operate per se to give rise to legal rights' because 'once the expression to be given to an idea has been accepted in the form of a particular regime or system, its legal incidents are those of the regime or system'.[28] In its *Namibia* pleadings ultimately rejected by the relevant part of the *Namibia* advisory opinion, South Africa also took issue with any attempt to elevate the concepts set out in the first paragraph of Article 22 to the status of norms of international law that could be directly applied to South Africa, arguing that these concepts were merely 'descriptive of the idealistic or humanitarian objectives involved in the mandates system' and that the 'juridical content of the mandates system' could only be drawn from 'the more detailed provisions' in later paragraphs of Article 22.[29]

It is accordingly safe to conclude that, for almost 10 years, one of the most important issues before the Court was whether it should ascertain the international legal norms opposable to South Africa by looking at the objectives of the concepts broadly set out at the start of Article 22 of the Covenant or instead at the terms of the more detailed provisions in the later paragraphs of Article 22 and the 1920 Mandate. This was clearly not an interpretative issue in the narrow sense of interpretation within which the problem of intertemporal linguistics is contained. The dispute did not concern the meaning of specific terms of the treaty, but instead which terms should be looked at and whether they should be understood according to their apparent terms or underlying objectives.

Paragraphs 44–54 of the *Namibia* advisory opinion clearly establish the *Namibia* Court's position on this important issue. The *Namibia* Court favoured the teleological and progressive approach and, as Judge Lachs subsequently revealed, those paragraphs were manifestly dedicated to taking a strong position on this important jurisprudential issue that had divided the Court for so long. Indeed, paragraphs 44–54 of the *Namibia* advisory opinion do not even mention the more specific terms of paragraph 6 of Article 22 or the 1920 mandate at all. Instead they focus entirely on understanding the concepts in Article 22(1) in the most progressive manner possible. This approach, achieved through a broad application of the teleological method, is most obvious when the Court rejects a South African interpretation of Article 22 on the basis that it constitutes 'a construction at variance with its object and purpose',[30] as well as when it concludes the paragraph 53 dictum by asserting that recent developments 'leave little doubt that the *ultimate objective* of the sacred trust was the self-determination and independence of the peoples concerned'.[31]

[28] *South West Africa Cases (Ethiopia v South Africa; Liberia v South Africa)* (Second Phase), Judgment [1966] ICJ Reports 6, 35 (§ 54).

[29] 'Pleadings, Oral Arguments, Documents', *Legal Consequences for States of the Continued Presence of South Africa in Namibia (South West Africa) notwithstanding Security Council Resolution 276 (1970), Advisory Opinion*, vol 1 (1970) 559.

[30] *Namibia*, Advisory Opinion (n 2) 30 (§ 50).

[31] ibid 31 (§ 53) (emphasis added).

In the end, however, one need only look at the terms of paragraph 53 itself to see that the *Namibia* Court was more focused on laying the foundations for a more modern and progressive jurisprudence than on canonising a new principle of treaty interpretation. Statements proclaiming an interpretative principle, such as Fitzmaurice's statement of the principle of contemporaneity, are generally made in narrow, technical and almost mechanical terms. The *Namibia* dictum is, by contrast, expressed in broad, foundational and almost poetic terms. Moreover, the *Namibia* Court did not confine the principle by naming it, defining it or linking it to the quite specific facts that the *Namibia* situation and the interpretation of Article 22 of the Covenant presented. Indeed, the Court could easily have followed some notable international lawyers including Bowett,[32] who had insisted that a different, more flexible interpretative method should be used for the special case of constitutive document of major international organisations, such as the Covenant of the League of Nations, but chose not to limit the scope of the doctrine in such a way. Instead the *Namibia* Court left its very broadly-stated principle open, vague and undefined, perhaps deliberately so in light of the fact that it may have appeared to ground a new principle of treaty interpretation, but was actually intended to lay the foundations for international courts and tribunals to make more progressive decisions.

II. SPLITTING OF THE DOCTRINE INTO DISTINCT INTERPRETATIVE AND PROGRESSIVE FORMS

A. An Initially Limited Doctrine Focusing on Treaty Interpretation Through Time

The hybrid nature of the *Namibia* dictum recognised as the fountainhead of the evolutionary treaty interpretation doctrine did not initially create any conceptual problems. Those who referred to the paragraph 53 dictum as the foundation of a doctrine of dynamic, evolutive or evolutionary interpretation focused on its interpretative aspects, while those who focused on its progressive aspects did not link them to the doctrine of evolutionary treaty interpretation.

Indeed, two *Namibia* case notes already published in the same year that the opinion was handed down themselves constitute examples of careful demarcation between the two different strands of the '*Namibia* doctrine'.

In the first of these, Brigitte Stern, writing then as Brigitte Bollecker, spoke of – indeed seems to have coined – the evolutionary interpretation doctrine, but isolated it from the progressive features of the *Namibia* advisory opinion. She fully observed the progressive elements of the same parts of the advisory opinion, but confined mention of them to two other interpretative theories she

[32] Bowett (n 1) 307–08.

believed had emerged from it, namely 'extensive interpretation' and 'teleological interpretation'. 'Evolutive interpretation' was accordingly insulated from the progressive approach and mostly confined to the temporal and interpretative sense relevant to the problem of intertemporal linguistics, Stern speaking of it as a principle that applied only to 'notions that are themselves evolutionary by nature' that thereby allowed 'old treaties to be instilled with the new spirit of the law'.[33]

Other authors speaking of evolutionary interpretation in the first 15 years after *Namibia* invariably sought to confine it to the interpretation of only certain types of terms, certain types of treaties and/or certain types of changes. Bernhardt's 1973 note on the case appears to constrain the types of change that evolutionary interpretation may respond to even more tightly than the '*principes juridiques en vigueur*' ('legal principles in force') used in Stern's definition,[34] speaking purely of the apparently more consequential '*Wandlungen der internationalen Ordnung*' ('changes to the international order').[35] Views expressed by other noted international lawyers of that era, including the Institute of international Law's Wiesbaden resolution on the inter-temporal law[36] and Jiménez de Aréchaga's Hague Course[37] also confined the interpretative doctrine *Namibia* had spawned by limiting its operation to the acceptance of later emerging *legal rules* applicable between the parties.

It is salient that Bernhardt's 1973 article also confined the application of the doctrine to 'at least some international treaties',[38] with his compatriot Bruno Simma, considering in 1983, that 'evolutionary interpretation' was only appropriate for treaties like the League of Nations Covenant and European Convention on Human Rights that are 'meant to remain in force for a long time'.[39] Following the *Namibia* Court's characterisation of key treaty terms as 'by definition evolutionary', Simma also stated that 'evolutionary interpretation of a treaty provision' would only be permissible where the terms are so 'open or evolutionary ... that their content *must* be adjusted'.[40] This latter limitation on the doctrine was then repeated by some of the first judges to mention the doctrine explicitly, the seven judges who dissented to the European Court of Human

[33] Bollecker(-Stern) (n 3) 292 (present author's translations).

[34] ibid 290–91.

[35] Bernhardt (n 5) 33, 34, 36.

[36] IDI (n 8) 368–69 (Septième séance plénière: lundi 11 août 1975 [après-midi], per Yasseen, Rosenne and Rapporteur Sørensen).

[37] Institut de droit international, 'Le problème intertemporel en droit international public – Résolution' (Wiesbaden, 1975) 2 (operative para 4).

[38] Bernhardt (n 5) 36, present author's translation from the German 'zumindest bei einem Teil der völkerrechtlichen Verträge'.

[39] Bruno Simma, 'Consent: Strains in the Treaty System' in Ronald StJ Macdonald and Douglas M Johnston (eds), *The Structure and Process of International Law: Essays in Legal Philosophy, Doctrine, and Theory* (The Hague, Martinus Nijhoff Publishers, 1983) 495.

[40] ibid 495–96.

Rights ('ECtHR')'s parallel *Feldbrugge* and *Deumeland* judgments of 1986 and notably stated:

> An evolutive interpretation allows variable and changing concepts already contained in the Convention to be construed in the light of modern-day conditions ... but it does not allow entirely new concepts or spheres of application to be introduced into the Convention: that is a legislative function...[41]

All these early texts speaking explicitly of evolutionary interpretation not only focused on the interpretative aspects of paragraph 53 of the *Namibia* advisory opinion, but also chose to read it more narrowly than the terms required. Significantly, they limited the breadth of the interpretative statement to the facts of the *Namibia* proceedings, when the Court itself had chosen not to.

In the second of the prominent *Namibia* case notes already published in 1971, Dugard quotes extensively from paragraph 53 of the advisory opinion, but emphasises its progressive and teleological features without alluding to the emergence of any new doctrine regarding how to interpret treaties through time.[42] In a similar vein, Lachs's 1983 article invokes the paragraph's statements not as evidence of a new doctrine of treaty interpretation, but instead as evidence of a wider, progressive jurisprudential view 'reject[ing] the claim that law can stand still and stress[ing] the close relationship between law and life'.[43] Since the literature focusing on the progressive aspects of the key *Namibia* paragraph steered clear of linking those aspects of it to any temporal interpretation doctrine, the two strands of the so-called *Namibia* dictum remained separate and the evolutionary treaty interpretation doctrine remained isolated from its strongly progressive overtones – at least initially.

More than 30 years later, the confined scope and strictly interpretative purity of the evolutionary interpretation doctrine has long since been lost. Its application is no longer confined to legal changes and to special types of terms in particular types of treaties. Indeed, in their more recent texts, authors such as Stern and Bernhardt have notably expanded their definitions of the doctrine.[44] Evolutionary interpretation is not only no longer understood as relating to interpretation in the narrow sense of assigning meanings to treaty terms, but is also associated with judicial acts that are not interpretative at all. Critically, the doctrine has increasingly come to refer to so much more than simply choosing to assign a treaty term its later-emerging – instead of original – meaning.

[41] *Feldbrugge v The Netherlands* (Merits), Joint Dissenting Opinion of Judges Ryssdal, Bindschedler-Robert, Lagergren, Matscher, Sir Vincent Evans, Bernhardt and Gersing (European Court of Human Rights (Plenary), 8562/79, 29 May 1986) 25 (§ 24).

[42] John Dugard, 'The Opinion on South-West Africa (Namibia): The Teleologists Triumph' (1971) 88 *The South African Law Journal* 460, 472.

[43] Lachs (n 16) 261.

[44] See, eg Rudolf Bernhardt, 'Evolutive Treaty Interpretation, Especially of the European Convention on Human Rights' (1999) 42 *German Yearbook of International Law* 11, 12 ff; Stern (n 2) 119 ff.

B. Evolutionary Interpretation and the Living Instrument as a Doctrine of Progressive Adjudication

The gradual expansion of the notion of evolutionary treaty interpretation began in the case law of international human rights courts. As explained above, the *Namibia* advisory opinion had left this possibility open by stating the principle in broad and unrefined terms and perhaps even prompted an identification of the doctrine with progressive adjudication by comingling statements of the dynamic interpretative approach with exhortations to follow an instrumentalist judicial approach. However, the *Namibia* advisory opinion did not even use the 'evolutionary interpretation' moniker, let alone apply it to the instrumentalist aspects of its opinion that in fact have little to do with interpretation of treaties through time at all. Moreover, that ill-advised link – which continues to plague the evolutionary interpretation literature today – was initially made not by the *Namibia* commentators coining the evolutionary treaty interpretation doctrine, nor by the immediately subsequent case law of the International Court of Justice, but rather by international human rights judges alone.

The story of how evolutionary treaty interpretation came to denote progressive adjudication rather than interpreting a treaty according to its later-emerging meaning is a drama that played out in five acts over a 30-year period. It began with the ECtHR's *Golder* judgment of 1975 and ended with the 2005 sentence handed down by five esteemed international lawyers in the inter-State arbitration concerning the *Iron Rhine Railway*. As will be seen, at all of the crucial points in this development of the doctrine, judges expert in international human rights were the primary protagonists.

i. Post-codification Confirmation of the ECtHR's Progressive Judicial Approach

In the story's first act, the ECtHR confirmed its progressive and instrumentalist approach to interpreting and applying the European Convention on Human Rights ('ECHR') in a world in which the law of treaties had just been essentially codified by the VCLT.

In 1969, the same year that the VCLT was adopted, the inmate Sidney Golder, who had been falsely accused of participating in a prison riot by a prison guard, lodged a claim against the denial of his alleged right to sue the guard for libel. The case came before the Court in September 1973, by which time the VCLT had been adopted and already ratified or acceded to by just under half of the number of States required for it to enter into force, including the *Golder* Respondent State, the United Kingdom.[45]

[45] treaties.un.org/pages/ViewDetailsIII.aspx?src=TREATY&mtdsg_no=XXIII-1&chapter=23&Temp=mtdsg3&clang=_en.

In a 1975 judgment handed down by a nine-to-three majority of a plenary sitting of the court, the ECtHR decided to consider, as the parties before it had done, that interpretations of the Convention should be guided by the interpretative rules in VCLT articles 31–33 on the basis that they 'enunciate[d] in essence generally accepted principles of international law'.[46] Then, in purported application of the VCLT's interpretative rules, it granted Mr Golder relief by reading an unenumerated right into ECHR Article 6(1).

The relevant sentence of Article 6(1) provides that '[i]n the determination of his civil rights and obligations or of any criminal charge against him, everyone is entitled to a fair and public hearing within a reasonable time by an independent and impartial tribunal established by law'.[47] Mr Golder claimed that this provision gave him a general right of access to the courts. However, as Gerald Fitzmaurice noted in his strident separate opinion, it was common ground before the Court in *Golder* that neither the Convention itself nor Article 6(1) of it expressly provided for a 'specific general substantive right of access to the courts', so the right alleged by Mr Golder could only be granted via a process of inference.[48] This did not dissuade the majority of the *Golder* Court from finding that the right of access claimed by Mr Golder was 'inherent in the right stated by Article 6 para 1'.[49]

By reading an unenumerated right into the fabric of the Convention, the 1975 *Golder* judgment laid the foundations for the instrumentalist and progressive judicial approach that the Strasbourg court has overwhelmingly followed ever since. The ECtHR clearly did not want to see Mr Golder denied a right that it considered he should possess just because the drafters of the 1950 Convention had failed to specifically provide for it. Even if the *Golder* majority did not consider itself to be pushing the limits of treaty interpretation,[50] its judgment clearly bears, especially when juxtaposed against the separate opinion of Sir Gerald Fitzmaurice, all the hallmarks of legal instrumentalism and a rejection of the legal formalism that denies any attempts to read unenumerated rights into a treaty.

ii. The Statement and Confirmation of the 'Living Instrument' Doctrine

The second act in the emergence of a new form of the evolutionary interpretation doctrine at international human rights courts was largely performed by the six members of a seven-member Chamber of the ECtHR who proclaimed the

[46] *Golder v The United Kingdom* (Merits and Just Satisfaction), Judgment (European Court of Human Rights (Plenary), 4451/70, 21 February 1975) 9–10 (§ 29).

[47] European Convention for the Protection of Human Rights and Fundamental Freedoms, as amended by Protocols Nos 11 and 14 1950 (213 UNTS 222), art 6(1).

[48] *Golder v The United Kingdom* (Merits and Just Satisfaction), Separate Opinion of Judge Fitzmaurice (European Court of Human Rights (Plenary), 4451/70, 21 February 1975) 38–39 (§ 25).

[49] *Golder*, Judgment (n 46) 14 (§ 36).

[50] ibid (§ 36).

'living instrument' doctrine in the 1978 *Tyrer v The United Kingdom* judgment. In a much-quoted statement which bears many affinities with the ICJ's *Namibia* dictum in both its form and context, the *Tyrer* Court said:

> The Court must also recall that the Convention is a living instrument which, as the Commission rightly stressed, must be interpreted in the light of present-day conditions. In the case now before it the Court cannot but be influenced by the developments and commonly accepted standards in the penal policy of the member States of the Council of Europe in this field.[51]

Like the *Namibia* dictum, this statement of principle was made in broad terms without any reference – despite its insistence that the principle must be 'recall[ed]' – to any prior case law, international legal scholarship or the VCLT that had been adopted a few years earlier and followed in the ECtHR's earlier *Golder* judgment. As Bjorge notes, it appears that the notion of the Convention being a 'living instrument' was drawn from a report penned by none other than Max Sørensen in 1975.[52] However, Sørensen only stated that this meant the provisions of the ECHR '*are capable of* being interpreted in such a way as to keep pace with social pace',[53] it was the *Tyrer* Court that went the extra step to proclaim that they '*must be* interpreted in the light of present-day conditions'.[54]

Moreover, just as the *Namibia* Court's statement of what was subsequently labelled the evolutionary treaty interpretation doctrine was made in a dual-purpose context and not actually necessary for reaching any of the ICJ's dispositive findings in that case, the *Tyrer* Court's promulgation of the living instrument doctrine was not necessary for its progressive finding that the birching of a 15-year-old offender by Manx police constituted 'degrading punishment' within the meaning of Article 3 of the ECHR.[55] The presence of the word 'also' at the start of the oft-quoted paragraph extracted above itself indicates that the living instrument point was made merely as an additional argument to buttress the Court's findings, while the context confirms that it was not adduced in favour of any preference for a legal, social, moral or political notion that had only emerged after the Convention was concluded in 1950.

Indeed, the living instrument argument was made in response to the Respondent's argument that 'the judicial corporal punishment at issue in this case was

[51] *Tyrer v The United Kingdom* (Merits), Judgment (European Court of Human Rights (Chamber), 5856/72, 25 April 1978) 12 (§ 31).

[52] Eirik Bjorge, *The Evolutionary Interpretation of Treaties* (Oxford, Oxford University Press, 2014) 12.

[53] M Sørensen, 'Do the Rights Set forth in the European Convention on Human Rights in 1950 have the Same Significance in 1975? Report presented by Max Sørensen to the Fourth International Colloquy about the European Convention on Human Rights, Rome 5–8 November 1975': reprinted in Max Sørensen, *A Bibliography* (Aarhus, Aarhus University Press, 1988), 23, 54–55 (emphasis added).

[54] *Tyrer*, Judgment (n 51) 12 (§ 31) (emphasis added).

[55] ECHR, art 3.

not in breach of the Convention since it did not outrage public opinion in the Island',[56] an argument that apparently invoked Manx public opinion not just of 1978, but of all times back to and including 1950, the year of the Convention's conclusion. To reject the United Kingdom's argument, the Court did not need to open the terms of the treaty to later-emerging Manx public opinion, but to public opinion existing in other States in which the Convention applied. After declaring the Convention to be a living instrument, the *Tyrer* Court expanded the scope of its inquiry to take into account 'the developments and commonly accepted standards in the penal policy of the member States of the Council of Europe in this field'.[57] The mention of the living character of the Convention and how it must be interpreted therefore served as a bridge from a claim about how birching was regarded in the jurisdiction concerned, to the consideration of how it is regarded in the wider community of the Council of Europe's Member States; a spatial link, not a temporal one.

Finally, just as the broad, unsupported and non-applied nature of the *Namibia* dictum did not dissuade subsequent general international lawyers from invoking it in support of a new doctrine of evolutionary treaty interpretation, the broad, unsupported and non-applied nature of the *Tyrer* dictum did not prevent international human rights judges from declaring it to have established the living instrument doctrine as an integral part of international human rights law. Many subsequent ECtHR cases simply stated their view that the Convention was a living instrument that must be interpreted in the light of present-day conditions with a bare citation of an existing authority. The *Marckx* judgment of June 1979 declared the living instrument doctrine an established principle citing the *Tyrer* judgment,[58] the 1986 *Johnston v Ireland* judgment proceeded in the same way but cited *Marckx*,[59] as did the *Soering* judgment (by citing *Tyrer*),[60] and the *Sigurjónsson* judgment (by citing *Soering*).[61] By the time of the *Loizidou* preliminary objections judgment of 1995, the ECtHR was expressly noting just how entrenched the living instrument doctrine had become, saying:

> That the Convention is a living instrument which must be interpreted in the light of present-day conditions is firmly rooted in the Court's case-law (see, *inter alia*, the *Tyrer v the United Kingdom* judgment of 25 April 1978, Series A no 26, pp 15–16, para 31).[62]

[56] *Tyrer*, Judgment (n 51) 12 (§ 31).
[57] ibid (§ 31).
[58] *Marckx v Belgium* (Merits and Just Satisfaction), Judgment (European Court of Human Rights (Plenary), 6833/74, 13 June 1979) 15 (§ 41).
[59] *Johnston and Others v Ireland* (Merits and Just Satisfaction), Judgment (European Court of Human Rights (Plenary), 9697/82, 18 December 1986) 18 (§ 53).
[60] *Soering v The United Kingdom* (Merits and Just Satisfaction), Judgment (European Court of Human Rights (Plenary), 14038/88, 7 July 1989) 33 (§ 102).
[61] *Sigurdur A Sigurjónsson v Iceland* (Merits and Just Satisfaction), Judgment (European Court of Human Rights (Chamber), 16130/90, 30 June 1993) 12 (§ 35).
[62] *Loizidou v Turkey* (Preliminary Objections), Judgment (European Court of Human Rights (Chamber), 15318/89, 23 March 1995) 21 (§ 71).

A Grand Chamber of the Court made the same statement word-for-word in the *Matthews* judgment of 1999 citing *Loizidou* in place of *Tyrer*,[63] while judgments of the Court including those in the cases of *Selmouni*, *Colas* and *Vo* all simply cited authority in support of a statement that the Convention was a living instrument that must be interpreted in the light of present-day conditions.[64]

Through a quite banal process of accretion on the base of a vague and unsupported statement, the living instrument had thus become, without any thoroughgoing analysis, a central tenet of ECtHR practice and European human rights law.

iii. Treatment of the Living Instrument and Evolutionary Treaty Interpretation Doctrines as Synonymous

Of course, the emergence and consolidation of this doctrine of human rights law would have been largely inconsequential for the development of the evolutionary interpretation doctrine examined in this chapter if it had remained a separate doctrine known only as the 'living instrument' doctrine. Soon after its emergence, however, the living instrument doctrine began being regarded as synonymous with the evolutionary interpretation doctrine that had emerged from the *Namibia* advisory opinion in general international law. This constitutes the third act in our story.

Interestingly, the first Strasbourg judges to mention the evolutionary interpretation doctrine by one of its names were all dissenters who, with one exception, advocated a constrained view of the doctrine in opposition to ECtHR judgments apparently expanding the scope of ECHR Article 6(1), the same provision into which the *Golder* court had famously read the right to bring civil proceedings.

In the *Albert and Le Compte v Belgium* case decided in 1983, a sixteen-to-four majority of an ECtHR plenary somewhat hesitantly found that the applicants' rights to continue to practise the medical profession as private doctors constituted a 'a civil right' within the meaning of ECHR Article 6(1), a provision that thereby granted them – following *Golder* – 'the benefit of the "right to a Court"'.[65] In a strongly-worded dissenting opinion, Judge Matscher expressed the view that the Court's finding went 'beyond the limits of an "evolutive" interpretation', which he simultaneously accepted, but sought to limit to interpreting

[63] *Matthews v The United Kingdom* (Merits and Just Satisfaction), Judgment (European Court of Human Rights (Grand Chamber), 24833/94, 18 February 1999) 14 (§ 39).

[64] *Selmouni v France* (Merits and Just Satisfaction), Judgment (European Court of Human Rights (Grand Chamber), 25803/94, 28 July 1999) 31 (§ 101); *Société Colas Est and Others v France* (Merits and Just Satisfaction), Judgment (European Court of Human Rights (Second Section), 37971/97, 16 April 2002) 14 (§ 41); *Vo v France* (Merits), Judgment (European Court of Human Rights (Grand Chamber), 53924/00, 7 August 2004) 37 (§ 82).

[65] *Albert and Le Compte v Belgium* (Merits), Judgment (European Court of Human Rights (Plenary), 7299/75 7496/76, 2 October 1983) 10–11 (§§ 28–29).

'general and undefined terms (for example, "necessary in a democratic society") ... in line with the evolution of social conceptions in the member countries'.[66]

In the parallel *Feldbrugge* and *Deumeland* cases of 29 May 1986, ECtHR majorities decided that the claims regarding health and accident insurance allowances respectively also constituted 'the determination of ... civil rights' within the meaning of ECHR Article 6(1).[67] It was again in the context of a dissenting opinion insisting on the 'limits to evolutive interpretation', that the evolutionary interpretation doctrine was mentioned.[68] Crucially, however, the *Feldbrugge* and *Deumeland* seven-judge joint dissents explicitly tied it to the living instrument doctrine, not only by a definition of 'evolutive interpretation' with terms that recalled those used in *Tyrer*, but also with a direct citation of the paragraphs of the *Tyrer*, *Marckx* and *Dudgeon* judgments asserting that doctrine.[69]

The other 1980s opinion to mention the doctrine, while also a dissenting opinion to a judgment on the applicability of ECHR Article 6, is the exception to the extent that it does not seek to limit, but instead unequivocally supports the 'evolutive interpretation of the Convention'.[70] It was very significant that its author, Rudolf Bernhardt, a renowned general international lawyer[71] who had notably explored aspects of the Problem in his 1963 *Habilitationsschrift*[72] and had referred to the doctrine's emergence in a case note on the *South West Africa-Namibia* complex of cases,[73] knowingly equated, already in 1984, the Strasbourg court's living instrument case law with general international law's evolutionary treaty interpretation doctrine.

By late 1986, it was not just dissenting opinions but judgments of the ECtHR that were treating these two doctrines as one and the same thing.[74] This continued in later cases such as *Colas*,[75] *Stafford*[76] and *Vo*.[77]

[66] *Albert and Le Compte v Belgium* (Merits), Partly dissenting opinion of Judge Matscher (European Court of Human Rights (Plenary), 7299/75 7496/76, 2 October 1983) 24 (§ 3).

[67] *Feldbrugge v The Netherlands* (Merits), Judgment (European Court of Human Rights (Plenary), 8562/79, 29 May 1986) 3–7 (§§ 11–21); *Deumeland v Germany* (Merits and Just Satisfaction), Judgment (European Court of Human Rights (Plenary), 9384/81, 29 May 1986) 14–15 (§§ 43–45).

[68] *Feldbrugge*, Joint Dissenting Opinion (n 41) 25 (§ 24).

[69] ibid (§ 24).

[70] *Öztürk v Germany, Judgment (Merits)*, Dissenting Opinion of Judge Bernhardt (European Court of Human Rights (Plenary), 8544/79, 21 February 1984) 34.

[71] Bernhardt later commented in relation to the acceptance of these two doctrines in the human rights field that 'a considerable number of the persons working and deciding in the European Court are not specialists in international law and are often more familiar with State constitutions, with the internal legal order of States' (Bernhardt [n 44] 24), but he certainly did not himself fall into the category of a human rights specialist without knowledge of general international law.

[72] Rudolf Bernhardt, *Die Auslegung völkerrechtlicher Verträge insbesondere in der neueren Rechtsprechung internationaler Gerichte* (Köln, Carl Heymanns Verlag, 1963).

[73] Bernhardt (n 5).

[74] *Johnston*, Judgment (n 59) 18 (§ 53).

[75] *Colas*, Judgment (n 64) 14 (§ 41).

[76] *Stafford v The United Kingdom* (Merits and Just Satisfaction), Judgment (European Court of Human Rights (Grand Chamber), 46295/99, 28 May 2002) 17 (§ 68).

[77] *Vo*, Judgment (n 64) 37 (§ 82).

The Inter-American Court of Human Rights ('IACtHR') followed the same path from the other end, eventually coming to speak of the living instrument doctrine and evolutionary interpretation of a human rights treaty synonymously. In the first decision in which it explicitly raised the temporal aspects of interpretation, the advisory opinion on the *Interpretation of the American Declaration of the Rights and Duties of Man* of 1989, the IACtHR did not mention the living instrument doctrine, but instead quoted the ICJ's famously dynamic dictum in the *Namibia* advisory opinion in favour of an approach rejecting the 'the normative value and significance which [the American Convention] was believed to have had in 1948'.[78] The Court's *Right to Information on Consular Assistance* advisory opinion of 1999 then both quoted the ECtHR's living instrument authorities and paragraph 53 of the *Namibia* advisory opinion as reflective of 'evolutive interpretation',[79] with the concurring opinion of Judge Cançado Trindade, then of the Inter-American Court, confirming the link in general statements that took a strongly anti-formalist stance on treaty interpretation.[80] Immediately subsequent IACtHR judgments extracted support from both doctrines with *Villagrán* and *Mayagna*, for example, referring to both apparently synonymously,[81] before several more recent judgments all expressly associated the two doctrines by following up their statement of the living instrument doctrine with the words '*[t]al interpretación evolutiva*' ('[t]his evolutive interpretation').[82]

It is therefore very clear that both major international human rights courts consider the living instrument and evolutive or dynamic treaty interpretation doctrines to be one and the same thing. Distinguished commentators on this case law confirm this. Letsas, for example, followed a statement of the living instrument doctrine by saying that '[t]his method [is] also called evolutive or

[78] *Interpretation of the American Declaration of the Rights and Duties of Man*, Advisory Opinion [1989] Inter-Am Ct HR (Ser A) No 10 11–12 (§ 37).

[79] *The Right to Information on Consular Assistance in the Framework of the Guarantees of the Due Process of Law*, Advisory Opinion [1999] Inter-Am Ct HR (Ser A) No 16 (1999) 58 (§ 114).

[80] *The Right to Information on Consular Assistance in the Framework of the Guarantees of the Due Process of Law*, Concurring Opinion of Judge Cançado Trindade [1999] Inter-Am Ct HR (Ser A) No 16 (1999) 1–6 (§§ 2–15).

[81] *Case of the 'Street Children' (Villagran-Morales et al) v Guatemala* (Merits), Judgment [1999] Inter-Am Ct HR (Ser C) No 77 46 (§ 193); *Case of the Mayagna (Sumo) Awas Tingni Community v Nicaragua* (Merits, Reparations and Costs), Judgment [2001] Inter-Am Ct HR Series C No 79 78 (§ 146).

[82] See *Case of the Yakye Axa Indigenous Community v Paraguay* (Merits, Reparations and Costs), Judgment [2005] Inter-Am. Ct. H.R. (Ser. C) No. 125 74 (§ 125); *Case of the "Mapiripán Massacre" v Colombia* (Merits, Reparations and Costs), Judgment [2005] Inter-Am. Ct. H.R. (Ser. C) No. 134 90 (§ 106); *Case of the Ituango Massacres v Colombia* (Preliminary Objections, Merits, Reparations and Costs), Judgment [2006] Inter-Am Ct. HR (Ser C) No 148 74 (§ 155); *Case of Atala Riffo and Daughters v Chile* (Merits, Reparations and Costs), Judgment [2012] Inter-Am Ct HR (Ser C) No 239 29 (§ 83); *Case of the Kichwa Indigenous People of Sarayaku v Ecuador* (Merits and Reparations), Judgment [2012] Inter-Am Ct HR (Ser C) No. 245 43 (§ 161); *Case of Artavia Murillo et al ('In Vitro Fertilization') v Costa Rica* (Preliminary Objections, Merits, Reparations and Costs), Judgment [2012] Inter-Am Ct HR (Ser C) No 257 76 (§ 245).

dynamic interpretation',[83] while Brölmann characterised the 'living instrument doctrine' as a well-known principle of Strasbourg case law before adding that: 'In current parlance, the notion appears synonymous to "evolutive treaty interpretation" or "dynamic interpretation", through which a treaty "can change its meaning in accordance with developments in State and society"'.[84] The two doctrines are so regularly conflated that one now even sees them referred to synonymously in the decisions and opinions of international courts and tribunals of general jurisdiction. Judge Cançado Trindade's *Whaling in the Antarctic* separate opinion presents what is currently the clearest example of this phenomenon, mixing references to 'evolutionary interpretation' (and the scarce ICJ case law supporting evolutionary interpretation) with countless references to the living instrument doctrine (and the many human rights cases supporting the living instrument doctrine).[85]

iv. Human Rights Courts' Use of the Doctrines for Progressive Adjudication, Not Temporal Interpretation

For international lawyers studying evolutionary interpretation, the synonymous treatment of the living instrument and evolutionary treaty interpretation doctrines constitutes a blessing. Instead of having to extract conclusions about the meaning and effects of the latter doctrine from an inherently limited number of ICJ cases and State-to-State arbitrations, they can now draw on the considerably larger body of interpretative case law produced by international human rights courts. Indeed, it is notable that some of the leading contemporary studies of evolutionary treaty interpretation rely heavily on human rights case law. In Malgosia Fitzmaurice's two-part and 82-page 2009–10 *Hague Yearbook* study of the 'Dynamic (evolutive) Interpretation of Treaties', by far the longest section – the 33-page section 4.2 – is dedicated to 'Human rights and the ECtHR',[86] while Bjorge, in his 2014 monograph on *The Evolutionary Interpretation of Treaties*, cites on an impressively broad range of international case law, but noticeably leans on human rights cases in many of the most important parts of his study.[87]

For a book going behind the evolutionary treaty interpretation doctrine to the specific problem of intertemporal linguistics, however, the conflation of the

[83] George Letsas, 'Intentionalism and the Interpretation of the ECHR' in Malgosia Fitzmaurice, Olufemi Elias and Panos Merkouris (eds), *Treaty Interpretation and the Vienna Convention on the Law of Treaties: 30 Years On* (Leiden, Martinus Nijhoff Publishers, 2010) 263.

[84] Catherine M Brölmann, 'Limits of the Treaty Paradigm' in Matthew Craven and Malgosia Fitzmaurice (eds), *Interrogating the Treaty: Essays in the Contemporary Law of Treaties* (Nijmegen, Wolf Legal Publishers, 2005) 8.

[85] *Whaling in the Antarctic (Australia v Japan; New Zealand intervening)*, Separate Opinion of Judge Cançado Trindade [2014] ICJ Reports 348, 358–360 (§§ 29–34).

[86] Malgosia Fitzmaurice, 'Dynamic (Evolutive) Interpretation of Treaties, Part I' (2009) *Hague Yearbook of International Law* 101; Malgosia Fitzmaurice, 'Dynamic (Evolutive) Interpretation of Treaties, Part 2' (2010) *Hague Yearbook of International Law* 3.

[87] Bjorge (n 52).

living instrument and evolutionary treaty interpretation doctrines is not even a mixed blessing, but a curse. One of the key points of this book is that, when many international lawyers speak of interpreting a living instrument or applying the doctrine of evolutionary treaty interpretation, they are not taking a position on the Problem at all. By conducting non-temporal and sometimes even non-interpretative progressive adjudication in the name of evolutionary treaty interpretation, international courts and tribunals have so greatly expanded the notion of evolutionary treaty interpretation that texts writing about it are no longer focused on the narrow temporal and uniquely interpretative issue at the core of this study.

Since the mid-1980s, human rights courts have increasingly invoked the living instrument/evolutionary treaty interpretation doctrine not to give a treaty term its later-emerging – rather than original – meaning, but to undertake different activities to achieve distinct, but invariably progressive, ends.[88] There are too many decisions playing a part in this fourth act of our drama for them all to be afforded a spoken part, so this important shift will be demonstrated through the analysis of two sets of sample decisions. The first set will show how the doctrine is used to go beyond the treaty to apply more modern and progressive law external to the treaty (section (a)), while the second will reveal how human rights courts applying the doctrine now openly consider themselves to be improving, rather than interpreting, human rights law (section (b)).

a. To Apply More Modern and Progressive External Law

In the early-1990s case of *Sigurjónsson v Iceland*, the applicant was a taxi driver who, after being forbidden from supplying taxi services in a certain area if he was not a member of a particular trade union, sought to enforce a so-called 'negative freedom of association'.[89] His claim relied on ECHR Article 11, the terms of which explicitly grant the 'right to form and join trade unions', but not the right not to.[90] By asking the ECtHR to read an unenumerated right into a provision that clearly did not provide for it, Sigurjónsson's claim mirrored Golder's. However, the Court presiding over this case did not refer to the teleology of the

[88] It is salient that, in his recent functional reconstruction of the ICJ and ECtHR case law on evolutive interpretation practice, Djeffal's efforts to find a case that used the doctrine to *decrease* the level of human rights protection leads him (a) back behind the last 30 years of ECtHR judgments citing the living instrument/evolutionary interpretation doctrine to a 1981 Report of the Commission and (b) a 2014 ECtHR judgment which not only fails to refer to the doctrine, but by Djeffal's own admission, 'cannot be considered as an evolutive interpretation' – Christian Djeffal, *Static and Evolutive Treaty Interpretation: A Functional Reconstruction* (Cambridge, Cambridge University Press, 2016) 312, 356; *McVeigh v The United Kingdom*, Report of the Commission (European Commission of Human Rights, 8022/77, 8025/77 and 8027/77, 18 March 1981); *Hassan v The United Kingdom* (Merits and Just Satisfaction), Judgment (European Court of Human Rights (Grand Chamber), 29750/09, 16 September 2014).

[89] *Sigurjónsson*, Judgment (n 61) 3–5 (§§ 7–17).

[90] ECHR, art 11.

provision (which probably would not have helped the applicant), but instead to various other instruments that dealt with the freedom of association in general, including documents issued well after the 1950 conclusion of the Convention.[91] It then immediately segued from this external body of law to its finding by invoking the living instrument doctrine:

> In this connection, it should be recalled that the Convention is a living instrument which must be interpreted in the light of present-day conditions (see, amongst other authorities, the *Soering v. the United Kingdom* judgment of 7 July 1989, Series A no 161, p 40, para 102). Accordingly, Article 11 must be viewed as encompassing a negative right of association.[92]

In the quite similar *Scoppola v Italy (No 2)* case that was decided in 2009, the applicant sought to have his sentence modified on the basis of a subsequently-issued legislative decree that reduced penalties for the offence he had committed.[93] Before an ECtHR Grand Chamber, he argued that a right to have his sentence reduced could be read into the State's obligation not to impose a 'heavier penalty … than the one that was applicable at the time the criminal offence was committed' in Article 7 of the Convention.[94] The *Scoppola (No 2)* Court openly recognised that the Convention contained no express provision for the right invoked by the applicant and that his request could only be granted through a process inferring the existence of that right.[95] It was nonetheless prepared to make that inference, speaking of the two notions as mirroring principles of non-retrospectiveness and retrospectiveness,[96] this despite the fact that one is an obligation applying only where penalties increase and the other has the distinct character of a right that applies only in the very different situation where penalties decrease.

To reach this conclusion, the *Scoppola (No 2)* Court invoked what it called 'a dynamic and evolutive approach',[97] using it in several ways, all of which were progressive, but none of which involved selecting the later meaning of a treaty term. Like the *Sigurjónsson* Court, it utilised the evolutionary interpretation doctrine to 'tak[e] into account … developments' reflected in instruments outside the treaty including the European Union's Charter of Fundamental Rights of 2000, the ECJ's 2005 *Berlusconi and Others* judgment, the 1998 Rome Statute of the International Criminal Court and the ICTY's 2005 *Dragan Nikolic* judgment.[98] The *Scoppola (No 2)* majority even admitted that it was

[91] *Sigurjónsson*, Judgment (n 61) 11–12 (§ 35).
[92] ibid 12 (§ 35).
[93] *Scoppola v Italy (No 2)* (Merits and Just Satisfaction), Judgment (European Court of Human Rights (Grand Chamber), 10249/03, 17 September 2009).
[94] ECHR, art 7(1).
[95] *Scoppola (No 2)*, Judgment (n 93) 29 (§ 107).
[96] ibid (§ 109).
[97] ibid 28 (§ 104).
[98] ibid 28–29 (§ 105).

leaving the terrain of interpreting the applicable treaty provision when it openly conceded that the provisions of these external laws differ from the applicable law, the EU's Charter even specifically providing for a right to retrospectiveness that is not included in the Convention.[99] Manifestly, in that 2009 judgment, the ECtHR was not simply using the various post-treaty developments it cited to illuminate the meaning of treaty terms before it, but was actually applying the law reflected in those subsequent developments directly.

In the 2002 *Colas* judgment,[100] the ECtHR went even further, using the doctrine not only to infer a right that could be viewed as the flipside of a positive freedom or obligation, but simply to expand the scope of the Convention's application beyond its clear and express terms. After their offices were raided by French authorities in 1985, a group of companies claimed a violation of their ECHR Article 8 right to the inviolability of their 'home'.[101] Yet the word 'home' clearly did not extend to business premises, another European court, the ECJ, having even specifically stated that as much in its 1989 judgment in the case of *Hoechst v Commission*.[102] This did not deter the ECtHR from finding that ECHR Article 8, with its reference to a person's 'home', also applied to business premises, putatively on the basis of the living instrument doctrine and a dynamic interpretation of Article 8:

> The Court reiterates that the Convention is a living instrument which must be interpreted in the light of present-day conditions. ... Building on its dynamic interpretation of the Convention, the Court considers that the time has come to hold that in certain circumstances the rights guaranteed by Article 8 of the Convention may be construed as including the right to respect for a company's registered office, branches or other business premises ...[103]

The statements made by a number of judges in the subsequent *Öcalan* case[104] provide a more extreme example of the same phenomenon, because they apparently considered that the evolutionary interpretation doctrine could not only expand the terms of a treaty provision into a gap, but also sanction the de facto amendment of a manifestly clear ECHR provision. Öcalan's case, which was heard by both a Chamber in 2003 and a Grand Chamber in 2005, raised the issue of whether the use of the death penalty violated the Convention by virtue of being inhuman or degrading treatment under ECHR Article 3, despite

[99] ibid 28 (§ 105).
[100] *Colas*, Judgment (n 64).
[101] See ibid 10 (§ 28).
[102] *Hoechst AG v Commission of the European Communities*, Judgment [1989] European Court Reports 2859, 2924 (§ 18).
[103] *Colas*, Judgment (n 64) 14 (§ 41).
[104] *Öcalan v Turkey, Judgment (Merits and Just Satisfaction), Partly dissenting opinion of Judge Türmen* (European Court of Human Rights (First Section), 46221/99, 3 December 2003); *Öcalan v Turkey* (Merits and Just Satisfaction), Judgment (European Court of Human Rights (Grand Chamber), 46221/99, 5 December 2005).

the specific terms of ECHR Article 2 that apparently authorised the death penalty by providing that: 'No one shall be deprived of his life intentionally save in the execution of a sentence of a court following his conviction of a crime for which this penalty is provided by law'.[105]

The 1989 judgment in the similar case of *Soering*[106] had invoked the living instrument doctrine in a manner consistent with its narrower, traditional sense, to find that ECHR Article 3's notion of 'inhuman or degrading treatment' now covered the provision of the death penalty.[107] However, it went on to conclude that the use of the death penalty did not violate the convention, because ECHR Article 2's express and specific sanctioning of the death penalty acted as a 'textual limit on the scope for evolutive interpretation of Article 3'.[108]

For the Chamber that first decided the *Öcalan* case in 2003, however, the living instrument doctrine allowed the Court to view the post-1989 internal developments pursuant to which the death penalty had almost completely been abolished in the Council of Europe 'as signalling the agreement of the Contracting States to abrogate, or at the very least to modify, the second sentence of Article 2§1'.[109] The majority of the Grand Chamber, for its part, mostly avoided the issue posed by ECHR Article 2 potentially overruling a violation of Article 3 by finding that Öcalan had been sentenced to death following an unfair trial which fell outside the scope of Article 2's authorisation of 'legally valid' death penalties.[110] However, on the specific issue of whether, through the operation of the living instrument/evolutionary interpretation doctrine, the 'abolitionist trend' that had become prevalent in Europe could potentially amend a provision of the Convention expressly contrary to it, the Grand Chamber quoted the Chamber's obiter dicta on this point extensively and approvingly before saying that even the Contracting Parties' parallel legislative programme (Protocol of No 13 of 3 May 2002) did 'not necessarily run counter to the view that Article 2 has been *amended* in so far as it permits the death penalty in times of peace'.[111]

One could easily debate the judiciousness of a court making such statements in a situation which simultaneously presented the benefits of recognising a palpable shift in values (including in the Respondent State) to the dangers of interfering with a legislative process and *pacta sunt servanda* by effectively applying protocols not applicable to the facts being assessed. But those questions

[105] ECHR, art 2.

[106] See especially *Soering*, Judgment (n 60) 24–25 (§§ 80–82); see also Colin Warbrick, 'Coherence and the European Court of Human Rights: The Adjudicative Background to the Soering Case' (1990) 11 *Michigan Journal of International Law* 1073, 1086–87.

[107] *Soering*, Judgment (n 60) 33 (§ 102).

[108] ibid 34 (§ 103).

[109] *Öcalan v Turkey* (Merits and Just Satisfaction), Judgment (European Court of Human Rights (First Section), 46221/99, 3 December 2003) 51 (§§ 193–96); see also *Öcalan*, Judgment (Grand Chamber) (n 104) 46–47 (§ 163).

[110] *Öcalan*, Judgment (Grand Chamber) (n 104) 48–51 (§§ 165–75).

[111] ibid 47 (§ 164) (emphasis added).

are not relevant here. For present purposes, these judicial statements made in the course of the *Öcalan* case merely serve to show that the living instrument/evolutionary interpretation doctrine has come to be understood in a manner so estranged from its original, strictly interpretative sense, that it is now perceived as potentially allowing subsequent developments to even amend – rather than simply inform the meaning of – applicable treaty terms.

It should be apparent, even from this small sample of ECtHR decisions, that contemporary human rights courts understand the evolutionary interpretation doctrine to go well beyond the assigning of a later-emerging meaning to an interpreted treaty term. In all of *Sigurjónsson*, *Scoppola (No 2)* and *Colas*, the Court effectively applied, as treaty norms, rules and principles that emerged after the treaty and outside of the treaty. In *Öcalan*, several judges went so far as to contemplate these external subsequent developments overruling or de facto amending express terms of an applicable treaty.

Other than their citation of the living instrument/evolutionary interpretation doctrine, these decisions have two things in common: (a) they apply rules, principles and values that emerged after the ECHR was concluded in 1950; and (b) they reach a socially progressive outcome. If evolutionary treaty interpretation were understood as a doctrine that enabled reference to any source of law or values post-dating the treaty's conclusion – whether or not they affect a treaty term's meaning – to support the adoption of any legally or socially progressive finding – however it is ultimately reached – then all these cases would come within the frame of the living instrument/evolutionary interpretation doctrine that they cite. Yet, in that form, the doctrine no longer merely constitutes the taking of a dynamic position on the problem of intertemporal linguistics, but instead a broad and powerful doctrine allowing judges charged with interpreting and applying a treaty to progressively develop international law; a doctrine of *progressive adjudication*.

b. To Progressively Develop the Treaties

Those accustomed to broadly teleological interpretation, including of treaties, may consider that the form of the doctrine being labelled progressive adjudication, while partially characterised by its progressiveness, is still interpretative, so should at least be referred to as 'progressive treaty interpretation'. However, contemporary human rights courts so often cite the doctrine in circumstances that are so far removed from even a broad and teleological interpretative process, that they cannot be characterised as instances of treaty interpretation. Moreover, while these courts now only rarely refer to the terms and even objects and purposes of the treaties themselves, they increasingly emphasise their intention to progressively develop the law.

In keeping with the progressive and non-interpretative sense of the doctrine that has emerged, a number of living instrument/evolutionary interpretation cases have used it simply to justify departing from what they consider bad or outdated prior case law.

In its 28 May 2002 *Stafford* judgment, for example, the ECtHR was much more concerned with using the evolutionary interpretation doctrine to move away from the non-distinguishable 1994 *Wynne* judgment than to interpret any treaty term. It is even unclear which ECHR provision the *Stafford* Court could have been interpreting. The parts of the judgment referring to *Tyrer*, *Cossey* and 'a dynamic and evolutive approach' all occur in a section of the judgment on paragraph 1 of ECHR Article 5, but speak most about the almost identical *Wynne* case decided uniquely under the quite distinct paragraph 4 of ECHR Article 5. Commentary of the decision is equally unsure. Mowbray, for example, cites *Stafford* as one of the judgments in which 'the living instrument doctrine enabled the Court to creatively update the interpretation of [the] Convention Articles', but speaks simply of compatibility with ECHR Article 5 in general.[112] It is much clearer on the face of the judgment that the *Stafford* court wanted to depart from the *Wynne* authority that had distinguished between mandatory and discretionary sentences and thereby found in favour of the Respondent State and that it invoked the evolutionary interpretation doctrine in this context:

> While the Court is not formally bound to follow any of its previous judgments, it is in the interests of legal certainty, foreseeability and equality before the law that it should not depart, without cogent reason, from precedents laid down in previous cases. Since the Convention is first and foremost a system for the protection of human rights, the Court must however have regard to the changing conditions in Contracting States and respond, for example, to any emerging consensus as to the standards to be achieved … It is of crucial importance that the Convention is interpreted and applied in a manner which renders its rights practical and effective, not theoretical and illusory. A failure by the Court to maintain a dynamic and evolutive approach would risk rendering it a bar to reform or improvement.
>
> … Although there is no material distinction on the facts between this case and *Wynne*, having regard to the significant developments in the domestic sphere, the Court proposes to reassess 'in the light of present-day conditions' what is now the appropriate interpretation and application of the Convention (see *Tyrer v the United Kingdom*, judgment of 25 April 1978, Series A no 26, pp 15–16, § 31, and subsequent case-law).[113]

Within three months of the *Stafford* judgment, other international human rights decisions had invoked the doctrine in the same way. The 11 July 2002 judgment of the same court in *Goodwin v The United Kingdom* invoked the doctrine in

[112] Alastair Mowbray, 'The Creativity of the European Court of Human Rights' (2005) 5 *Human Rights Law Review* 57, 69; cited approvingly by: Fitzmaurice, 'Dynamic (Evolutive) Interpretation of Treaties, Part I' (n 86) 134.

[113] *Stafford*, Judgment (n 76) 17 (§§ 68–69).

almost identical terms as part of its move away from prior case law finding that Contracting States did not interfere with the ECHR Article 8 right to respect for private life by failing to legally recognise the changed gender of post-operative transsexuals.[114]

Less than a month later, the Human Rights Committee met to evaluate whether Canada had breached ICCPR articles 6 or 7 by deporting the US-national Robert Judge to his home State where he had been sentenced to death for double-homicide. Clearly troubled by its prior *Kindler v Canada* decision finding on very similar facts that there could be no such violation, the *Judge* Court explicitly seized on the living instrument doctrine that had developed at the ECtHR: (a) to depart, like *Stafford*, from a prior authority; and (b) to recognise, like ECtHR decisions including *Stafford* and *Goodwin*, an 'emerging' or 'broadening' societal consensus on the issue.[115]

As if to entrench this new use of the living instrument/evolutionary interpretation doctrine, the ECtHR 2005 *Mamatkulov* judgment used the doctrine to depart from previous decisions of the Court determining that a power to order binding interim measures could not be inferred from ECHR Article 34's (former Article 25's) granting of the 'right to judicial protection'.[116]

All these decisions betrayed a somewhat ironic consistency in not only their use of the doctrine to depart from existing authority, but also the terms in which they stated they were doing this. The *Mamatkulov* Court, for example, presented a collage of the *Stafford* and *Goodwin* dicta,[117] before going on to find that a failure by a Contracting State to comply with interim measures hindered the effective exercise of an individual applicant's right of application under ECHR Article 34.[118] Yet it did so not through any unpacking of the meaning of the terms of that provision, but rather through a series of reflections on the function of interim measures and the nature of the European system of human rights protection. Indeed, there is no suggestion that the meaning of any of the terms of ECHR Article 34 had changed over time and the judgment does not identify any treaty terms that it considers itself to be interpreting.

From both its immediate and wider context, therefore, the *Mamatkulov* judgment's reference to the living instrument doctrine, like those of *Stafford*, *Goodwin* and *Judge* appears to have been made not in support of any treaty interpretation, but simply to move away from earlier authority that the Court did not

[114] *Christine Goodwin v The United Kingdom* (Merits and Just Satisfaction), Judgment (European Court of Human Rights (Grand Chamber), 28957/95, 7 November 2002).

[115] *Roger Judge v Canada*, Communication No 829/1998 [2002] UN Doc CCPR/C/78/D/829/1998 (2003).

[116] *Mamatkulov and Askarov v Turkey* (Merits and Just Satisfaction), Judgment (European Court of Human Rights (Grand Chamber), 46827/99 46951/99, 2 April 2005) 33–34 (§§ 118–21), departing from: *Cruz Varas and Others v Sweden*, Judgment (European Court of Human Rights (Plenary), 15576/89, 20 March 1991).

[117] *Mamatkulov*, Judgment (n 116) 34 (§ 121).

[118] ibid 36 (§§ 128–29).

wish to follow on bases that may or may not have been valid, but were certainly not interpretative. In this light, it is surprising to read that the *Mamatkulov* judgment 'focused on an evolutive interpretation of the Convention'[119] or 'applied the "living instrument" approach to the procedural provisions' of the Convention,[120] unless, of course, one accepts the emergence of a more progressive and less interpretative form of the doctrine.

These dicta from the relatively recent case law are not only valuable for showing just how far the doctrine has moved from the core task of interpretation, but also for affirming, through express statements, that human rights judges openly equate an application of the living instrument/evolutionary interpretation doctrine with an effort to develop and improve human rights law. For example, the previously mentioned *Scoppola (No 2)* judgment of 2009 extracted and combined the overtly progressive sentences emerging from the *Stafford*, *Goodwin* and *Mamatkulov* courts' invocation of the doctrine, saying:

> It is of crucial importance that the Convention is interpreted and applied in a manner which *renders its rights practical and effective*, not theoretical and illusory. A failure by the Court to maintain a dynamic and evolutive approach *would risk rendering it a bar to reform or improvement* ...[121]

As should now be clear, these cases undoubtedly focus on going beyond a mere interpretation of the treaty to enhance the treaty's role and to use it for the betterment of society. Over the last 15–20 years, judicial slogans in the form of the quotations above have been increasingly repeated and the overtly progressive approach in the name of the living instrument/evolutionary interpretation doctrine has become a feature of both ECtHR case law and the field of international human rights in general.

We have now reached a point where international human rights courts are essentially expected to progressively develop the treaty they are charged with interpreting and applying. In light of the nature of human rights treaties, this is relatively unremarkable. What is more significant, particularly for present purposes, is that these courts routinely justify their progressive approaches by appealing to a doctrine regarding treaty interpretation through time, even where they do not engage with temporal issues of treaty interpretation at all.

There was always a risk that an ill-defined doctrine of treaty interpretation emerging from the special circumstances of the *Namibia* advisory opinion and

[119] Vassilis P Tzevelekos, 'The Use of Article 31(3)(c) of the VCLT in the Case Law of the ECtHR: An Effective Anti-Fragmentation Tool or a Selective Loophole for the Reinforcement of Human Rights Teleology – Between Evolution and Systemic Integration' (2010) 31 *Michigan Journal of International Law* 621, 656.

[120] Daniel Rietiker, 'The Principle of "Effectiveness" in the Recent Jurisprudence of the European Court of Human Rights: Its Different Dimensions and Its Consistency with Public International Law – No Need for the Concept of Treaty Sui Generis' (2010) 79 *Nordic Journal of International Law* 245, 264.

[121] *Scoppola (No 2)*, Judgment (n 93) 28 (§ 104) (emphasis added).

its broadly-termed and dual-purpose paragraph 53 would come to be understood in a manner that diverges markedly from the original form of the doctrine that took a position on the problem of intertemporal linguistics. Through the agency of international human rights courts, this risk was realised and evolutionary treaty interpretation *qua* progressive adjudication fully emerged.

v. Cross-fertilisation of the Human Rights Conception into General International Law and Other Treaties

The fifth and final act in the tale of how evolutionary interpretation came to be more readily associated with progressive adjudication than a position on the problem of intertemporal linguistics is a story of cross-fertilisation.

While it had human rights aspects to it, the *Namibia* advisory opinion constituted a prominent case of general international law and the evolutionary interpretation doctrine was extracted from its terms by general international lawyers such as Stern, Bernhardt and Simma. Indeed, in the area of general international law, the evolutionary treaty interpretation doctrine received little attention and scant support throughout the quarter-century after its 1971 proclamation.

The general international case law remained tightly confined to the narrow interpretative task of giving meaning to a treaty term, with the controversies in which it was raised focused on the meaning that should be given to specific treaty terms such as 'relating to the territorial status of Greece',[122] 'Canadian fishery regulations',[123] 'exclusive economic zone' and 'continental shelf'.[124] In these decisions, there was some indication that the doctrine was coming to be understood as capable of integrating changes other than just the legal changes which international lawyers of the 1970s considered it to refer to. However, there was no indication that general international lawyers of this period were coming to understand the doctrine more broadly than that. In particular, under the general international law of the 1970s, 1980s and 1990s, the evolutionary treaty interpretation doctrine did not appear to allow for any adjudicatory act other than assigning a contested treaty term its later-emerging – rather than original – meaning.

In addition, by contrast to international human rights courts, the general international law literature of this period not only understood the doctrine narrowly, but also to be far from established as a principle of international law.

[122] *Aegean Sea Continental Shelf (Greece v Turkey)*, Judgment [1978] ICJ Reports 3; see further s 6.II.B(i) below.

[123] *Filleting within the Gulf of St Lawrence between Canada and France ('La Bretagne')*, Award (1986) XIX RIAA/RSA 225; *Filleting within the Gulf of St Lawrence between Canada and France ('La Bretagne')*, Dissenting Opinion of Donat Pharand (1986) XIX RIAA/RSA 266.

[124] *Case concerning the delimitation of maritime boundary between Guinea-Bissau and Senegal*, Decision of 31 July 1989 (1989) XX RIAA/RSA 119.

For example, Sergio Aly's admirable and oft-neglected study of *l'interprétation évolutive en droit international public* considered, in 1997, that the doctrine would have to be – and should not be – *elevated* to the rank of an established method of interpreting international law.[125] In 1999, even Rudolf Bernhardt, by then a proponent of the dynamic approach, had to admit that:

> It seems that textbooks and treatises on public international law still primarily refer to the traditional or conservative rule of treaty interpretation, and they stress the view that the original intentions and the understanding of treaty clauses at the time of the conclusion of the treaty are in principle decisive.[126]

In 2002, a few years after the WTO Appellate Body's *Shrimp* report now frequently said to have established the dynamic approach at that institution had been handed down, Pauwelyn, a specialist in that field, nonetheless made plain the still uncertain view of the doctrine, openly questioning which of the principle of contemporaneity and evolutionary treaty interpretation was the rule and which was the exception.[127]

Against this backdrop, the *Iron Rhine* award of 2005 was already remarkable for so wholeheartedly and unequivocally throwing its support behind the evolutionary interpretation doctrine. Not only did the Tribunal explicitly note 'a general support among the leading writers today for evolutive interpretation of treaties',[128] but it also characterised many of its most important findings as an application of that doctrine.[129] Penned by a distinguished group of five general international lawyers, including three who were ICJ judges at the time, this unanimous award in a PCA arbitration between Belgium and the Netherlands almost had the de facto influence of a judgment of the world court itself, so constituted a pioneering development.

However, what makes the *Iron Rhine* award even more remarkable – and much more important for this book – is that the notion of evolutionary interpretation invoked and putatively applied by the *Iron Rhine* Tribunal was not the narrow, strictly interpretative general international law notion of it, but the much broader, progressive adjudication form of the doctrine that had developed at international human rights courts over the course of the prior 27 years.

The Iron Rhine or *Izeren Rijn* is the name given to a railway linking the Belgian port city of Antwerp to the Rhine basin in Germany through the Dutch provinces of Noord-Brabant and Limburg.[130] When Belgium separated from the

[125] Sergio Aly, *L'"interprétation évolutive" en droit international public* (Mémoire de DEA, Institut universitaire de hautes études internationales, Genève, 1997) 82–83.

[126] Bernhardt (n 44) 16.

[127] Joost Pauwelyn, 'The Nature of WTO Obligations' (2002) 1 *Jean Monnet Working Papers* 1, 31–34.

[128] *Iron Rhine ('Ijzeren Rijn') Railway between the Kingdom of Belgium and the Kingdom of the Netherlands*, Award (2005) XXVII RIAA/RSA 35, 73 (§ 81).

[129] ibid (§ 80).

[130] See further ibid 47–48 (§ 16).

Netherlands in the 1830s, it ensured that its right to transit over Dutch territory was expressly provided for in the 1839 Treaty of Separation between the two States.[131]

The *Iron Rhine* dispute arose during negotiations over the re-activation of the line that took place in the late 1990s and early 2000s. During the 1990s, the Netherlands had designated areas through which the line passed as nature reserves.[132] It insisted that it would only agree to the line being re-activated if it was done using noise barriers and tunnelling, expensive undertakings that understandably made the costs of any re-activation works an important issue between the parties.[133]

As part of its effort to shift these costs onto Belgium, the Netherlands argued that the Belgian demand for reactivation of the railways amounted to a request for a '*nouvelle route*' within the meaning of Article XII of the 1839 Treaty of Separation and that Belgium thereby bore the financial obligations for the works as set out in that provision.[134] Belgium, by contrast, argued that its request for reactivation did not amount to a request for a '*nouvelle route*' within the meaning of Article XII and that it was not this treaty, but other parts of the 'conventional regime' for the Iron Rhine railway that determined who would bear the cost of works it characterised as 'use, restoration, adaptation and modernisation'.[135] Article XII of the Treaty of Separation relevantly provided as follows:

> *Dans le cas où* il aurait été construit en Belgique *une nouvelle route*, ou creusé *un nouveau canal*, qui aboutirait à la Meuse vis-à-vis le canton néerlandais de Sittard, alors il serait loisible à la Belgique de demander à la Hollande, qui ne s'y refuserait pas dans cette supposition, que la dite route ou le dit canal *fussent prolongés* d'après le même plan, entièrement aux frais et dépens de la Belgique, par le canton de Sittard, jusqu'aux frontières de l'Allemagne.[136]

In paragraph 78 of its award, the Tribunal indicated that it understood that the applicability of this provision depended on the meaning of '*une nouvelle route*' and considered that, to determine this, it needed 'other principles

[131] Traité entre la Belgique et la Hollande, relatif à la séparation de leurs territoires respectifs 1839, art 12.

[132] See *Iron Rhine*, Award (n 128) 49 (§ 20).

[133] See ibid 49–51 (§§ 22–25).

[134] 'Counter-Memorial of the Kingdom of the Netherlands', *Arbitration regarding the Iron Rhine ('Ijzeren Rijn') Railway between the Kingdom of Belgium and the Kingdom of the Netherlands* (Permanent Court of Arbitration, 2004) 43 (§ 3.3.4.5); see also *Iron Rhine*, Award (n 128) 114 (§ 217).

[135] 'Memorial of the Kingdom of Belgium', *Arbitration regarding the Iron Rhine ('Ijzeren Rijn') Railway between the Kingdom of Belgium and the Kingdom of the Netherlands* (Permanent Court of Arbitration, 2003) 100–07 (§§ 85–94); see also *Iron Rhine*, Award (n 128) 113 (§ 213).

[136] Traité entre la Belgique et la Hollande, relatif à la séparation de leurs territoires respectifs, art 12 (emphasis added): '*In the case that* in Belgium a *new road* would have been built or a *new canal* dug, which would lead to the Maas facing the Dutch canton of Sittard, then Belgium would be at liberty to ask Holland, which in that hypothesis would not refuse it, that the said road, or the said canal *be extended* in accordance with the same plan, entirely at the cost and expense of Belgium, through the canton of Sittard, up to the borders of Germany.' (*Iron Rhine* tribunal's translation – *Iron Rhine*, Award (n 128) 58 (§ 32)).

of interpretation'.[137] Through its immediately subsequent paragraphs, the award extensively addresses the doctrine of evolutionary treaty interpretation, citing the *Nationality Decrees*, *Namibia*, *Aegean Sea*, *Gabčíkovo* and *Shrimp* authorities for the doctrine, while also referring to the closely related notions of 'generic terms' and treaties of unlimited and fixed duration.[138]

However, this part of the *Iron Rhine* award also gives clear indications that the Tribunal was not applying the narrower form of the doctrine limited to interpretations preferring the later-emerging meanings of evolutionary treaty terms, but instead the broader form of the doctrine that had emerged in international human rights courts. It is significant, for example, that the only piece of scholarship that the relevant part of the award cites is Rudolf Bernhardt's 1999 *German Yearbook* article on 'Evolutive Treaty Interpretation, Especially of the European Convention on Human Rights'.[139]

Most notably, however, the award states:

> In the present case it is not a conceptual or generic term that is in issue, but rather new technical developments relating to the operation and capacity of the railway. But here, too, it seems that an evolutive interpretation, which would ensure an application of the treaty that would be effective in terms of its object and purpose, will be preferred to a strict application of the intertemporal rule.[140]

The admission that the treaty term itself was not 'in issue' and strong implication that the evolutionary interpretation doctrine was being applied to 'technical developments' makes it very clear that the Tribunal was using the doctrine, like many international human rights courts, in a manner that strays a long way from the terms of the applicable treaty. Like the decisions of those courts invoking the broader form of the doctrine, the *Iron Rhine* Tribunal is not at all clear which treaty term it purported to interpret using the 'evolutive interpretation' doctrine, causing difficulty for subsequent readers. For example, in his Declaration appended to the ICJ's 2009 *Related Rights* judgment, Gilbert Guillaume could not identify a specific term interpreted dynamically so argued simply that 'an evolutionary interpretation was also given to the 1839 Treaty between Belgium and the Netherlands'.[141]

Moreover, by speaking of evolutionary treaty interpretation 'ensur[ing] an application of the treaty that would be effective in terms of its object and purpose', the September 2005 *Iron Rhine* award was evidently following the several ECtHR judgments that had, in dicta regarding the same doctrine, announced that the European Convention should be 'interpreted and applied in a manner which renders its rights practical and effective, not theoretical or

[137] *Iron Rhine*, Award (n 128) 72 (§ 78).
[138] ibid 72–74 (§§ 79–82); see further ss 9.II and 9.VI below.
[139] ibid 74 (§ 81).
[140] ibid 73 (§ 80).
[141] *Related Rights*, Guillaume Declaration (n 2) 296 (§ 12) (ICJ translation).

illusory' including the above-cited *Stafford* (May 2002), *Goodwin* (July 2002) and *Mamatkulov* (February 2005) judgments.

It is unsurprising that an arbitral tribunal presided over by Rosalyn Higgins was aware of developments in the field of international human rights law. She had, after all, joined the Human Rights Committee in 1984 and only left it in 1995 when she was elected to the ICJ.[142] She had also demonstrated an interest in intertemporal interpretation issues both curially[143] and extra-curially.[144] It is notable in this regard that another prominent ICJ judge with a strong human rights background, the former judge and President of the IACtHR, Judge Cançado Trindade, has consistently been an agitator for the use of the evolutionary interpretation doctrine in the more recent case law of the World Court, even quoting extensively from ECtHR and IACtHR living instrument cases on occasion.[145]

Overall, the *Iron Rhine* award's most prominent feature is its reliance on a broadly teleological approach to reach an undeniably progressive outcome. The Tribunal concluded its 'normal' interpretation of Article XII, by finding that Belgium's request for a reactivation of the long dormant line was not to be regarded as a request for a '*nouvelle route*'.[146] Yet it nonetheless went on: (i) to find that 'the entirety of Article XII, with its careful balance of the rights and obligations of the Parties, remains in principle applicable to the adaptation and modernisation requested by Belgium';[147] and (ii) to require Belgium to bear the costs of building the new line, including those imposed by the need to protect the Meinweg national park.[148]

These key findings were all reached through teleological considerations, the Tribunal stating for example that it believed 'that it would be incompatible with the *object and purpose* of the earlier treaty to read those declarations as stating that further work and requests were to be regarded as *en dehors* Article XII'.[149] It is crucial though that, throughout section II.C.4 of the award, the dynamic or evolutionary approach is expressly linked to these teleological considerations, including by quoting Bernhardt's association of the two approaches in his article on evolutionary treaty interpretation at the ECtHR.[150]

[142] See Rosalyn Higgins, 'Ten Years on the UN Human Rights Committee: Some Thoughts Upon Parting' (1996) 6 *European Human Rights Law Review* 570, 576ff.

[143] *Kasikili/Sedudu Island (Botswana/ Namibia)*, Declaration of Judge Higgins [1999] ICJ Reports 1113, 1113 (§ 2).

[144] Rosalyn Higgins, 'Some Observations on the Inter-Temporal Rule in International Law' in Jerzy Makarczyk (ed), *Theory of International Law at the Threshold of the 21st century: Essays in Honour of Krzysztof Skubiszewski* (The Hague, Kluwer Law International, 1996).

[145] *Dispute regarding Navigational and Related Rights (Costa Rica v Nicaragua)*, Judgment [2009] ICJ Reports 213; *Whaling*, Trindade Separate Opinion (n 85) 358–60 (§§ 29–34).

[146] *Iron Rhine*, Award (n 128) 74–75 (§ 84).

[147] ibid 74 (§ 83).

[148] ibid 125 (§ 244(e)).

[149] ibid 74 (§ 82) (emphasis added).

[150] ibid 73–74 (§§ 80–81).

The *Iron Rhine* award's findings were progressive because they sought to make the parties subject to existing and emerging norms of international environmental law, a fast-moving, avant-garde sub-field of international law *en pleine croissance* in latter half of the 1990s and early 2000s. Indeed, it is perhaps relevant that the two non-human-rights decisions of the 1990s most prominently referring to the evolutionary interpretation doctrine, the ICJ's 1997 *Gabčíkovo* judgment and the WTO's 1998 *Shrimp* report, also presented environmental issues. While the *Gabčíkovo* Court did not specifically state nor rely on the evolutionary interpretation doctrine, it did indicate that it might be relevant by speaking of the relevant treaty terms as 'evolving provisions' and characterising the treaty, with a nod to *Namibia*'s paragraph 53, as 'not static' and 'open to adapt to emerging norms of international law'.[151] Some signs of the resurgence of the doctrine in general international law are also apparent in the separate *Gabčíkovo* opinion of the manifestly progressive and environmental Judge Weeramantry, who, despite confusing the evolutionary interpretation doctrine with the principle of contemporaneity, cited, among other things, paragraph 53 of the *Namibia* Advisory Opinion and *Tyrer* case to insist on the application of the environmental 'standards in force at the time of application'.[152] The very next year, the WTO Appellate Body's famous *Shrimp* report famously declared: 'the generic term "natural resources" in Article XX(g) is not "static" in its content or reference but is rather "by definition, evolutionary"', adding a footnote referring to the *Namibia* dictum and other 1970s authorities for the evolutionary treaty interpretation doctrine.[153]

The *Iron Rhine* award may thus have consolidated an emerging trend to bring back the notion of evolutionary treaty interpretation for the purposes of making international environmental law norms applicable, but it also went much further than previous 'environmental' cases. The *Gabčíkovo* and *Shrimp* cases both involved interpreting treaties with provisions directed at environmental protection, whereas the 1839 Treaty of Separation did not even allude to such an objective. The treaty provisions interpreted in *Gabčíkovo* impliedly allowed for the incorporation of modern environmental norms, whereas Article XII of the Treaty of Separation certainly did not. In the *Iron Rhine* decision, the link between the environmental norms to be applied and the treaty was thus considerably more forced than it had been in all previous general international law cases invoking evolutionary interpretation. Importantly, that link could only be drawn through the agency of the evolutionary interpretation doctrine if that doctrine were understood in the very broad, almost non-interpretative sense that had emerged in international human rights courts.

[151] *Gabčíkovo-Nagymaros Project (Hungary/Slovakia)*, Judgment [1997] ICJ Reports 7, 66–67 (§ 112).

[152] *Gabčíkovo-Nagymaros Project (Hungary/Slovakia)*, Separate Opinion of Vice-President Weeramantry [1997] ICJ Reports 88, 115.

[153] *United States – Import prohibition of certain shrimp and shrimp products*, Report (WTO Appellate Body, WT/DS58/AB/R, 12 October 1998) 48 (§ 130).

The *Iron Rhine* Tribunal was accordingly the first general international law court or tribunal to both unequivocally accept the evolutionary interpretation doctrine and to clearly invoke it in its broad, progressive-adjudication form. Its significance to the development of the evolutionary interpretation doctrine is unquestionable, particularly because it extends the application of the broad form of evolutionary interpretation beyond human rights treaties. Indeed, that form of the doctrine had previously only been applied in cases arising from the interpretation and application of human rights treaties, often through an emphasis on their unique teleological aspects.

Indeed, it is very significant that the treaty the *Iron Rhine* Tribunal was purporting to interpret and apply, the 1839 Treaty of Separation, was clearly not for the guaranteeing of human rights and not a 'living instrument'. It was not even a constitutive treaty like the League of Nations Covenant at issue in *Namibia*, nor a law-making, nor even multilateral treaty. By the Tribunal's own admission, it was of a fixed, not unlimited duration and did not present a contested term of a conceptual or generic nature previously regarded by general international law authorities to be more open to an evolutionary approach.[154] The Treaty of Separation was the opposite of all those things, a plain vanilla and mostly commercial bilateral cooperation treaty between two neighbouring countries.

The teleological and progressive aspect of the evolutionary interpretation doctrine now appears to have become so pronounced under general international law that an ILC Special Rapporteur has even referred to it as 'a form of purpose-oriented interpretation'[155] that can now be used 'for multilateral as well as bilateral treaties, and even for unilateral declarations'.[156] In her 1996 article 'Some Observations on the Inter-Temporal Rule in International Law', Higgins had even explicitly referred to the *Tyrer* dictum as part of an evaluation of whether it could be said that human rights treaties should, 'because of their nature, … be interpreted in accordance with contemporary international law or conditions in society'.[157] With the unanimous *Iron Rhine* award handed down under her presidency, she ensured that the living instrument doctrine emerging from *Tyrer* would be used much more widely.

For the purposes of this study, however, the principal significance of the *Iron Rhine* award lies in how it imported into general international law, from the case law of international human rights courts, a broader variant of the evolutionary treaty interpretation doctrine. It accordingly constitutes the denouement in our

[154] *Iron Rhine*, Award (n 128) 73–74 (§§ 80, 82–83).

[155] International Law Commission, 'Report of the work of the sixty-third session' (New York, United Nations, 2011) Supplement No 10 (A/66/10) 281.

[156] International Law Commission and Georg Nolte, 'Introductory Report for the Study Group on Treaties over Time: Jurisprudence of the International Court of Justice and arbitral tribunals of ad hoc jurisdiction relating to subsequent agreements and subsequent practice' in Georg Nolte (ed), *Treaties and Subsequent Practice* (Oxford, Oxford University Press, 2013) 187.

[157] Higgins (n 144) 175–76.

important story of how international law's evolutionary interpretation doctrine came to diverge from the problem of intertemporal linguistics.

III. JETTISONING A DOCTRINE NO LONGER SUFFICIENTLY LINKED TO THE PROBLEM

A. The Distinct Narrow and Broad Forms of the Evolutionary Interpretation Doctrine

Having described the saga by which a new, broader form of the doctrine focused on progressive adjudication has emerged and become consolidated throughout international law, we can now make the important observation that, in present-day international law, there are two distinct notions regularly masquerading as the doctrine of evolutionary interpretation.

The first or 'narrow' notion focuses on ascertaining the meaning of treaty terms, a task close to the core of treaty interpretation because all theories of treaty interpretation, ranging from the textualist to the broadly teleological and subjectivist, at some stage look to – and seek to understand – some part of the text of the treaty. In this sense, the first variant of the evolutionary treaty interpretation is narrowly interpretative. It is also overtly temporal in the sense that it ascertains the meaning of the treaty term in light of how it came to be understood after the treaty was concluded. As the counterpoint doctrine to the principle of contemporaneity, it opts for a later-emerging, rather than original, meaning of the applicable treaty's term. It should be clear that this form of the doctrine is not only clearly relevant to the problem of intertemporal linguistics, but patently takes a dynamic approach to the Problem.

The second or 'broad' notion of evolutionary treaty interpretation is much less concerned about the meaning of a treaty terms and only interpretative to the extent that one accepts a wide teleological view of interpretation that allows interpreters to themselves flesh out general objects and purposes that they read into a treaty provision. It is more obviously progressive than it is temporal, manifestly seeking the improvement of the system by applying not *later* law and values, but *better* law and values. By straying from the terms of the treaty and the subset of changes that affect the meaning of its terms, this broad variant of the doctrine has become estranged from the problem of intertemporal linguistics.

Applications of the doctrine in both its forms usually have one thing in common: they identify the law by taking rules, policies or values that emerged after conclusion of the treaty into account. In the narrow variant, those subsequent developments impact on the original meaning of the treaty term, producing a problem of intertemporal linguistics. In the broad variant, those subsequent developments advance the legal, political, social or moral framework that can then be fed back into the treaty regime.

Beyond this apparent parallel, the two notions of evolutionary treaty interpretation share very little; indeed, they are structurally and functionally very distinct.

They are structurally distinct primarily because, while the narrow notion involves an act that assigns meanings to specific treaty terms, the broad notion involves an act that seeks to improve the treaty regime or resolve the case appropriately – irrespective of what the treaty says. For example, the *Aegean Sea* judgment's use of the narrow form of the doctrine stayed very close to the terms of the treaty by focusing on whether 'the expression "relating to the territorial status of Greece"' should 'be understood as a generic term' and enquiring into what it 'denot[ed]'.[158] By contrast, the IACtHR's 1989 advisory opinion on the *Interpretation of the American Declaration of the Rights and Duties of Man*, applying the broad form of the doctrine, admitted that it did not reach its finding through treaty interpretation, avoided saying that Article 64(1) of the Convention authorised it to interpret the relevant type of advisory opinion and preferred to conclude, vaguely and without reference to a treaty basis, that it was 'authorized, within the framework and limits of its competence, to interpret the American Declaration' and did not 'lack[] the power to interpret it'.[159]

The two forms of the evolutionary interpretation are functionally distinct because the narrow notion results in assigning a treaty term a later-emerging – rather than original – *meaning*, whereas the broad notion simply leads to a progressive – rather than regressive – *outcome*.

While using a later-emerging meaning of a treaty term will frequently lead to a progressive outcome, it is a fallacy to think that it always will. This follows logically from similar observations to those laid out below in relation to why a teleological approach does not always entail taking a dynamic approach to a problem of intertemporal linguistics. Essentially, whether following a change in meaning will lead to a progressive result depends on a host of factors, including (i) the directionality of the meaning change (eg narrowing or broadening), (ii) the directionality of the particular treaty term (eg obligation or exception), (iii) the nature of the provision in which it occurs (eg procedural or substantive), as well as the extent to which each of these aligns with current values and ideals. In a progressive treaty, a change in meaning involving the broadening of a term that defines the scope of an exception, for example, is likely to produce a regressive outcome. There are enough variables involved for it to be impossible to conclude that the impact of meaning change on a contested treaty term will always be progressive – even when disregarding the subjectivity as to what constitutes 'progress'.

For this book, the most significant difference between the two forms of the evolutionary interpretation doctrine lies in the fact that uses of the broad

[158] *Aegean Sea*, Judgment (n 122) 31–32 (§ 76).
[159] *Rights of Man*, Advisory Opinion (n 78) (§§ 44, 47).

variant only rarely involve an interpretative act that prefers the later-emerging meaning of a treaty term over its original meaning. Among the several decisions cited above that apply the broad form of the doctrine, the ECtHR's *Colas* judgment is particularly illustrative of this. When the Court effectively found the word 'home' in ECHR Article 8(1) to extend to 'business premises', it was not acknowledging any change in the meaning of that treaty term. The meaning of the word 'home' had not taken on this new meaning – or undergone any change in meaning at all – between 1950 when the Convention was concluded and either 1985 when the French authorities' raids were carried out and the treaty fell to be applied or 2002 when the ECtHR came to interpret it. Indeed, the *Colas* judgment, like the 1992 *Niemietz* judgment which had decided a similar case in the same way without referring to the living instrument/evolutionary doctrine, appears to have reached its finding on the basis of a clearly non-temporal linguistic argument, noting that the word '*domicile*' in Article 8 of the equally authentic French version of the European Convention 'has a broader connotation'.[160] This may be true, but there is nothing to suggest that if '*domicile*' has such a broad connotation, it did not already have it in 1950 when the Convention was concluded, so the *Colas* judgment was adopting a broader – not later – meaning of the treaty term.

Of course, the many cases applying the broad variant of the evolutionary interpretation doctrine that do not even interpret a treaty term also fail to assign a later-emerging – rather than original – meaning to a term of a treaty. The IACtHR's landmark 1999 *Right to Information on Consular Assistance* advisory opinion, like many human rights decisions in the tradition of *Golder*, goes beyond the terms of the treaty provision to the objective that it was ostensibly pursuing and then interprets that objective. Both the judgment[161] and the concurring opinion of Judge Cançado Trindade[162] invoked the evolutionary treaty interpretation doctrine to flesh out the right to 'due process', a concept that was two steps removed from the Article 14 ICCPR treaty provision it was purporting to interpret and apply.[163] In this type of decision, the judges may be applying the doctrine of evolutionary interpretation, potentially even by using a later-emerging meaning, but they do not prefer the later-emerging meaning of a *treaty term* over its original meaning.

[160] *Colas*, Judgment (n 64) 14 (§ 40); *Niemietz v Germany* (Merits and Just Satisfaction), Judgment (Court (Chamber), 13710/88, 16 December 1992) 10 (§ 30).

[161] *Right to Information*, Advisory Opinion (n 79) 58–59 (§§ 114–17).

[162] *Right to Information*, Cançado Trindade Concurring Opinion (n 80) 1–6 (§§ 2–15).

[163] International Covenant on Civil and Political Rights 1966 (999 UNTS 171) 176, art 14. The Court quite tenuously claimed that 'due process' came within ICCPR Article 14 because that provision should be read in light of the second paragraph of the ICCPR's preamble which in turn, by speaking of 'civil and political rights' that 'everyone may enjoy' if 'the ideal of free human beings enjoying civil and political freedom' is to be achieved, indirectly 'recognizes the right to due process of law' – *Right to Information*, Advisory Opinion (n 79) 58–59 (§ 116).

B. Conceptual and Definitional Difficulties Arising from the Failure to Distinguish between the Two Forms of the Doctrine

Having now observed the oft-neglected fact that evolutionary treaty interpretation has split into two different doctrines of which only one clearly takes a position on the problem of intertemporal linguistics, we must decide whether the doctrine remains useful for this study.

Of course, if the case law and scholarship recognised that there are two different forms of the doctrine and distinguished between them, we would simply be able to put that which refers to the broad variant to one side and, as part of our inquiry into the problem of intertemporal linguistics, exclusively use the case law and scholarship referring to the narrow variant. Unfortunately, however, contemporary international lawyers continue to conflate these two structurally and functionally distinct forms of evolutionary treaty interpretation, speaking of them as if they are but one and the same thing.

This confusion is most apparent in the attempts of contemporary authors writing on evolutionary treaty interpretation to define the phenomenon. Indeed, the emergence of the broad variant the doctrine, together with the persistence of the narrow variant, has rendered the notion of evolutionary treaty interpretation so wide-ranging that authors are forced to resort to extremely imprecise statements when defining it. For example, a 2013 doctoral study bravely chose to explicitly define 'evolutionary interpretation' ('*evolutive Auslegung*'), but found itself impelled to define it very broadly as 'every method which takes into account, for the determination of how the norm to be interpreted should be understood, the changes in conditions and values that have occurred after the conclusion of the treaty'.[164] In 2011, Pierre-Marie Dupuy could only describe the phenomenon in even vaguer – and less interpretative – terms as 'modifications to a treaty that take into account the passing of time' through which a 'judge is often requested to redefine the meaning of a treaty without altering its nature'.[165]

Even the descriptions of evolutionary treaty interpretation that are most structured like a definition are riddled with terms and expressions too vague to define it adequately. For example, Antoine Martin's admirable attempt to set out a test through which instances of evolutionary interpretation could be identified casts the net very wide in terms of what change it must 'take into account' ('*prend[re] en considération*'), referring to all of 'the evolutionary process of

[164] Katharina Böth, *Evolutive Auslegung völkerrechtlicher Verträge: Eine Untersuchung zu Voraussetzungen und Grenzen in Anbetracht der Praxis internationaler Streitbeilegungsinstitutionen* (Berlin, Duncker & Humblot, 2013) 17–18 (present author's translation).

[165] P-M Dupuy, 'Evolutionary Interpretation of Treaties: Between Memory and Prophecy' in Enzo Cannizzaro (ed), *The Law of Treaties Beyond the Vienna Convention* (Oxford, Oxford University Press, 2011) 125.

law, ideas, society, or even … the meaning of concepts and terms (legal, technical or other) contained in international treaties'.[166]

Several other authors writing on the doctrine have clearly been so overwhelmed by the diversity of judicial activity to which it now lends its name that they studiously avoid providing a clear definition of it. Even Malgosia Fitzmaurice's lengthy two-part study of the 'Dynamic (evolutive) interpretation of Treaties', which begins by noting the confusion accompanying the notion and the need to identify and differentiate it,[167] never actually does so, preferring to discuss, with the aid of quotations from a range of international decisions, the relevance of original intentions and the role of the intertemporal law.[168]

In contemporary descriptions of the doctrine, we hear of what '[a]n evolutive interpretation *allows*',[169] the 'premise that it *proceeds on*',[170] what the 'interpretation is *based on*',[171] and when the 'question *arises*',[172] and of something which 'draws upon'[173] or 'takes account of'[174] changes in language or law. We do not, however, hear what evolutionary treaty interpretation in fact *is*. The now bifurcated doctrine has simply become too diffuse to be able to be encapsulated by a precise definition.

Even the most conceptually astute international adjudicators have, when discussing evolutionary treaty interpretation, encountered the difficulty caused by the divergence between the two forms of the doctrine. Judge Mohammed Bedjaoui's separate opinion to the ICJ's *Gabčíkovo* judgment remains one of the most sophisticated and nuanced pieces of international case law on the evolutionary interpretation doctrine, but nonetheless suffers from this problem. Having served as one of three members on two different 1980s arbitral tribunals addressing the temporal aspects of treaty interpretation,[175] Bedjaoui was well-placed to engage with the *Gabčíkovo* judgment's references to this doctrine. He addresses it at length and, already in 1997, he seems to have detected – albeit not expressly – the apparent bifurcation of the notion of evolutionary

[166] A Martin, 'L'interprétation dite évolutive des termes insérés dans des traités intemationaux. Regards sur un arrêt du Tribunal fédéral suisse' in Université de Neuchâtel, Faculté de droit et des sciences économiques (ed), Jacques-Michel Grossen, *Mélanges en l'honneur de Jacques-Michel Grossen* (Bâle, Helbing & Lichtenhahn, 1992) 439 (present author's translation).

[167] Fitzmaurice, 'Dynamic (Evolutive) Interpretation of Treaties, Part I' (n 86) 102.

[168] ibid 102–13.

[169] *Feldbrugge*, Joint Dissenting Opinion (n 41) 25 (§ 24) (emphasis added).

[170] Michael P Van Alstine, 'Dynamic Treaty Interpretation' (1998 1997) 146 *University of Pennsylvania Law Review* 687, 715 (emphasis added).

[171] See, eg Stern (n 2) 119 (emphasis added).

[172] Pauwelyn (n 127) 30 (emphasis added).

[173] Ulf Linderfalk, 'Doing the Right Thing for the Right Reason – Why Dynamic or Static Approaches Should be Taken in the Interpretation of Treaties' (2008) 10 *International Community Law Review* 109, 113.

[174] Böth (n 164) 17–18; Bjorge (n 52) 59.

[175] *Case concerning the delimitation of the maritime boundary between Guinea and Guinea-Bissau*, Decision of 14 February 1985 (1985) XIX RIAA/RSA 149; *Guinea-Bissau/Senegal*, Award (n 124).

interpretation. Indeed, in his preliminary section devoted to explaining what 'evolutionary interpretation' entails, Judge Bedjaoui appears to understand the doctrine in its narrow form and takes an undeniably static approach to the problem of intertemporal linguistics.[176] Yet Bedjaoui ultimately rendered a separate, not dissenting, opinion and ended up cautiously welcoming the taking of subsequent law into account in the *Gabčíkovo* situation. In paragraph 18 of his opinion, he cited legal policy reasons entirely separate from the question of whether a treaty term should be given its original or later-emerging meaning, including the need for the Court to align itself with '[i]nternational public opinion' in its 'first major case' presenting 'sensitive ecological' issues.[177] His opinion then appears to associate the 'the so-called principle of the evolutionary interpretation of a treaty' with the judgment's recognition of this need for progressive adjudication.[178]

Whether he himself considered the doctrine to support such judicial activity or merely that the majority of the *Gabčíkovo* Court did, Judge Bedjaoui clearly recognised that evolutionary treaty interpretation had started becoming linked to progressive approaches. Indeed, the only way to reconcile his assertion of the static approach in the name of evolutionary interpretation and acceptance of the Court's judgment as an application of evolutionary interpretation is to point to the fact that he was referring to functionally different forms of the doctrine. However, because Bedjaoui did not make this bifurcation of the doctrine explicit, the cogency of his otherwise excellent *Gabčíkovo* opinion is undermined by speaking of its two forms as if they were the same thing, with subsequent commentators left unsure as to whether he was advocating a static or dynamic approach to the how to interpret treaties through time. This further underscores to the danger inherent in using the bifurcated doctrine of evolutionary treaty interpretation to tackle the problem of intertemporal linguistics.

Ultimately, while the narrow form of the doctrine directly relevant to the Problem remains in existence, it is increasingly overshadowed by the many prominent uses of the wider, progressive form. As matters stand today, an international adjudicator or scholar of international law referring to evolutionary treaty interpretation may be speaking of a notion pursuant to which the later-emerging meaning of a treaty term should be preferred over its original meaning or may equally be speaking of a notion pursuant to which a treaty provision – or treaty regime – should be read so as to reach a decision in line with contemporary law and values and/or to progressively develop international law.

Sometimes, an international lawyer may even be indirectly speaking of both forms of the doctrine simultaneously, including by citing authorities adduced in support of the narrow form of the doctrine in order to take a decision that can

[176] *Gabčíkovo-Nagymaros Project (Hungary/Slovakia)*, Separate Opinion of Judge Bedjaoui [1997] ICJ Reports 120, 123 (§§ 13–14).
[177] ibid 124 (§ 18).
[178] ibid (§ 18).

only be relying on the broad form of the doctrine. Bjorge's leading 2014 study arguably falls into this trap, defining evolutionary interpretation in accordance with its narrow form,[179] but expounding on what it really means with heavy reliance on decisions invoking it in its broad form.[180] Equally, Djeffal's 2016 study defines 'evolutive interpretation' in the narrow sense relevant to the Problem,[181] but then speaks of it predominantly in its broad, progressive form, most notably where he links it to the dissenting opinions of Judge Alvarez.[182] These situations are clearly among the most dangerous and most damaging for the conceptual clarity and development of thinking regarding the temporal issues of treaty interpretation, including the problem of intertemporal linguistics. Books like Bjorge's and Djeffal's faithfully describe the evolutionary treaty interpretation doctrine, including from whence it draws its authority and the range of ways in which it is now used, but by mixing two distinct forms of the doctrine, they do not take a clear position on any single question to which the doctrine relates.

The present book is, by contrast, focused on one of these specific questions: the problem of intertemporal linguistics. It would accordingly be unwise to address that problem through an investigation of the bifurcated, much-expanded and now quite diffuse evolutionary interpretation doctrine most commonly associated with it. If we wish to hold our focus firmly trained uniquely on the issue of whether interpreters should give a treaty its original or later-emerging meaning, we cannot be distracted by a doctrine which often just authorises adjudication that leads to progressive results.

Even the foremost international law minds run the risk of being conceptually distracted by approaching the problem of intertemporal linguistics through the associated doctrines. The separate experiences of two ILC Special Rapporteurs who could – and arguably should – have addressed the problem of intertemporal linguistics 40 years apart is especially illustrative of this phenomenon.

We noted in chapter 2 above that an undue link of the static approach via the principle of contemporaneity to the intertemporal law doctrine, caused the ILC's Special Rapporteur on the Law of Treaties, Humphrey Waldock, to wrongly regard the *Grisbadarna* case – a classic intertemporal law case – as taking a position on the problem of intertemporal linguistics, when it clearly does not. This and further confusion generated by that association and a failure to appropriately define the temporal issues, ultimately led to the ILC's Law of Treaties Study Group's decision to propose a codification of the rules for treaty interpretation that avoided taking a position on the Problem.

[179] Bjorge (n 52) 59: '[T]he words "evolutionary interpretation" are taken to mean situations in which an international court or Tribunal concludes that a treaty term is capable of evolving, that it is not fixed once and for all, so that allowance is made for, among other things, developments in international law. This is, in other words, a situation where account is taken of the meaning acquired by the treaty terms when the treaty is applied.'

[180] See, eg ibid 8, 190.

[181] Djeffal (n 88) 27.

[182] ibid 248–49.

Approximately 40 years later, the International Law Commission decided, on the basis of an initial report submitted by Georg Nolte,[183] to re-examine the law of treaties through a study group, established in August 2008, dedicated to the topic 'Treaties over Time'. The scope of the project was initially cast broadly enough to cover the problem of intertemporal linguistics,[184] but, from its earliest days, the project seemed to come at the problem through the doctrine of evolutionary interpretation, and notably broad conceptions of it, with Nolte's preliminary report already citing the *Iron Rhine* award and the ECtHR's living instrument case law.[185] Very quickly, the Treaties over Time study group was paying less and less attention to general interpretative issues such as the problem of intertemporal linguistics and focusing more and more strongly on the issue of subsequent agreements and practice. By the 2012 session, the Commission formally legitimised the narrow direction the Treaties over Time study group's work had taken, renaming the topic 'Subsequent agreements and subsequent practice in relation to the interpretation of treaties'.[186] This project concluded in 2018 with 'Draft conclusions on subsequent agreements and subsequent practice in relation to the interpretation of treaties' that do not address the problem of intertemporal linguistics, raising the question in passing in the commentaries to conclusion 8, but addressing it only superficially and within the confines of the role played by subsequent agreements and subsequent practice.[187]

There are probably many reasons for the ILC Treaties over Time Study Group's ultimate decision not to address the problem of intertemporal linguistics. However, it is extremely likely that one of these was the conceptual complexity and confusion that surrounded the Problem, particularly after it had been approached through the lens of the bifurcated and befuddled evolutionary interpretation doctrine. International law's peak scholarly body, the ILC, has now failed twice-over to address and resolve the problem of intertemporal linguistics, both times on account of a failure to isolate and clearly define it. If this book also fails to do so, it will fall victim to the same fate.

For the navigator trying to work out when the vessel of treaty interpretation should dock at the port of an original meaning and when it should dock at the port of a later-emerging meaning, it is clearly not only time to jettison the principle of contemporaneity but also time to jettison the evolutionary interpretation doctrine, heavy cargo otherwise destined to take that vessel – and this study – off course.

[183] See International Law Commission, 'Report of the work of the sixtieth session' Supplement No 10, A/63/10 (New York, United Nations, 2008) 354–55 (§§ 351–353).

[184] International Law Commission and Georg Nolte, 'Annex I Treaties Over Time in Particular: Subsequent Agreement and Practice' in *Yearbook 2008, vol II, pt 2* (New York, United Nations, 2015) 152 (§§ 1–6).

[185] ibid 154 (§ 15).

[186] International Law Commission, 'Report of the work of the sixty-fourth session', Supplement No 10, A/67/10 (New York, United Nations, 2012) 6, 122 and 133 (§§ 22, 227 and 269 respectively).

[187] International Law Commission, 'Draft conclusions on subsequent agreements and subsequent practice in relation to the interpretation of treaties, with commentaries', A/73/10 (United Nations, 2018) 64, commentaries to Conclusion 8.

4

Refocusing on and Defining the Static and Dynamic Approaches to the Problem of Intertemporal Linguistics

I. THE NEED FOR ANALYTICAL DEFINITIONS OF THE PROBLEM AND THE APPROACHES TO IT

IN CHAPTER 1, we noted that there are, broadly-speaking, two possible ways of resolving the problem of intertemporal linguistics: the 'static approach' and the 'dynamic approach'. Having now cut the static approach free from the principle of contemporaneity (and its associations) and the dynamic approach free from the doctrine of evolutionary interpretation (and its associations), it falls to chapter 4 of this book to define these two approaches in the tightest terms possible. Only definitions which outline the precise situation in which the problem of intertemporal linguistics arises and what the static and dynamic approaches to it specifically entail will ensure that we do not lapse into the error of looking at case law and scholarship that purports to take a position on the Problem when it actually does not.

In a complex area characterised by the inexact use of broad, undefined notions, an analytic approach strongly recommends itself. Analytic philosophers of all persuasions seek to bring an almost scientific clarity to complex phenomena, frequently by breaking them down into as many small, certain and clearly-definable pieces as possible.[1] Moreover, when different scholars writing in this area of international law seem to be asking and purporting to answer quite different questions, there is a patent need to observe the first demand of analytic philosophy and clearly define the question to be answered.

[1] See, eg Scott Soames, *Philosophical Analysis in the Twentieth Century, Volume 1: The Dawn of Analysis* (Princeton NJ, Princeton University Press, 2005); Michael Beaney, 'Analysis' in Edward N Zalta (ed), *The Stanford Encyclopedia of Philosophy*, Summer 2018 Edition – plato.stanford.edu/archives/sum2018/entries/analysis/.

One of the key proponents of the analytic tradition, GE Moore could just as easily have been speaking about the problem of how to interpret treaties through time as he was about ethics when, in the preface to his *Principa Ethica* of 1903 he said that:

> [T]he difficulties and disagreements, of which its history is full, are mainly due to a very simple cause: namely to the attempt to answer questions, without first discovering precisely what question it is which you desire to answer. … At all events, philosophers seem, in general, not to make the attempt; and, whether in consequence of this omission or not, they are constantly endeavouring to prove that 'Yes' or 'No' will answer questions, to which neither answer is correct, owing to the fact that what they have before their minds is not one question, but several, to some of which the true answer is 'No,' to others 'Yes'.[2]

In keeping with this sound advice, chapter 4 of this study will endeavour to state the problem of intertemporal linguistics and to define the static and dynamic approaches using relationships of certain, objectively ascertainable variables.

II. PRELIMINARY REFINEMENTS OF THE NATURE OF THE PROBLEM

When Rosenne labelled the issue to which this book is dedicated the 'problem of intertemporal linguistics', he did not define it. Instead, after referring to the *US Nationals in Morocco* case which he understood to exemplify the Problem, he stated almost in passing that it referred to a 'conflict' or 'choice' between 'the meaning of words at the time used and when interpreted'.[3]

This brief and vague description of the problem obviously needs considerable refinement. We have already, in paraphrasing it for the purposes of the previous chapters, spoken of 'treaty *terms*', rather than 'words'. We have also generalised out from what Rosenne had called meaning at 'the time used' and 'when interpreted' to 'original meaning' and 'later-emerging meaning' respectively, leaving the precise times at which the meaning is relevant to the problem of intertemporal linguistics deliberately open. Our first steps along the path to precise, formal definitions of the static and dynamic approaches to the problem of intertemporal linguistics are therefore: (a) to explain why the Problem concerns 'terms' and not 'words'; (b) to define exactly what we mean by 'original meaning'; (c) to define what we mean by 'later-emerging' meaning; and (d) to describe what a choice between these two competing meanings implies.

[2] GE Moore, *Principia Ethica* (Cambridge, Cambridge University Press, 1903) vii (Moore's emphasis).

[3] Institut de droit international and Max Sørensen, 'Le problème dit du droit intertemporel dans l'ordre international – Rapport provisoire' (12 February 1973) *Annuaire* 1, 80–81 (observations of Shabtai Rosenne dated 10 July 1969, § 9).

A. The Problem Concerns how we Understand Treaty *Terms*

International law texts on interpretation differ in terms of the precise textual unit of which a treaty interpreter must ascertain the meaning. Some focus on single or small groups of words. Chang's 1933 study on treaty interpretation, for example, refers to 'the particular *terms* in a treaty',[4] while Judge de Castro's *Aegean Sea* dissenting opinion speaks of 'ascertain[ing] the meaning of the *words* used …'.[5] Others speak more generally of the entire article of the treaty. Bernhardt's *Habilitationsschrift*, for example, speaks of 'determining the content of *legal provisions*',[6] while Kolb's detailed study defines interpretation as 'seeking to discover and give legal meaning to a *provision*'.[7] The VCLT's interpretative rules are also ambiguous in this respect, referring to interpreting '[a] treaty' in general, but then of 'the ordinary meaning to be given to the *terms* of the treaty in their context and in the light of its object and purpose'.[8]

In the specific context of the problem of intertemporal linguistics, the meanings that differ are not those that the interpreter ascertains, but, as will be demonstrated below, those which are capable of changing through time outside the treaty. For such change to occur, the series of words used by the treaty must be sufficiently used outside the frame of the treaty for it to be capable of undergoing semantic change in some external context. The precise sequences of words making up both entire treaties and entire treaty provisions of all but the shortest length are extremely unlikely to have a meaning assigned to them outside of the treaty. By contrast, fixed expressions of only a few words will frequently have a meaning external to the treaty and the individual words used by a treaty will almost always have such an external meaning. What matters is whether the relevant sequence of words used by the treaty has an external meaning.

Fortunately, the English expression 'treaty term', a favourite of many definitions and doctrines of treaty interpretation, refers precisely to single or small groups of words that have a defined meaning. The Oxford English Dictionary defines this sense of 'term' as meaning 'any word or phrase expressing a particular idea or concept, or denoting a particular object; an expression

[4] See Yi-Ting Chang, *The Interpretation of Treaties by Judicial Tribunals* (New York, Columbia University Press, 1933) 182: 'the sense in which the contracting parties actually employed particular terms in a treaty' (emphasis added).

[5] *Aegean Sea Continental Shelf (Greece v Turkey)*, Dissenting Opinion of Judge de Castro [1978] ICJ Reports 62, 68 (emphasis added).

[6] Rudolf Bernhardt, *Die Auslegung völkerrechtlicher Verträge insbesondere in der neueren Rechtsprechung internationaler Gerichte* (Köln, Carl Heymanns Verlag, 1963) 1 (emphasis added) (present author's translation of *'die Feststellung des Gehalts der Rechtsvorschriften'*).

[7] Robert Kolb, *Interprétation et création du droit international: Esquisses d'une herméneutique juridique moderne pour le droit international public* (Bruxelles, Bruylant, 2006) 25 (emphasis added) (present author's translation of 'cherche à découvrir et à donner un sens juridique à une disposition').

[8] Vienna Convention on the Law of Treaties 1969 (1155 UNTS 331), art 31 (emphasis added).

(for something)',[9] while the French *TLFi* defines its second meaning of the equivalent '*terme*' as a 'word or a set of words having, in a given language, a precise meaning and expressing a defined idea'.[10] Legal dictionaries pick up on the same key criterion, Black's law dictionary of 1910 defining this sense of term as '[a] word or phrase; an expression; particularly one which possesses a fixed and known meaning in some science, art or profession'.[11]

It is accordingly necessary to refine Rosenne's description of the problem of intertemporal linguistics slightly to reflect that it arises from a difference between the original and later-emerging meaning of treaty *terms*, not words.

B. The Original Meaning is the Meaning at the Time of the Treaty's *Conclusion*

The case law and scholarship advocating resolution of the problem of intertemporal linguistics through the selection of a treaty term's original meaning is not consistent in which meaning it considers 'original'. Vattel's very early mention of the static approach referred to both the time of the treaty's drafting and the time of its conclusion,[12] while Waldock's two separate 1964 draft provisions intended to reflect the principle of contemporaneity spoke variously of the time that the treaty was 'drawn up',[13] and the 'time of its conclusion'.[14] The main authorities for the static approach only serve to confuse the issue. The *North Atlantic Fisheries* Tribunal focused on the moment of negotiation,[15] which could be more proximate to the drafting or the conclusion of the treaty, as did the paraphrasing of the principle of contemporaneity in the recent *Daimler* award.[16] The *Rights of US Nationals in Morocco* spoke of two different times of conclusion, with one closer to the time the applicable treaty provision was drafted, by considering that treaty terms in the applicable 1836 treaty drawn almost verbatim from a 1787 treaty should be given the meaning they held at the conclusion of the

[9] 'term, n.', *OED Online* – www.oed.com/view/Entry/199409, sense 11(b).

[10] 'terme(2), subst. masc.', *Le TLFi – Trésor de la langue française informatisé* – stella.atilf.fr/Dendien/scripts/tlfiv5/visusel.exe?14;s=1687921245;r=1;nat=;sol=3 (present author's translation of '*[m]ot ou ensemble de mots ayant, dans une langue donnée, une signification précise et exprimant une idée définie*').

[11] Henry Campbell Black, *A Law Dictionary Containing Definitions of the Terms and Phrases of American and English Jurisprudence, Ancient and Modern* 2nd edn (St Paul MN, West Publishing Co, 1910) 1145.

[12] Emer de Vattel, *Le droit des gens, ou principes de la loi naturelle appliqués à la conduite et aux affaires des nations et des souverains*, vol I (Paris, J-P Aillaud, 1835) 468 (livre II, chapitre XVII, §272).

[13] International Law Commission, 'Yearbook 1964, vol II' (New York, United Nations, 1965) 8 (Sir Humphrey Waldock's Third Report on the Law of Treaties).

[14] See ibid 199.

[15] *The North Atlantic Coast Fisheries Case (Great Britain/United States)*, Award (1910) XI RIAA/RSA 167, 195–96.

[16] *Daimler Financial Services AG v Argentina* (Jurisdiction), Award (ICSID Tribunal, ARB/05/1, 22 August 2012) 90 (§220).

earlier treaty.[17] Other cases linked to the problem of intertemporal linguistics are simply too vague to be helpful in this regard. In the *La Bretagne* arbitration of 1986, one arbitrator, Donat Pharand spoke of '*le sens du mot "pêche" dans son acception d'alors*',[18] while in the *Laguna del Desierto* arbitration of 1994, Reynaldo Galindo Pohl associated the 'principle of contemporaneity' with 'the interpretation of … terms in the meaning which they had at the time when they were used'.[19]

Both of the main approaches, setting the meaning as that which it had at the time of the treaty's drafting and that which it had at the time of the treaty's conclusion, each come with their advantages and disadvantages.

Focussing on the moment of drafting has the clear advantage of being temporally closest to the communicative act of which the static approach seeks to identify the meaning. It also accords nicely with a subjective approach to treaty interpretation which considers the meaning of a treaty term to be that which it possessed in the mind of the person uttering it. Roberto Ago, for example, appears to have been a partisan of this approach as he is reported as having said at a May 1964 meeting of the ILC's Law of Treaties Study Group:

> In interpreting a treaty, it was impossible not to take into consideration the legal concepts which the parties had had in mind when they *drew it up*, and that applied even more strongly to the legal terms used in the treaty, which must necessarily be taken in the sense in which they had been used when it was *drafted*.[20]

However, by focusing on the drafters so much, this approach partially distances the inquiry from the inter-subjective, common intention that most modern authors consider the most important to the meaning of a legal text such as a treaty. Choosing the meaning as that prevailing at the earlier point in time also renders the practical task of an interpreter more difficult because the precise moment at which the treaty terms were committed to paper is often unknown.

The alternative which focuses on the time of the treaty's conclusion is clearly built on Fitzmaurice's emphasis on when the treaty was concluded in his 1957 definition of the principle of contemporaneity as privileging the 'meaning … possessed … at the time when the treaty was originally concluded'.[21] It cures the

[17] *Case concerning Rights of Nationals of the United States of America in Morocco (France v United States of America)*, Judgment [1952] ICJ Reports 176, 189 ('at the times when the two treaties were concluded').

[18] *Filleting within the Gulf of St Lawrence between Canada and France ('La Bretagne')*, Dissenting Opinion of Donat Pharand (1986) XIX RIAA/RSA 266, 275 (§31). In English: 'the meaning of "pêche" as it might have been then understood' (translation from *Dispute Concerning Filleting within the Gulf of St Lawrence ('La Bretagne')* (1986) 82 ILR 590, 648).

[19] *Boundary dispute between Argentina and Chile concerning the frontier line between boundary post 62 and Mount Fitzroy ('Laguna del Desierto')*, Dissenting Opinion of Reynaldo Galindo Pohl (1994) XXII RIAA/RSA 53, 56 (part I, §9).

[20] International Law Commission, 'Yearbook 1964, vol I' (New York, United Nations, 1965) 39 (per Ago, 729th meeting – 22 May 1964, §50) (emphasis added).

[21] Gerald Fitzmaurice, 'The Law and Procedure of the International Court of Justice 1951–4: Treaty Interpretation and Other Treaty Points' (1957) 33 *British Year Book of International Law* 203, 212.

main defects of focussing on the time of drafting, by highlighting a precise point in time known to all: the official date upon which the treaty was concluded. Moreover, it responds to a more inclusive and less subjective notion of the intention underlying the terms of a treaty: that which was shared by all parties when they concluded it.

In light of the VCLT's reticence vis-à-vis the subjectivist approach and emphasis of the importance of the moment of a treaty's conclusion in several of its interpretative rules,[22] it seems appropriate to consider the original meaning of a treaty term to be that which obtained at the time of the treaty's *conclusion*. In the rare cases where that moment in time is temporally quite distant from the time the treaty was drafted and a change in a treaty term's meaning intervened during that period, it does not seem unreasonable to assume that the parties concluding the applicable treaty had an opportunity to revise the terms or clarify the meaning of the treaty prior to its conclusion.[23]

C. The Later-emerging Meaning is the Meaning at the Time of the Treaty's *Application*

There are also two main alternatives for the precise point in time referred to by what we have thus far called the 'later-emerging' meaning: (i) the time of the treaty's application and (ii) the time of the treaty's interpretation.

In his brief description of the problem of intertemporal linguistics, Rosenne spoke of the time 'when interpreted',[24] but more considered scholarly views of the issue have preferred to speak of the time when the treaty is applied. For example, in the very IDI study as part of which Rosenne wrote his letter describing the problem of intertemporal linguistics, Rapporteur Sørensen sought to reflect *Namibia*'s apparently dynamic approach by speaking of '*son acception au moment de l'application*'[25] and the IDI's final resolution ultimately implored

[22] VCLT art 31(2) considers agreements and instruments 'in connection with the conclusion of the treaty' to be part of its context, thereby implying that the treaty made its statement at the time of conclusion. Equally, VCLT arts 31(3)(a) and 31(3)(b) have now been authoritatively defined as referring to agreements or conduct 'after the conclusion of a treaty', indicating that the moment of the communicative intention upon which subsequent agreements and subsequent practice may shed light is the moment of the treaty's conclusion – see further International Law Commission, 'Draft conclusions on subsequent agreements and subsequent practice in relation to the interpretation of treaties, with commentaries', A/73/10 (United Nations, 2018) 27–28, Conclusion 4 and commentary thereto.

[23] *United States – Import prohibition of certain shrimp and shrimp products*, Report (WTO Appellate Body, WT/DS58/AB/R, 12 October 1998) 48 (§ 129) where the Appellate Body impliedly asserted the importance of the time of the relevant covered agreement's conclusion, as opposed to the time of its drafting, by referring to the 1994 awareness of the 1994 signatories and to 1994 contextual elements including the WTO preamble.

[24] IDI and Sørensen (n 3) 80–81 (observations of Shabtai Rosenne dated 10 July 1969, § 9).

[25] ibid 99–100: 'its sense at the time of application' (present author's translation).

interpreters to take into account relevant rules of international law applicable between the parties '*au moment de l'application*'.[26]

Equally, while the *Namibia* dictum often considered to have founded the dynamic approach spoke of interpreting an international instrument within the framework 'prevailing at the time of the interpretation',[27] cases in which the time of application and time of interpretation did not coincide, have overwhelmingly focused on the time of the treaty's application.

For example, in the *La Bretagne* arbitration, Canada implicitly suggested that the meaning of the expression 'Canadian fishery regulations' in a 1972 treaty with France moved in accordance with the body of regulations that its Ministry of Fisheries had enacted. It was only on 26 June 1985, five months *after* the event giving rise to the dispute (Canada's refusal to allow the French-registered ship to fillet fish in the Gulf of St Lawrence), but a year *prior* to the hearing and deciding of the dispute in the Northern summer of 1986, that an amendment was introduced into the body of Canadian fishery regulations which explicitly concerned the treatment of fish.[28] While the Tribunal ultimately found for France on other bases, it is notable that it drew attention to the date of application rather than interpretation by saying that the amendment was introduced 'after the ... dispute arose'.[29]

Later, in the *Gabčíkovo* case frequently regarded as an instance of the dynamic approach being applied, two judges penning separate opinions, in 1997, explicitly laid emphasis on the moment of the treaty's application. Judge Weeramantry's dynamic view considered it to be 'vitally important that the standards in force *at the time of application* would be the governing standards',[30] while Judge Herzcegh highlighted 1989, the year in which the juridical fact being assessed (Hungary's suspension and abandonment of the works) took place, saying 'the protection of nature was to be ensured in a manner commensurate with the requirements of the day, that is to say, in 1989'.[31]

Moreover, established doctrines of international law, including the *nullum crimen sine lege* principle, the notion of jurisdiction *ratione temporis*, the

[26] Institut de droit international, 'Le problème intertemporel en droit international public – Résolution' (Wiesbaden, 1975) 2 (operative para 4) : 'at the time of application' (present author's translation).

[27] *Legal Consequences for States of the Continued Presence of South Africa in Namibia (South West Africa) notwithstanding Security Council Resolution 276 (1970)*, Advisory Opinion [1971] ICJ Reports 16, 31 (§53).

[28] *Filleting within the Gulf of St Lawrence between Canada and France ('La Bretagne')*, Award (1986) XIX RIAA/RSA 225, 250 (§41).

[29] ibid 251 (§42) (translation from *Dispute Concerning Filleting within the Gulf of St Lawrence ('La Bretagne')* (1986) 82 ILR 590, 623).

[30] *Gabčíkovo-Nagymaros Project (Hungary/Slovakia)*, Separate Opinion of Vice-President Weeramantry [1997] ICJ Reports 88, 115 (emphasis added).

[31] *Gabčíkovo-Nagymaros Project (Hungary/Slovakia)*, Dissenting Opinion of Judge Herczegh [1997] ICJ Reports 176, 178.

Critical Date concept so crucial to territorial disputes, the non-retroactivity of treaties principle in VCLT Article 28 and the intertemporal law doctrine, all emphasise that the moment at which the law should be assessed is the moment at which it falls to be applied, not interpreted. Clearly, if the law that counts is that which obtains at the moment of the treaty's application, then it should not be retrospectively given a meaning that it only came to have at the later moment of interpretation.

If we are to respect the well-established intertemporal law doctrine and the bulk of the applicable case law and literature, we should therefore specify the 'later-emerging meaning' of a treaty term to be its meaning at the time of the treaty's *application*.

D. For the Problem to Arise, these Two Meanings must be *Different*

Irrespective of whether one understands the problem of intertemporal linguistics as a conflict, like Sørensen, or a mere interpretative choice, like Rosenne, it necessarily implies a difference between (a) the meaning of a treaty term at the time of the treaty's conclusion and (b) the meaning of a treaty term at the time of the treaty's application. Clearly, there is only a problem in the first place if these two meanings differ.

One of the main flaws in approaching the problem of intertemporal linguistics through the associated doctrines is that interpretations are considered static or dynamic when they occur in a context of no relevant meaning change, so do not even raise the problem of intertemporal linguistics in the first place.

For example, the *Alaska Boundary* award, which centred on interpreting the words '*côte*' and '*océan*' in a 1825 treaty, was cited by Rousseau as an example of the principle of contemporaneity even though there was no evidence of the (relevant type of) meaning of these terms changing between 1825 and 1903, when the Tribunal was called upon to apply it.[32] Likewise, in the *Related Rights* case so regularly cited as an authority for the dynamic approach, the meaning of the treaty term 'commerce' ('*comercio*') did not relevantly change such that tourist services were considered outside its scope when the treaty was concluded in 1848, but within its scope when it was applied in 2009.[33]

These important cases present but two of many examples of interpretations regarded as static or dynamic even though there is no apparent difference between the original and later-emerging meaning of a treaty term that is relevant to the disputing parties' disagreement. In a situation of unchanging

[32] *The Alaska Boundary Case (Great Britain/United States)*, Award (1903) XV RIAA/RSA 481, see further s 2.II.A.i above.

[33] *Dispute regarding Navigational and Related Rights (Costa Rica v Nicaragua)*, Judgment [2009] ICJ Reports 213; and see further s 6.II.B.iii below.

meaning, there is no choice to be made between the meaning at the time of conclusion and the meaning at the time of application, so the problem of intertemporal linguistics does not arise and the court or tribunal's approach will not be static or dynamic in any meaningful sense.

It is accordingly necessary to state the existence of a difference between the original and later-emerging meanings as a condition sine qua non for the problem of intertemporal linguistics arising and therefore also for the taking of a static or dynamic approach to the Problem. Our definitions of the static and dynamic approaches to the Problem are accordingly each made up of two cumulative necessary conditions: one of which is common to both of them and the second of which is specific to each of them, as seen in Figure 1.

Figure 1 Conditions for the Static and Dynamic Approaches to the Problem (First Iteration)

	S1: <u>Static</u> Approach to the Problem	**D1: <u>Dynamic</u> Approach to the Problem**
Common Condition	The meaning of the treaty term at the time of the treaty's conclusion differs from the meaning of the treaty term at the time of the treaty's application. ($x_{t(conclusion)} \neq x_{t(application)}$)	
	&	&
Specific Conditions	The interpretation chooses the meaning that the treaty term had at the time of the treaty's **conclusion.** ($x_{identified} = x_{t(conclusion)}$)	The interpretation chooses the meaning that the treaty term had at the time of the treaty's **application.** ($x_{identified} = x_{t(application)}$)

While provisional, these definitions of the static and dynamic approaches to the Problem are already more technical than the simpler definitions that much of the pertinent practice and literature implies. Of course, the latter definitions are manifestly vague – and necessarily so – because they are descriptive of a diffuse and heterogenous set. They try to include all cases regarded as, for example, instances of evolutionary treaty interpretation in both its narrow and broad forms and, in achieving their aims, end up with an unmanageable multitude of different types of decisions out of which very little sense can ultimately be made.

By exactly specifying matters that are inherent to the Problem, the definitions proposed here provide an extremely valuable filter. The common condition, for example, may seem obvious and banal. However, it merits being specifically identified because it helps us filter out the many interpretations that do not actually choose between the original and later-emerging meaning of a treaty term, leaving us with a more manageable set of cases to analyse and therefore greater chances of solving the problem of intertemporal linguistics.

Yet, these definitions of the static and dynamic approaches to the Problem are still too inexact. They leave two major issues unclarified, namely: (a) what do we mean by meaning? and (b) when are two meanings different?

III. USING LINGUISTICS TO REFINE THE KEY NOTION OF 'DIFFERENT MEANINGS'

A. For Treaty Interpretation Generally, the 'Meaning' is '*Semantic-pragmatic Content*'

In order to be able to answer the essential question of whether the meaning of a treaty term at the time of the treaty's conclusion differs from the meaning of a treaty term at the time of the treaty's application, we need first to clearly understand what we mean by the 'meaning of a treaty term'.

Unfortunately, both legal science and even the branches of linguistics dedicated to the study of meaning only rarely define what they mean by 'meaning' itself. One book review from this field commented that, '[o]f all phases of language, that about which the least is known so far is meaning'.[34] Moreover, the 'meaning of meaning' is itself tied up with complex philosophical questions about the nature of speech, the mind and the world, with most linguists appearing to favour, since the early twentieth century, a position linked to the philosophical movement of idealism,[35] much like one of the few international law authorities tackling this abstruse question, Judge Galindo Pohl's 1994 *Mount Fitzroy* dissenting opinion.[36]

The notion of meaning is central to many fields of intellectual inquiry beyond the bounds of law. Many of these, including moral philosophy, ontology or existentialism, use special notions of meaning that stray from the legal sense of meaning relevant to the present study. This indicates that only observations on the nature of meaning from legal theory or any overtly linguistic fields such as the philosophy of language, linguistics, semiotics, hermeneutics and semantics are of potential assistance in clarifying the issue discussed here.

One important observation, coming from the field of linguistics but sometimes used in legal theory, is the distinction between *semantics* and *pragmatics*. Semantics ignores context and focuses solely on lexical and sometimes syntactic

[34] Charles F Hockett, 'Review of "The Principles of Semantics" by Stephen Ullmann' (1959) 61 *American Anthropologist* 158, 158.

[35] See, eg Gustaf Stern, *Meaning and Change of Meaning* (Bloomington IN, Indiana University Press, 1931) 1, see also 9 ('The term meaning is here taken as denoting certain elements of the mental events occurring in connection with words in the minds of people thinking, speaking, writing, hearing or reading the words. The study of meanings, as of all psychic phenomena, belongs to psychology.').

[36] *Laguna del Desierto*, Galindo Pohl Dissenting Opinion (n 19) 102 (§4.1) ('According to the theory of meaning, at least in its most simple and customary form, words represent perceptible forms of ideas, and the ideas represent the immediate meaning of the words themselves.').

meaning, while pragmatics emphasises context and also takes into account other matters relevant to what the author was trying to convey such as specific intentions or general purposes. In the words of the linguistic psychologists, Huang and Snedeker:

> Semantics refers to the aspects of the interpretation that can be directly calculated from the meanings of words and the structural relationships between them. In contrast, pragmatics refers to the aspects of interpretation that are inferred through an analysis of the context and the communicator's goals.[37]

The meaning that an interpretation seeks to ascertain can accordingly be semantic content, pragmatic content or a combination of the two.

The sense of meaning with which this study is concerned is, of course, the meaning given through a process of treaty interpretation. Most international lawyers speak of the thing that must be ascertained through interpretation as the 'meaning' or 'sense' of a word, its '*sens*', '*portée*' or '*Gehalt*'. It is salient that several French-speaking authors supplement their reference to '*sens*' in this context with the mention of the '*sens juridique*' or '*portée*' of the definition,[38] perhaps betraying a concern that the connotation of the French word '*sens*' might alone be a little too narrow to reflect the true nature of interpretation. It is also significant that German-speaking international lawyers giving prominent definitions of interpretation steered clear of the German word for meaning, '*Bedeutung*', and instead employed the more general and legally relevant term '*Gehalt*', which broadly translates into English as 'content'.[39]

These authorities suggest that the meaning identified by the process of treaty interpretation is not just the semantic content of a treaty term and extends to the semantic and pragmatic content of the term. This accords with other areas of law, as analysed by the linguistic branch of legal theory. As the renowned theorist Soames explains, '[t]he first and most important task of interpretation is to discern what a text says … its meaning is only one of the determinants of this'.[40] What interpretation seeks to ascertain, '[t]hat content, which encompasses everything conveyed or asserted by the text' in Soames' words, 'often includes information that goes well beyond the semantic content of the sentences involved';[41] what linguists sometimes refer to as 'semantic-pragmatic content'.[42]

[37] Yi Ting Huang and Jesse Snedeker, 'Semantic Meaning and Pragmatic Interpretation in 5-Year-Olds: Evidence From Real-Time Spoken Language Comprehension' (2009) 45 *Developmental Psychology* 1723, 1723.

[38] Serge Sur, *L'interprétation en droit international public* (Paris, Pichon Durand-Auzias, 1974) 67; Charles E Rousseau, *Droit international public* (Paris, Sirey, 1970) 241; see also Kolb (n 7) 25.

[39] See, eg Bernhardt (n 6) 1.

[40] Scott Soames, 'Interpreting Legal Texts: What is, and What is Not, Special About the Law' (2009) 1 *Philosophical Essays* 403, 421 ff.

[41] ibid 1–2, 8–15.

[42] Or sometimes 'semantic/pragmatic content', see, eg Michael Israel, 'Saying Less and Meaning Less' in Betty J Birner and Gregory Ward (eds), *Drawing the Boundaries of Meaning: Neo-Gricean Studies in Pragmatics and Semantics in Honor of Laurence R Horn* (Amsterdam, John Benjamins Publishing, 2006) 139.

The conclusion that treaty interpretation identifies the semantic-pragmatic content of a treaty term is strongly supported by how the Vienna Convention on the Law of Treaties codifies this task. As has been widely-remarked upon, the interpretative provisions in articles 31 and 32 of the VCLT contain a wide range of interpretative considerations – perhaps as a result of a compromise between competing interpretative ideologies or perhaps as a testimony to the inherently multi-faceted and flexible nature of interpretation. The terms of these two articles allow reference to as many as nine different factors as part of the interpretation of a treaty. All of these are, it is submitted, capable of revealing – in some circumstances – the semantic-pragmatic content of a treaty term, expression or provision. Only two of them are purely semantic: 'ordinary meaning' (Article 31(1)) and 'special meaning' (Article 31(4)). The remainder are largely pragmatic, ranging from 'context' (Article 31(1) and Article 31(2)) and 'object and purpose' (Article 31(1)), through 'subsequent agreement' (Article 31(3)(a)), 'subsequent practice' (Article 31(3)(b)) and external 'relevant rules' (Article 31(3)(c)) to the supplementary means of 'the preparatory work of the treaty' (Article 32) and 'the circumstances of its conclusion' (Article 32). That the VCLT allows for consideration of this many pragmatically supplied indicia confirms that it is aimed at the ascertainment of a meaning extending beyond mere semantic content to semantic-pragmatic content.

With this realisation in mind, we can, with Figure 2, further refine our statement of the conditions and the definitions of the static and dynamic approaches to the Problem, by replacing the word 'meaning' and the variable '*x*', with the more precise expression 'semantic-pragmatic content' and the variable '*y*'.

Figure 2 Conditions for the Static and Dynamic Approaches to the Problem (Second Iteration)

	S2: <u>Static</u> Approach to the Problem	**D2: <u>Dynamic</u> Approach to the Problem**
Common Condition	The **semantic-pragmatic content** of the treaty term at the time of the treaty's conclusion differs from the **semantic-pragmatic content** of the treaty term at the time of the treaty's application. $(y_{t(conclusion)} \neq y_{t(application)})$	
	&	&
Specific Conditions	The interpretation chooses the **semantic-pragmatic content** that the treaty term had at the time of the treaty's conclusion. $(y_{identified} = y_{t(conclusion)})$	The interpretation chooses the **semantic-pragmatic content** that the treaty term had at the time of the treaty's application. $(y_{identified} = y_{t(application)})$

B. The Problem Implies a Difference in *Semantic* Content Only

If meaning is to be understood as containing all of a term's semantic and pragmatic components, it follows that the meanings of two terms can differ on the basis of semantic and/or pragmatic differences between them.

Since the pragmatic meaning of a term is inherently related to the contextual features of the utterance or the text in which it occurs, it may only change where the word is used in a different context, for a different purpose or to a different audience. For changes in pragmatic meaning to occur, the same words must be re-used in a new situation on a new occasion. In the context of the problem of intertemporal linguistics, however, the contextual features of the treaty under investigation have almost invariably not changed between the time of the treaty's conclusion and the time of the treaty's application. The words have only been committed to paper once, in one situation accompanied by one sole set of pragmatic features. Leaving aside the rare situation of updated copy-and-paste treaties like the General Agreements on Tariffs and Trade (GATT) 1994,[43] or the marginal theory of the emergent purpose, the context, object, purpose, intentions and drafting history revealing the sense in which the relevant words were used does not change; it runs with the specific and unchangeable initial speech-act. Indeed, even in the more difficult cases of subsequent agreement or subsequent practice, there is a presumption that these facts merely serve to complete our knowledge of the contextual factors determining the meaning of the word as it was initially used. The constraints inherent to the Problem, which require an interpreter to opt for a new semantic-pragmatic meaning of a treaty term mentioned in one, unchanging context, mean that the change of meaning that a dynamic approach responds to cannot be pragmatic.

The semantic component of a treaty term is, on the other hand, drawn from factors external to the treaty act and therefore changeable over time. Indeed, we all know that the dictionary meanings of words – the main source of semantic meaning – can and frequently do change over time. The changed meanings of the English words 'deer' – which ceased to mean any wild animal on four legs (like its German cousin '*Tier*') and came to mean species in the Cervidae family – and 'spill' – the old meaning of which was 'to kill' rather than 'to cause or allow liquid to flow out' are examples of this, as are the more recent changes to the meaning of the words 'gay' or 'awesome'. It is therefore generally only the semantic part of the semantic-pragmatic meaning ascertained by treaty interpretation that can change in instances where the problem of intertemporal linguistics will arise.

[43] See s 6.II.C below.

In the language of the VCLT's interpretative provisions, the semantic content of a treaty term is either its ordinary or special meaning. Both are clearly subject to change over time, outside of the treaty and independently of the parties' actions.

It is on this basis that Distefano speaks of what we define as dynamic treaty interpretation as '*exogenous* evolutionary interpretation' ('*l'interprétation évolutive exogène*'), a phenomenon he contrasts with the '*endogenous* evolutionary interpretation' ('*l'interprétation évolutive endogène*') produced by subsequent agreement or practice.[44] For this accomplished international jurist, dynamic treaty interpretation refers to a phenomenon through which 'a change in the normative system surrounding the treaty … eventually affects the treaty'.[45] Once one accepts that the change in the system surrounding the treaty must be a change in meaning and not simply a change in, for example, values or circumstances, the treaty meaning affected can only be that which is not bound up with the specific use itself, namely the semantic content of the meaning term – its original or special meaning in the narrow sense.

In the context of static treaty interpretation too, there are strong indications that the most important element of meaning is the semantic content. In his seminal 1957 article pronouncing the principle of contemporaneity, Fitzmaurice focused on the meaning used in the community of language users: the meaning 'possessed, or … attributed … in the light of current linguistic usage, at the time when the treaty was originally concluded'[46] and 'the sense in which [treaty terms] were normally employed, at the date when the treaty was entered into'.[47] These statements of the static approach contain an implied, but inherent reference to the meaning outside of the treaty and therefore to semantic content. A similar focus on the semantic content of a treaty follows from other notably expressions of the static approach, including Rousseau's,[48] that learned author speaking of 'the meaning of the words' ('*le sens qu'avaient les mots*') in isolation and thereby referring to the semantic content of a treaty's terms.

We can accordingly conclude that it is the *semantic* – not *semantic-pragmatic* – content that must have changed for the problem of intertemporal linguistics to arise. Labelling the semantic content of the treaty term '*z*', we can refine our common condition accordingly to produce Figure 3a.

[44] Giovanni Distefano, 'L' interprétation évolutive de la norme internationale' (2011) 115 *Revue génerale de droit international public* 373, 374 ff.

[45] ibid (present author's translation of 'un changement dans le système normatif entourant le traité [… qui] finit par se répercuter [c'est l' idée de système] sur le traité').

[46] Fitzmaurice (n 21) 212.

[47] ibid 225.

[48] Rousseau (n 38) 282.

Figure 3a Conditions for the Static and Dynamic Approaches to the Problem (Third Iteration – Common Condition)

	S3: Static Approach to the Problem	**D3: Dynamic Approach to the Problem**
Common Condition	The **semantic content** of the treaty term at the time of the treaty's conclusion differs from the **semantic content** of the treaty term at the time of the treaty's application $(z_{t(conclusion)} \neq z_{t(application)})$	

Yet we cannot effect the same *y*-to-*z* substitution for the static and dynamic approaches to the problem because, as interpretative acts, they do not identify merely the *semantic* content, but the *semantic-pragmatic* content. We have, however, established that the essence of the static and dynamic approaches is that they respectively ignore or respond to purely *semantic* change. We can accordingly state, in Figure 3b, that the dynamic approach to the problem identifies a semantic-pragmatic content of the treaty term which is *congruent with* the semantic content of that term at the time of the treaty's application, whereas a static approach identifies a semantic-pragmatic content of the treaty term which is *congruent with* the semantic content of that term at the time of the treaty's conclusion.

Figure 3b Conditions for the Static and Dynamic Approaches to the Problem (Third Iteration – Specific Conditions)

	S3: Static Approach to the Problem	**D3: Dynamic Approach to the Problem**
Specific Conditions	The interpretation identifies a semantic-pragmatic content of the treaty term **congruent with the semantic content** of the treaty term at the time of the treaty's conclusion. $(y_{identified} \equiv z_{t(conclusion)})$	The interpretation identifies a semantic-pragmatic content of the treaty term **congruent with the semantic content** of the treaty term at the time of the treaty's application. $(y_{identified} \equiv z_{t(application)})$
Where: =: equivalence; ≠: difference; ≡: congruence; *y*: semantic-pragmatic content of term; *z*: semantic content of term		

The use of the concept of congruence is necessary owing to the fact that the semantic-pragmatic meaning identified by an interpretation is not necessarily equal or equivalent to the semantic content of the treaty term interpreted. Indeed, the pragmatic features, such as context, may have caused it to depart from the semantic meaning. The general meaning of 'congruent with' is 'in agreement or in harmony with' and a semantic-pragmatic meaning that uses an earlier or later version of the semantic content of a treaty term, modulated by a consideration of the pragmatic features accompanying the expression of that term, might not be equivalent to, but will likely be in harmony with the semantic meaning. Moreover, in the mathematical field, where congruence has a specific meaning, the non-equivalent numbers can be congruent according to a particular 'modulo'. Excepting the feature reflected in that 'modulo', here the pragmatic modulation, the two semantic-pragmatic contents are equal or at least equivalent. It is not a perfect analogy, but the concept of congruence is close enough make our definitions useful when they are applied to real-world decisions that purport to be instances of the static or dynamic approach being taken in response to the Problem.

C. The Semantic Content of Two Terms Differs after '*Semantic Change*'

When, as our common condition demands, the semantic content of a treaty term at the time of the treaty's conclusion differs from the semantic content of the same treaty term at the time of the treaty's application ($z_{t(conclusion)} \neq z_{t(application)}$), that term has necessarily undergone what linguists call 'semantic change'.

The apparently widespread view that any interpretation taking post-treaty change into account is an evolutionary treaty interpretation means that we must emphasise that the change giving rise to the problem of intertemporal linguistics is *semantic*. Indeed, one of the key differences between the doctrine of evolutionary interpretation understood broadly and a dynamic approach to the problem of intertemporal linguistics is that the former allows all types of change to influence the range of law being applied, while the latter does not.

Not all decisions or opinions that take heed of change will prefer the later-emerging meaning of a treaty term over its original meaning. For example, use of VCLT Article 31(3)(c), specific interpretative rules such as that appearing in Article 29(b) of the American Convention, or simply wide views of the evolutionary interpretation doctrine may result in the direct application of external and modern law.

Even more obviously, cases decided on the basis of treaties which include a *renvoi* to general international law rules and principles may have the relevant law 'updated' through a process that is technically related to those treaties, but barely involves interpreting them at all. The inherent mobility in customary international law means that the legal framework set up by treaties may be updated with the simple application of those cross-referencing provisions and ascertainment of the customary international law position contemporary with the relevant act or omission. In many instances, adjudicators or scholars have incorrectly associated the judicial processes undertaken in such cases as treaty interpretation taking a dynamic approach to the Problem – the *Gabčíkovo* case and a series of investment arbitrations on the customary law standard of fair and equitable treatment constituting illustrative examples in this regard.[49] However,

[49] See ss 6.II.B.ii and 9.III below.

there is, for example, no change in the meaning of a term which meant – both at the time of the treaty's conclusion and the time of its application – 'treat in accordance with what customary international law at the time of the relevant act or omission considered to be fair and equitable treatment'.

If the focus of intertemporal linguistics implies that the change responded to (dynamic approach) – or not responded to (static approach) – must be a change in the meaning of the treaty term, then the phenomenon of semantic change is central to understanding and solving it. Fortunately, semantic charge is the central problem of one branch of linguistics: historical semantics.[50] The best-known definition of the phenomenon in the world of semantics is that which was proposed by Ullmann: 'Semantic change will occur whenever a new name becomes attached to a sense and/or a new sense to a name'.[51] In this definition, a 'name' can be considered the equivalent of a word and a 'sense' roughly equivalent to each of the numbered instances describing what that word means in a dictionary. Cantos Gómez, for example, shows that the name 'bank' may be considered to have as many as 11 different senses, including several that are by no means synonymous such as 'land sloping up along each side of a river or canal' and 'an establishment for keeping money'.[52] In his book on lexical change,[53] Paul Gévaudan ably demonstrated that Ullmann's first case, the attaching of a new name to an existing sense, is actually just word building, not a change of meaning. Borrowing from Blank[54] and Geeraerts[55] he explained that semantic change actually only exists where there is *morphological continuity* (the word stays the same) and *semantic discontinuity* (the meaning changes).[56] This is precisely the event that gives rise to the problem of intertemporal linguistics.

Gévaudan also notes that, while the terms 'semantic change', '*changement sémantique*' and '*Bedeutungswandel*' suggest that some mutation akin to the transformation of milk to cheese has occurred, what has actually happened is much subtler and purely *semasiologic*.[57] Semasiology explores the different senses of a given word, name or, indeed, treaty term and only concerns itself with where that word or term has not undergone any significant lexical or morphological change. It is this type of change in meaning with which the

[50] See László Antal, 'Meaning and its Change' (1964) 2 *Linguistics* 14, 14 ff.

[51] Stephen Ullmann, *The Principles of Semantics* (New York, Philosophical Library, 1957) 171.

[52] See Pascual Cantos Gómez, *Lexical Ambiguity, Dictionaries and Corpora* (Murcia, Universidad de Murcia, 1996) 26–28.

[53] Paul Gévaudan, 'Klassifikation lexikalischer Entwicklungen: Semantische, morphologische und stratische Filiation' (PhD Thesis, Universität Tübingen, 2002) (later published as a monograph with the title: *Typologie des lexikalischen Wandels*).

[54] Andreas Blank, *Prinzipien des lexikalischen Bedeutungswandels am Beispiel der romanischen Sprachen* (Tübingen, Niemeyer, 1997) 113.

[55] Dirk Geeraerts, *Diachronic Prototype Semantics: A Contribution to Historical Lexicology* (Oxford, Oxford University Press, 1997).

[56] Gévaudan (n 53) 9–11.

[57] ibid 11–12.

problem of intertemporal linguistics is concerned: semantic change unaccompanied by any morphological or lexical change and pursuant to which the same morpheme, word or term operates as a frame inside which the semantic innovation occurs.[58]

Those semantic innovations can be of various types, including scope or value-oriented phenomena such as widening, narrowing, amelioration and pejoration.[59] Blank helpfully points out that there are two main categories: (a) where the term has come to describe a new sense – what he labels 'innovative semantic change' ('*innovativer Bedeutungswandel*'); or (b) where the term has ceased to describe a sense that it previously described – what Blank calls 'reductive semantic change' ('*reduktiver Bedeutungswandel*').[60]

This insight lends itself particularly well to the kinds of concepts and activities that frequently become the objects of treaty interpretation and, indeed, cases posing the problem of intertemporal linguistics. For example, in a series of GATT-WTO disputes determining whether the scope of the treaty term 'exhaustible natural resources' had expanded to include such things as dolphins and turtles,[61] the Problem arose through alleged '*innovative* semantic change'. When the ICJ had to determine, in the *Rights of US Nationals in Morocco* case, whether the treaty term '*différend*' in an 1836 treaty had lost the sense pursuant to which it described criminal actions and had come only to refer to civil disputes,[62] the Problem arose by virtue of an alleged '*reductive* semantic change'.

We are now one step closer to being able to precisely determine whether a case situation actually gives rise to the problem of intertemporal linguistics. However, we will still not be able to determine whether a treaty term has undergone semantic change through time unless we can precisely identify the semantic content of that term at each relevant time. As Hollman has commented: 'Studying semantic change presupposes a more general understanding of semantics. In order to grasp what it means for a meaning to change, we need to know what meanings are in the first place'.[63] It is for this reason that we dig further into what exactly semantic content is and introduce a further distinction from the field of linguistics, the difference between *intension* and *extension*.

In ordinary use, the context-neutral meaning of something, its semantic content, is found on ground between two extreme philosophical positions: idealism and direct reference theory. Words, expressions, even treaty terms are

[58] ibid 27.

[59] See, eg Paul Cook and Suzanne Stevenson, 'Automatically Identifying Changes in the Semantic Orientation of Words', Proceedings of the Seventh International Conference on Language Resources and Evaluation ('LREC 2010') (Luxembourg, European language resources distribution agency, 2010).

[60] Blank (n 54) 113.

[61] *US – Shrimp*, WTO AB Report (n 23) 48 (§ 130); see further s 6.II.C(i) below.

[62] *US Nationals in Morocco*, Judgment (n 17).

[63] Willem B Hollmann, 'Semantic Change' in Jonathan Culpeper and others (eds), *English Language* (London, Macmillan, 2009) 526.

regularly designed both to provoke a corollary internal idea (the psychological aspect) and to refer us to specific things in the world (the referential aspect).

Unfortunately, the field of semantics is also characterised by a long-running dispute as to how best to define what something means. Linguists traditionally followed the objectivist or truth-conditional theory of semantics that focused on the properties of 'semantic components' of a term in order to define it. Recently, this approach has lost ground to prototype-theoretical semantics, which focuses on finding a perfect category member or 'prototype' in order to explain the meaning of the term.[64]

A suitable compromise approach to what something means in a semantic sense is evident in dictionaries, the traditional repositories of semantic content that the non-specialist resorts to when asked about the content-independent meaning of a term. Law and lexicography are both heavily dependent on written language in which the meaning of words often must be explained using other words. Dictionary writers the world over wrestle constantly with this difficulty and know that the meaning of a term can either be explained using either words describing their qualities (what is called '*intensional* definition') or words describing a set of real-world referents ('*extensional* definition').

Since there are problems with extreme applications of either the truth-conditional theory of semantics or prototype-theoretical semantics, words are most commonly defined through a mixture of both properties (intension) and examples (extension)[65] with a 'genus + differentiae' style of definition.[66] Consider the English and French dictionary definitions of the words 'resource(s)' and '*ressources*' of consequence for the resolution of several cases decided under GATT Article XX.[67] The current edition of the Oxford English Dictionary defines 'resources' using a combination of qualities and examples,[68] while the French TLFi also defines the plural form of '*ressource*' using a combination of intension and extension.[69]

Unfortunately, international lawyers engaging with the problem of inter-temporal linguistics frequently adopt either a purely intensional or purely extensional understanding of the semantic content of a treaty term. As will now

[64] See ibid 526–27.

[65] Intension points us in the direction of the meaning of a word by setting out its properties, while extension uses examples (see further Norman Swartz, 'Definitions, Dictionaries, and Meanings' [*Norman Swartz – From My Notebooks*, 8 November 2010] – www.sfu.ca/~swartz/definitions.htm).

[66] H Jackson, *Lexicography: An Introduction* (London, Routledge, 2002) 94.

[67] See s 6.II.C below and cases cited therein.

[68] Oxford Dictionaries, "resource" – www.oxforddictionaries.com/definition/english/resource: 'NOUN 1 (usually resources) A stock or supply of money, materials, staff, and other assets that can be drawn on by a person or organization in order to function effectively …'.

[69] 'ressources, subst. pl.', *Le TLFi – Trésor de la langue française informatisé* – www.cnrtl.fr/definition/ressources: 'RESSOURCE, subst. fém. … II. – Le plus souvent au plur. A. – Moyens pécuniaires dont dispose une personne pour assurer son existence. Synon. économies, finances. Avoir de maigres ressources; être dénué de ressources; diminuer, augmenter ses ressources; disposer de ressources importantes. … B. – Moyens matériels dont dispose un pays, une région, une collectivité. Ressources hydrauliques, industrielles, minières, pétrolières d'un pays.'

be seen, both of these two ways of conceiving of semantic content have dangerous implications for the understanding of semantic change at the core of the Problem.

i. Purely Intensional Conceptions of Meaning Render Semantic Change Too Rare

Where a term is defined through intension alone and – following a frequent corollary of a purely intensional approach – in very abstract or general terms, the existence of significant semantic change can be obscured.

Indeed, it is through the presumption of general, exclusively intensional definitions that an international lawyer like Marko Milanovic appears to reach the conclusion that there has been no semantic change in key dynamic interpretation cases. He says, for example, that the meaning of the word 'cruel' did not change between 1789 and 2009 and uses quite an abstract definition of 'cruel' to substantiate this claim.[70] Yet today we find being 'cruel to animals' listed among one of the illustrative examples of the definitions of 'cruel',[71] a notion of cruelty that most likely did not exist in 1789 when cruelty was linked to inflicting pain on other *people* without compassion for them.

Such extremely intensional and general conceptions of the semantic content of a treaty term deny the existence of semantic change even where it seems to have occurred. On this approach, arguably any semantic change could be defined away and the problem of intertemporal linguistics would barely ever arise. Following Milanovic, we could, for example, assign a very general intensional definition to '*différend*', such as any matter in which two entities have opposing positions, and thereby ignore the fact that, by 1950, the meaning of the word '*différend*' had narrowed such that its extensional scope, by the ICJ's own admission, did not include situations where someone was subject to criminal charges.[72] If we understand everything according to its (intensional) characteristics and, worse still, limit our definition to its core characteristics or the term's most general features, we most obviously disavow instances of narrowing, a 'reductive' form of semantic change that, as the *Rights of US Nationals in Morocco* case shows, can easily create difficulties for treaty interpretation.

Broad intensional conceptions of semantic content also run the risk of disavowing 'innovative' semantic changes such as broadening. Indeed, it is Milanovic's intensional and somewhat arbitrary definition of commerce that led him to the conclusion that no change in meaning in the *Related Rights* case was possible,[73] when there is substantial evidence in the submissions made to the Court as

[70] Marko Milanovic, 'The ICJ and Evolutionary Treaty Interpretation' (*EJIL Talk!*, 14 July 2009) – www.ejiltalk.org/the-icj-and-evolutionary-treaty-interpretation/.

[71] See, eg 'cruel, adj.', *Lexico Dictionaries | English* – www.lexico.com/en/definition/cruel.

[72] See *US Nationals in Morocco*, Judgment (n 17) 189.

[73] Milanovic (n 70) 3–4: 'If … the term commerce in 1858, then as now, semantically denoted an activity for profit that involves an exchange for money, but the term as interpreted was only applied

part of that case, that there was at least some broadening – even if not relevant broadening – of the general semantic content of the term '*comercio*' over the relevant period of time.[74] Equally, an overly intensional approach could give the expression 'natural resources' a general intensional meaning such as 'anything occurring in nature that can be used' and thereby claim that the conclusion that a dolphin or turtle is a natural resource does not reveal any semantic change, even though this term was previously associated, extensionally, with items that can be used or traded by human beings for their subsistence.[75]

If we are going to take a meaningful view of the problem of intertemporal linguistics, we must accordingly understand the semantic content of a treaty term not just according to its properties (intension), but also according to the scope of things to which it actually refers (its extensional scope).

ii. Purely Extensional Conceptions of Meaning Render Semantic Change Too Common

It is, by the same token, dangerous to go to the other extreme and maintain that all changes in a term's extensional scope constitute semantic change. Some types of extensional change are a result of changes in the world – such as technological or institutional developments – so do not reflect a semantic change and therefore do not raise the problem of intertemporal linguistics. Indeed, if the slightest change in a term's set of real-world referents constituted semantic change, the problem of intertemporal linguistics would be ubiquitous and dynamic approaches to it pervasive.

Consider a gruesome but vivid example centred on the methods of torture and the semantic content of the treaty term 'torture' in Article 3 of the European Convention of Human Rights. In 1950, when the ECHR was concluded, common examples of torture might have included waterboarding and strappado, but would not have included the use of tasers or even a cattle prod. Someone setting out the extensional scope of the term 'torture' back then would not have thought of the systematic use of tasers, because they had not been invented. The new form of torture using them arose due to technological developments, yet falls – and would always have fallen – within the scope of torture. Critically, the meaning of 'torture' has not changed just because new techniques were invented that fall within its existing referential range. Indeed, the defining features of torture did not have to change between 1950 and 2015 in order to accommodate these new examples.

to situations involving trade in goods, as only such situations in fact occurred, then there is no obstacle in construing the term "commerce" more expansively to take into account the changing circumstances. This, however, has nothing to do with the changing meaning of the word, but with a change in the application or construction of that meaning.'

[74] See further s 6.II.B.iii below.

[75] See further s 6.II below.

There are also many case examples in which international lawyers impliedly understood the semantic content of a treaty term to change just because institutional or technological developments slightly expanded their extensional scope.

In the *Matthews* case, the ECtHR seemed to think it was breaking new ground for the living instrument doctrine through a somewhat radical dynamic interpretation of the treaty term 'choice of legislature'.[76] Commentators such as Letsas even cite the *Matthews* Court's interpretation as a 'fine example' of the ECtHR rendering 'a clear intention on the part of the drafters simply irrelevant'.[77] However, upon closer inspection with a sophisticated understanding of the semantic content of the term, it becomes clear that the facts did not even present the need for this term to be interpreted using the dynamic approach.

Matthews, a citizen of Gibraltar, had applied to be registered as a voter for the 1994 elections for the European Parliament and been refused.[78] In a case against the United Kingdom, she claimed that this breached Article 3 of Protocol No 1 of the Convention, which provides as follows:[79] 'The High Contracting Parties undertake to hold free elections at reasonable intervals by secret ballot, under conditions which will ensure the *free expression of the opinion of the people in the choice of the legislature*'.[80] Following the joint dissent of Weitzel, Rozakis, Pellonpää, Conforti and Bratza in the Commission,[81] a Grand Chamber of the Court ruled that European elections came within the scope of Article 3 of Protocol No 1 of the Convention, saying:

> That the Convention is a living instrument which must be interpreted in the light of present-day conditions is firmly rooted in the Court's case-law (see, *inter alia*, the *Loizidou v Turkey* judgment of 23 March 1995 (preliminary objections), Series A no 310, pp 26–27, §71, with further reference). The mere fact that a body *was not envisaged by the drafters of the Convention* cannot prevent that body from falling within the scope of the Convention. To the extent that Contracting States organise common constitutional or parliamentary structures by international treaties, the Court must take these mutually agreed structural changes into account in interpreting the Convention and its Protocols.[82]

For the present author, the *Matthews* Court is undoubtedly correct in its overall finding and also when it insists that 'structural changes [must be taken] into account in interpreting the Convention and its Protocols'.[83] However, despite

[76] *Matthews v The United Kingdom* (Merits and Just Satisfaction), Judgment (European Court of Human Rights (Grand Chamber), 24833/94, 18 February 1999) 14 (§39).

[77] George Letsas, 'Strasbourg's Interpretive Ethic: Lessons for the International Lawyer' (2010) 21 *European Journal of International Law* 509, 518.

[78] *Matthews*, Judgment (n 76) 3 (§7).

[79] See ibid 10 (§24).

[80] European Convention for the Protection of Human Rights and Fundamental Freedoms, as amended by Protocols Nos 11 and 14 1950 (213 UNTS 222), Protocol No 1, art 3 (emphasis added).

[81] See *Matthews v The United Kingdom* Report of the Commission (European Commission of Human Rights, 24833/94, 29 October 1997).

[82] *Matthews*, Judgment (n 76) 14 (§39) (emphasis added).

[83] ibid (§39).

the views of the ECtHR Grand Chamber, this approach is not required by any evolutionary interpretation (whether understood in the broad or narrow sense). Elections for the European Parliament came within the scope of ECHR Article 3 simply because factual developments in the world outside the treaty brought new things within existing categories set by the unchanged meaning of the relevant treaty terms. Indeed, the Court found that the European Parliament that Ms Matthews wanted to be able to vote for in 1994 possessed the overwhelming majority of the key features capable of bringing it within the ordinary meaning of 'legislature' not only now, but also when ECHR Protocol 1 was concluded in 1952.[84] Unless the meaning of the term is understood solely in terms of a precise 1950 set of referents, there was no change in the meaning of the term interpreted.

This example renders the dangers of understanding a treaty term according to its original referents plain to see. If, as for the Commission, the word 'legislature' were to mean 'all legislatures currently in existence', the rights contained in Article 3 of Protocol No 1 would only extend to the legislatures of States party to the Convention in 1952 when the Protocol was signed. This would in turn produce anachronistic outcomes such as Austria being allowed to deny its citizens free expression in the choice of the Austrian legislature on account of that country not existing as an independent State and a member of the Council of Europe until 1955–1956. Where there is no evidence of any reason to define and fix the content of a category extensionally using precise referents, we must avoid doing so, lest we create a problem of intertemporal linguistics and a need for a dynamic approach where there actually isn't one.

The WTO's 2009 *China – Publications & AV Products* dispute constitutes a paradigmatic example of a technological – rather than institutional – development being confused with semantic change and creating a putative need for a dynamic approach to a perceived problem of intertemporal linguistics. The interpretative question was whether the electronic distribution of sound recordings such as mp3 files over the internet came within the scope of China's commitment to provide national treatment to foreign 'sound recording distribution services'.[85] Before the Appellate Body, China argued that the meaning of this term 'should be based on definitions contemporaneous to the conclusion of the treaty' and considered that the Panel, in failing to do this, had 'followed an "evolutionary" approach to treaty interpretation'.[86] Rejecting this argument, the Appellate Body admitted that it based its analysis on the

[84] Note that two judges dissented from this finding on the basis of their different view of the nature of the 1994 European Parliament and whether it constituted a legislature, see *Matthews v The United Kingdom, Judgment (Merits and Just Satisfaction), Joint dissenting opinion of Judges Freeland and Jungwiert* (European Court of Human Rights (Grand Chamber), 24833/94, 18 February 1999) 23.

[85] The People's Republic of China – Schedule of Specific Commitments 2002 (GATS/SC/135) 21.

[86] See *China – Publications and Audiovisual Products*, Report (WTO Appellate Body, WT/DS363/AB/R, 21 December 2009) 22, 159 (§§47, 390).

meaning of the terms at the time of its decision,[87] and spoke in terms indicative of a dynamic or evolutionary approach, including by characterising the terms 'sound recording' and 'distribution' as 'sufficiently generic that what they apply to may change over time' and the WTO agreements as 'multilateral treaties with continuing obligations that WTO Members entered into for an indefinite period of time'.[88]

This has caused many commentators to cite *China – AV Products* as an example of evolutionary interpretation and, for those who take a narrow view of that doctrine, to deem it an instance of a dynamic approach being taken to the problem of intertemporal linguistics.[89] Bjorge even goes so far to state that this case proves the more general point that GATT and General Agreement on Trade in Services (GATS) schedules 'must be interpreted evolutionarily'.[90] Yet, the Appellate Body did not need to make an argument that, even if the semantic-pragmatic meaning of 'sound recording distribution services' did not extend to the distribution of sound recordings not held in a physical medium such as a compact disc back in 2001 when China concluded its GATS Schedule, it did by October 2007 when the compatibility of China's measures with the GATS fell to be assessed. By its own admission, even the 2001 scope of the 'term "sound recording", because it could 'refer to [all] "recorded content"', necessarily included mp3 files. On a more sophisticated notion of what (semantic) meaning is, the change that the Appellate Body is considered to have recognised through a dynamic approach, was not a change in meaning at all, because the scope of a category is not limited to the instantiations of that category in existence at the time it was first mentioned. Bjorge's subsequent comment that this decision constitutes an example of a situation which 'leaves very little scope or need for evolutionary interpretation'[91] is therefore much more accurate.

The view that proceeds from an overly extensional understanding of meaning to consider that dynamic interpretation is necessary to accommodate institutional or technological developments occurring inside the scope of a treaty term is quite prevalent among international lawyers. Regrettably, this view has even interfered with an assessment of the problem of intertemporal linguistics in cases most obviously calling for it to be analysed. For example, in the written and oral arguments in the most important modern-day case on

[87] ibid 160 (§396).

[88] ibid 161 (§396).

[89] See, eg Sondre Torp Helmersen, 'Evolutive Treaty Interpretation: Legality, Semantics and Distinctions' (2013) 6 *European Journal of Legal Studies* 127, 131–32; Paolo Palchetti, 'Interpreting "Generic Terms": Between Respect for the Parties' Original Intention and the Identification of the Ordinary Meaning' in Nerina Boschiero and others (eds), *International Courts and the Development of International Law: Essays in Honour of Tullio Treves* (The Hague, Asser Press, 2013) 93.

[90] Eirik Bjorge, *The Evolutionary Interpretation of Treaties* (Oxford, Oxford University Press, 2014) 126.

[91] ibid 140.

the Problem, the *Related Rights (Costa Rica v Nicaragua)* case before the ICJ between 2005 and 2009, the two parties often spoke at cross-purposes in relation to the Problem as a result of this failure to appreciate the intensional and extensional aspects of (semantic) meaning. One of the counsel for Costa Rica, Professor Marcelo Kohen, understood Nicaragua to be arguing that a static interpretation of '*comercio*' required restricting its scope to the activities that were known to be within its scope in 1858, most notably advocating a dynamic approach before saying: 'If not, will it be argued for each trade and navigation treaty, that their scope should be fixed with respect to commercial activities existing only at the time of their conclusion?'[92] In its written submissions, Nicaragua appeared to put its finger on the fact that a term can accommodate changes its set of real-world referents, without losing all the inherent limits on its scope:

> It should also be acknowledged that the articles of trade, merchandise and goods being transported are subject to change over time. It would be unreasonable to seek a limitation to only the products concerned in 1858. But if the 'articles' can change, they nonetheless have to continue being 'articles'.[93]

Unfortunately, Nicaragua's oral pleadings than rehabilitated the idea that mere technological development necessitated dynamic interpretation by connecting the second sentence of this very argument to the dynamic approach, citing not only the *Namibia* notion of terms being 'not static, but by definition evolutionary', but also the so-called evolutionary interpretation authorities handed down in the *La Bretagne* and *Iron Rhine* arbitrations.[94] While Professor Alain Pellet's oral submissions for Nicaragua on the problem of intertemporal linguistics were generally quite conceptually astute, the link he drew between technological developments and the dynamic interpretation doctrine – even if it was actually designed to discredit the Costa Rican argument by labelling it as overly dynamic – still revealed a partial misunderstanding of the notion of semantic change through which the Problem actually arises.

Just as Judge de Castro was perhaps guilty of failing to recognise in his *Aegean Sea* dissent, when he adopted a temporally static and exclusively extensional interpretation of 'disputes relating to the territorial status of Greece',[95] the question across the entire legal domain should be whether the thing itself

[92] *Dispute regarding Navigational and Related Rights* (*Costa Rica v Nicaragua*), Verbatim record of public sitting, 9 March 2009 at 10am, 35 (§58, see also §56, per Kohen for Costa Rica); see also *Dispute regarding Navigational and Related Rights* (*Costa Rica v Nicaragua*), Verbatim record of public sitting, 2 March 2009 at 10.15am, 68 (§§72–73, per Kohen for Costa Rica) (present author's translation from the original French).

[93] 'Counter-Memorial of Nicaragua', *Dispute regarding Navigational and Related Rights (Costa Rica v Nicaragua)* (International Court of Justice, 2007) 191–92 (§§4.3.23–4.3.24).

[94] *Dispute regarding Navigational and Related Rights* (*Costa Rica v Nicaragua*), Verbatim record of public sitting, 5 March 2009 at 10am, 51–52 (§6, per Pellet for Nicaragua).

[95] See *Aegean Sea*, De Castro Dissenting Opinion (n 5).

is included in the category designated by the term, not whether the users of the term were aware of the thing subsequent coming within the scope of that category. Whether the matters that subsequently arose were *aliquis de novo emergentibus* and not conceived or capable of being conceived at the time of the treaty's conclusion[96] is in fact not the end of the matter. If we were to consider those situations to constitute semantic change, institutional and technological developments would make semantic change ubiquitous and a dynamic approach – albeit in a softer sense – would constantly be called for simply by developments inherent to the very nature of life.

iii. The Hypothetical Original Interpreter Strikes a Balance between Intensional and Extensional Extremes

It is accordingly advisable to avoid the pitfalls of both purely intensional and purely extensional conceptions of the meaning of treaty terms and instead, like dictionary definitions, adopt an integrated approach pursuant to which the semantic content of a term resides in a combination of its intensional features and extensional scope. Semantic change is not precluded from occurring simply because one of the possible intensional definitions of a term still applies. Equally, it does not exist every time the extensional set of referents to which a term applies happens to change. It hovers somewhere in between, where there has been a significant change to one or both of (a) the term's intensional characteristics and (b) its extensional scope relative to that which it had back when the treaty was concluded.

Both these observations point to one unifying consideration: what is the scope of things in the world to which the term naturally applies at the relevant time? The crux of semantic change is accordingly whether a referent now considered to come within the scope of a term, was not – or, if it did not exist earlier, *would not have been* – considered part of its scope at that relevant earlier point in time.

In his study of meaning and changes of meaning, Gustaf Stern introduces the valuable concept of the 'range' of a word.[97] The notion of a word's 'referential range', in his words 'the totality of referents that may be denoted by it', is particularly useful for present purposes.[98] Whether this range is described by its properties (intensionally), through examples (extensionally) or a combination of both, the key issue is whether the object, activity or anything else that a party is trying to bring within or exclude from the scope of a treaty term

[96] See ibid 70; *China – Publications and Audiovisual Products*, Report (WTO Panel, WT/DS363/R, 12 August 2009) 376–77 (§§7.1246–7.1247).
[97] Stern (n 35) 42–44.
[98] ibid 42.

comes within its referential range. Indeed, only those cases in which one or other party pleads that the referential range of a treaty term has been extended or curtailed to include or exclude something of importance to the outcome of the case can present a problem of intertemporal linguistics in a practically relevant sense.

This inherent consequence of operating in the dispute settlement context makes our task in subsequent parts of this study much more manageable. We do not need to evaluate whether the meaning of *any* of the terms in a cited treaty have been subject to semantic change, but only if the *contested* treaty term's meaning has changed. Moreover, we do not even need to set out all the possible senses of that contested treaty term at the time the treaty was concluded and compare them to all its senses at the time the treaty falls to be applied. We only need to consider whether the object, activity of whatever else a party to the dispute claims is inside – or outside – the scope of a treaty term was part of its referential range at each of these moments in time. In the rest of this book, we will refer to this as '*relevant* semantic change'.

When we are dealing, as we usually are in the legal context, with conceptual categories or kinds of things and activities, the interpretative question boils down to: is *C* a *B*?[99] For example, is a criminal dispute a *différend*?[100] Is a turtle an exhaustible natural resource?[101] Often the answer will be influenced by all sorts of other factors relevant to treaty interpretation that impact on the meaning of the treaty term such as the context, the object and purpose of the treaties or the known intentions of the parties. Yet, because the parties' pleadings give us both the candidate object or activity and the particular treaty term, we can largely escape such complexity through the use of some hypothetical reasoning. We simply need to put ourselves in the shoes of a hypothetical 'original interpreter' and (less hypothetical) 'later interpreter' and respectively ask two questions:

> (Q1) Would a treaty interpreter on the day of the conclusion of the treaty, our 'original interpreter', have thought, for example, that *C* was a *B*?

and

> (Q2) Would a treaty interpreter on the day the treaty falls to be applied, our 'later interpreter', have thought, for example, that *C* was a *B*?

[99] In different situations, this might be 'is *C* equal to *B* ($C = B$)?' or 'is *C* part of the set denoted by *B* ($C \in B$)?'

[100] See *US Nationals in Morocco*, Judgment (n 17).

[101] See *US – Shrimp*, WTO AB Report (n 23) 48 (§ 130).

These observations open the path for reliably determining whether a term's meaning has changed along the lines of the hypothetical or idealised process of rational deliberation Rawls and others use as part of their meta-ethical constructivism.[102] In our necessarily restricted legal and dispute-resolution context, we can use the device of the Hypothetical Original Interpreter, a simple thought experiment, to bypass the complexities of semantics and lexicography and conveniently approximate the application of the linguistic definition of semantic change outlined above. In so doing, we can determine whether the meaning of a treaty term has, for the purposes of any particular case situation, *relevantly* changed.

Assuming our Hypothetical Original Interpreter is a representative interpreter and cognisant of the right information, the answer to the first hypothetical question set out just above will indicate whether the proposed object, activity or whatever else comes within the referential range of the treaty term at the time of the treaty's conclusion. If the answer is 'yes', then the object or activity *C* was included, potentially by analogy, in the meaning of the treaty term *B* and the intensional properties associated with the meaning of the treaty term at that time were wide enough for *C* to come within its scope. If the answer is 'no', then it can be fairly safely concluded that the object or activity *C* was not a *B* or did not belong to the set *B* at the time the treaty was concluded. Of course, if the answer to Q2 differs to the answer to Q1, there is strong evidence that the meaning of the treaty term *B* has relevantly changed between the time of the treaty's conclusion and the time at which it is applied, because its referential range was either extended or curtailed over that period of time. It is only in these cases that the common condition of relevant semantic change set out in the above definitions of both the static approach and the dynamic approach will be met. It is only in these cases that we can truly say that an interpreter has taken a static or dynamic approach to a problem of intertemporal linguistics.

It can readily be admitted that the idea of a Hypothetical Original Interpreter considering the relevant question on the day of the treaty's conclusion is likely to cause some unease among readers wary of the role of counterfactuals in the context of interpretation. However, the present author is not proposing that the interpretation of a treaty term be decided by what the Hypothetical Original Interpreter would have thought of it, but merely proposing the use of

[102] See John Rawls, *Political Liberalism* (New York, Columbia University Press, 1996) 99–107; see also Samuel Freeman, 'Constructivism, Facts, and Moral Justification' in Thomas Christiano and John Christman (eds), *Contemporary Debates in Political Philosophy* (Malden MA, Wiley-Blackwell, 2009).

this device for the much more restricted purpose of determining whether the problem of intertemporal linguistics arises in the first place. In the terms used by the US constitutional interpretation literature, this use of the device may be counterfactual, but it is not normative.[103]

Though the purposes for which the Hypothetical Original Interpreter device is advanced are modest, it has great practical merit. By revealing changes in extensional scope over time, it guards against failures to recognise semantic change which are caused by associating the meaning of a term exclusively with its intensional and, regularly, most general qualities. Birching is unlikely to have been considered 'degrading punishment' by the ECHR's Hypothetical Original Interpreter in 1950, yet had clearly become repugnant to Member States and within the meaning of 'degrading punishment' by 1972 when young Tyrer was subjected to it. Dolphins are extremely unlikely to have been considered 'natural resources' within the meaning of GATT Article XX(g) by a Hypothetical Original Interpreter back in 1947 when the GATT was first concluded, yet were held to be within the meaning of this term in 1994. Indeed, the fact that the hypothetical original and later interpreters would have responded differently to the key interpretative issue in the *Tuna – Dolphin II* dispute of 1994 reveals that this GATT Panel decision, so widely neglected by the evolutionary treaty interpretation literature, actually constitutes a clear instance of the dynamic approach being taken to the problem of intertemporal linguistics.[104] Moreover, using the Hypothetical Original Interpreter ensures that we do not, in resisting purely intensional and overly general understandings of what a term means, move so far to the extensional side of the spectrum that we come to characterise simple technological or other factual developments – such as that which occurred in the music distribution market in the 2000s – as establishing the existence of semantic change.

To properly appreciate the problem of intertemporal linguistics, we must therefore adopt a view of semantic content that is neither too intensional nor too extensional. The constructivist device of the Hypothetical Original Interpreter gives us a workable method for finding the middle-ground between these two extremes and accordingly for identifying the situations actually presenting the Problem. It also directs our attention to only the relevant semantic change. This in turn allows us to produce in Figure 4, with one small modification to their non-symbolic form and a small amount of set theory, our final definitions of the static and dynamic approaches to the Problem.

[103] See Randy E Barnett, 'Interpretation and Construction' (2011) 34 *Harvard Journal of Law and Public Policy* 12, 70–72.

[104] See s 6.II.C.iii below.

Figure 4 Conditions for the Static and Dynamic Approaches to the Problem (Fourth and Final Iteration)

<table>
<tr><th></th><th>S4: Static Approach to the Problem</th><th>D4: Dynamic Approach to the Problem</th></tr>
<tr><td>Common Condition</td><td colspan="2">The semantic content of the treaty term at the time of the treaty's conclusion relevantly differs from the semantic content of the treaty term at the time of the treaty's application,
$(z_{t(conclusion)} \neq^* z_{t(application)})$
meaning that, where these semantic contents take the sets $B_{t(conclusion)}$ and $B_{t(application)}$ respectively, for a relevant C, $(C \in B_{t(conclusion)}$ & $C \notin B_{t(application)})$ OR $(C \notin B_{t(conclusion)}$ & $C \in B_{t(application)})$</td></tr>
<tr><td></td><td>&</td><td>&</td></tr>
<tr><td>Specific Conditions</td><td>The interpretation identifies a semantic-pragmatic content of the treaty term congruent with the semantic content of the treaty term at the time of the treaty's conclusion
$(y_{identified} \equiv z_{t(conclusion)})$</td><td>The interpretation identifies a semantic-pragmatic content of the treaty term congruent with the semantic content of the treaty term at the time of the treaty's application
$(y_{identified} \equiv z_{t(application)})$</td></tr>
<tr><td colspan="3">Where: $=$: equivalence; $\neq$: difference; $\equiv$: congruence; $\neq^*$: relevant difference
y: semantic-pragmatic content of term; z: semantic content of term</td></tr>
</table>

Part II

The Misconceptions – Casting Aside the Conventional Wisdom

5

The VCLT's Interpretative Rules do not Solve the Problem

ONE OF THE major misconceptions surrounding the problem of intertemporal linguistics is that the VCLT's interpretative rules enable us to solve it.

Case law on the matter of how to interpret treaties through time is replete with statements arguing – or at least implying – that VCLT Articles 31 and 32 require one of the two diametrically opposed approaches to the Problem to be used. This view is most prominently stated by the Inter-American Court of Human Rights which has in several cases stated plainly that 'evolutive interpretation is consistent with the general rules of treaty interpretation established in the 1969 Vienna Convention'.[1] Other international adjudicators have made similar claims. For example, in a passage of the *Mondev* award penned by Ninian Stephen, James Crawford and Stephen Schwebel, that illustrious group of common-law jurists stated that '[a] reasonable evolutionary interpretation of Article 1105(1) is consistent both with the *travaux* [and] with normal principles of interpretation'.[2]

Many scholars of international law also consider that the VCLT's interpretative rules help resolve the problem of intertemporal linguistics. Arato, for example, makes the broad claim that the VCLT's interpretative provisions, to use his words, 'implicitly endorse' evolutive or dynamic treaty interpretation.[3]

Yet there are also international courts and tribunals that consider the same interpretative rules to support an apparently static approach. For example,

[1] See, in particular: *The Right to Information on Consular Assistance in the Framework of the Guarantees of the Due Process of Law*, Advisory Opinion [1999] Inter-Am Ct HR (Ser A) No 16 (1999) 58 (§ 114); see also *Case of the Gómez-Paquiyauri Brothers v Peru* (Merits, Reparations and Costs), Judgment [2004] Inter-Am Ct HR (Ser C) No 110 59 (§ 165); *Case of the 'Street Children' (Villagran-Morales et al) v Guatemala* (Merits), Judgment [1999] Inter-Am Ct HR (Ser C) No 77 46 (§ 193).

[2] *Mondev International Ltd v United States of America*, Award (ICSID(AF) Tribunal constituted under NAFTA Chapter 11, ARB(AF)/99/2, 11 October 2002) 43 (§ 123).

[3] Julian Arato, 'Subsequent Practice and Evolutive Interpretation: Techniques of Treaty Interpretation Over Time and Their Diverse Consequences' (2010) 9 *Law & Practice of International Courts and Tribunals* 443, 446.

the very detailed interpretative analysis conducted by a WTO Panel in the *EC – Chicken Cuts* dispute includes the following statement:

> The Panel infers from this that … the 'ordinary meaning' is to be assessed at the *time of conclusion of the treaty* in question, being the time which is at the focus of both Articles 31 and 32 of the Vienna Convention.[4]

The present chapter will briefly evaluate such claims. After verifying that, despite some statements to the contrary, the VCLT's interpretative rules are in fact temporally neutral (section I), it will turn to explaining why international lawyers nonetheless insist that its Articles 31 and 32 endorse a dynamic – or static – approach to the Problem. Two main reasons are identified. First, several modern-day international lawyers believe that the VCLT – at least as it is now understood – authorises a progressive adjudicatory approach and, in keeping with the above-noted confusion between the narrow and broad forms of the evolutionary treaty interpretation doctrine, confuse progressive outcomes with the narrowly interpretative outcome taken by a dynamic approach to the problem of intertemporal linguistics (section II). Second, many of the statements linking the VCLT's rules for treaty interpretation to the static or dynamic approaches consider that the VCLT rules help solve the Problem by providing scope for positions on it to be justified ex post, when only something that provides ex ante guidance can actually solve the Problem (section III).

I. THE VCLT'S INTERPRETATIVE PROVISIONS ARE TEMPORALLY NEUTRAL

The fact that international adjudicators, practitioners and scholars regularly invoke the VCLT's interpretative provisions in support of taking a static or dynamic approach to the Problem is, in light of the history behind those provisions, somewhat surprising. After all, in chapter 2 above, we established that the ILC Law of Treaties Study Group expressly avoided taking a position on the issue of how to interpret treaty terms when their meaning has changed through time.

The result of this was, of course, that the VCLT neither address the temporal issue of treaty interpretation explicitly,[5] nor mentions any of the doctrines indicating what to do in situations of change relevantly affecting the meaning of a treaty term. All of the principle of contemporaneity, static treaty interpretation, dynamic, evolutive and evolutionary treaty interpretation, and even the

[4] *European Communities – Customs Classification of Frozen Boneless Chicken Cuts*, Report (WTO Panel, WT/DS269/R WT/DS286/R, 30 May 2005) 41–42 (§ 7.99) (emphasis added).

[5] Oliver Dörr and Kirsten Schmalenbach, 'Article 31. General Rule of Interpretation' in Oliver Dörr and Kirsten Schmalenbach (eds), *Vienna Convention on the Law of Treaties: A Commentary* (Berlin, Springer, 2012) 533 (§ 23).

intertemporal law doctrine commonly considered to take a particular stance on the issue, do not appear in the text of the Convention. In addition, the terms of Articles 31 and 32 of the VCLT are deliberately neutral as to whether a term should be given the meaning it had at the time of the treaty's conclusion or the meaning it had at the time of the treaty's application. Such temporal neutrality – and the deliberateness of it – is clearest in the parts of VCLT Articles 31 and 32 that are the most relevant to the Problem: (a) the ordinary/special meaning rule and (b) the rule requiring account to be taken of 'relevant rules of international law' in VCLT Article 31(3)(c).

A. Ordinary and Special Meaning

As explained in chapter 4, ordinary meaning, along with special meaning, points to the semantic content of the treaty term being interpreted. International lawyers have willingly recognised that the ordinary or special meaning of a treaty term may change through time. Already in a 1922 advisory opinion, the Permanent Court of International Justice indirectly acknowledged the possibility of a change in the meaning of the French words '*industrie*' and '*industriel*' by referring to how they were 'most commonly used' '[a]t the present-day'.[6] More recently, Villiger, a noted writer on treaty law, elegantly noted that '[a] term may have a number of ordinary meanings, which may even change over time'.[7] Indeed, it is when there is a relevant difference in that ordinary – or, alternatively, special – meaning between the time of the treaty's conclusion and the time at which the treaty falls to be applied that the problem of intertemporal linguistics arises. The Problem accordingly occurs within the concepts of ordinary special meaning, the question being: which ordinary/special meaning – the original or later-emerging one? Paying heed to a rule emphasising the ordinary or special meaning of a treaty term therefore *raises* the problem of intertemporal linguistics, it does not solve it.

The history of some of the most prominent statements on the Problem demonstrates that only more detailed and temporally qualified expressions of the ordinary and special meaning rules are capable of taking a position on it. As we saw in chapter 2, Wolff, for example, qualified something very similar to the ordinary meaning according to how it is used in its time (the 'usu[s] loquendi *ejus temporis*')[8] and Vattel specified that the word usage of which we

[6] *Competence of the ILO in regard to International Regulation of the Conditions of the Labour of Persons Employed in Agriculture*, Advisory Opinion [1922] PCIJ Reports (Series B) No 2, 35.

[7] Mark E Villiger, 'The Rules on Interpretation: Misgivings, Misunderstandings, Miscarriage? The "Crucible" Intended by the International Law Commission' in Enzo Cannizzaro (ed), *The Law of Treaties Beyond the Vienna Convention* (Oxford, Oxford University Press, 2011) 109.

[8] Christian Wolff, *Jus naturae: methodo scientifica pertractatum*, vol 6 (Halle, Renger, 1746) 328 (bk VI, ch III, § 471).

are speaking in the context of ordinary meaning is that of the time in which the treaty was drawn up and concluded.[9]

The members of the ILC's Law of Treaties Study Group were also keenly aware of the fact that the ordinary or special meanings could change through time and thus create an issue over whether the earlier or later version of that meaning should be used. Bartoš, for example, asked the Commission to note that '[t]he "ordinary meaning" might not always continue to be what it had been at the time of the treaty's conclusion'.[10] Yet, for reasons of complexity and lack of time, the ILC Law of Treaties study group chose to speak of 'ordinary meaning' (in what became VCLT Article 31(1)) and 'special meaning (in what became VCLT Article 31(4)) in temporally unqualified terms. Clearly the ordinary meaning and special meaning rules, as they are stated in VCLT Article 31, do not take a position on the problem of intertemporal linguistics.

B. VCLT Article 31(3)(c)

The provision in VCLT Article 31(3)(c) requiring that '[t]here ... be taken into account, together with the context ... any relevant rules of international law applicable in the relations between the parties'[11] expressly relates to how legal changes through time affect interpretation. It is thus regularly considered to lie at the heart of the temporal interpretation issue surrounding the problem of intertemporal linguistics. Böth, for example, was so convinced of its importance in this context that, in her monograph *Evolutive Auslegung völkerrechtlicher Verträge*, she even took the view that 'the only valid instances of dynamic treaty interpretation are those that come within the scope of VCLT Article 31(3)(c)'.[12]

Yet Article 31(3)(c) was also deliberately stated in temporally neutral terms. As Mansfield and McLachlan pointed out when analysing this provision as part of the ILC study on the fragmentation of international law, Article 31(3)(c) arose from a very compact and quite controversial synthesis of positions on two highly-controversial debates dominating international law at that time: treaty interpretation and the intertemporal law doctrine.[13] When the ILC ultimately

[9] Emer de Vattel, *Le droit des gens, ou principes de la loi naturelle appliqués à la conduite et aux affaires des nations et des souverains*, vol I (Paris, J-P Aillaud, 1835) 468 (livre II, chapitre XVII, § 272).

[10] International Law Commission, 'Yearbook 1966, vol I, pt 2' (New York, United Nations, 1967) 192 (per Bartos, 870th meeting – 15 June 1966, § 89).

[11] Vienna Convention on the Law of Treaties 1969 (1155 UNTS 331), art 31(3)(c).

[12] Katharina Böth, *Evolutive Auslegung völkerrechtlicher Verträge: Eine Untersuchung zu Voraussetzungen und Grenzen in Anbetracht der Praxis internationaler Streitbeilegungsinstitutionen* (Berlin, Duncker & Humblot, 2013) 172 (present author's translation).

[13] International Law Commission William Mansfield and Campbell McLachlan, 'Study on: "The interpretation of treaties in the light of 'any relevant rules of international law applicable in the relations between the parties' (article 31(3)(c) of the Vienna Convention on the Law of Treaties) in the context of general developments in international law and concerns of the international community"', ILC(LVI)/SG/FTL/CRD.3/Rev 2 (United Nations, 2005) 14 (§§ 43–44).

decided not to take a position on the problem of intertemporal linguistics, it did so primarily in the context of whether what became VCLT Article 31(3)(c) should be temporally qualified. Special Rapporteur Waldock's formulation of this provision in the first draft ILC articles on treaty interpretation (then numbered Article 69(1)(b)) required interpretation '[i]n the light of the rules of international law in force at the time of its conclusion'.[14] As first drafted, this provision therefore incorporated a *static* approach to treaty terms that might be influenced by subsequent changes in law. When this temporal qualification of the rules to be considered relevant was ultimately removed, what became VCLT Article 31(3)(c) was left deliberately ambiguous on the matter of whether interpreters should take post-treaty changes in rules applicable to the parties into account.

Despite this, many now take the view that VCLT Article 31(3)(c) implies a *dynamic* approach where the meaning of a treaty term is affected by post-treaty developments in the legal framework applicable to the parties. As we saw in chapter 3, the Institute of International Law felt obligated to incorporate the *Namibia* doctrine into its 1975 resolution on the 'problem of the inter-temporal law', so temporally qualified the article 31(3)(c) rule in the opposite direction to how Waldock originally had done so, declaring that '[a]ny interpretation of a treaty must take into account all relevant rules of international law which apply between the parties *at the time of application*'.[15] This reflected a similar movement in the international case law, albeit over a significantly larger expanse of time. When a principle equivalent to VCLT Article 31(3)(c) was discussed in the 1905 *Boutres de Mascate* case,[16] it was given a firmly static connotation. Exactly 100 years later, the *Iron Rhine* award gave this principle a strongly dynamic connation.[17] It is, however, a measure of the rule's temporal neutrality than it can be – and has been – spun in both static and dynamic directions.

Moreover, in the form in which it is expressed in the VCLT, this provision's neutrality on the problem of intertemporal linguistics is patent. Prominent recent studies have confirmed this. The ILC's 2006 Fragmentation Report, for example, noted that '[t]he sub-paragraph contains no temporal provision' and that '[i]t does not state whether the applicable rules of international law are to be determined as at the date on which the treaty was concluded, or at the date on which the dispute arises',[18] while Thirlway has noted:

> Th[e] text [of Article 31(3)(c)] does not resolve the intertemporal problem, whether it is the rules of international law as they stand at the date of conclusion of the treaty

[14] See International Law Commission, *Yearbook 1964, vol II* (New York, United Nations, 1965) 199–200.

[15] Institut de droit international, 'Le problème intertemporel en droit international public – Résolution' (Wiesbaden, 1975) (emphasis added).

[16] *Affaire des boutres de Mascate (France/Grande-Bretagne)*, Award (1905) XI RIAA/RSA 83, 94.

[17] *Iron Rhine ('Ijzeren Rijn') Railway between the Kingdom of Belgium and the Kingdom of the Netherlands*, Award (2005) XXVII RIAA/RSA 35, 72–75 (§§ 78–84).

[18] International Law Commission and Martii Koskenniemi, 'Fragmentation of International Law: Difficulties arising from diversification and expansion of international law', A/CN.4/L.682 (Geneva, United Nations, 2006) 213 (§ 426).

which are relevant, or the rules in force at the time of the interpretation: indeed, it is not even immediately apparent that the text has anything to do with that question.[19]

C. The Philosophy and General Tenor of the VCLT's Interpretative Provisions

The fact that the parts of the VCLT most obviously relevant to the Problem were deliberately stated in temporally neutral terms has not dissuaded many international lawyers from declaring that they help solve the Problem. Many simply consider that the philosophy or general tenor of the VCLT's interpretative provisions supports a static or dynamic approach.

In the *RosInvest* arbitration, noted international investment lawyers acting for the claimant argued that treaties should be considered 'not to be static documents rooted eternally to the context in which they were concluded',[20] because 'the original intention of the authors of a treaty is not ascribed central importance' in Articles 31(1), 31(3) and 32 of the Vienna Convention on the Law of Treaties.[21] The Tribunal noted that, when

> [p]ressed to specify the basis in the [VCLT] for this interpretative technique, Counsel explained that the Claimant was not relying on the provisions of Articles 31 and 32 of that Convention in a formal sense, but rather as *general indications that the philosophy* of the Vienna Convention is to look at what happens after the conclusion of the treaty.[22]

Other international lawyers have considered the general tenor of the same provisions to imply a *static* approach. For example, Judge de Castro asserted, in his *Aegean Sea* opinion, that a static approach was required in light of not only the general rule in VCLT Article 31, but also Article 32's mention of the 'circumstances of [a treaty's] conclusion'.[23] In its 2005 *EC – Chicken Cuts* report, a WTO Panel made a similar point, advocating a static approach on the basis that:

> [T]he various sources to which a treaty interpreter may have regard under Articles 31 and 32 of the Vienna Convention are, in general terms, identified by reference to when they were created, finalized and/or existed as compared to when the treaty being interpreted was concluded.[24]

Arguments that the VCLT interpretative provisions as a whole – or the philosophy generally underpinning them – favours either the static or the dynamic approach are, however, not compelling.

[19] Hugh Thirlway, 'The Law and Procedure of the International Court of Justice 1960–1989: Part Three' (1992) 62 *British Yearbook of International Law* 1, 58.

[20] See *RosInvestCo UK Ltd v Russia* (Jurisdiction), Award (Stockholm Chamber of Commerce Tribunal, V079/2005, October 2007) 68 (§ 100).

[21] ibid 69 (§ 100, citing Claimant's First Memorial on Jurisdictional Issues, §§ 162 ff).

[22] ibid 41 (§ 37) (emphasis added).

[23] *Aegean Sea Continental Shelf (Greece v Turkey)*, Dissenting Opinion of Judge de Castro [1978] ICJ Reports 62, 68.

[24] *EC – Chicken Cuts (Panel)* (n 4) 41–42 (§ 7.99).

They are, first of all, contradicted by the accepted historical background to these provisions. The ILC's Law of Treaties Study Group and the representatives of the States present at the Vienna Conferences clearly intended to leave the final interpretative rules open as regards the Problem.[25] There is, moreover, no evidence that these drafters of the VCLT imbued the philosophy underlying its interpretative rules with a dynamic – or for that matter, static – preference.

Second, these arguments are often highly selective in their choice of the relevant interpretative elements, constructing a dynamic bias out of the interpretative elements suited to that position, while ignoring those that seem to imply a more static philosophy – or vice versa. For example, when the *RosInvest* claimant argued that the general philosophy of the VCLT provisions accommodates change, it appears to have relied upon the importance ascribed by VCLT Article 31(3) to events occurring after the conclusion of a treaty,[26] yet ignored the parts of VCLT Articles 31 and 32 that emphasise events happening prior to or at the moment of the treaty's conclusion such as the references to the Parties' preamble,[27] annexes[28] and (concrete) intentions,[29] as well as the preparatory work and circumstances of conclusion focused on as supplementary means of interpretation.[30] If the underlying philosophy of the VCLT's interpretative provisions is to be determined from the temporal nature of the elements it refers to, there are as many elements pointing to an underlying static philosophy as there are pointing to an underlying dynamic philosophy. Claims such as those made by counsel for the claimant in *RosInvest* therefore only stand if one takes an unduly selective view of VCLT Articles 31 and 32. Those provisions do not generally disclose a philosophy that favours either the dynamic or the static approach.

The fact that VCLT Articles 31 and 32 can be invoked for two such contrasting approaches to the Problem attests to the generality and flexibility of the VCLT's interpretative rules. Indeed, this flexibility arguably even demonstrates itself that the rules do not take a general position on the Problem. Just as there is nothing within VCLT Articles 31 or 32 specifically authorising, requiring or advocating a dynamic approach, there is also nothing within their terms binding the interpreter to consideration of a treaty term's meaning at the time at which the treaty was concluded. Overall, the VCLT's interpretative rules are neutral on this question and – as was established in chapter 2 above – deliberately so.

This acknowledgement of the VCLT's neutrality on the Problem is backed up by a thorough analysis of the ILC debates, the Vienna Conference sessions and the text of the Convention itself. The recent study of Djeffal focuses on

[25] See further s 2.II.A above.
[26] VCLT, art 31(3).
[27] ibid, art 31(2).
[28] ibid, art 31(2).
[29] ibid, art 31(4).
[30] ibid, art 32.

providing a 'functional reconstruction' of the VCLT's interpretative rules in relation to a question which presents a very similar dichotomy to the problem of intertemporal linguistics and 'resulted in the conclusion that the VCLT is intertemporally open'.[31] The conclusion is inescapable and apparently confirmed not only by historical and textual analysis, but also simple deduction from the amount of debate surrounding intertemporal questions of treaty interpretation today. After all, if the so-called 'treaty of treaties' – an instrument widely ratified and generally considered to reflect the state of customary international law, including in relation to interpretation – had taken a clear position on the problem of intertemporal linguistics, there would not be an ongoing debate about whether treaty terms should be interpreted statically or dynamically.

II. BY AUTHORISING PROGRESSIVE ADJUDICATION, THE VCLT DOES NOT ENDORSE A DYNAMIC APPROACH TO THE PROBLEM

If the VCLT's interpretative provisions are temporally neutral, but international lawyers are continuing to invoke them in support of static and particularly dynamic interpretation, it seems that they might be talking about those provisions holding an interpretative bias of a non-temporal kind.

In chapter 3 of this book, we saw that the notion of evolutionary treaty interpretation has bifurcated, such that a broad, progressive but less obviously interpretative form of the doctrine is now very prevalent. Upon closer inspection, it appears that many international lawyers who link the VCLT's interpretative rules to dynamic, evolutive or evolutionary interpretation are not arguing that these rules endorse choosing a treaty's later-emerging meaning over its original meaning, but instead that they endorse achieving a progressive rather than regressive outcome.

In this regard, it is significant that the oft-repeated IACtHR statement of the consistency between the VCLT's interpretative rules and 'evolutive interpretation' occurs in a part of the *Right to Information* advisory opinion that refers predominantly to the more teleological part of the *Namibia* dictum and comes just after a sentence in which the Court states that 'international human rights law … has made great headway thanks to an evolutive interpretation of international instruments of protection'.[32] These are, after all, obvious allusions to the progressive and outcome-oriented form of the doctrine.

The prominent 2014 study of Bjorge also seems to link the VCLT's interpretative rules to a form of evolutionary interpretation more akin to a doctrine of progressive adjudication than a dynamic approach to the problem of

[31] Christian Djeffal, *Static and Evolutive Treaty Interpretation: A Functional Reconstruction* (Cambridge, Cambridge University Press, 2016) 357.

[32] *Right to Information*, Advisory Opinion (n 1) 57–58 (§§ 113–14).

intertemporal linguistics. Bjorge pointedly relies very heavily on two particular elements of VCLT Article 31(1), namely the requirements that a treaty be interpreted (a) in good faith and (b) in the light of its object and purpose. As will now be demonstrated, each of these elements often supports progressive outcomes in keeping with the instrumentalist variant of the evolutionary interpretation doctrine, but is neutral on the narrower and distinct issue of original or later-emerging meaning.

A. Good Faith

The appearance of arguments emphasising the good-faith element of VCLT Article 31 in this context is itself surprising. While good faith is an important notion across international law, it is typically most relevant to the 'creation and performance of legal obligations',[33] and is understood as 'not itself a source of obligation where none would otherwise exist', but merely complementing the application of other rules, principles, rights or obligations.[34] Moreover, while the words 'in good faith' appear in the VCLT's golden rule for treaty interpretation, the 'exact contours of how to interpret a treaty in good faith are difficult',[35] and the 'interpreted in good faith' requirement has never been applied by major international courts and tribunals as a self-standing principle of treaty interpretation. Indeed, it is noteworthy that Bjorge's claim that the good-faith requirement 'has received universal acceptance in legal doctrine' is backed up by quotations that speak of the demand to *perform* treaties in good faith and *execute* all obligations of international law in good faith.[36] As a purely interpretative consideration, the role of good faith is far from established.

Since good faith operates in concert with other rules and principles of international law, and as a non-controlling partner, it is *generally* neutral on all interpretative questions. Just as good faith may require a restrictive interpretation in some situations and an expansive interpretation in others, it may, with other elements, seem to require a static approach to the Problem in some situations and a dynamic approach in others.

Indeed, it is notable that good faith has been invoked as an element supporting both static and dynamic treaty interpretations.

In the *Loizidou* case before the European Court of Human Rights, counsel for Turkey argued that ECHR Articles 25 and 46 had to be 'interpreted with

[33] *Nuclear Tests (Australia v France)*, Judgment [1974] ICJ Reports 253, 268 (§ 46).

[34] *Border and Transborder Armed Actions (Nicaragua v Honduras)* (Jurisdiction and Admissibility), Judgment [1988] ICJ Reports 69, 105 (§ 94).

[35] Steven Reinhold, 'Good Faith in International Law' (2013) 2 *UCL Journal of Law and Jurisprudence* 40, 61.

[36] Eirik Bjorge, *The Evolutionary Interpretation of Treaties* (Oxford, Oxford University Press, 2014) 66.

reference to their meaning when the Convention was being drafted' because the 'principle of contemporaneous meaning is part of the "good faith" interpretation embodied in Article 31 of the Vienna Convention on the Law of Treaties'.[37] In his detailed 2004 book on the interpretation of tax treaties, Engelen also considered that good faith required a *static* approach to the Problem, saying:

> [G]ood faith requires that one party should be able to place confidence in the words of the other, as a reasonable man might be taken to have understood them in the circumstances, and this means that where a party proposes to include in the treaty certain terms, they 'are presumed to have been used in the contemporary and general sense in which the other party would have understood them at the time the treaty was concluded'.[38]

While it seems logical from a certain perspective that good faith would, at least in some cases, require focus on how words were understood at the time they were first committed to writing, it can appear to be equally logical, in other cases, for good faith to require 'by definition evolutionary' treaty concepts to be interpreted in the sense that they take on sometime after the treaty's conclusion. There is no authority in support of the principle that the good-faith requirement generally tips the interpretative scales to the static side. Indeed, it is salient that Engelen's argument that the 'principle of contemporaneity … is based on the principle of good faith' resorts to citing the static interpretation of '*différend*' in the *Rights of US Nationals of Morocco* judgment, even though that decision never referred to good faith in this context.[39]

Most texts invoking the good-faith requirement in relation to temporal issues of treaty interpretation, however, consider it to require a *dynamic* approach. No text on evolutionary treaty interpretation relies on the requirement that a treaty be interpreted in good faith as much as Bjorge's 2014 monograph. Bjorge devotes an entire section of his third chapter to 'Evolutionary Interpretation and Good Faith',[40] and argues that 'evolutionary interpretation must be seen as being closely linked to the principle of good faith' and may even be 'required by good faith'.[41]

The 'interpreted in good faith' requirement would seem, at most, to add what Reinhold calls 'an element of 'reasonableness' to interpretations and to act as a security against interpretations that are so unreasonable that they can be

[37] *Loizidou v Turkey* (Preliminary Objections), Judgment (European Court of Human Rights (Chamber), 15318/89, 23 March 1995) 20 (§ 67).

[38] Franciscus Antonius Engelen, *Interpretation of Tax Treaties under International Law: A Study of Articles 31, 32, and 33 of the Vienna Convention on the Law of Treaties and Their Application to Tax Treaties* (Amsterdam, International Bureau of Fiscal Documentation, 2004) 134.

[39] ibid 135; see also *Case concerning Rights of Nationals of the United States of America in Morocco (France v United States of America)*, Judgment [1952] ICJ Reports 176, 189.

[40] See Bjorge (n 36) 63–76.

[41] ibid 64.

considered in bad faith.[42] Originally, good-faith interpretation was most often insisted upon as a security against formalism and, particularly, textualism in interpretation. In a world where legal interpretation was still partly dominated by the scholastic approaches of Savigny's historical school, good-faith interpretation guarded against excessive use of the text and advocated consideration of under-used non-textual factors. Used this way, the good-faith interpretation requirement renders treaty interpretation more flexible, liberal and often more progressive. If one understands more progressive approaches to treaty-based cases as dynamic or evolutionary treaty interpretation, then good-faith interpretation of this kind can manifestly play a role.

Bjorge's argument that good faith supports evolutionary interpretation draws attention to this by being most obviously anti-textualist, but also teleological and, in its application, clearly progressive. His argument justifying what are habitually called instances of evolutionary treaty interpretation relies on the way in which good faith authorises an interpreter to reject the ordinary meaning of the treaty's terms in favour of an implied common teleological 'intention'. For Bjorge, good faith 'is the most important element that goes into the crucible of treaty interpretation' and operates as a 'permanent gravitation point which draws the interpretation of treaty texts in the direction of the object of the treaty as well as the spirit by which the treaty is underlain'.[43] Bjorge is not the only author devoting substantial attention to evolutionary treaty interpretation to make the link between that doctrine and the requirement that a treaty be interpreted in good faith. In his lengthy CISG-focused article on 'Dynamic Treaty Interpretation', Van Alstine betrays a progressive conception of the evolutionary interpretation doctrine when he says that, as a general principle with 'neither a preordained nor an immutable content', good faith implies 'an active role for the judiciary in ... guid[ing] the future development of the law'.[44]

Such arguments link the good-faith interpretation requirement to teleological and effectiveness-inspired progressive constructions of treaty texts, that is, to instances of evolutionary interpretation *qua* progressive adjudication. They do not link the requirement to the instances of evolutionary treaty interpretation directly relevant to the problem of intertemporal linguistics, namely interpretations of treaty terms that favour the meaning the term had at the time of its application over that which it had at the time of its conclusion. Where he relies on good faith, Bjorge's focus is clearly on the type of decisional outcome reflective of the progressive adjudication doctrine rather than the interpretative and purely semantic type of outcome produced by a dynamic approach to the Problem. For example, he highlights the ICJ's reference to 'determin[ing] the

[42] Reinhold (n 35) 61.
[43] Bjorge (n 36) 67–68.
[44] Michael P Van Alstine, 'Dynamic Treaty Interpretation' (1998) 146 *University of Pennsylvania Law Review* 687, 693.

meaning of a treaty for purposes of good-faith *compliance* with it',[45] and speaks of '[g]ood faith [that …] may steer the interpretation away from what could be termed wrong-footed conservatism'.[46] For Bjorge, it appears, the relevance of good faith to evolutionary treaty interpretation lies in its ability to adapt the terms of a treaty to the exigencies of a situation so as to arrive at a fairer outcome. This is akin to the interpretative role played by the principle of '*Treu und Glauben*' – translated as 'good faith' – in the German Civil Code,[47] not of any specifically temporal interpretative rule.

Even if the 'interpreted in good faith' requirement indeed required progressive constructions to be given to treaties,[48] this would not mean that it would require a dynamic approach to the problem of intertemporal linguistics. As the next sub-section will demonstrate, just because an interpretation makes a treaty more effective in a certain way or brings it more closely into line with the parties' deemed objectives, does not mean that it necessarily adopts the meaning a treaty term had at the time of the treaty's application over the meaning it had at the time of its conclusion. Even if Bjorge is right that the good-faith requirement effectively subordinates the ordinary or special meaning of a treaty term to the drafters' intended purposes, he is only showing that good faith supports (a type of) teleological interpretation, but not demonstrating the quite different point that good faith – and with it VCLT Article 31 – requires a dynamic approach to the Problem. Temporally, VCLT Article 31's reference to good faith is clearly neutral.

B. Object and Purpose

The interpretative element of VCLT Articles 31 and 32 that is the most commonly linked to static or dynamic interpretation is the requirement that a treaty be interpreted in the light of its object and purpose. The renowned international

[45] *Dispute regarding Navigational and Related Rights (Costa Rica v Nicaragua)*, Judgment [2009] ICJ Reports 213, 242 (§ 63) (emphasis added).

[46] Bjorge (n 36) 74.

[47] German Civil Code (BGB) 2002, art 242.

[48] Bjorge never fully establishes that good faith supports evolutionary treaty interpretations *qua* progressive adjudication. In his three-step argument from good faith to teleological intentions and on to effectiveness-oriented objectives and then to a progressive outcome, even the first two steps may encounter difficulty. Bjorge does not demonstrate that good faith is granted the importance in treaty interpretation that he claims it is and cannot convincingly show that it implies a focus on the teleological intention. Indeed, while Bjorge is correct in noting that the requirement of good faith in treaty interpretation guards against bad-faith literal interpretations (Bjorge [n 36] 68–69), he fails to explain why the good-faith interpretation requirement would not also guard against bad-faith insistence on the underlying common intentions of the parties such as those recorded in a treaty's preparatory work, or indeed teleological interpretations that go so far from the terms of the treaty that they too could be considered inconsistent with the requirement to interpret a treaty in good faith.

lawyer and writer on this subject, Rudolf Bernhardt, explained the commonly perceived connection between the object and purpose of a treaty and dynamic treaty interpretation as follows:

> The object and purpose of a treaty plays, as shown in previous quotations, a central role in treaty interpretation. This reference to object and purpose can he understood as entry into a certain dynamism. If it is the purpose of a treaty to create longer lasting and solid relations between the parties or to guarantee personal freedoms to citizens as well as foreigners, it is hardly compatible with this purpose to eliminate new developments in the process of treaty interpretation. Multilateral treaties creating international organizations and human rights conventions are outstanding examples for the need of evolutive treaty interpretations.[49]

Another author has even gone so far as to say that, at least in relation to human rights treaties, '[t]he evolutionary approach … can be understood as a particular application of the Vienna Convention's object-and-purpose test'.[50] The popularity of this view is, moreover, by no means limited to those working in the field of international human rights law. Benedek considered the object and purpose of the GATT ('*die Verwirklichung der Ziele und Aufgaben des GATT*') to justify dynamic interpretation in the context of international trade law,[51] while, in the context of United Nations law, Damrosch has stated:

> Gradual growth in the Security Council's powers is fully consistent with methodologies of treaty interpretation, widely accepted in international law, that take into account the purposes of an instrument and practice under it; interpretation can accordingly be dynamic and teleological rather than static and literal.[52]

The insistence on this link is not merely a feature of the doctrine. Several international cases invoking the evolutionary interpretation doctrine cite VCLT Article 31(1)'s reference to the 'object and purpose' of the treaty as a basis for the dynamic interpretation being carried out. One of the most prominent of these is the above-described *Iron Rhine* award, in which an esteemed group of international lawyers invoked 'effective[ness] in terms of a treaty's object and purpose' as one of the main justifications for adopting an 'evolutive interpretation'.[53]

[49] Rudolf Bernhardt, 'Evolutive Treaty Interpretation, Especially of the European Convention on Human Rights' (1999) 42 *German Yearbook of International Law* 11, 16–17.

[50] Anthea Roberts, 'Power and Persuasion in Investment Treaty Interpretation: The Dual Role of States' (2010) 104 *The American Journal of International Law* 179, 202.

[51] Wolfgang Benedek, *Die Rechtsordnung des GATT aus völkerrechtlicher Sicht* (Graz, Springer, 1990) 145: 'If the objectives and tasks of the GATT are to be attained, dynamic-evolutive interpretation is justified wherever there is no interference with the established legal positions of the Contracting Parties. Since only a functioning legal order can effectively protect the mutual rights of the Contracting Parties, the functional development of the GATT through the multilateral agreement to international organization is in line with the intertemporal law.' (present author's translation).

[52] Lori Fisler Damrosch, 'Concluding Reflections' in Lori Fisler Damrosch (ed), *Enforcing Restraint: Collective Intervention in Internal Conflicts* (New York, Council on Foreign Relations Press, 1993) 358.

[53] *Iron Rhine*, Award (n 17) 73 (§ 80).

As these quotations and their sources indicate, the object-and-purpose element is linked to teleological interpretations and onward to progressive outcomes. Both links are contestable, the first link relying on a broad reading of 'in its object and purpose' in VCLT Article 31(1) and the second assuming that the object and purpose of a treaty will always be progressive. Yet for present purposes, the general validity of these links is irrelevant. Even if the link between 'in the light of its object and purpose' and progressive constructions were established, this would still not prove a general link between that part of VCLT Article 31 and a dynamic approach to the problem of intertemporal linguistics. For a study recognising the difference between a narrow variant of the evolutionary interpretation doctrine insisting on the later-emerging meaning of a treaty term and a broad variant insisting on progressive adjudication, it is quite evident that the international lawyers quoted above are speaking of the latter. For example, Bernhardt's text was focused on evolutionary interpretation at the European Court of Human Rights, an institution where the broader variant of the doctrine dominates, while the *Iron Rhine* award was, as described above, highly progressive but barely interpretative.[54] As will now be explained, the 'object and purpose' requirement may support a broad teleological approach and thus evolutionary treaty interpretation *qua* progressive adjudication, but even progressive adjudication does not itself take a general position on the problem of intertemporal linguistics.

In the choice between original and later-emerging meaning with which we are here concerned, the outcome produced by interpretative reliance on the treaty's object and purpose varies according to the openness of that object and purpose to change, the directionality of the external meaning change that alters the semantic content of the treaty term (ie whether it is socially progressive or regressive) and the role played by the treaty term in the context of the treaty (for example, whether it is a positive obligation or an exception). Indeed, it is not difficult to think of situations in which the object and purpose of a treaty, even if it endorses a broad teleological approach, would prompt an interpreter to select the original – rather than later-emerging – meaning of a treaty term subject to semantic change over the relevant time.

The degree to which a teleological or progressive interpretative approach substantively intersects with a dynamic approach to the Problem depends principally on the practical role played by the treaty term subject to semantic change. Whether an interpretative outcome is in-line with certain objectives or progressive is not only a matter of values, but also a matter of real-world outcome. This type of interpretation – or really construction – first takes a position at the very end-point of the inquiry where the practical outcome has come into view, whereas the problem of intertemporal linguistics seeks the elaboration of a position to be taken earlier, initially oblivious to the practical outcome it produces and how that outcome fits with the world-view of the interpreter.

[54] See further s 3.II.B.v above.

Crucially, while most relevant semantic change follows social developments and is prima facie socially progressive (such as the broadening of the meaning of the words 'torture', 'commerce' or 'natural resources'), a dynamic approach to interpreting the word will only produce a progressive outcome where it appears in the 'right way' in the context. For example, an interpreter consistently acknowledging the semantic broadening of the term 'natural resources' beyond products of economic utility to all things present in nature will produce an (environmentally) progressive outcome where that term appears as part of a provision imposing an obligation on States to protect their natural resources, but an (environmentally) regressive outcome where that term appears as part of a treaty restricting international trade in some natural products but granting a State, as an exception to that prohibition, a right to sell unlimited quantities of 'natural resources'.

The lack of correlation between a teleological interpretation and a dynamic approach to the Problem is also demonstrated by situations in which different facts would require different teleological interpretations of the same provision, one in keeping with the static and the other with the dynamic approach to the Problem. Consider the provision guaranteeing the right to life 'from the moment of conception'[55] that was at issue in the *Artavia Murillo* case decided by the IACtHR in 2012. For the *Artavia* Court, it was clear that, when the provision was drafted, the moment of conception was understood as implantation,[56] but also that the development of in-vitro fertilisation ('IVF') had 'transformed the discussion on how the phenomenon of "conception" [was] understood' such that 'the definition of "conception" ha[d] changed' to include the earlier moment of fertilisation.[57] On the facts of the *Artavia* case, in which the court was asked to determine the legality of Costa Rica's prohibition of IVF, an acknowledgement of this semantic change – a dynamic approach to the Problem – would have served the objective of maximising respect for human rights by giving those seeking to be parents a right to use IVF. However, it is easy to imagine a fact situation, involving a prohibition on the use of post-rape contragestive drugs, for example,[58] that would reduce the scope of human rights by denying rape victims the right to interfere with a fertilised but non-implanted ovum. A teleological approach aimed at maximising the rights of the potential mother would thus appear to favour interpreting Article 4 of the American Convention using a dynamic approach in a case about the first law and a static approach in a case about the second law.

[55] American Convention on Human Rights ('Pact of San José, Costa Rica') 1969 (1144 UNTS 123), art 4.

[56] *Case of Artavia Murillo et al ('In Vitro Fertilization') v Costa Rica* (Preliminary Objections, Merits, Reparations and Costs), Judgment [2012] Inter-Am Ct HR (Ser C) No 257 57 (§ 187).

[57] ibid 53 (§ 179).

[58] See, eg Kathleen Mary Raviele, 'Levonorgestrel in Cases of Rape: How Does it Work?' (2014) 81 *The Linacre Quarterly* 117.

As these examples show, the key fact is the context in which the contested and semantically changing treaty term appears. The outcome of a dynamic approach in terms of the treaty's object and purpose will obviously be very different depending not only on the facts to which the semantically changing term will be applied, but also on where in the treaty that term appears. This extends beyond the obvious situation of a semantically changing treaty term appearing in an obligation or an exception. For example, where the treaty term appears in a clause defining the scope of a provision's applicability, semantic change might render a provision that was previously applicable to that situation inapplicable, which could in turn undermine the treaty's ability to achieve its objectives. Ironically, if the *Namibia* court had given a dynamic interpretation to the expression 'inhabited by peoples not yet able to stand by themselves under the strenuous conditions of the modern world' in Article 22(1) of the Covenant of the League of Nations, it would probably have determined Namibia's peoples as able to stand by themselves under the strenuous conditions of the modern world, thereby potentially leaving Article 22 of the Covenant inapplicable and imposing no 'sacred trust' on South Africa as the mandatory and therefore no risk of the apartheid policy breaching that sacred trust;[59] a manifestly regressive outcome.

In a jurisdictional context, (dynamic) acknowledgement of semantic broadening in reservations to acceptances of jurisdiction – along with the principle of reciprocity – can mean that States will avoid being required to account for their violations of a treaty before a third-party dispute settlement body. In the *Aegean Sea* case, Turkey objected to the ICJ's jurisdiction by invoking – through the doctrine of reciprocity – the Greek reservation to the General Act of matters 'relating to the territorial status of Greece'. Attention fell on whether the meaning of the treaty expression 'territorial status of Greece' had changed through time and many authors consider the Court to have opted for a dynamic interpretation of it, taking the broader meaning prevailing in 1975, rather than the narrower meaning prevailing at the time the reservation was made in 1931.[60] The General Act was clearly focused – like a progressive international legal philosophy – on bringing as many international disputes within the jurisdiction of peaceful third-party dispute settlement mechanisms as possible, especially

[59] See especially *South West Africa Cases (Ethiopia v South Africa; Liberia v South Africa)* (Second Phase), Dissenting Opinion of Judge Jessup [1966] ICJ Reports 325, 440; *South West Africa Cases (Ethiopia v South Africa; Liberia v South Africa)* (Preliminary Objections), Judgment [1962] ICJ Reports 319, 329; *Legal Consequences for States of the Continued Presence of South Africa in Namibia (South West Africa) notwithstanding Security Council Resolution 276 (1970)*, Advisory Opinion [1971] ICJ Reports 16, 31–32 (§ 53).

[60] See, eg International Law Commission and Georg Nolte, 'Introductory Report for the Study Group on Treaties over Time: Jurisprudence of the International Court of Justice and arbitral tribunals of ad hoc jurisdiction relating to subsequent agreements and subsequent practice' in Georg Nolte (ed), *Treaties and Subsequent Practice* (Oxford, Oxford University Press, 2013) 199. For various reasons, the present author does not agree with this characterisation of the Court's interpretative finding (see s 6.II.B.i below).

in tense situations such as that which existed between Greece and Turkey in the mid-1970s. This means that a dynamic approach to interpreting 'territorial status' would have undermined that treaty's object and purpose by putting Greece's claim within the scope of the reservation and therefore outside the jurisdiction of the Court, whereas a static approach following the same term's narrower 1931 meaning would have produced the outcome that would have been the most effective in terms of the General Act's object and purpose.

These examples show how, despite being so regularly associated with a dynamic approach to the Problem, teleological and progressive approaches to interpretation can also imply a static approach that prefers a semantically changing treaty term's original meaning. In the circumstances, it simply cannot be said that VCLT Article 31's requirement that a treaty be interpreted in the light of its object and purpose gives treaty interpreters the general instruction to grant a semantically changing treaty term the meaning it had at the time of the treaty's application, rather than conclusion.

III. ONLY EX ANTE GUIDANCE CAN SOLVE THE PROBLEM, MERE EX POST JUSTIFICATION CANNOT

We have now established that the VCLT's interpretative rules are intended to be – and actually are – temporally neutral and also that, while they might support evolutionary treaty interpretation *qua* progressive adjudication, this does not mean that they generally support taking a dynamic approach to the problem of intertemporal linguistics.

It is therefore somewhat odd to see that the link between the VCLT rules and a dynamic approach to the Problem is still made by many international lawyers, including even those who acknowledge the temporal openness of these rules and apparently understand evolutionary interpretation in its narrow form relevant to intertemporal linguistics. The conclusions Djeffal reaches in this regard in his 2016 book are particularly curious. He focuses on providing a functional reconstruction of the VCLT's interpretative rules in relation to a question which presents a very similar dichotomy to the problem of intertemporal linguistics and quite skilfully reaches the (correct) conclusion that these rules are temporally open. Yet he immediately follows this by saying that they nonetheless constitute 'part of the solution' to the problem of how to interpret treaties through time.[61] Djeffal thus appears to have gone half-way to recognising how the conventional wisdom misconceives the role played by the VCLT rules in relation to intertemporal interpretation questions, then stopped. If even writers recognising the 'intertemporal openness' of the VCLT nonetheless consider that it helps adjudicators interpret treaties through time, the conventional wisdom must be

[61] Djeffal (n 31) 357–58.

well-entrenched. This clearly points to a different understanding of what can constitute a 'solution' to the problem of original or later-emerging meaning, one which does not involve guiding the interpreter to a selection of one of these two competing meanings.

The best clue to solving this riddle is found in the notion of 'consistency'. Many of the decisions linking the VCLT's interpretative rules with a static or dynamic approach speak of how those rules are *consistent with* the approach ultimately taken. Indeed, both the oft-repeated IACtHR statement: 'evolutive interpretation is consistent with the general rules of treaty interpretation established in the 1969 Vienna Convention',[62] and the important *Mondev* award dictum penned by Stephen, Crawford and Schwebel: '[a] reasonable evolutionary interpretation of Article 1105(1) is consistent both with the *travaux* [and] with normal principles of interpretation',[63] can be read as narrow consistency claims. Importantly, a dynamic approach will in many cases be *consistent with* the VCLT rules, without being *prompted by* those rules.

To say that a dynamic interpretation is consistent with a set of rules is, interpreted narrowly, merely to say: (a) that within the set of rules 'S', there is a rule *x* which supports the adoption of the dynamic approach; and (b) that, within the set of rules 'S', there is no rule *y* which operates so as to exclude the adoption of the dynamic approach. Of course, the VCLT rules are famously open-textured and include various different approaches without expressly prohibiting any interpretative approaches.[64] This means that there is likely to be, in all situations, at least one interpretative rule – one member of the set S – supporting the particular interpretation proffered, with no interpretative rule expressly denying it. However, it also means that, while a dynamic approach to the Problem is likely to be supported or even justified by a VCLT rule, an alternative, static approach will generally be equally as likely to be supported or justified by another VCLT rule.

In such circumstances, the claim that a dynamic approach is consistent with – or even justified by – the VCLT rules is strictly correct, but so weak that it is not meaningful. Indeed, because the opposing static approach would also likely be consistent with or justified by the VCLT rules, the rules cannot be said to discriminate between the two approaches. In other words, while the rules might offer support to an interpreter looking for an ex post justification of a particular interpretative position reached on other grounds, they do not offer any guidance at all to an interpreter facing the problem of intertemporal linguistics with an open mind.

In philosophical terms, the rules, in general terms, provide a range of *normative* reasons pointing in different and often opposing directions, but are

[62] See, eg *Right to Information*, Advisory Opinion (n 1) 58 (§ 114); see also *Gómez-Paquiyauri*, Judgment (n 1) 59 (§ 165); *Street Children*, Judgment (n 1) 46 (§ 193).

[63] *Mondev*, Award (n 2) 43 (§ 123).

[64] See, eg Ian Sinclair, *The Vienna Convention on the Law of Treaties* (Manchester, Manchester University Press, 1984) 1.

generally incapable of providing a *motivating* reason for the taking of the static or, alternatively, dynamic approach in response to the Problem.[65] Only interpretative rules which obviously favoured a particular interpretative approach by, for example, failing to mention other approaches or creating a hierarchy between the approaches, could potentially provide the clear ex ante guidance the present part of this study is searching for.

Djeffal willingly accepts that his conclusion 'might prove to be unsatisfactory to lawyers and legal scholars if they prefer guidance over discretion' and that his inquiry 'has taken another stance'.[66] Most of all, however, it betrays a facile view of what constitutes a solution to the problem of how to interpret treaties through time. To privilege 'discretion' and then say that '[t]he choice between static and evolutive results is situated within competing attitudes'[67] may be seen as abdicating from the responsibility of trying to solve the Problem. This very soft, almost timorous notion of a 'solution' enables Djeffal to avoid contradicting the important body of international case law and scholarship that asserts, at least impliedly, that the VCLT helps solve the problem of intertemporal linguistics. However, for reasons including the temporal openness of the VCLT interpretative provisions that he himself adroitly identified, this conventional wisdom must now be cast aside. The VCLT may provide ex post justification to a static or dynamic approach, but it does not provide the ex ante guidance necessary to resolve contests between original and later-emerging meanings and thus solve the problem of intertemporal linguistics.

IV. CONCLUSIONS

The somewhat controversial nature of these contentions means that they merit some brief final remarks.

First, a rejection of the conventional wisdom that the VCLT helps solve the Problem does not equate to a rejection of the case law or scholarship invoking the VCLT's interpretative rules as part of a justification for the static or dynamic approach being taken. Those rules are notoriously flexible and unquestionably applicable to the vast majority of situations in which the Problem arises. That international adjudicators, including the many who, as Kolb has noted, often know where they want to end up before they look at the rules that are designed to point them in the right direction,[68] justify their findings through reference to these rules is clearly to be welcomed. That scholars focusing on evolutionary treaty interpretation note how both the narrow and broad forms of the doctrine

[65] See, eg Jonathan Dancy, *Practical Reality* (London, Oxford University Press, 2004) 2–4.

[66] Djeffal (n 31) 357.

[67] ibid.

[68] Robert Kolb, *Interprétation et création du droit international: Esquisses d'une herméneutique juridique moderne pour le droit international public* (Bruxelles, Bruylant, 2006) 169.

can be propped up by different interpretative rules is equally understandable and commendable. This study simply comes from a different starting point with a different perspective and finds ex post justifications of a pre-ordained approach to be of no utility to the particular task of deciding, independently of other factors, whether a treaty interpreter should use the original or later-emerging meaning of a treaty term subject to relevant semantic change.

Second, a rejection of the conventional wisdom that the VCLT helps solve the problem of intertemporal linguistics is in fact not the slight to the VCLT and the members of the ILC that it may initially appear to be. It is not as if the esteemed international jurists in the ILC's Law of Treaties study group tried to solve the Problem but failed to. On the contrary, they struggled, by their Special Rapporteur's own admission, to deal with the 'immense difficulties' presented the Problem in the short time they had available and 'abandoned the attempt to cover the point in the draft'.[69] Indeed, it would have been remarkable if, without even trying to, the VCLT had managed to solve the problem of intertemporal linguistics, especially when its drafters did not have the benefit of the many international decisions raising the Problem that have emerged in the 50 years since it was concluded.

[69] UN Conference on the Law of Treaties, 'Official Records, First Session, Vienna' (Vienna, United Nations, 1968) 184 (per Sir Humphrey Waldock [Expert Consultant], Thirty-third meeting – 22 April 1968, § 74).

6

*The Post-*Namibia *International Case Law does not Provide a General Solution to the Problem*

AT THE TIME of writing, the prevailing view among international lawyers is that there is no longer any contest between the original and the later-emerging meaning of a treaty term. The static approach – represented by the principle of contemporaneity – is regularly ignored and barely ever posited as a principle of modern-day international law, while the dynamic approach – associated with the burgeoning evolutionary treaty interpretation doctrine – is not only increasingly written about, but also increasingly accepted.

In 2005, the *Iron Rhine* award appeared to crystallise the triumph of evolutionary interpretation in the doctrine, noting 'a general support among the leading writers today for evolutive interpretation of treaties'.[1] Then, in 2009, the ICJ's *Related Rights* judgment was generally deemed to have crystallised the triumph of the same principle in the case law of international courts and tribunals. Both of these decisions spawned a great body of scholarship, much of it focused on the evolutionary interpretation doctrine. By continually explaining it, international adjudicators and scholars alike have helped to entrench that doctrine into the fabric of contemporary international law. By defining it as reflecting – or otherwise associating it with – the dynamic approach to the problem of intertemporal linguistics, modern-day international lawyers have strongly implied that the dynamic approach is the only one which today's international courts and tribunals will or should apply to the Problem.

A review of contemporary case law and scholarship thereby leaves the undeniable overall impression that the temporal issues of treaty interpretation were fought by the principle of contemporaneity against the evolutionary interpretation doctrine – and that the latter has clearly won. Bernhardt's 1999 article provides an illustrative example of how some prominent commentators focusing on the emergence and consolidation of the evolutionary treaty interpretation

[1] *Iron Rhine ('Ijzeren Rijn') Railway between the Kingdom of Belgium and the Kingdom of the Netherlands*, Award (2005) XXVII RIAA/RSA 35, 73 (§ 81).

doctrine, particularly in the human rights field, have extended themselves to concluding that the doctrine provides a dynamic answer to the Problem:

> Static or evolutive interpretation? Conservation of the original intentions of the drafters of the Convention or relevance of changing conditions and opinions in State and society? These questions need a basic answer. The answer has been given by the European Court of Human Rights in many judgments ...[2]

Ultimately, while there is some recognition among commentators of the fact that the principle of contemporaneity and the static approach may have prevailed in cases prior to *Namibia* and in a handful since, a clear consensus has emerged that, in the five decades since that advisory opinion, the evolutionary interpretation doctrine and, with it, the dynamic approach to the Problem has firmly taken the reins.

This view, it must be emphasised, is based on the contemporary commentary of the case law relevant to the Problem, principally that which is found in secondary literature, but also in adjudicatory opinions referring to prior case law. That commentary is characterised by two important features that, it is submitted, have skewed international lawyers' understandings of the state of the relevant authorities.

First, the commentary giving rise to this popular view is overwhelmingly dedicated to the *evolutionary interpretation doctrine*, not to the distinct issue of original or later-emerging meaning. It therefore focuses on cases containing statements that clearly advocate evolutionary treaty interpretation rather than on cases taking a position on the problem of intertemporal linguistics. In doing so, the bulk of the recent commentary directs too much attention to cases that are not relevant to the Problem, such as those advocating the progressive-adjudication variant of the doctrine, and too little attention to many of the cases that are relevant to the Problem, particularly those of institutions other than the ICJ and ECtHR that advocate a static approach. Once attention is redirected towards the distinct set of cases actually relevant to the Problem, the view that international courts and tribunals now generally prefer a dynamic approach to the Problem finds itself resting on substantially shakier ground.

Second, the commentary upon which this view is based relies very heavily on judicial *statements* advocating an approach to the Problem, not on evidence of how the modern-day international courts and tribunals actually respond to the Problem. In this area of international law, as in many others, adjudicators, practitioners and scholars alike often fall victim to the temptation of taking eminently quotable judicial statements at face value and out of context. When the judicial different statements relied upon are analysed in their full decisional context with less focus on what international adjudicators say they will do and more focus on what they actually did, the state of the authorities appears far less 'dynamic' than is commonly thought.

[2] Rudolf Bernhardt, 'Evolutive Treaty Interpretation, Especially of the European Convention on Human Rights' (1999) 42 *German Yearbook of International Law* 11, 17.

This chapter presents two substantive sections dedicated to showing in more detail how each of these features of the contemporary commentary of the case law has propped up the popular view that international courts and tribunals now favour a dynamic approach. Together, they demonstrate that this conception is in fact a misconception that cannot be maintained in the face of a more comprehensive and deeper analysis of the modern-day case law truly relevant to the problem of intertemporal linguistics.

I. THE CONCEPTION IS BASED ON THE WRONG SET OF INTERNATIONAL CASES

Over the course of the past five decades, adjudicatory statements advocating evolutive, evolutionary or dynamic treaty interpretation have become an increasingly prevalent feature of the case law of international courts and tribunals. The ICJ's statements to this effect, including in the famous paragraph 53 of the *Namibia* advisory opinion,[3] in paragraph 77 of the *Aegean Sea* judgment,[4] in paragraph 112 of the *Gabčíkovo* judgment[5] and in paragraph 66 of the *Related Rights* judgment,[6] are particularly well-known and oft-quoted,[7] as are the various statements made by the *Iron Rhine* arbitrators on pages 73 and 74 of their award.[8] In the field of international human rights, statements that a human rights treaty 'is a living instrument which must be interpreted in the light of present-day conditions', that the relevant Convention must be 'interpreted and applied in a manner which renders its rights practical and effective, not theoretical and illusory' and that a 'failure by the Court to maintain a dynamic and evolutive approach would risk rendering it a bar to reform or improvement'

[3] *Legal Consequences for States of the Continued Presence of South Africa in Namibia (South West Africa) notwithstanding Security Council Resolution 276 (1970)*, Advisory Opinion [1971] ICJ Reports 16, 31–32 (§ 53).

[4] *Aegean Sea Continental Shelf (Greece v Turkey)*, Judgment [1978] ICJ Reports 3, 32 (§ 77): 'once it is established that the expression "the territorial status of Greece" was used in Greece's instrument of accession as a generic term denoting any matters comprised within the concept of territorial status under general international law, the presumption necessarily arises that its meaning was intended to follow the evolution of the law and to correspond with the meaning attached to the expression by the law in force at any given time'.

[5] *Gabčíkovo-Nagymaros Project (Hungary/Slovakia)*, Judgment [1997] ICJ Reports 7, 67–68 (§ 112): 'By inserting these evolving provisions in the Treaty, the parties recognized the potential necessity to adapt the Project. Consequently, the Treaty is not static, and is open to adapt to emerging norms of international law.'

[6] *Dispute regarding Navigational and Related Rights (Costa Rica v Nicaragua)*, Judgment [2009] ICJ Reports 213, 243 (§ 66): 'It is founded on the idea that, where the parties have used generic terms in a treaty, the parties necessarily having been aware that the meaning of the terms was likely to evolve over time, and where the treaty has been entered into for a very long period or is "of continuing duration", the parties must be presumed, as a general rule, to have intended those terms to have an evolving meaning.'

[7] See, eg Eirik Bjorge, *The Evolutionary Interpretation of Treaties* (Oxford, Oxford University Press, 2014) 1, 119, 136.

[8] *Iron Rhine*, Award (n 1) 73–74 (§§ 79–82).

have been so regularly repeated that they have almost become articles of faith. At the WTO, the same two Appellate Body statements, in paragraph 130 of the *US – Shrimp* report[9] and paragraph 396 of the *China – AV Products* report,[10] are regularly quoted and relied upon.[11]

Modern-day international lawyers approaching the problem of intertemporal linguistics through the prism of the evolutionary treaty interpretation doctrine tend to call on this same set of supposedly authoritative statements to demonstrate that the doctrine – and with it the dynamic approach to the Problem – has become established in contemporary international law. This is readily understandable. For a study assessing, in isolation, whether the evolutionary interpretation doctrine has become an established part of international law, it is perfectly normal to focus on all the judicial statements made in relation to that doctrine and those statements alone. Difficulty only arises when these studies proceed to use that set of cases and decisions to expressly or impliedly take a view on the related but distinct matter of how international courts and tribunals respond to the problem of intertemporal linguistics.

For a study directed towards the problem of intertemporal linguistics, the fact that modern-day commentary of the case law relevant to the Problem is dominated by evolutionary interpretation literature is problematic. The latter focus has, it is submitted, caused views of the state of the relevant authorities to be skewed towards the view that the dynamic approach has prevailed in at least three distinct ways.

A. Cases with Statements Advocating the Irrelevant Broad Variant of the Evolutionary Interpretation Doctrine

First, several judicial statements made in support of evolutionary interpretation are, as demonstrated in chapter 3, actually referring to a broad variant of

[9] *United States – Import prohibition of certain shrimp and shrimp products*, Report (WTO Appellate Body, WT/DS58/AB/R, 12 October 1998) 48 (§ 130): 'From the perspective embodied in the preamble of the WTO Agreement, we note that the generic term "natural resources" in Article XX(g) is not "static" in its content or reference but is rather "by definition, evolutionary". It is, therefore, pertinent to note that modern international conventions and declarations make frequent references to natural resources as embracing both living and non-living resources.' (Appellate Body's footnotes omitted).

[10] *China – Publications and Audiovisual Products*, Report (WTO Appellate Body, WT/DS363/AB/R, 21 December 2009) 161 (§ 396): 'More generally, we consider that the terms used in China's GATS Schedule ("sound recording" and "distribution") are sufficiently generic that what they apply to may change over time. In this respect, we note that GATS Schedules, like the GATS itself and all WTO agreements, constitute multilateral treaties with continuing obligations that WTO Members entered into for an indefinite period of time, regardless of whether they were original Members or acceded after 1995.'

[11] See, eg Paolo Palchetti, 'Interpreting "Generic Terms": Between Respect for the Parties' Original Intention and the Identification of the Ordinary Meaning' in Nerina Boschiero and others (eds), *International Courts and the Development of International Law: Essays in Honour of Tullio Treves* (The Hague, Asser Press, 2013) 93.

that doctrine which is focused on progressive adjudication and does not take a position on the problem of intertemporal linguistics. We have already seen that the important *Namibia* and *Iron Rhine* dicta so often relied upon to assert the new-found dominance of the dynamic approach fall squarely within this category. In addition, the many judgments of human rights courts that invoke the evolutionary interpretation doctrine to render 'rights practical and effective' and to avoid making those courts 'a bar to reform or improvement' are not, for the reasons set out in chapter 3 above, advocating a general preference for the later-emerging meaning of a treaty term over its original meaning. Such statements may lend support to claims that the evolutionary interpretation doctrine has become established, but not to the separate claim often made as a corollary, namely that in a contest between the meaning of a treaty term at the time of the treaty's conclusion and the time of the treaty's application, modern-day international courts and tribunals routinely favour the latter.

In this regard, it is salient that Bernhardt followed his statement of a dynamic answer having been given to the '[s]tatic or evolutive interpretation?' question by describing the ECtHR's *Golder* judgment. That decision, already described in section 3.II.B.i above, was so clearly progressive that it could be considered the founding judgment of the Strasbourg court's judicial philosophy now assimilated to the wider variant of the evolutionary interpretation doctrine, but, by Bernhardt's own admission,[12] it did not even make any reference to the evolutionary interpretation doctrine and, by reading an unenumerated rights into a provision rather than giving a later-emerging meaning to a semantically changing treaty term, did not take a position on the Problem at all.

Helmersen's 2013 article on evolutive treaty interpretation also clearly displays substantial reliance on adjudicatory statements advocating only the broader variant of the doctrine. In a series of footnotes in support of his statement that 'evolutive interpretations are found in "decisions" from various international tribunals',[13] Helmersen cites eight decisions from international courts and tribunals other than the ICJ. Among these, he includes several decisions speaking uniquely of evolutionary interpretation in a progressive adjudication sense, including some of those identified as such in chapter 3, such as the IACtHR's *Right of Information on Consular Assistance* advisory opinion,[14] the Human Rights Committee's *Judge v Canada* communication[15] and the 2005 *Iron Rhine* award.[16]

[12] Bernhardt (n 2) 18.

[13] Sondre Torp Helmersen, 'Evolutive Treaty Interpretation: Legality, Semantics and Distinctions' (2013) 6 *European Journal of Legal Studies* 127, 131–32.

[14] ibid 132, fn 31; *The Right to Information on Consular Assistance in the Framework of the Guarantees of the Due Process of Law*, Advisory Opinion [1999] Inter-Am Ct HR (Ser A) No 16 (1999).

[15] Helmersen (n 13) 132, fn 32; *Roger Judge v Canada*, Communication No 829/1998 [2002] UN Doc CCPR/C/78/D/829/1998 (2003).

[16] Helmersen (n 13) 132, fn 34; *Iron Rhine*, Award (n 1).

Having discerned two variants of the evolutionary interpretation doctrine and determined only one of them to relate to the Problem, this study urges readers of the evolutionary interpretation literature to determine which version of the evolutionary interpretation doctrine the judicial statements appear to be advocating, before jumping to the conclusion that, by supporting evolutionary interpretation, they endorse a dynamic approach to the problem of intertemporal linguistics.

Figure 5 Cases on the Doctrine and the Problem – Euler Diagram

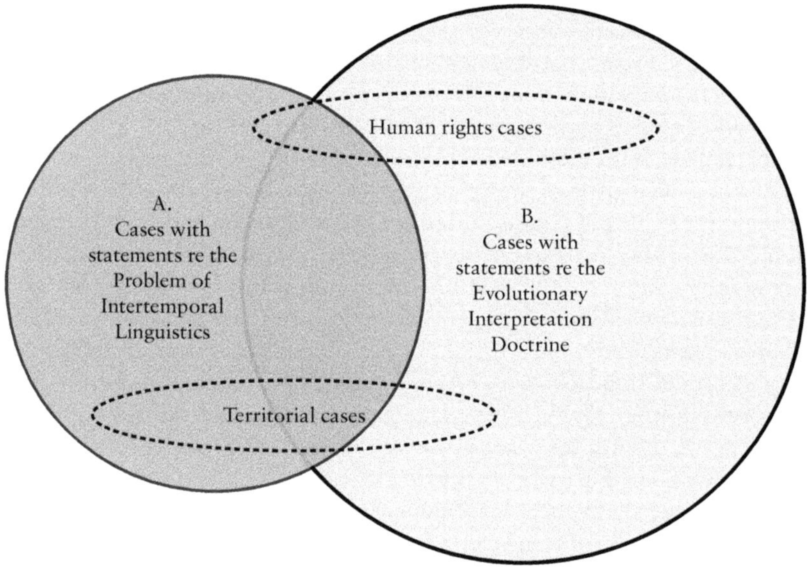

In the Euler diagram presented as Figure 5 above, the cases containing statements that advocate only the progressive-adjudication variant of the evolutionary interpretation doctrine are those in the right-hand circle that do not overlap with those in the left-hand circle. Once this (large) subset of cases is put to one side, the weight of evolutionary treaty interpretation authority clearly advocating the dynamic approach to the Problem (the overlapping area representing the subset of B that is (A ∩ B)) is much less imposing – even as a proportion of the relatively small number of international decisions actually taking a position on the problem of intertemporal linguistics. This observation itself, a corollary of this study's important discernment of two different forms of the evolutionary interpretation doctrine, points to one of the reasons why we must now call into question the popular view that the dynamic approach to the Problem has prevailed in the recent case law of international courts and tribunals.

B. Cases Selectively Chosen from Particular Courts and Types of Treaties

Second, the all-encompassing focus on the evolutionary interpretation doctrine has caused modern-day international lawyers touching on the problem of intertemporal linguistics to direct disproportionate amounts of their attention to cases decided by particular international courts and tribunals and in relation to particular types of instruments.

While much of it does not, some of the recent international case law and scholarship dedicated to evolutionary treaty interpretation admirably makes an effort to put the doctrine in its context by referring to cases apparently advocating a static approach to the Problem. However, because they remain inherently focused on the evolutionary interpretation doctrine, the studies that come closest to surveying recent practice often concentrate on (a) the case law of the international courts and tribunals most responsible for the emergence and consolidation of that doctrine and (b) interpretations of the types of treaties most capable of prompting resort to the doctrine.

For example, Malgosia Fitzmaurice's 81-page, two-part study of dynamic treaty interpretation devotes approximately 47 pages to reviewing the relevant case law, 37 of which analyse the interpretative practice either of the ECtHR or in relation to 'multilateral environmental agreements'.[17] Even the rare studies openly dedicated to both the static and dynamic approaches still focus on the case law most relevant to the emergence of the ever-magnetic evolutionary interpretation doctrine. Djeffal's 2016 book on 'Static and Evolutive Treaty Interpretation', for example, has a wider focus closer to this study's, but still restricts its survey of practice to the case law of the ICJ and the ECtHR alone.[18]

In an era of ever more abundant international dispute settlement and ever tighter word limits on the scholarship dedicated to commenting on it, contemporary authors cannot be faulted for restricting their attention to merely a couple of international courts and only a few types of treaty. However, such sampling necessarily renders general conclusions more fragile, especially when the samples taken are somehow skewed towards a particular approach. From the perspective of whether contemporary international courts and tribunals generally favour a static or dynamic approach to the problem of intertemporal linguistics, samples restricted to ICJ and ECtHR case law and predominantly to interpretations of human rights and environmental treaties are inherently skewed towards a conclusion that the dynamic approach is preferred.

A focus on the case law of the ECtHR makes the sample particularly unrepresentative. That particular court undoubtedly evinces more support for the

[17] Malgosia Fitzmaurice, 'Dynamic (Evolutive) Interpretation of Treaties, Part I' (2009) *Hague Yearbook of International Law* 101, 121–53; Malgosia Fitzmaurice, 'Dynamic (Evolutive) Interpretation of Treaties, Part 2' (2010) *Hague Yearbook of International Law* 3, 3–7.

[18] Christian Djeffal, *Static and Evolutive Treaty Interpretation: A Functional Reconstruction* (Cambridge, Cambridge University Press, 2016) 214–344.

dynamic approach than the case law of other courts and tribunals. Indeed, at the ECtHR, evolutionary or dynamic interpretation is so well regarded that interpretations taking a static position and dissents to judgments applying a dynamic approach are not justified by an invocation of the static approach, nor a rejection of the dynamic approach, but instead by reference to a need to impose some limits on the dynamic interpretation of the Convention.[19]

Moreover, the ECtHR's interpretative practice is almost exclusively focused on the interpretation of a now almost 70-year-old treaty of a quite particular kind. Higgins has gone so far as to claim that human rights treaties require an exception to be made from the general rules affecting the temporal aspects of treaty interpretation,[20] while Dörr and Schmalenbach describe it as a 'particular application of the dynamic approach … founded on … the quasi-constitutional character of the ECHR and the need to receive directions from it for effectively implementing human rights guarantees in a modern world'.[21] Some prominent international lawyers have made similar comments in relation to environmental treaties, Judge Weeramantry's *Gabčíkovo* separate opinion, for example, stating that '[e]nvironmental rights are human rights' and arguing that environmental treaties must therefore be 'understood at the time of their application'.[22] There is a manifest danger that what international courts and tribunals consider appropriate modes for interpreting these treaties will differ from how they are likely to interpret the myriad of other types of treaties to be interpreted and applied by contemporary international courts and tribunals, so general conclusions should not be drawn from how these particular types of treaties alone are interpreted.

A restriction to the case law of the ICJ is more defensible, not because of that institution's prestige and status as a principal organ of the UN,[23] but rather on account of the generality of its jurisdiction and the concomitant fact that, unlike international courts and tribunals in specialised sub-fields of international law, the ICJ deals with disputes and treaties of many different kinds. However, the case law of the ICJ by no means covers all interpretative decisions that do not fall within the special jurisdiction of international dispute settlement bodies belonging to sub-fields of international law. Many States choose

[19] See, eg *Khamidov v Russia* (Merits and Just Satisfaction), Judgment (European Court of Human Rights (Fifth Section), 72118/01, 15 November 2007) 31 (§ 131); *Pretty v The United Kingdom* (Merits), Judgment (European Court of Human Rights (Fourth Section), 2346/02, 29 April 2002) 31 (§ 54); *X and Others v Austria* (Merits and Just Satisfaction), Joint Partly Dissenting Opinion of Judges Casadevall, Ziemele, Kovler, Jočienė, Šikuta, de Gaetano and Sicilianos (European Court of Human Rights (Grand Chamber), 19010/07, 19 February 2013) 58 (§ 23).

[20] Rosalyn Higgins, 'Time and the Law: International Perspectives on an Old Problem' (1997) 46 *International & Comparative Law Quarterly* 501, 517–18.

[21] Oliver Dörr and Kirsten Schmalenbach, 'Article 31. General rule of interpretation' in Oliver Dörr and Kirsten Schmalenbach (eds), *Vienna Convention on the Law of Treaties: A Commentary* (Berlin, Springer, 2012) 535 (§ 27).

[22] *Gabčíkovo-Nagymaros Project (Hungary/Slovakia)*, Separate Opinion of Vice-President Weeramantry [1997] ICJ Reports 88, 114.

[23] Djeffal (n 18) 214–15.

to take disputes raising issues of treaty interpretation to State-to-State arbitration, particularly, though not exclusively, in relation to the delimitation of their boundaries. Indeed, in a detailed study of the general jurisdiction cases most clearly raising the Problem since *Namibia*, the present author identified six ICJ judgments and almost as many (five) arbitral awards.[24] Moreover, given that five of the six ICJ judgments apparently most relevant to the Problem did not resolve the matter before them by giving a treaty term its original or later-emerging meaning, a larger sample of 'general jurisdiction' decisions would clearly enable safer conclusions to be drawn.

It is particularly regrettable that, by focusing on the ICJ and ECtHR alone, an author such as Djeffal does not discuss territorial decisions decided by distinguished arbitral panels that have a direct bearing on the problem of inter-temporal linguistics. Of these, the *La Bretagne* arbitration decided in 1986 and the *Guinea-Bissau/Senegal* arbitration decided in 1989 are particularly important for an analysis of the Problem, as they present applications of the static and dynamic approaches to the facts and also explicit views of the Problem that differ according to the inclinations of the individual judge and the term being interpreted.[25] Equally, by focusing on recent ICJ case law, authors such as Helmersen and Djeffal consider the static approach's flag to be flown by a group of cases that ultimately constitute only very weak authorities for that position, including a judgment which interpreted an old award rather than a treaty[26] and two judgments which barely referred to the approach and only used it to uncontroversially determine the parties to have been referring to, respectively, the same thing in two authentic languages[27] and a static geographical border point.[28] If these authors had instead opened up their enquiries to, for example, the case law of arbitral tribunals adjudicating disputes under investment treaties, they would have had access to much fuller statements of the static approach, including the assertion and use of the principle of contemporaneity to interpret the term 'treatment' in the *Daimler* and *ICS* awards of 2012.[29]

[24] Julian Wyatt, 'An Original or Modern-Day Meaning for Treaty Terms? The Problem of Inter-temporal Linguistics in the Case Law of International Courts and Tribunals' (Doctorat en droit, University of Geneva, 2017) 401–510 – archive-ouverte.unige.ch/unige:102376 (chs 10 and 11).

[25] *Filleting within the Gulf of St Lawrence between Canada and France ('La Bretagne')*, Award (1986) XIX RIAA/RSA 225; *Case concerning the delimitation of maritime boundary between Guinea-Bissau and Senegal*, Decision of 31 July 1989 (1989) XX RIAA/RSA 119.

[26] *Boundary dispute between Argentina and Chile concerning the frontier line between boundary post 62 and Mount Fitzroy ('Laguna del Desierto')*, Award (1994) XXII RIAA/RSA 3.

[27] *Kasikili/Sedudu Island (Botswana/ Namibia), Judgment* [1999] International Court of Justice 98, ICJ Reports 1045 (on Thalweg).

[28] *Land and Maritime Boundary between Cameroon and Nigeria (Cameroon v Nigeria: Equatorial Guinea intervening)* (Merits), Judgment [2002] ICJ Reports 303.

[29] *Daimler Financial Services AG v Argentina* (Jurisdiction), Award (ICSID Tribunal, ARB/05/1, 22 August 2012) 90 (§ 220); see also almost identical terms in *ICS Inspection and Control Services Limited v Argentina* (Jurisdiction), Award (Permanent Court of Arbitration Tribunal, PCA Case No 2010-9, 10 February 2012) 96 (§ 289).

One should accordingly be careful not to extrapolate from studies that restrict their analysis to specific courts and certain types of treaties a general view regarding the state of the authorities on the problem of intertemporal linguistics.

By focusing on a narrower question than other studies in this area, the research endeavour giving rise to this book made a wider-ranging review of international case law manageable. When it is defined rigorously, the problem of intertemporal linguistics only arises in a small number of international cases, significantly fewer cases than the number mentioning evolutionary treaty interpretation and other doctrines associated with the Problem. This permitted the author to conduct a thoroughgoing comparative analysis of the case law of a number of different international courts and tribunals that covered the vast majority of the international case law[30] touching on the problem of intertemporal linguistics.[31]

The fruits of that analysis were manifold. It revealed interesting divergences between the different branches of the increasingly complex and specialised international dispute settlement system, including contrasting approaches to the interpretation across time for different types of treaties in different types of fact situations. It also uncovered the full quota of generally applicable insights regarding how to solve the problem of intertemporal linguistics – irrespective of which international court or tribunal they emanated from. This wider range of insights and divergences was then used to fortify the conclusions drawn in Part III of this book, particularly chapter 9's efforts to identify a default position on the Problem in different situations. For the purposes of this chapter, however, it suffices to note that the review conducted had the benefit of revealing the popular view that contemporary international courts and tribunals generally favour the dynamic approach to the problem of intertemporal linguistics to be a misconception based largely on an inherently skewed survey of the case law.

C. Cases Referring to the Evolutionary Interpretation Doctrine Instead of Cases Addressing the Problem

Third, even where the focus on the evolutionary interpretation doctrine does not prevent contemporary international lawyers from surveying an area of

[30] By 'international case law', the author is referring to the case law of truly international courts and tribunals. An analysis of the case law of domestic courts and tribunals raising the Problem would have either been too focused on one system to be representative of international practice or so unwieldy that it would have undermined the study's corollary quest for insights into the international adjudicatory function. By 'international courts and tribunals', the author is referring to all third-party dispute settlement mechanisms that exist outside of the apparatus of any one State, hear disputes involving States as at least one of the parties in each dispute, and consider issues and rules of international – rather than internal – law. This stipulation excludes courts such as the Judicial Committee of the Privy Council and the Court of Justice of the European Communities from the scope of the analysis, because the bulk of the work of those supranational courts involves the hearing of appeals, including between non-State parties, on matters of domestic law that have come up from the judicial systems of, respectively, certain Commonwealth and certain European States.

[31] See Wyatt (n 24) 53–138, 401–642.

international case law relevant to the Problem, this focus still regularly prompts them to pay substantially lesser attention to decisions that do not mention the doctrine. By filtering the case law according to whether it refers to the doctrine, the bulk of the commentary relevant to the Problem effectively filters out many of the cases and statements that, because they advocate the static approach, do not mention the doctrine. Such in-built selectivity in turn tips the balance of the authorities towards observing a preference for the dynamic approach.

In one of the few books looking specifically at the interpretation of treaties through time in a particular sub-field of international law, Eva Greschek's 2012 *Die evolutive Auslegung voelkerrechtlicher Vertraege am Beispiel des GATT*,[32] a focus on cases referring to the evolutionary interpretation doctrine by name is the most reasonable explanation for the author's failure to mention the *EC – Chicken Cuts* dispute, a case in which the panel report dealt extensively with the problem of intertemporal linguistics and took a manifestly static approach to it.[33] Greschek is not alone in her neglect of this decision. The vast majority of the case law and literature referring to how the WTO adjudicatory bodies interpret the covered agreements through time only mentions the supposedly dynamic *US – Shrimp* and *China – AV Products* authorities and also ignores the *EC – Chicken Cuts* dispute. Obviously, no conclusion regarding the WTO bodies' position on the Problem can safely be drawn on the basis of a text that discusses only the reports that take a dynamic approach to it and ignores a detailed statement and application of the static approach.

One should equally avoid drawing any general conclusions from scholarly contributions so dedicated to locating the judicial support for the doctrine that they fail to mention the decisions and opinions asking for limits to be placed on its use. Malgosia Fitzmaurice's 2010 book chapter on 'Dynamic (Evolutive) Interpretation of Treaties and the European Court of Human Rights',[34] for example, neglects to engage with the concern expressed about the overreach of evolutionary interpretation in the *Johnston*,[35] *Pretty*[36] and *Khamidov*[37] cases handed down before the publication of her otherwise quite comprehensive article. Those decisions, along with the more recent but still much-neglected

[32] Eva Greschek, *Die evolutive Auslegung voelkerrechtlicher Vertraege am Beispiel des GATT* (Frankfurt, Peter Lang, 2012).

[33] *European Communities – Customs Classification of Frozen Boneless Chicken Cuts*, Report (WTO Panel, WT/DS269/R WT/DS286/R, 30 May 2005); *European Communities – Customs Classification of Frozen Boneless Chicken Cuts*, Report (WTO Appellate Body, WT/DS269/AB/R WT/DS286/AB/R, 12 September 2005), see further s 6.II.C below.

[34] Malgosia Fitzmaurice, 'Dynamic (Evolutive) Interpretation of Treaties and the European Court of Human Rights' in Alexander Orakhelashvili and Sarah Williams (eds), *40 Years of the Vienna Convention on the Law of Treaties* (London, British Institute of International and Comparative Law, 2010).

[35] *Johnston and Others v Ireland* (Merits and Just Satisfaction), Judgment (European Court of Human Rights (Plenary), 9697/82, 18 December 1986).

[36] *Pretty*, Judgment (n 19).

[37] *Khamidov*, Judgment (n 19).

seven-judge *X & Others* dissenting opinion,[38] are undoubtedly helpful for determining the precise scope and modalities of the dynamic approach at the ECtHR.

Among contemporary texts on evolutionary treaty interpretation in general, a precious few commendably refer to cases endorsing the competing static approach. However, because their focus nonetheless remained trained on evolutionary interpretation cases, they give the static interpretation cases short shrift, especially when the respect afforded to them is juxtaposed against that which is afforded to the dynamic interpretation cases. The admirable 2013 article of Helmersen, for example, contains one short paragraph noting that '[t]here are examples of tribunals using explicitly static interpretations' and citing three decisions, before returning to a more detailed analysis of a much larger number of cases explicitly stating the evolutionary approach.[39]

Bjorge's treatment of the main authorities for 'contemporaneous interpretation' in a two-page section of his enormously valuable 2014 book on *The Evolutionary Interpretation of Treaties* presents a further example of this phenomenon. While his study has the merit of even referring to the main two pre-VCLT authorities for the static approach, he does not try to fit them into his theory apparently advocating a general use of an evolutionary or dynamic approach, but instead dismisses them quite summarily. The *North Atlantic Coast Fisheries* arbitration is dismissed on the basis that a static approach was 'only natural' where the 'provisions in issue' were 'concerned with the distribution or grant of territorial rights',[40] even though the provision being interpreted was not concerned with the distribution or grant of *in rem* territorial rights but rather with *in personam* fishery rights.[41] Bjorge also accords the ICJ's *Rights of US Nationals* less 'authority [than] more recent pronouncements' simply because 'the heavy US political and economic interests involved [in the case] had made the International Court's job in the case a particularly difficult one'.[42] Yet, even if this were a valid criterion for dismissing a case as an authority, it would also need to be applied to politically-charged and difficult cases advocating the dynamic approach, notably including what was one of the ICJ's most politically sensitive cases, the *Namibia* advisory proceedings upon which Bjorge and all authors advocating evolutionary interpretation doctrine heavily rely. Bjorge's focus on building a structure to support the use of evolutionary interpretation as it is broadly defined also causes him to cite interpretation cases that actually contain some support for the diametrically opposed approach to the Problem, without referring to their important statements of the static approach. For example, he cites paragraph 85 of the *Guinea-Bissau/ Senegal* award in the context of separate points about the importance of intention in the interpretation

[38] *X & Others*, Joint Partly Dissenting Opinion (n 19).

[39] Helmersen (n 13) 132–33.

[40] Bjorge (n 7) 125.

[41] See *The North Atlantic Coast Fisheries Case (Great Britain/United States)*, Award (1910) XI RIAA/RSA 167.

[42] Bjorge (n 7) 123 (footnotes omitted).

of treaties and the intertemporal law doctrine, without ever referring to its important – and partially static – statements in relation to the problem of intertemporal linguistics.[43] His treatment of the 2012 *Daimler v Argentina* award is similar. Section VI.C.3.c of that award contains a prominent statement and relatively detailed application of the principle of contemporaneity,[44] but Bjorge's book only quotes a different part of it in support of a subsidiary point he makes about treaties as expressions of consent.[45]

These observations regarding the favouring of dynamic over static authorities are not provided as criticisms of the above-mentioned authors; such cursory treatment of judicial statements and international cases favouring a static approach is perfectly understandable for articles and books dedicated to evolutionary treaty interpretation. Instead, they are provided to show how we should be careful to draw conclusions about the state of the authorities on the problem of intertemporal linguistics from texts which, by focusing on the evolutionary interpretation doctrine, provide an overview of the recent cases that is inherently slanted towards those favouring a dynamic approach.

At a time when discussion of the case law in relation to the Problem is dominated by studies of the evolutionary interpretation doctrine, the popular view that the dynamic approach to the Problem has prevailed is inevitably based largely on these studies' necessarily skewed selection of the relevant authorities and, particularly, the most quotable statements within them. A wider and less skewed survey of the authorities reveals even the explicit statements made in relation to the Problem by adjudicators in different international courts and tribunals to be more finely balanced between the static and dynamic approaches than commonly thought.

In courts and tribunals of general jurisdiction, the famously dynamic statements in the *Aegean Sea*, *Gabčíkovo* and *Related Rights* judgments are largely counteracted by oft-ignored statements endorsing a *static* approach in the *Young Loan* award,[46] certain parts of the *La Bretagne* award,[47] in one of the two interpretations carried out by the *Guinea-Bissau/Senegal* tribunal,[48] in the *Jan Mayen* judgment,[49] in Judge Bedjaoui's very sophisticated *Gabčíkovo* separate opinion,[50] in the *Eritrea/Ethiopia Border Delimitation*[51] and, albeit in relation to

[43] *Guinea-Bissau/Senegal*, Award (n 25) 151 (§ 85).

[44] *Daimler*, Award (n 29) 88–92 (§§ 217–24).

[45] Bjorge (n 7) 56–57.

[46] *Belgium, France, Switzerland, UK and USA v Germany ('Young Loan Arbitration')*, Award (1980) XIX RIAA/RSA 67, 93–94 (§ 19).

[47] *La Bretagne*, Award (n 25) 247, 251–52 (§§ 37, 43).

[48] *Guinea-Bissau/Senegal*, Award (n 25) 151 (§ 85) (Tribunal's references omitted).

[49] *Maritime Delimitation in the Area between Greenland and Jan Mayen (Denmark v Norway)*, Judgment [1993] ICJ Reports 38, 50–51 (§ 27).

[50] *Gabčíkovo-Nagymaros Project (Hungary/Slovakia)*, Separate Opinion of Judge Bedjaoui [1997] ICJ Reports 120, 123 (§§ 13–14) (Judge Bedjaoui's emphasis).

[51] *Decision regarding delimitation of the border between Eritrea and Ethiopia*, Decision of 13 April 2002 (2002) XXV RIAA/RSA 83, 110 (§ 3.5).

the interpretation of an award rather than a treaty, in both the award and erudite Galindo Pohl dissenting opinion handed down in the *Laguna del Desierto* case.[52]

At the WTO, the seminal statements of the evolutionary approach made in the *US – Shrimp* report,[53] together with the apparent confirmation of this approach for the purposes of GATS schedules in the *China – AV Products* report,[54] are partially counteracted by the widely-ignored but tremendously detailed and quite cogent statement of the need to use a static approach in the *EC – Chicken Cuts* panel report.[55]

In the field of investment law often neglected by the literature on treaty interpretation, the most prominent statements made in relation to the problem of intertemporal linguistics actually advocate a static approach, with panels presided over by the distinguished general international lawyer Pierre-Marie Dupuy expressly favouring 'the classical rule of interpretation known as the principle of contemporaneity'.[56] Statements of the dynamic approach are also present, including in the *Mondev* award,[57] as well as the *ADF* and *Waste Management* awards that followed it,[58] but the general recognition of the applicability of the principle of contemporaneity, particularly in cases raising the MFN-DR issue since *Daimler* and *ICS*,[59] militates against any finding that a dynamic approach to the Problem prevails in the recent case law of investment tribunals.

Ultimately, even at the superficial level of judicial statements made in relation to the Problem, the view that international courts and tribunals now generally favour the dynamic approach cannot be sustained – at least not without the skewed perspective lent by a discernible focus on the case law relevant to the evolutionary interpretation doctrine. As will now be seen, that view becomes even less defensible when one considers those statements in their context.

[52] *Laguna del Desierto*, Award (n 26) 42–43 (§§ 127–30); *Boundary dispute between Argentina and Chile concerning the frontier line between boundary post 62 and Mount Fitzroy ('Laguna del Desierto')*, Dissenting Opinion of Reynaldo Galindo Pohl (1994) XXII RIAA/RSA 53, 56 (§§ 9–11).

[53] *US – Shrimp*, WTO AB Report (n 9) 48–50 (§§ 129–31).

[54] *China – AV Products*, WTO AB Report (n 10) 161 (§§ 396–397).

[55] *EC – Chicken Cuts (Panel)* (n 33) 41–42 (§ 7.99 including fn 144).

[56] *Daimler*, Award (n 29) 90, 110 (§§ 220, 264); see also almost identical terms in *ICS*, Award (n 29) 96, 107 (§§ 289, 317).

[57] *Mondev International Ltd v United States of America*, Award (ICSID(AF) Tribunal constituted under NAFTA Chapter 11, ARB(AF)/99/2, 11 October 2002) 43 (§ 123).

[58] *ADF Group Inc v United States of America*, Award (ICSID(AF) Tribunal constituted under NAFTA Chapter 11, ARB(AF)/00/1, 9 January 2003) 277 (§ 179). *Waste Management Inc v Mexico*, Award (ICSID(AF) Tribunal constituted under NAFTA Chapter 11, ARB(AF)/00/3, 30 April 2004) 32 (§ 92).

[59] The issue of whether most-favoured nation ('MFN') clause(s) can be applied to an investment treaty's provision(s) on dispute resolution ('DR'). See, eg *Philip Morris Brands Sàrl, Philip Morris Products SA and ABAL Hermanos SA v Uruguay*, Decision on Jurisdiction (ICSID Tribunal, ARB/10/7, 2 July 2013) 28 (§ 90); *Kiliç İnşaat İthalat İhracat Sanayi ve Ticaret Anonim Şirketiv Turkmenistan*, Award (ICSID Tribunal, ARB/10/01, 2 July 2013) 28–30 (§§ 3.3.27–3.3.33); *Garanti Koza LLP v Turkmenistan*, Decision on the Objection to Jurisdiction for Lack of Consent (ICSID Tribunal, ARB/11/20, 3 July 2013) 27 (§§ 55–56).

II. SEEN IN THEIR DECISIONAL CONTEXTS, THE AUTHORITIES FOR THE VIEW DO NOT ADEQUATELY SUPPORT IT

The view asserting that contemporary international courts and tribunals now generally take a dynamic approach to problems of intertemporal linguistics is supported primarily by weighty judicial statements apparently advocating the dynamic approach. Of course, that material does indeed support the conclusion that, in the abstract, international courts prefer the dynamic approach. Yet, it does not prove that they actually take a dynamic approach in concrete situations raising the problem of intertemporal linguistics.

Even if modern-day international courts and tribunals had universally stated an abstract preference from the dynamic approach, they would not have solved the Problem. International courts and tribunals would only solve the problem by developing and consolidating the use of a method that can be generally applied to a situation in which the meaning of a contested treaty term has relevantly changed between the time of the treaty's conclusion and the time of its application. Of course, the consistent adoption of a treaty term's later-emerging meaning over its different original meaning – the dynamic approach – would constitute such a method that, if established, would indeed solve the Problem. However, when they are analysed in their full context, even decisions vehemently advocating the dynamic approach are revealed not to have ended up applying it. In other words, when we focus less on what contemporary international courts and tribunals *say* in relation to the Problem and more on what they actually *do* when they come face-to-face with it, the picture becomes incredibly mixed,[60] so the view that those courts and tribunals now routinely favour the dynamic approach must be discarded.

A. The Problem with Relying on Judicial Statements Alone

While it may seem ironic in a study of treaty interpretation to have to remind ourselves that the meaning and scope of a statement can only properly be appreciated in its context, we must attempt to counteract the tendency to isolate statements advocating a particular approach from the factual and decisional circumstances in which they were made. The taking of judicial statements out of context is regrettably not only a feature of the case law and scholarship relating to the temporal issues of treaty interpretation, but across the field of international law in general. It is, moreover, not merely a recent phenomenon, Sir Robert Jennings noting already in 1987 that:

> The tendency all too often, of both writers and of courts, is to cite isolated passages from judgments, with little or no attempt to qualify their meaning in relation to the

[60] See Wyatt (n 24) 53–138, 401–642.

> submissions and arguments of the parties, or to the facts of the particular case, or to the context of the entire judgment in which the passage occurs. By such use of selected citations from decisions, almost any proposition can be given the appearance of being vested with judicial authority.[61]

The proposition that contemporary international courts and tribunals have solved the problem of intertemporal linguistics by providing a dynamic answer to it might appear well supported by isolated passages from their judgments, but finds no basis in their actual practice. Indeed, when carefully analysed in their context, most of the statements of the dynamic approach in fact provide scant authority for the proposition that an interpreter should always use a treaty term's later-emerging meaning instead of its relevantly different original meaning.

An understanding of the decisional context of a judicial statement can impact on the weight of the authority it lends to the dynamic approach in several different ways.

First, an analysis of this context might reveal what are likely to be the adjudicator's true reasons for the finding made or personal understanding of the rules and principles cited. Through a study of how adjudicators applied the rules they stated to the facts, we can uncover exactly what they understand the rule to entail. For example, the context might reveal a decision that prominently endorses the evolutionary interpretation doctrine not to have assigned any particular meaning to a treaty term, but to have reached a modern, fair and socially progressive outcome. In such a situation, we will be able to conclude that the adjudicators were invoking the broad variant of the evolutionary interpretation doctrine, not the narrow variant which is relevant to the problem of intertemporal linguistics. We have, after all, already used context to identify many decisions of this kind in prior chapters of this book.

Second, the context may reveal that the court or tribunal ultimately decided the relevant issue by applying a legal rule or principle other than the dynamic approach that it stated. By way of example, an international tribunal might purport to use dynamic approach to follow the evolution of a treaty, but ultimately end up simply applying external and more recent law on the basis of a treaty provision that makes that law directly applicable.[62] Such non-application

[61] Robert Jennings, 'The Judicial Function and the Rule of Law in International Relations' in *Le droit international à l'heure de sa codification: études en l'honneur de Roberto Ago*, vol III (Milan, Giuffre, 1987) 143.

[62] See, eg the series of IACtHR judgments which refer to the need to interpret the American Convention evolutionarily, yet ultimately reach their findings not by acknowledging a change in the meaning of any treaty term, but instead by using its Art 29(b) to effectively apply external human rights laws of the State party directly (*Case of the Yakye Axa Indigenous Community v Paraguay* (Merits, Reparations and Costs), Judgment [2005] Inter-Am Ct HR (Ser C) No 125; *Case of the Mayagna (Sumo) Awas Tingni Community v Nicaragua* (Merits, Reparations and Costs), Judgment [2001] Inter-Am Ct HR Series C No 79; *Case of the Ituango Massacres v Colombia* (Preliminary Objections, Merits, Reparations and Costs), Judgment [2006] Inter-Am Ct HR (Ser C) No 148); see also American Convention on Human Rights ('Pact of San José, Costa Rica') 1969 (1144 UNTS 123) 153, art 29(b).

impacts on the weight of the relevant judicial statement because an international adjudicator who makes a statement of principle then applies it to the facts to produce a finding in favour of one or other party has likely thought through the merits, mechanics and implications of that principle. By contrast, an adjudicator who states a principle without applying it, or in a fact situation where it could never have had any substantive effect on the rights and duties of the parties, has likely thought less deeply about whether and when an application of the principle is justified.

One might argue that, in the system of public international law, the existence of a short statement that seems to favour a dynamic approach to the Problem is enough and that any requirement that this statement be backed up by a considered application or reasoned explanation unduly imports common-law-style distinctions between rationes decidendi and obiter dicta. It is true that international law has no formal doctrine of precedent and does not officially observe this distinction;[63] a point made or approach advocated in a decision of an international court or tribunal technically has the same status irrespective of whether it is a ratio decidendi or an obiter dictum, with the latter sometimes even ending up more influential than the former.[64] However, both international law and basic canons of deliberative rhetoric accord greater weight to statements of principle that are then applied to a fact situation than those that are spoken and then left hanging in the wind. The authoritative statement of the sources of international law in the ICJ statute includes as 'subsidiary means for the determination of international law' what it calls 'judicial decisions'.[65] A mere statement of a rule in a judicial context does not equate to a 'judicial decision' in the sense of Article 38 of the ICJ Statute, only a statement of rule accompanied by an application of that rule to a particular situation will have this character. As Abi-Saab noted in his *Hague Course*:

> [T]he judge must establish which general rules are applicable and how they concretely apply to the case at hand. It is this reasoning, the *ratio decidendi*, linking the general rule or objective law by a sort of logical breadcrumb trail to subjective situations, that constitutes the second component of the judicial decision, the *reasons*. It is the reasons that create the precedent, by shedding specific light on the content of the rules in general, beyond the limits of *res judicata* in the particular case.[66]

[63] Statute of the International Court of Justice (annexed to the Charter of the United Nations) 1945, art 59; see also Alain Pellet, 'Article 38' in Andreas Zimmermann, Christian Tomuschat and Karin Oellers-Frahm (eds), *The Statute of the International Court of Justice: A Commentary* (Oxford, Oxford University Press, 2006) 784–90.

[64] See, eg Gernot Biehler, *Procedures in International Law* 1st edn (Berlin, Springer, 2008) 285.

[65] ICJ Statute, art 38(1)(d).

[66] Georges Abi-Saab, *Cours général de droit international public* (The Hague, Martinus Nijhoff, 1996) 129 (Abi-Saab's emphasis, present author's translation of: '[L]e juge doit établir quelles sont les règles générales applicables et comment elles s'appliquent concrètement en l'espèce. C'est ce raisonnement, la *ratio decidendi,* reliant la règle générale, ou le droit objectif, par une sorte de fil d'Ariane logique, aux situations subjectives, qui constitue la seconde composante de la décision judiciaire, les *motifs*. Ce sont les motifs qui créent le précédent, en apportant un éclairage particulier sur la teneur des règles en général, au-delà des limites de la *res judicata* en l'espèce.')

In many of the cases cited in support of the putatively predominant dynamic approach, the international adjudicator has stated that approach as a rule, but, by failing to apply it to a fact situation, has not arrived at a 'judicial decision'. Such incomplete judicial acts are not capable of creating international legal precedent or providing important insight into the specific content of the rule. At best, they possess the status of arguments made by well-regarded scholars of international law. Yet scholarly arguments are only as weighty as they are persuasive and great persuasiveness will rarely be achieved by short and undeveloped statements of principle. In practice, only a very clear and systematic explanation of a mere statement of principle will rival the persuasiveness of decision that not only states the approach, but also clearly and methodically applies it to the real-world facts.[67] This basic fact of (deliberative) rhetoric is finding ever greater acceptance in the field of international law, both through the increasing use of the case-based method of teaching that is already highly prevalent in common law jurisdictions and through the case-based approach to proving the state of international law used by influential instruments such as the commentaries to the seminal 2001 Articles to State Responsibility[68] and the WTO Analytical Index.[69] Statements of the legal rules applied to facts as part of judicial decisions are clearly more capable of supporting a view on the state of the authorities on the Problem than mere statements of principle.

Third, an analysis of the context of the relevant judicial statement might reveal that, while the interpretative approach contributed to the interpretative finding made, it still did not constitute an instance of the dynamic approach being applied. By way of example, an international tribunal might purport to use the dynamic approach to follow the changes in the meaning of a generic treaty term, but ultimately arrive at an interpretation of that term that is congruent with not only its meaning at the time of the treaty's application, but also its meaning at the time of its conclusion.[70] In such a case, the dynamic approach has not actually been applied any more than the static approach has been, so the adjudicatory decision made cannot be used as a basis for the view that the relevant tribunal – or even the specific decision-makers for that particular case – will generally apply the dynamic approach to problems of intertemporal linguistics.

The definition work done in chapter 4 of this book leaves us very well placed for identifying such interpretations that appear prima facie to be dynamic, but are in fact not instances of the dynamic approach. As will be seen, many of the interpretations apparently advocating a dynamic approach interpret treaty terms that do not meet what we have labelled the 'common condition' for static and dynamic approaches to the Problem, because there is no difference between

[67] See, eg Pellet (n 63) 789 (§ 316).

[68] 'Articles on Responsibility of States for Internationally Wrongful Acts with commentaries' in International Law Commission, 'Yearbook 2001, vol II, pt 2' (New York, United Nations, 2001).

[69] World Trade Organization, *WTO Analytical Index: Guide to WTO Law and Practice* (Cambridge, Cambridge University Press, 2012).

[70] See, eg *China – AV Products*, WTO AB Report (n 10).

treaty term's semantic content at the time of the treaty's conclusion and at the time of the treaty fell to be applied.

International decisions advocating the evolutionary approach may also fall foul of the specific condition for a dynamic approach to the Problem by failing to give the interpreted treaty term a semantic-pragmatic content congruent with its semantic content at the time of application, even where the term has undergone semantic change. The *La Bretagne* award quite frequently cited as an instance of the evolutionary approach to treaty interpretation constitutes an example of this substantially rarer phenomenon.[71] The scope of what was meant by the treaty term 'fishery regulations' had likely changed between the 1972 treaty's time of conclusion and the time of its application in 1985. The tribunal was, moreover, keen to incorporate those changes into its interpretative endeavour.[72] Yet the tribunal ultimately arrived at an interpretation of the term that, by excluding the on-board filleting of fish from the scope of 'fishery regulations',[73] was actually more congruent with the original semantic content of the contested treaty term.

Fourth, in our specific context inherently involving changes in the meaning of a treaty term, the probative value of the static or dynamic approach to the Problem will be affected by the extent of the relevant meaning change, something that can only be determined by carefully analysing how the interpretative issue was dealt with in its full context. For example, an overtly static statement in relation to an interpretation ultimately preferring the meaning that a treaty term had at the time of its conclusion to the very similar meaning that it had at a time just before the treaty's conclusion,[74] is clearly not as probative of the desirability of the static approach to the Problem as the same kind of statement made in relation to an interpretation ultimately preferring a treaty term's meaning at the time of the treaty's conclusion over its very different meaning at the much later time of its application.[75]

Ultimately, judicial statements advocating the dynamic approach to problems of intertemporal linguistics do not themselves suffice to substantiate the view that contemporary international courts and tribunals have given the Problem a firmly dynamic answer. If they were accompanied by applications of the principle that adjudicated between the parties' interests by preferring a treaty term's later-emerging meaning over its quite different original meaning, then they would adequately support this widely held view. However, as will now be seen,

[71] See, eg Joost Pauwelyn, 'The Nature of WTO Obligations' (2002) 1 *Jean Monnet Working Papers* 1, 32.

[72] *La Bretagne*, Award (n 25) 247 (§ 37).

[73] ibid 251–52 (§ 43).

[74] See, eg *Affaire des boutres de Mascate (France/Grande-Bretagne)*, Award (1905) XI RIAA/RSA 83, 94; *EC – Chicken Cuts (Panel)* (n 33) 40–43 (§§ 7.95–7.103).

[75] See, eg *Case concerning Rights of Nationals of the United States of America in Morocco (France v United States of America)*, Judgment [1952] ICJ Reports 176.

very few of the cases invoked to support the use of the dynamic approach to the Problem actually even applied it.

B. The ICJ Cases Regularly Quoted do not Apply the Dynamic Approach

For most international lawyers, the cases decided by international courts and tribunals of general jurisdiction will be the most important for determining the prevailing approach to the Problem among modern-day international adjudicators.

The general international law cases from the post-1971 period are usually considered to offer significant support for the evolutionary interpretation doctrine and a dynamic approach to the problem of intertemporal linguistics, with the case law and scholarship relying particularly heavily on statements made by the ICJ in three post-*Namibia* judgments, namely those handed down in the *Aegean Sea*, *Gabčíkovo-Nagymaros* and *Related Rights* cases. Yet none of these cases constitutes a clear instance of the dynamic approach being applied to resolve an interpretative dispute.

i. Aegean Sea Continental Shelf (Greece v Turkey) *(ICJ – 1978)*

There is a popular conception that the Court in the *Aegean Sea* case was called upon merely to interpret the term 'territorial status', interpreted it dynamically to include the continental shelf and therefore found that it did not have jurisdiction over Greece's claim.[76] This assessment of the judgment tallies nicely with the judicial statements clearly advocating a dynamic approach in its paragraphs 77 and 80. However, the interpretative issue in the *Aegean Sea* case did not centre around the meaning of 'territorial status', but rather of 'disputes relating to the territorial status of Greece' and the Court reached its finding on the reservation through a broad interpretation of 'relating to', not a dynamic interpretation of 'territorial status'. Indeed, in the very first paragraph in which the Court embarks upon the application of its interpretation to the facts of the case, the paragraph immediately following the Court's statement that the treaty expression '"disputes relating to the territorial status of Greece" must be interpreted in accordance with the rules of international law as they exist today and not as they existed in 1931',[77] the judgment reminds readers that:

> The question is not, as Greece seems to assume, whether continental shelf rights are territorial rights or are comprised within the expression 'territorial status'. The real

[76] See, eg International Law Commission and Georg Nolte, 'Introductory Report for the Study Group on Treaties over Time: Jurisprudence of the International Court of Justice and arbitral tribunals of ad hoc jurisdiction relating to subsequent agreements and subsequent practice' in Georg Nolte (ed), *Treaties and Subsequent Practice* (Oxford, Oxford University Press, 2013) 199.

[77] *Aegean Sea*, Judgment (n 4) 33–34 (§ 80).

> question for decision is, whether the dispute is one which *relates* to the territorial status of Greece.[78]

Once the Court had equated 'relating to' with 'not entirely extraneous to',[79] Greece had little chance of placing a dispute regarding sovereign rights over the continental shelf abutting its territory outside the scope of the reservation that had been invoked against it. A dynamic interpretation of 'territorial status' was accordingly unnecessary for reaching the findings on the interpretative issue in relation to which it was invoked. Indeed, it seems that even if the meaning of 'territorial status' had, pursuant to the static and restrictive interpretation advanced by Greece, been restricted to matters regarding who had sovereignty over what *land*, then the continental shelf claim would still have been related to it under the Court's wide interpretation of 'relating to'.

There was, in any event, considerable evidence that, between the time of Greece's 1931 reservation to the General Act and the 1978 application of it in the *Aegean Sea* case, the meaning of 'territorial status' had not expanded sufficiently to include matters relating to the continental shelf – Judge ad hoc Stassinopoulos and Judge de Castro even used modern authorities to make this point in their dissenting opinions.[80] It is accordingly likely that a dynamic interpretation of the treaty term at issue was not only unnecessary for, but also incapable of affecting the outcome of this part of the dispute.

The *Aegean Sea* judgment's support for the dynamic approach was accordingly mere obiter dicta. Given that it was made without any implication for the issue of the case and indeed never applied to the facts before the Court, one must be careful not to lean too heavily on it as an authority for how the ICJ – and international courts and tribunals in general – in fact respond to the problem of intertemporal linguistics.

ii. Gabčíkovo-Nagymaros Project (Hungary/Slovakia) *(ICJ – 1997)*

The fact that several international lawyers have cited the *Gabčíkovo-Nagymaros* case as an authority for the dynamic approach to the Problem[81] illustrates even more clearly international lawyers' tendency to focus on what international courts say about an issue, rather than what they in fact do when confronted by it. All of the famous judgment itself, two lengthy separate opinions and a dissenting opinion refer to evolutionary interpretation and insist upon the relevance of international environmental law norms and principles that emerged after the

[78] ibid 34 (§ 81) (the Court's emphasis).
[79] ibid 35 (§§ 82–84).
[80] *Aegean Sea Continental Shelf (Greece v Turkey)*, Dissenting Opinion of Judge de Castro [1978] ICJ Reports 62; *Aegean Sea Continental Shelf (Greece v Turkey)*, Dissenting Opinion of Judge ad hoc Stassinopoulos [1978] ICJ Reports 72.
[81] See, eg Duncan French, 'Treaty Interpretation and the Incorporation of Extraneous Legal Rules' (2006) 55 *International and Comparative Law Quarterly* 281, 296; Martin Dawidowicz, 'The Effect of the Passage of Time on the Interpretation of Treaties: Some Reflections on Costa Rica v. Nicaragua' (2011) 24 *Leiden Journal of International Law* 201, 219; Helmersen (n 13) 132.

conclusion of the 1977 treaty being interpreted and applied. Yet none of these four judicial opinions ever engages in an interpretative act that takes a position on the Problem.[82]

In the section of the judgment introducing what has since been considered by many to be a dynamic approach to the interpretation of the 1977 Treaty, the Court did not focus on, or even mention, the *interpretation* of the 1977 Treaty at all, but instead its *implementation* and *application*. Indeed, it is clear from its specific comment that such norms are 'relevant for the implementation of the Treaty',[83] that the Court did not consider itself to be conducting a properly interpretative enterprise when integrating norms of environmental law into the treaty. The Court stated that it is 'through the *application* of Articles 15, 19 and 20' that these norms were 'incorporate[d]' 'by agreement'.[84] The Court's characterising of Articles 15, 19 and 20 as 'evolving provisions'[85] is quite misleading, because there is little scope for semantic change in 'shall ensure ... that the quality of the water in the Danube is not impaired' (Article 15) or 'shall ... ensure compliance with the obligations for the protection of nature' (Article 19).[86] Unless one uses an overly extensional understanding of meaning, these two commitments meant the same thing in 1977 as they did in 1997, namely 'we won't do anything that makes the water worse' and 'anything that we must legally do to protect the environment, we should make sure we do that when building these installations'. As Judge Bedjaoui pointed out in his separate opinion, the *means* of protecting nature or the environment might have changed over time, but the provisions did not refer to the means and the meaning of the words 'nature' and the 'environment' did not change over time.[87] The provisions relied upon to invoke post-treaty environmental norms were not interpreted dynamically, but instead applied in the forward-looking manner in which they were intended. Rather than recognising semantic change, the *Gabčíkovo* Court consistently described a situation in which it was presented with treaty provisions that had a known semantic content, but whose application called for – and thereby incorporated – norms external to the treaty.

In addition, the Court only ever held the environmental concerns to be relevant in the *prescriptive* rather than declaratory parts of its judgment that, rather than making legal findings, merely implored the parties to take the action the Court considered that they ought to take.[88] Following its famous statement of

[82] The separate and dissenting opinions either refer to evolutionary interpretation in a manner that understands it in its broad form reflecting a doctrine of progressive adjudication or in a manner which understands it as following explicit references in the treaty to external norms of customary international law.

[83] *Gabčíkovo-Nagymaros*, Judgment (n 5) 67–68 (§ 112).

[84] ibid 67 (§ 112).

[85] ibid (§ 112).

[86] Treaty between the Hungarian People's Republic and the Czechoslovak Socialist Republic concerning the Construction and Operation of the Gabčíkovo – Nagymaros System of Locks 1977.

[87] *Gabčíkovo-Nagymaros*, Bedjaoui Separate Opinion (n 50) 123 (§§ 10–11).

[88] See especially *Gabčíkovo-Nagymaros*, Judgment (n 5) 67–68, 77–78 (§§ 112, 140–41).

the relevance of the 'concept of sustainable development',[89] the Court did not interpret a term of the 1977 Treaty in light of this concept, but merely stated that:

> It is for the Parties themselves to find an agreed solution that takes account of the objectives of the Treaty, which must be pursued in a joint and integrated way, as well as the norms of international environmental law and the principles of the law of international watercourses.[90]

As Dupuy has pointed out, by merely suggesting compliance with more recent environmental law, the *Gabčíkovo* judgment did not impose that post-treaty law on the parties.[91] The surprising decision not to read the new-found environmental obligations into the treaty even had implications for the outcome of the underlying case, Judge Herczegh's dissenting opinion bemoaning the fact that the Court's failure to regard them as substantive law prevented Hungary from claiming their violation as a ground for its termination of the treaty.[92]

Together these two contextual features of the *Gabčíkovo* judgment reveal just how deferential the judges were to the original concrete intentions of the parties, a consideration more readily associated with a static than a dynamic approach to the Problem. Even in a situation where the parties had themselves called for the application of later-emerging environmental law, the Court still chose not to officially require them to abide by it. There can be little doubt that, in the light of the treaty provisions almost explicitly calling for the application of later environmental norms and the majority's decision to only include those norms in a set of suggestions rather than its findings, the *Gabčíkovo* judgment does not constitute a strong authority for the dynamic approach to the Problem or even an instance of dynamic interpretation at all.

iii. Dispute regarding Navigational and Related Rights (Costa Rica v Nicaragua) *(ICJ – 2009)*

The various documents produced over the course of the *Related Rights* case contain a more sophisticated analysis of how to interpret treaty terms with meanings that change through time than the vast majority of the prior international case law, making the case tremendously valuable for other parts of this study. However, the arguments, opinions and judgment emerging from the case are sufficiently nuanced that attempts to cast them as evidence of the

[89] ibid 78 (§ 140).

[90] ibid 77–78 (§§ 140–41).

[91] Pierre-Marie Dupuy, 'Evolutionary Interpretation of Treaties: Between Memory and Prophecy' in Enzo Cannizzaro (ed), *The Law of Treaties Beyond the Vienna Convention* (Oxford, Oxford University Press, 2011) 129–30.

[92] *Gabčíkovo-Nagymaros Project (Hungary/Slovakia)*, Dissenting Opinion of Judge Herczegh [1997] ICJ Reports 176, 176–79.

consecration of the dynamic approach at international courts and tribunals oversimplifies the matter.

Even the much-quoted dynamic statements of the judgment itself are, when seen in their context, less supportive of the dynamic approach to the Problem than commonly thought. Once again, the dynamic interpretative approach outlined probably did not need to be applied. Article VI of the 1858 Treaty of Limits granted Costa Rica a perpetual right of free navigation over the San Juan river '*con objetos de comercio*',[93] a phrase the Court understood as meaning 'for the purposes of commerce'.[94] However, the context in which this treaty term occurred left the word '*comercio*' underdetermined for the purposes of the issue that the Court had to resolve, namely whether '*navegación … con objetos de comercio*' extended to tourist services on the river.

The vast majority of the many authors picking up on the judgment's lengthy and fertile statement of the problem of intertemporal linguistics and endorsement of a dynamic approach consider that the dynamic approach was applied to the meaning of the word '*comercio*' such that tourist services not included within the scope of the term in 1858 came within the scope of that term when it was applied in 2009. Indeed, early in the relevant section of its judgment, the Court implicitly acknowledged the broadening of this term by rejecting a Nicaraguan interpretation it considered 'based on the assertion that "commerce" should be given the *narrow meaning it had when the Treaty was entered into*'.[95] Then, after a review of the authorities on the problem of intertemporal linguistics, the judgment explicitly stated that it was using the dynamic approach in its interpretation of the treaty term, saying: 'Thus, even assuming that the notion of "commerce" does not have the same meaning today as it did in the mid-nineteenth century, it is the present meaning which must be accepted for purposes of applying the Treaty'.[96] Prima facie, this seems to constitute a perfectly valid, almost paradigmatic application of the dynamic approach to what appeared to be a problem of intertemporal linguistics. The Court unanimously found that the transport of tourists came within the scope of the treaty term 'commerce' and therefore awarded Costa Rica the right to provide tourist services. Unlike many other supposed authorities for the dynamic approach, the *Related Rights* judgment clearly decided a part of the issues in dispute between the parties by assigning a certain meaning to a specific treaty term. Moreover, the interpretation to which the dynamic approach was applied was an interpretation in the narrow sense and part of the judgment's 'decision' or ratio decidendi.

However, under the discerning light of the analytic definitions elaborated in chapter 4 of this book, the *Related Rights* judgment's decisive interpretation of

[93] Tratado de Limites entre Nicaragua y Costa Rica (Tratado Cañas – Jerez) 1858; see *Related Rights*, Judgment (n 6) 233–36 (§§ 37, 43–44).

[94] *Related Rights*, Judgment (n 6) 238–40 (§§ 50–56).

[95] ibid 242 (§ 62) (emphasis added).

[96] ibid 244 (§ 70).

the treaty term '*comercio*' does not appear to have actually ended up taking a dynamic approach to a problem of intertemporal linguistics.

While the Court sometimes seems to have thought that the semantic content of '*comercio*' in 1848 differed from its semantic content in 2009, there are many indications that the two did not relevantly differ, so the common condition of our definitions again comes into play. In the *Related Rights* case, the interpretative 'is C a B?' question to be posed of the Hypothetical Original Interpreter was simply: 'are tourist services commerce'? There was little doubt that tourist services ('C') were within the set denoted by the word 'commerce' in 2009 ($C \in B_{t(application)}$), so, for a relevant semantic difference and the Problem to truly arise, tourist services would *not* have fallen within the set denoted by the word 'commerce' in 1858 ($C \notin B_{t(conclusion)}$). Yet there is substantial evidence to suggest, including from both parties' pleadings in the case, that tourist services actually did fall within the scope of 'commerce' back in 1858 ($C \in B_{t(conclusion)}$), including in the relevant region.

This observation is supported by the fact that the party seeking a wider reading of the disputed treaty term, Costa Rica, never relied on a dynamic approach. As noted by the Court, Costa Rica's interpretative position was based largely on dictionary definitions of '*comercio*',[97] with Costa Rica's memorial revealing the cited dictionary to have been published in 1852, a few years prior to the conclusion of the 1858 Treaty.[98] Other important evidence of the broader meaning of '*comercio*' advanced by Costa Rica was also contemporaneous with the 1858 Treaty and therefore put forward as an argument as to the semantic content of the term already at the time of the treaty's conclusion.

Equally, Nicaragua relied much more heavily on temporally neutral arguments that tourism was not '*navegación … con objetos de comercio*' at *any* relevant point in time than it did on a static approach, the Court's somewhat unfair characterisation of its interpretation as based on a narrow original meaning[99] notwithstanding. Indeed, Nicaragua specifically made the claim that tourist services were still not included within the scope of the word '*comercio*' in 2009 in both its Counter-Memorial[100] and the oral submissions of its lead counsel.[101]

[97] ibid 241 (§ 59).

[98] 'Memorial of Costa Rica', *Dispute regarding Navigational and Related Rights (Costa Rica v Nicaragua)* (International Court of Justice, 2006) 67 (§ 4.56).

[99] *Related Rights*, Judgment (n 6) 28 (§ 62).

[100] 'Counter-Memorial of Nicaragua', *Dispute regarding Navigational and Related Rights (Costa Rica v Nicaragua)* (International Court of Justice, 2007) 190 (§ 4.3.19): 'If we apply this reasoning to the case at hand, we will easily reach the conclusion that the reference to commerce in Article VI of the Jerez-Canas Treaty comprised in 1858, and still comprises today, traffic in commodities and not services unrelated to said traffic' – the key words being 'and still comprises today'.

[101] *Dispute regarding Navigational and Related Rights (Costa Rica v Nicaragua)*, Verbatim record of public sitting, 5 March 2009 at 10am, 53 (§ 8, per Pellet for Nicaragua) : 'Nul ne pouvait envisager que les touristes, à l'époque seulement de riches et curieux oisifs, pourraient être définis comme des marchandises (en admettant que ce soit le cas aujourd'hui – quod non)' – with the key words being 'quod non'; also see his use of the present tense in the following phrase: 'des touristes ne peuvent être assimilés à des "objets de commerce"' (§ 9, per Pellet for Nicaragua).

It therefore seems that neither party considered there to have been any relevant change in the meaning of the term '*comercio*' in the 150 years between the time of the treaty's conclusion and the time of its application. This is perhaps why, when Nicaragua nonetheless tried to stigmatise Costa Rica's argument as relying on an evolutionary interpretation of the treaty term,[102] Costa Rica's counsel dismissively replied: 'If you were to listen to them, Costa Rica would like to give an evolutionary interpretation to the Cañas-Jerez Treaty. That, of course, is not the problem'.[103] The fact that neither party's pleadings consistently acknowledged a relevant semantic change suggests that there wasn't one, a hypothesis confirmed by a closer look at the detail of the relevant facts. As the Court noted in paragraph 58 of its judgment,[104] Nicaragua had, in its Counter-Memorial, expressly (a) admitted that the transportation of passengers for money along the San Juan river was, in 1858, not only well-known, but also commercially very important;[105] and (b) deemed this activity to be 'the nearest equivalent of the tourist trade' at that point in time.[106] The Court was never going to hold that a service provided for profit was not commerce back in 1858, so Nicaragua's best argument was that river transportation and tourism in exchange for money were unknown and unthought-of in 1858. By conceding that passenger services had been provided for profit on that very river at that time, Nicaragua denied itself the opportunity to convincingly make that argument. In circumstances where the Court's judges understandably saw no reason to distinguish passenger services and tourism services,[107] this concession indirectly brought tourism services within the scope of '*comercio*' at all relevant times. Indeed, if our Hypothetical Original Interpreter had have been asked in 1858 if ferrying passengers down the river in exchange for payment was '*navegación … con objetos de comercio*', it seems fairly certain that he or she would have responded 'yes'.

The *Related Rights* judgment attempts to rescue the need for the application of a dynamic approach by using the word 'nowadays' in the statement 'as the activity of transporting persons can be commercial in nature nowadays'.[108] Yet in

[102] 'Rejoinder of Nicaragua', *Dispute regarding Navigational and Related Rights (Costa Rica v Nicaragua)* (International Court of Justice, 2008) 155 (§ 3.96).

[103] *Dispute regarding Navigational and Related Rights (Costa Rica v Nicaragua)*, Verbatim record of public sitting, 2 March 2009 at 10.15am, 68 (§§ 71–72, per Kohen for Costa Rica). Original: 'À les entendre, le Costa Rica voudrait donner une interprétation "évolutive" au traité Cañas-Jerez. Le problème, bien entendu, n'est pas là'. Note also that this appears to have been mentioned in passing by Caflisch when he said – in the context of Nicaragua's claims that certain modern-day international environmental law standards play a role – that Nicaragua resists attempts at interpreting the 1858 Treaty in an evolutionary manner (*Dispute regarding Navigational and Related Rights (Costa Rica v Nicaragua)*, Verbatim record of public sitting, 3 March 2009 at 10am, 25 (§ 10, per Caflisch for Costa Rica)).

[104] *Related Rights*, Judgment (n 6) 240 (§ 58).

[105] 'Counter-Memorial of Nicaragua' (n 100) 161 (§ 4.1.37).

[106] ibid 186 (§ 4.3.9).

[107] *Related Rights*, Judgment (n 6) 244 (§ 71); *Dispute regarding Navigational and Related Rights (Costa Rica v Nicaragua)*, Declaration of Judge ad hoc Guillaume [2009] ICJ Reports 290, 298 (§ 16).

[108] *Related Rights*, Judgment (n 6) 244 (§ 71).

circumstances where it had accepted that the transportation of persons on the very same river 150 years earlier had been very profitable, it surely cannot be read as implying that a profitable transportation of persons was not commercial in nature back in 1858. In this part of the judgment, the Court appears to be labouring to justify its statement of a dynamic approach when the facts simply did not require it.

Finally, the lack of relevant semantic change in the meaning of the word commerce between 1858 and 2009 is confirmed by the fact that Judges Guillaume and Skotnikov, despite refusing to take a dynamic approach, both still found with the majority on the issue of whether Costa Rica had the right to conduct tourist services because, back in 1858, the scope of the term already extended to transporting people for profit.[109] Clearly, if judges adopting a static approach reach the same interpretative outcome as those adopting a dynamic approach, there was no relevant semantic change between the time of the treaty's conclusion and the time of its application.

The absence of any relevant semantic change means that the Court could have decided the case with a temporally neutral approach and saved itself the trouble of engaging with the problem of intertemporal linguistics. The fact that it chose not to exercise judicial economy and to clearly state the dynamic approach could be seen as revealing just how confident the Court was that a term like '*comercio*' should be interpreted dynamically. Yet this does not itself mean that, by 2009, the approach had become widely accepted. Indeed, in this very case, the Nicaraguan team led by the distinguished professor of international law and regular ICJ advocate, Professor Alain Pellet, had clearly surmised that the dynamic approach was still controversial, trying to undermine Costa Rica's strong interpretative argument by saying that it required accepting a dynamic or evolutionary approach.[110]

Ultimately, the fact that the *Related Rights* judgment's prominent statement of the dynamic approach was made in a context in which it was not needed detracts from the weight that this judgment exerts as an authority for the view that contemporary international courts and tribunals are now prepared to impose post-treaty changes in meaning on litigant State parties and to generally follow a dynamic approach to the problem of intertemporal linguistics.

C. The GATT/WTO Cases Regularly Quoted do not Apply the Dynamic Approach

The two WTO decisions most commonly cited as authorities for the dynamic approach are also clearly selected on account of how obviously they refer to the doctrine of evolutionary interpretation, rather than how closely they interacted

[109] *Related Rights*, Guillaume Declaration (n 107) 298–99 (§ 16); *Dispute regarding Navigational and Related Rights (Costa Rica v Nicaragua)*, Separate Opinion of Judge Skotnikov [2009] ICJ Reports 283, 284–285 (§§ 5–10).

[110] 'Rejoinder of Nicaragua' (n 102) 155–57 (§§ 3.96–3.99).

with the problem of intertemporal linguistics. When the *US – Shrimp* and *China – AV Products* Appellate Body reports are analysed in their context, it becomes clear that neither actually responded to a problem of intertemporal linguistics by using a dynamic approach.

i. United States – Import prohibition of certain shrimp and shrimp products *(WTO AB – 1998)*

The difficulties in reading the famous *Shrimp-Turtle* report as an instance of the dynamic approach being applied to the Problem are already apparent in one of report's two oft-quoted statements advocating that approach.

> The words of Article XX(g), 'exhaustible natural resources', were actually crafted more than 50 years ago. They must be read by a treaty interpreter in the light of contemporary concerns of the community of nations about the protection and conservation of the environment. While Article XX was not modified in the Uruguay Round, the preamble attached to the WTO Agreement shows that the signatories to that Agreement were, in 1994, fully aware of the importance and legitimacy of environmental protection as a goal of national and international policy.[111]

At first blush, this dictum appears to constitute a direct challenge to the static approach and endorsement of the dynamic approach, placing emphasis on the terms of GATT Article XX(g) being drafted in 1946–47 and unambiguously stating that these terms must be interpreted in light of contemporary international concerns.

However, the peculiar history and status of the GATT creates a more complex legal situation. The GATT was drafted in 1946–47 and, as the so-called 'GATT 1947', governed international trade relations for almost half a century as a separate agreement left orphaned by the ultimate failure of the ECOSOC-sponsored attempt to create an International Trade Organization (ITO) to complement other Bretton Woods institutions through the UN Conference on Trade and Employment.[112] However, the agreement being interpreted and applied by the Appellate Body in the *Shrimp* dispute was not the GATT 1947, but the 'legally distinct' 'GATT 1994' that had been incorporated into the over-arching WTO agreement as an annex.[113]

[111] *US – Shrimp*, WTO AB Report (n 9) 48 (§ 129).

[112] See John H Jackson, 'History of the General Agreement on Tariffs and Trade' in Rüdiger Wolfrum, Peter-Tobias Stoll and Holger Hestermeyer (eds), *WTO – Trade in Goods* (Leiden, Martinus Nijhoff Publishers, 2011) 9 (§§ 23–24); Holger P Hestermeyer and Andrew J Grotto, 'Preamble GATT' in Peter-Tobias Stoll, Rüdiger Wolfrum and Holger P Hestermeyer (eds), *WTO – Trade in Goods* (Leiden, Martinus Nijhoff Publishers, 2011) 45–46 (§§ 7–12); see also Ernst-Ulrich Petersmann, 'Internationales Recht und Neue Internationale Wirtschaftsordnung' (1978) 18 *Archiv des Völkerrechts* 17.

[113] Marrakesh Agreement establishing the World Trade Organization 1994 (1867 UNTS 3) 155, art II(4); General Agreement on Tariffs and Trade (1994), Annex 1A of the Marrakesh Agreement establishing the World Trade Organization 1994 (190 UNTS 1995), art 1.

The third sentence of the above-quoted statement manifestly moves away from the time the reiterated GATT Article XX(g) was drafted to the later time when the agreement being interpreted and applied, the GATT 1994, was concluded. Moreover, by referring to the WTO Agreement's preamble that was drafted in 1994 and neglecting to mention the different GATT preamble drafted in 1947, the Appellate Body again appears to be focusing on ascertaining the meaning of the relevant treaty term in 1994, rather than 1947.

The *Shrimp* report is accordingly ambiguous as to whether it needs to determine the 1947 meaning of 'exhaustible natural resources' or the 1994 meaning of the same treaty term, with such ambiguity not being cleared up by temporally very imprecise statements later in the report such as 'we believe it is too late in the day to suppose that Article XX(g) of the GATT 1994 may be read as referring only to the conservation of exhaustible mineral or other non-living natural resources'.[114] However, the terms of the Dispute Settlement Understanding that vested the Appellate Body with jurisdiction in the *Shrimp* dispute clearly determined that the agreement to be interpreted was the GATT 1994. The time relevant for the static approach, the time of the treaty's conclusion,[115] was accordingly 1994 and the report discloses no semantic change in the meaning of the term 'exhaustible natural resources' between that time and 1998, the short time later that the treaty fell to be applied.

In the absence of any evidence of a relevant change to the semantic content of 'exhaustible natural resources' in the four-year period between the GATT 1994's conclusion and application, it is more accurate to conclude that the *Shrimp* report applies neither a static, nor a dynamic approach to the problem of intertemporal linguistics. What chapter 4 highlighted as the *condition sine qua non* common to both approaches, relevant semantic difference between the original and later-emerging semantic contents of the term, is clearly not satisfied in this case.

Moreover, the Appellate Body's *Shrimp* report is, relative to other treaty interpretations carried out by the WTO's adjudicatory bodies, quite perfunctory.[116] Many interpretative considerations are raised without being fully developed or placed in an overarching framework. In the end, it is unclear whether the Appellate Body reached its interpretative finding on the basis of the WTO Agreement's preamble, VCLT Article 31(3)(c), the principle of effective interpretation or even the broad variant of evolutionary treaty interpretation that actually just provides for progressive adjudication. Any one or more of these interpretative

[114] GATT 1994, art 1.

[115] See above s 4.II.C.

[116] The relevant section contains only eight paragraphs and runs over a mere 4.5 pages, a far cry from the 40 paragraphs and 13 pages dedicated specifically to explaining the relevance of just VCLT art 31(3)(c) in, for example, *European Communities – Measures Affecting the Approval and Marketing of Biotech Products*, Report [2006] WT/DS291/R WT/DS292/R WT/DS293/R 328–41 (§§ 7.49–7.89).

rules or doctrines may have ultimately brought the scope of provision designed to protect sea turtles within the scope of the GATT Article XX(g), but a dynamic approach preferring the later-emerging meaning of a treaty term over its relevantly different original meaning certainly did not.

ii. China – Publications and Audiovisual Products *(WTO AB – 2009)*

The other main statement of the WTO Appellate Body that is regularly adduced in support of the dynamic approach was also uttered in the context of an interpretation that did not require – and did not actually apply – a dynamic approach to the Problem. When, in the *China – AV Products* dispute, the Appellate Body followed technological developments occurring within the scope of the expression 'sound recording distribution services' in China's 2001 schedule of GATS commitments, it did not, as explained in chapter 4 above, depart from the original meaning of that term. The scope of 'sound recording distribution services', unless it is defined in an unduly extensional manner, has always been large enough to cover both emerging sound recording technologies and distribution technologies. On any reasonable view of the semantic scope of that term, there was accordingly no relevant semantic difference capable of meeting chapter 4's common condition for the existence of both the static and dynamic approaches to the Problem.

Indeed, in the paragraph of the *China – AV Products* report immediately prior to the two sentences so regularly quoted in support of the dynamic approach, the Appellate Body even appears to admit that the 'distribution' part of the treaty term not only covered the provision of intangibles in 2009, but 'would equally have done so in 2001',[117] the year when the relevant treaty commitment was effectively concluded.[118] If that was the case, than a dynamic approach to the interpretation of the term was clearly not necessary. In this light, the words '[m]ore generally' that then appear at the start of the statement of the dynamic approach are more readily understandable.[119] The Appellate Body was effectively indicating that it was making an entirely obiter statement, not stating a rule that it needed to apply to resolve the interpretative issue between the parties.

[117] *China – AV Products*, WTO AB Report (n 10) 161 (§ 395), the WTO Panel in the dispute also reaching this conclusion and thereby avoiding any recourse to evolutionary interpretation, see *China – Publications and Audiovisual Products*, Report (WTO Panel, WT/DS363/R, 12 August 2009) 376–77 (§§ 7.1245–7.1247).

[118] See The People's Republic of China – Schedule of Specific Commitments 2002 (GATS/SC/135). While this document is dated 14 February 2002, the relevant treaty was effectively concluded in 2001, when this schedule of commitments was included as a schedule to China's WTO Accession Protocol, see Protocol on the Accession of the People's Republic of China 2001.

[119] *China – AV Products*, WTO AB Report (n 10) 162 (§ 396).

iii. Other GATT/WTO Decisions Actually More Relevant to the Problem

The popular view of the state of the GATT/WTO authorities on the problem of intertemporal linguistics illustrates the perils of focusing on what international adjudicators say about the Problem, rather than what they actually do when confronted with it.

First, by focusing on the cases advocating a dynamic approach, but not actually taking it, the case law and literature neglects the decisions that actually take a dynamic approach, even if they do not expressly describe themselves as doing so. We have now seen that the *US – Shrimp* report did not interpret 'exhaustible natural resources' dynamically, because it was interpreting Article XX(g) in its GATT 1994 instantiation. However, that same expression has in fact been interpreted dynamically in other GATT/WTO disputes decided prior to the reiteration of Article XX(g) in that much more recent treaty.

There is substantial evidence to suggest that, at the time the GATT 1947 was concluded, the meaning of 'natural resources' extended beyond classic mineral resources to all things of economic and day-to-day importance for human populations, but stopped short of items without subsistence or economic value. The preparatory work for associated provisions, circumstances of conclusion and general context of the GATT 1947 reveal that its Article XX(g) was not initially regarded as an *environmental* exception allowing contracting parties to protect all items in the natural environment, but as a *resource* exception allowing contracting parties to protect all items of (significant) subsistence or economic use to them.[120] International conservation efforts at the time were essentially limited to species of sufficient use to human populations that they were threatened by over-exploitation,[121] most notably fish (a food source),[122] 'birds useful to agriculture',[123] seals (for fur)[124] and whales (for their meat and oil).[125] Dictionaries from this time limited the semantic content of the English word 'resource' to a 'means of supplying some want or deficiency' and a 'stock or reserve upon which one can draw when necessary',[126] and the semantic content of the French '*ressource(s)*' to '*des moyens pécuniaires*' and '*des moyens matériels d'existence*', even citing as examples the '*[r]essources d'un pays*' and '*[l]es ressources en énergie thermique, en minéraux*'.[127]

[120] See Steve Charnovitz, 'Exploring the Environmental Exceptions in GATT Article XX' (1991) 25 *Journal of World Trade* 37, 40–43.

[121] P Van Heijnsbergen, *International Legal Protection of Wild Fauna and Flora* (Amsterdam, IOS Press, 1997) 8–17.

[122] See, eg Convention for Regulating the Police of the North Sea Fisheries 1882 (160 CTS 219).

[123] See, eg Convention for the Protection of Birds Useful to Agriculture 1902 (51 LNTS 221).

[124] See, eg Convention for the preservation of the fur seal and sea otter in the North Pacific Ocean and Bering Sea 1911 (214 CTS 80).

[125] International Convention for the Regulation of Whaling 1946 (161 UNTS 72).

[126] 'resource, n.', *Oxford English Dictionary (Online)*, 2nd edn (1989) 1000 – www.oed.com/oed2/00204199.

[127] Paul Robert, *Dictionnaire alphabétique et analogique de la langue française: les mots et les associations d'idées*, vol 6 (Paris, Littré, 1964) 154.

If 'natural resources' had this meaning at the time of the GATT 1947's conclusion, then by the time the *Tuna-Dolphin II* panel interpreted it to include dolphin species not being eaten or traded within or by the United States,[128] the treaty term was being interpreted using a dynamic approach to the Problem. The meaning the GATT panel impliedly gave 'natural resources' was congruent with a significantly broader semantic content than that which it had in the same context in 1947.[129] The relevant part of the GATT panel's *Tuna/Dolphin II* report did not explicitly engage with the problem of intertemporal linguistics, nor openly apply a dynamic approach. However, this does not mean that it should not be studied as an example of the dynamic approach actually being applied. Indeed, such applications of the approach are probably a better reflection of how GATT/WTO dispute settlement bodies respond to the Problem than statements of principle ultimately left unapplied, like the overtly dynamic *Shrimp* dicta.

Second, by focusing on the *Shrimp* report's statements, non-trade lawyers saw a dynamic interpretation case where trade law specialists focused on how the *Shrimp* report actually interpreted Article XX(g) did not. The *Shrimp* report's paragraph 130 statement immediately prompted a wide range of international law experts to declare that the dynamic approach had become established at the WTO. For example, the ILC's 2006 Fragmentation Report understood its acknowledgement of the UNCLOS of 1982 to be a result of an evolutionary interpretation of 'natural resources' and 'exhaustible',[130] and sought in some detail to explain why these terms had to be interpreted dynamically, all the while misunderstanding the US import ban in dispute as aimed at the protection of shrimp, rather than sea turtles.[131] The eminent arbitrators handing down the 2005 *Iron Rhine* award, for their part, also characterised the *Shrimp* report as a 'finding' that the meaning of 'natural resources' in GATT Article XX(g) 'was intended to follow the evolution of the law'.[132]

Yet, at roughly the same time, the WTO-based diplomats making submissions to the *EC – Chicken Cuts* panel, true specialists in this sometimes-abstruse sub-field of international law, all appeared to consider that the meaning of terms within the WTO covered agreements should not evolve. On the specific issue of the relevant '[t]ime-frame for interpretation', no party argued for a dynamic approach, the dispute between them centring on whether the relevant time for (a static) interpretation was the time of the instrument's drafting or conclusion.[133] As part of its response to a specific question from the Panel, Thailand's

[128] *United States – Restrictions on Imports of Tuna*, Report [1994] DS29/R (GATT Panel).

[129] See especially ibid 49 (§ 5.13).

[130] International Law Commission and Martii Koskenniemi, 'Fragmentation of International Law: Difficulties arising from diversification and expansion of international law', A/CN.4/L.682 (Geneva, United Nations, 2006) 223 (§ 443).

[131] ibid 243 (§ 478(b)).

[132] *Iron Rhine*, Award (n 1) 73 (§ 79).

[133] *EC – Chicken Cuts (Panel)* (n 33) 40–41 (§§ 7.95–7.97).

representatives even explicitly read the *Shrimp* report as an instance of the *static* approach being applied to the Problem,[134] a reading impliedly affirmed by the Panel when it accepted the complainants' position that the EC Schedule should be interpreted according to the meaning it had on 15 April 1994.[135]

According to the *EC – Chicken Cuts* litigants and panellists, therefore, the *US – Shrimp* report so often cited in support of the dynamic approach actually took a static approach to the interpretation of the GATT 1994, while unilateral commitments similar to those putatively interpreted dynamically by the *China – AV Products* report should be interpreted according to the meaning they had when they were concluded.

This does not serve to show that one approach to the Problem is better than the other, nor even that some cases were more correctly decided than others, but simply that, when the dicta cited in support of the dynamic approach are considered in their context, they provide a far less persuasive endorsement of that position. Away from the glare of the elegant statements of the dynamic approach so often quoted by the case law and scholarship about treaty interpretation, the picture presented by the case law – even the very decisions containing those statements – is complex, unclear and manifestly incapable of sustaining a general view that contemporary international courts and tribunals generally favour the dynamic approach to the Problem.

III. CONCLUSIONS

Once the static and dynamic approaches to the Problem have been carefully defined, there turn out to be substantially fewer interpretations in the international case law that actually take a position on the Problem than might be imagined. However, the need to go beyond the small set of cases referring to evolutionary interpretation to all those which not only speak about the Problem more generally, but also impliedly take a position on it, implies a substantial research endeavour. This, together with the requirement that each such interpretation not merely be taken at face-value, but also carefully considered in its full context, renders the task of presenting the right picture of the state of the authorities on the Problem laborious, lengthy and therefore outside the constraints of this book project.

Suffice to say that a comprehensive analysis of the relevant case law leads to an overall conclusion that does not differ from the snapshot provided by the present chapter: the authorities on the problem of intertemporal linguistics are mixed. Once the dynamic approach generally taken to the interpretation of semantically changing terms in provisions granting human rights has been

[134] ibid 40 (§ 7.95).
[135] ibid 41–43 (§§ 7.98–7.103).

juxtaposed against the static approach generally taken to the interpretation of semantically changing terms in provisions fixing the scope of a State's boundary or consent to jurisdiction, it becomes clear that there is little prospect of being able to reliably draw a general conclusion as to how contemporary international courts and tribunals respond to the Problem.

Fortunately, the present chapter was not dedicated to determining which of the static and dynamic approaches is most supported by this rich and varied adjudicatory tapestry, but instead to the much more manageable task of demonstrating that the relevant international case law has not provided a clear, generally applicable and dynamic answer to the Problem. The above observations and examples are themselves sufficient to show that the view that the case law does provide such an answer in fact rests on shaky foundations. Like several other components of the conventional wisdom in this area of international law, this popular view should now be cast aside.

Part III

The Solution – Innovating Inside International Law

7

The Problem of Intertemporal Linguistics as an Issue of Ambiguity, Not Vagueness

In Parts I and II, we saw that the scholarship on the problem of intertemporal linguistics is too distracted by the doctrines associated with it and generally too confused and too heterogenous to reveal a solution to the Problem. The same can be said for the post-VCLT international case law, while the VCLT's interpretative rules are so multi-faceted and flexible that they do not offer interpreters faced with the Problem any useful guidance on how to solve it. Having now extricated it from the doctrines muddying our analysis of it, formally defined it and cast aside the misconceptions in relation to it, this book must now turn to *solving* the problem of intertemporal linguistics.

Developing a proposed solution to the Problem is undoubtedly the book's most ambitious enterprise and one that some might consider the author foolish to even attempt. It is notable that most authors writing in relation to the Problem have studiously avoided trying to solve it. Most often, this is achieved by focusing on explaining and justifying the doctrine of evolutionary treaty interpretation and the decisions invoking that doctrine, rather than the question of which of a static or dynamic approach should be taken to a defined legal problem. Yet, even the rare studies devoted to the question, rather than a doctrine, never attempt to solve it. We have seen that the ILC's *Treaties over Time* project ended up redefining the scope of its study to focus on subsequent agreement and practice, thereby eschewing the need to deal with the Problem in any detail and therefore any attempt to solve it. We have also seen that Djeffal's recent book on *Static and Evolutive Treaty Interpretation* merely seeks to 'reorganis[e] and restat[e]' the very similar static-versus-evolutive problem 'in a faithful manner so that it can be better dealt with',[1] but by his own admission does not attempt to provide guidance for how to solve it.[2]

The search for a solution to the Problem is not, however, a forlorn enterprise. When Djeffal says that '[t]he choice between static and evolutive results

[1] Christian Djeffal, *Static and Evolutive Treaty Interpretation: A Functional Reconstruction* (Cambridge, Cambridge University Press, 2016) 71–72.

[2] ibid 357.

is situated within competing attitudes … different general political mindsets (conservative/progressive) or different philosophical standpoints on language (intentionalist/pragmatist)' and that '[i]t is very hard to find a solution that mitigates between these views once and for all', he is, it is submitted, talking about the choice between following and not following the multi-faceted doctrine of evolutionary treaty interpretation, not merely the narrower and less value-laden choice between the static and dynamic approaches to the problem of intertemporal linguistics. Yet while the taking of a position on whether a treaty interpreter should favour a progressive or formalistic interpretation of a treaty inherently implies a particular jurisprudential mindset, taking a position on the problem of intertemporal linguistics does not. As this book has gone to great pains to point out, the battles over evolutionary treaty interpretation and the problem of intertemporal linguistics are carried out with different weapons on different terrains. One of the benefits of describing the Problem as one of intertemporal linguistics is that it emphasises that the problem is linguistically loaded, but value neutral. Solutions can accordingly be offered without falling into the morass of moral or jurisprudential relativity.

It is incumbent on a study in the field of international law to try to answer this 'how should international adjudicators respond?' question from *within* the existing framework of international law. One could, of course, answer this question while being completely oblivious to the constraints imposed on international adjudicators including those provided by the interpretative rules or principles they should apply, the scope of their adjudicatory function and the nature and best interests of the international legal system. Such an argument would draw its rhetorical strength from outside of international law. It could have political, sociological, philosophical or even linguistic bases, but would not have a *legal* basis. A solution developed from within the field in which a problem emerges will, it is submitted, always be more appropriate and more palatable to the actors confronting that problem.

Regrettably, the international law relevant to the Problem has so far revealed itself to be incapable of providing a clear and simple solution to it. Together, case law and scholarship yield a number of insights relevant to the Problem, but no ordered framework capable of guiding interpreters faced with a choice between the original and later-emerging meaning of a treaty term. Our only hope of finding a solution from within international law is by using new concepts to arrange those insights into a system capable of providing the desired guidance. Such a reorganising notion or principle would itself seem to have to come from outside the field of international law, for if it were already present within international law, it would already have been used to provide the solution.[3]

[3] As demonstrated in ch 5, efforts to locate an organising principle lurking implied beneath the text of the temporally-neutral VCLT rules for treaty interpretation – including Bjorge's very teleological notion of 'intention' – run into difficulty by de facto elevating one or more of the interpretative elements within the VCLT above others that are intended to sit on the same level.

Moreover, as this study has shown, modern-day international legal debate relating to the problem of intertemporal linguistics is somewhat undisciplined and conceptually confused.

In our quest for the conceptual clarity that might lead us to a solution, we must accordingly go back to first principles. For a question of interpretation, linguistics is an obvious source of those principles, something that many legal theorists dealing with questions of legal interpretation readily acknowledge. Moreover, the field of linguistics provides concepts that render the Problem more intelligible at a sufficiently abstract level for them not to replace, but rather to structure and reorganise the more directly relevant material from the field of international law, including the insights emerging from the international decisions and adjudicatory opinions most relevant to the Problem.

I. INTERPRETATION RESOLVES EITHER VAGUENESS OR AMBIGUITY

'"Interpretation" is', as Bos noted in his two-part 1980 study of treaty interpretation, 'a term very differently understood by different authors' and 'neither the scope nor content of it is commonly agreed upon'.[4] While international law scholars' definitions of 'interpretation' differ as to the nature of the outcome that interpretations should produce,[5] they ultimately tend to understand its essence in the same way as it has been understood for centuries and across countless systems of law, namely as ascertaining the content or meaning of a text or act.[6]

Echoing Vattel's famous first general maxim of interpretation,[7] the renowned legal theorist Endicott has noted that the need for interpretation only arises where there is 'doubt or contention' such that 'arguments can be made in favour

[4] Maarten Bos, 'Theory and Practice of Treaty Interpretation (Part I)' (1980) 27 *Netherlands International Law Review* 3, 6.

[5] For a prominent example of a very functional definition of interpretation in international law, see Charles de Visscher, *Problèmes d'interprétation judiciaire en droit international public* (Paris, Pedone, 1963) 14; see also Robert Kolb, *Interprétation et création du droit international: Esquisses d'une herméneutique juridique moderne pour le droit international public* (Bruxelles, Bruylant, 2006) 24.

[6] See, eg Rudolf Bernhardt, *Die Auslegung völkerrechtlicher Verträge insbesondere in der neueren Rechtsprechung internationaler Gerichte* (Köln, Carl Heymanns Verlag, 1963) 1; Charles E Rousseau, *Droit international public* (Paris, Sirey, 1970) 241; Francis Lieber, *Legal and Political Hermeneutics or Principles of Iinterpretation and Construction in Law and Politics with Remarks on Precedents and Authorities* (Boston MA, Charles C Little and James Brown, 1839) 115; Mark E Villiger, 'The Rules on Interpretation: Misgivings, Misunderstandings, Miscarriage? The "Crucible" Intended by the International Law Commission' in Enzo Cannizzaro (ed), *The Law of Treaties Beyond the Vienna Convention* (Oxford, Oxford University Press, 2011) 106; and see generally Kolb (n 5) 25.

[7] Pursuant to which one should not interpret that which does not need to be interpreted ('qu'il n'est pas permis d'interpréter ce qui n'a pas besoin d'interprétation') – Emer de Vattel, *Le droit des gens, ou principes de la loi naturelle appliqués à la conduite et aux affaires des nations et des souverains*, vol I (Paris, J-P Aillaud, 1835) 461 (§ 263).

of different conclusions as to the meaning of a communicative act';[8] in other words when the legal instrument is, in the relevant context, 'inconclusive'.[9]

Solan points out that, while lawyers generally use 'ambiguity as a blanket term that covers all of the[] problems' of inconclusiveness, '[l]inguists, philosophers and psychologists distinguish between vagueness and ambiguity as different phenomena, resulting largely from distinct psychological processes'.[10] One of the better-known statements explaining this important distinction also comes from the world of legal theory, Dickerson saying: 'Whereas 'ambiguity' in its classical sense refers to equivocation, 'vagueness' refers to the degree to which, independently of equivocation, language is uncertain in its respective application to a number of particulars'.[11] Another legal theorist, Poscher, summed it up by saying that '[a]mbiguity ... is about multiple meanings; vagueness is about meaning in borderline cases'.[12]

Modern linguists appear to agree that vagueness is better defined by an absence of precision or granularity at the heart of the sorites paradox.[13] A vague expression, Pinkal says, 'allows for gradual differentiation and can be transduced to its opposite by imperceptible transitions'.[14] This is a key respect in which vagueness can be distinguished from ambiguity. Whereas vague expressions allow 'for gradual differentiation' and 'infinitely many precisifications', 'ambiguous expressions can assume an arbitrarily but finitely large number of readings'.[15]

As linguists point out, the difference between ambiguity and vagueness is so clear that it is reflected in how each is instinctively dealt with in everyday

[8] Timothy Endicott, 'Interpretation and Indeterminacy: Comments on Andrei Marmor's Philosophy of Law' (2014) 10 *Jerusalem Review of Legal Studies* 46, 51–52.

[9] Endicott himself does not use a term to describe the attribute of the legal instrument being interpreted that renders interpretation necessary, but criticises Marmor – Andrei Marmor, *Interpretation and Legal Theory* 2nd edn (Oxford, Hart Publishing, 2005) – for using the term 'indeterminacy' in this context, see Endicott (n 8). 'Inconclusiveness' seems to reflect Endicott's notion of a conclusion not being able to be reached on the basis of the text and will be used by the remainder of this study.

[10] Lawrence M Solan, 'Vagueness and Ambiguity in Legal Interpretation' in Vijay Kumar Bhatia and others (eds), *Vagueness in Normative Texts*, vol 23 (Bern, Peter Lang, 2005) 74.

[11] F Reed Dickerson, *The Interpretation and Application of Statutes* (Boston MA, Little Brown, 1975) 49.

[12] Ralf Poscher, 'Ambiguity and Vagueness in Legal Interpretation' in Peter M Tiersma and Lawrence M Solan (eds), *The Oxford Handbook of Language and Law* (Oxford, Oxford University Press, 2012) 129; see also Solan (n 10) 73.

[13] This paradox, attributed to Eubulides of Miletus, starts with a heap (soros/σωρός) of grains and, removing one by one, asks when the heap ceases to become a heap. The paradox arises from never knowing at what point it can be said not to be a heap, but knowing that with only one grain left it clearly is not a heap. For linguists, the paradox arises due to the vagueness inherent in the word 'heap' (see further Dominic Hyde, 'Sorites Paradox' in Edward N Zalta (ed), *The Stanford Encyclopedia of Philosophy*, Winter 2014 Edition – plato.stanford.edu/archives/win2014/entries/sorites-paradox/).

[14] Manfred Pinkal, *Logic and Lexicon* (Geoffrey Simmons tr, Dordrecht, Springer Science+Business Media, 1995) 73.

[15] ibid 73–75.

human communication: ambiguity must be resolved, but vagueness need not be.[16] An addressee will inevitably disambiguate whether the speaker saying 'bank' is referring to a river bank or a savings bank but, once it has determined that the latter of the two senses was being used, will usually not need or try to exactly determine what institutions qualify and do not qualify as 'banks'. In other words, ambiguous terms instantly and inherently demand a primary level of clarification irrespective of the use to which they are put, even if it involves invoking more than one meaning as in the case of poetry or paronomasia (puns). Vague terms are, by contrast, not only common, but also commonly tolerated. They only demand clarification – on a more thoroughgoing level – when put to particular uses that reveal the problematic aspects of their vagueness.

Ambiguity and vagueness constitute very distinct phenomena and it is truly remarkable that the distinction is so rarely observed by interpreters of legal text, notably including public international lawyers. Helmersen's 2013 article constitutes a rare exception, noting that treaty interpretation can exist on the level of resolving each of these two distinct types of inconclusiveness.[17] However, since his article is dedicated to explaining instances of both the narrow and broad forms of evolutionary interpretation, his use of the distinction is essentially limited to trying to characterise these instances as resolutions of ambiguity or resolutions of vagueness. Courts' and tribunals' treaty interpretations invariably involve a resolution of vagueness (sometimes in addition to a resolution of ambiguity), so Helmersen concludes with the descriptive and therefore somewhat banal statement that '[a]ll the ICJ's evolutive interpretations have concerned vagueness'.[18] Unfortunately, his focus on evolutionary interpretations has him look back at the interpretative process from its end-point, so his conclusions stop at the parts of the interpretative process most proximate to the interpretative outcome and miss earlier parts of that process – including those involving the necessary resolution of any ambiguity.

This study, by contrast, does not look back down a path already taken, but starts at the fork-in-the road where the open question posed by the problem of intertemporal linguistics first arises. Crucially, it is here, at the start of the interpretative process, well prior to determining borderline cases of whether a fact comes within the vague scope of a designated term, that the choice between the static and the dynamic approaches to the Problem is made. As will now be demonstrated, this choice, the very essence of the problem of intertemporal linguistics, constitutes a resolution of ambiguity, not a resolution of vagueness.

[16] Moshe Azar, 'Transforming Ambiguity into Vagueness in Legal Interpretation' in A Wagner, WG Werner and D Cao (eds), *Interpretation, Law and the Construction of Meaning: Collected papers on legal interpretation in theory, adjudication and political practice* (Dordrecht, Springer, 2007) 128.

[17] Sondre Torp Helmersen, 'Evolutive Treaty Interpretation: Legality, Semantics and Distinctions' (2013) 6 *European Journal of Legal Studies* 127, 142–44.

[18] ibid.

II. THE CHOICE BETWEEN AN ORIGINAL AND LATER-EMERGING MEANING CALLS FOR THE RESOLUTION OF AMBIGUITY, NOT VAGUENESS

In chapter 4, we arrived at definitions of the static and dynamic approaches to the problem of intertemporal linguistics that revealed the core of the Problem to lie in the difference between a treaty term's semantic contents at two different moments in time. With our condition common to the two approaches, we saw that the Problem can only be properly said to have arisen where the semantic content of a treaty term changes between the time the treaty was concluded and the time that it falls to be applied. The choice between the static and dynamic approaches to the Problem also centres around the differing semantic contents of the original and later meaning of the treaty term, the specific condition of the static approach resulting in an identified meaning congruent with the original semantic content and the specific condition of the dynamic approach resulting in an identified meaning congruent with the semantic content of the term at the time of the treaty's application.

As explained above, semantic content is narrower than what is generally regarded as meaning. The semantic content is the context- and utterance-neutral part of meaning; the content of a word or expression that can be directly calculated merely from the stored common knowledge of what that word may mean (lexical component of meaning) and the structural relationship between that word and others (the syntactic component of meaning).[19] The change in meaning that concerns us when analysing the problem of intertemporal linguistics occurs outside of the particular context of the treaty, affecting the relevant expressions as they are used in a variety of contexts. It is therefore wholly semantic; it results from the change in the meaning of an expression, not a change to the treaty.

Features inherent to the process of treaty interpretation allow us to narrow down the Problem even further. When we observe that the meaning of a word or expression has changed, we are talking about the kind of change that is reflected in a dictionary: a lexical change. A common form of lexical change involves broadening, when a term is given a new sense, such as when the English term 'bird', which originally referred merely to fowl (farmyard birds bred for consumption), came to denote all winged creatures. At least in the initial phase of semantic change, if not indefinitely, two senses of the same word co-exist, meaning that it may be unclear in which sense the term was used when it is written or spoken. Semantic change produces competing senses ('meaning variants' or 'lexico-semantic variants') for the same lexeme: one sense has the lexeme's original semantic content and another sense has the lexeme's later semantic content. In the treaty context, the problem of intertemporal linguistics arises when there is semantic change to a treaty term. There is one sense that is the

[19] See, eg Yi Ting Huang and Jesse Snedeker, 'Semantic Meaning and Pragmatic Interpretation in 5-Year-Olds: Evidence From Real-Time Spoken Language Comprehension' (2009) 45 *Developmental Psychology* 1723, 1723 and see further s 4.III.A above.

treaty term's semantic content at the time of the treaty's conclusion and another sense that is the treaty term's semantic content at the time of the treaty's application. Linguistics tells us that, where there are competing senses of the same word or expression, there is ambiguity. The problem of intertemporal linguistics is therefore a problem of ambiguity.

There are various types of ambiguity. The ambiguity produced by the semantic change that concerns us in this study of the problem of intertemporal linguistics is 'lexical ambiguity'[20] and, almost invariably, polysemy. It is lexical – not phonetic or syntactic – ambiguity because, by occurring in a written form in a fixed context, it does not arise from different words sounding the same in oral speech,[21] nor from ambiguity in the grammatical analysis of a sentence,[22] but is 'due solely to the alternative meanings of an individual lexical item'.[23] It involves polysemy – rather than true homonymy – because over relatively short periods of time in mature languages, the most common types of semantic change (eg narrowing, widening, metonymy, hyperbole, metaphor and synecdoche) spawn new, but invariably related meanings. Already in the nineteenth century, Bréal had shown that changes in meaning, by adding or subtracting senses from existing words, generally involve polysemy because the same word will either gain or lose one of two or more meanings.[24]

Semantic change therefore creates – and the problem of intertemporal linguistics therefore presents – lexical ambiguity between the original and later sense of the same treaty term, each of which has its own semantic content. The fact that one or both of those competing senses of the treaty term is vague does not mean that they are not ambiguous in relation to each other. Terms can be, and often will be, both ambiguous *and* vague. It does not even matter if one sense fully includes the other, they are still different.[25] Expressions that 'can assume an arbitrarily but finitely large number of readings' are 'ambiguous expressions'.[26] Treaty terms that can assume either their (semantic) meaning at the time of the treaty's conclusion or their relevantly different (semantic) meaning at the time of the treaty's application can assume two different readings, so are ambiguous between their original and later meanings.

[20] Note that some authors consider lexical ambiguity to include syntactic ambiguity, defining 'semantic lexical ambiguity' as the form of lexical ambiguity that is not syntactic – see, eg Steven L Small Garrison W Cottrell and Michael K Tanenhaus, 'Preface' in Steven L Small, Garrison W Cottrell and Michael K Tanenhaus (eds), *Lexical Ambiguity Resolution: Perspective from Psycholinguistics, Neuropsychology and Artificial Intelligence* (San Mateo CA, Morgan Kaufmann, 1988) 4 ff.

[21] For example, differently spelt homophones like the English words 'saw' and 'sore' or 'storey' and 'story' present *phonetic* ambiguity.

[22] Morphologically deficient expressions like 'he ate the cookies on the couch' or 'Dusko wants to buy a big dog treat' produce *syntactic* ambiguity.

[23] David Crystal, *A Dictionary of Linguistics and Phonetics* 6th edn (Malden MA, Blackwell Publishers, 2008) 23.

[24] Michel Bréal, *Essai de sémantique (science des significations)* (Paris, Hachette, 1897) 154–56, 171–72.

[25] Pinkal (n 14) 73.

[26] ibid 75.

III. THE VCLT RULES ARE FOCUSED ON RESOLVING VAGUENESS, BUT IMPLICITLY RECOGNISE THE AMBIGUITY/VAGUENESS DISTINCTION

A. Rules of Legal Interpretation Generally

In all systems of law, the rules and principles for interpreting legal texts focus on resolving vagueness rather than on resolving ambiguity. This is completely understandable. Vagueness is extremely prevalent in the law and almost ubiquitous in dispute settlement.[27] Important legal concepts are notoriously vague. As examples, Solan cites the important common law concept of 'reasonableness',[28] while Kluck cites key civil law notions such as 'good cause' ('*aus wichtigem Grund*') in the context of employment contracts and 'good faith' ('*Treu und Glauben*') in the law of obligations.[29]

Even those legal terms that are not vague in-and-of-themselves often turn out to be vague under the microscope of a legal dispute. We saw above that vagueness is defined by a lack of precision or granularity. Yet whether sufficient precision or granularity is lacking is clearly, as Hobbs has pointed out, determined by what we need to determine in a precise situation.[30] Legal situations very often involve determinations of whether some fact or situation falls within the scope of a particular word. To make such determinations, lawyers need to be able to sketch the parameters of a word or concept in finer detail than is usually necessary in everyday speech. For example, one does not need a precisely defined notion of what is 'tall' in order to explain to a young child the difference between a house and a tall building, but one is likely to need a much more precisely defined notion of what tall means when interpreting and applying fire regulations specific to 'tall buildings'. Dispute settlement inherently focuses on borderline cases that are routinely apt to reveal the lack of precision that characterises vagueness. To develop this example further, courts are unlikely to be faced with the question of what constitutes a tall building in a case about whether a fire regulation applies to a 200-metre high building – it will be accepted by the parties that it does. Where, however, there is a case involving the potential application of such a regulation to a 25-metre high building, it is more likely to come before the courts and the vagueness inherent in the term 'tall' is much more likely to be revealed.

Relative to vagueness, ambiguity is rarely an issue in legal contexts. Language users can always avoid linguistic ambiguity if they are aware of it and wish to

[27] Lawrence Solum, 'Legal Theory Lexicon: Vagueness & Ambiguity' (*Legal Theory Blog*, 28 June 2015) – lsolum.typepad.com/legaltheory/2015/06/legal-theory-lexicon-vagueness-ambiguity.html; see also Poscher (n 12) 14.

[28] Solum (n 27).

[29] Nora Kluck, *Der Wert der Vagheit* (Berlin, Walter de Gruyter, 2014) 145.

[30] See Jerry R Hobbs, 'Granularity', Proceedings of the 9th International Joint Conference on Artificial Intelligence, vol 1 (San Francisco, Morgan Kaufmann Publishers, 1985) – dl.acm.org/citation.cfm?id=1625219.

avoid it,[31] as the drafters of legal texts, including treaty drafters generally do. Moreover, as further explained below, an addressee, such as a judge, can usually resolve ambiguity in an incontestable manner by referring to readily available linguistic context. Disambiguation is particularly straightforward in legal contexts that feature lexical ambiguity in the forms of polysemy and, especially, true homonymy. No one is going to doubt that a financial services regulation using the word 'bank' is referring to financial institution rather than river banks, just as a French-language agricultural treaty using the word 'avocats' is more likely to be speaking about avocados, while a French code of ethical conduct to be displayed before courts of law is much more likely to be speaking about lawyers. Azar notes that '[p]ractically, it is very rare to find in normal communication a misunderstanding or an interpretation dispute caused by lexical or morphological homonymy';[32] it is perhaps even rarer in the law.

It is only natural, with vagueness being a more common and substantially more intractable type of inconclusiveness faced by legal systems than ambiguity, that the rules for legal interpretation focus on resolving vagueness and often do not even consider the possibility of ambiguity being the problem instead. As Solan notes, the function of law is such that it is 'much more concerned with finding the appropriate interpretation of a legal document than characterizing the linguistic problems that allowed multiple interpretations in the first instance'.[33] Yet, as he rightly asserts after reviewing a range of domestic law decisions resolving inconclusiveness, 'the distinction between vague and ambiguous language that philosophers and linguists use so routinely has some explanatory power [in the legal context] after all'.[34]

Whereas Solan considers that legal decision makers tacitly resolve ambiguity differently to how they resolve vagueness, other legal theorists believe that they conflate the two, at times even deliberately. The main legal theorists addressing this distinction at least appear to agree that it is simpler and therefore less dangerous (in terms of predictability) for legal decision makers to resolve ambiguity than it is for them to resolve vagueness. As Poscher points out, whereas ambiguity presents 'a choice between different pre-established alternatives', vagueness 'allows for creative concept formation even if pre-established concepts are around'.[35] This creative formation, what German theorists refer to as *richterliche Rechtsfortbildung* and what some English-language lawyers might be tempted to describe as 'judicial activism', is a cause for concern for some legal theorists. Decker, for example, worries that attempts to resolve vagueness involve 'a highly subjective mode of analysis that involves an

[31] Azar (n 16) 126.
[32] ibid 125.
[33] Solan (n 10) 74–75.
[34] ibid 75.
[35] Poscher (n 12) 11.

unpredictable assortment of paths a court might take in arriving at a ruling'.[36] Azar, for his part, is convinced that there is even a discernible tendency among judges 'to transform ambiguity cases into vagueness cases in order to make room for judicial discretion'.[37]

To the extent that the rules for resolving inconclusiveness – and the habits of adjudicators who resolve it – fail to distinguish between situations of ambiguity and vagueness, there is a risk that more uncertainty is being imported into the adjudicatory process than is linguistically required. Legal security is being unnecessarily undermined every time an adjudicator jumps out to the extraneous considerations that might be necessary to resolve the finest of issues posed by the vagueness of a word or phrase, even though he or she need only have resolved an ambiguity by looking at linguistic facts apparent on the face of the text.

Yet most rules for legal interpretation, and most decision makers, do not distinguish between inconclusiveness produced by ambiguity and inconclusiveness produced by vagueness. In most cases, this is because the interpretative rules which they apply make no such distinction.

B. The Vagueness-oriented International Law Rules for Treaty Interpretation

The rules for treaty interpretation are no exception to interpretative rules' general focus on resolving vagueness. This is clear from (a) the range of different interpretative elements in VCLT Article 31 and (b) the practice of the international courts and tribunals applying these rules.

Linguistic and legal theory analyses reveal that, while ambiguity may be resolved by linguistic facts visible within the very text where the ambiguous term appears, resolving vagueness regularly requires resort to linguistic and paralinguistic facts that are extraneous to the text. In the VCLT's general rule of interpretation, almost all facts to be taken into account by the treaty interpreter are either sometimes or always extraneous to the treaty text. *Good faith* is a vague concept with a source outside the treaty, while the injunction to interpret according to '*ordinary meaning*' is an invitation to textualism that, in a practical sense, impels many international courts and tribunals to refer to dictionaries,[38] themselves extraneous to the internal linguistic context of the treaty.[39] Both the *context* and *object and purpose* referred to in VCLT Article 31 extend beyond the textual context immediately surrounding the interpreted treaty term to other

[36] John F Decker, 'Addressing Vagueness, Ambiguity, and Other Uncertainty in American Criminal Laws' (2002) 80 *Denver University Law Review* 241, 243.

[37] Azar (n 16) 124 ff.

[38] The WTO's adjudicatory bodies' frequent resort to the Oxford English Dictionary is the best-known example of how VCLT art 31(1)'s elevation of 'ordinary meaning' can lead to going outside of a treaty, instead of staying within it.

[39] Azar (n 16) 135.

parts of the treaty and even other agreements. The interpretative considerations listed in VCLT Article 31(3), *subsequent agreement*, *subsequent practice* and *relevant rules applicable between the parties* are also, by definition, extraneous to the treaty text.

While such heavy reference to extraneous elements would alone be sufficient to show that the rules and principles for treaty interpretation are primarily dedicated to resolving vagueness rather than ambiguity, this observation is also confirmed by the interpretative practice of international courts and tribunals. Very many cases turn on whether a particular activity falls within the scope of a category. In other words, they involve the use of interpretative methods to bring the extra granularity to a treaty term such that a concrete situation can be qualified in a legally relevant manner. Examples of such cases include the ICJ's decision in the *Whaling in the Antarctic* case as to whether Japan's JARPA II programme was 'for purposes of scientific research' within the meaning of Article VIII of the Whaling Convention,[40] or the ECtHR's famous *Tyrer* decision seeking to determine whether 'birching' came within the scope of 'degrading punishment'.[41] In other cases, the interpreter will try to determine what specific real-world referent is signified by a treaty term, such as which of the north or south arms of the Chobe River constituted its 'main channel' in the *Kasikili/Sedudu* case.[42] The interpretative practice of international courts and tribunals, like the rules elaborated for that practice, is clearly quite heavily oriented towards resolving vagueness rather than ambiguity.

The fact that, in the treaty interpretation context, the rules are directed to resolving vagueness rather than ambiguity is not only standard, but also perfectly understandable. The question is not whether these rules and principles should be used in the many situations in which vagueness needs to be resolved, but instead whether they should be used as commonly as they are where the inconclusiveness to be resolved arises – at least in the first instance – from ambiguity rather than from vagueness.

C. VCLT Article 31(4)'s Implied Recognition of the Ambiguity and Vagueness Distinction

What is more atypical and, in the context of this chapter's analysis, quite remarkable about the rules for treaty interpretation is the fact that they contain one rule that, unlike all the others, is dedicated to resolving ambiguity rather than vagueness. Read together with VCLT Article 31(1), the sole sub-paragraph

[40] See *Whaling in the Antarctic (Australia v Japan; New Zealand intervening)*, Judgment [2014] ICJ Reports 226.

[41] *Tyrer v The United Kingdom* (Merits), Judgment (European Court of Human Rights (Chamber), 5856/72, 25 April 1978).

[42] See *Kasikili/Sedudu Island (Botswana/ Namibia)*, Judgment [1999] ICJ Reports 1045.

of VCLT Article 31 not mentioned above, VCLT Article 31(4), makes particular provision for the situation in which a term may have been used in either an ordinary or special sense:

> SECTION 3. INTERPRETATION OF TREATIES
>
> Article 31: General rule of interpretation
>
> 1. A treaty shall be interpreted in good faith in accordance with the ordinary meaning to be given to the terms of the treaty …
>
> 4. A special meaning shall be given to a term if it is established that the parties so intended.[43]

VCLT Article 31(4) has received scant attention from practitioners and scholars of international law. This is perhaps because it was only ever intended by its drafters to be used in quite exceptional circumstances,[44] because it explicitly mentions the controversial matter of the drafting parties' intentions, or because it is a mere 18 words in length. For the present study's efforts to solve the problem of intertemporal linguistics, however, VCLT Article 31(4) is extremely valuable by virtue of the fact that it seeks to resolve an ambiguity.

For many scholars of international law, ordinary and special meaning represent two different sides of a coin, always in conflict and never overlapping. For Engelen, for example, 'any meaning other than the ordinary meaning to be given to a term in the application of Article 31(1) VCLT is regarded as a special meaning'.[45] This echoes Linderfalk's statement that '[t]he relationship between the ordinary and the special meaning is converse: a non-ordinary meaning is by definition a special meaning, and a non-special meaning is by definition an ordinary meaning',[46] a statement which in turn draws on the celebrated writings of Sinclair for whom '[t]he converse of the "ordinary meaning" of a term is its special meaning'.[47] For Sur the two might even be contradictory ('*à la limite contradictoire*'),[48] while for Hummer they present a fundamental dichotomy ('*dicotomía fundamental*').[49]

[43] Vienna Convention on the Law of Treaties 1969 (1155 UNTS 331), art 31.

[44] International Law Commission, 'Yearbook 1966, vol I, pt 2' (New York, United Nations, 1967) 269 (per Jiménez de Aréchaga, 884th meeting – 5 July 1966, § 9); see also Carlos Fernández de Casadevante y Romani, *Sovereignty and Interpretation of International Norms* (Berlin, Springer, 2007) 50; Franciscus Antonius Engelen, *Interpretation of Tax Treaties under International Law: A Study of Articles 31, 32, and 33 of the Vienna Convention on the Law of Treaties and Their Application to Tax Treaties* (Amsterdam, International Bureau of Fiscal Documentation, 2004) 160.

[45] Engelen (n 44) 149; see also Mark E Villiger, 'Article 31 – General Rule of Interpretation' in Mark E Villiger, *Commentary on the 1969 Vienna Convention on the Law of Treaties* (Leiden, Martinus Nijhoff Publishers, 2009) 434; Mark E Villiger, 'The 1969 Vienna Convention on the Law of Treaties: 40 Years After' (2011) 344 *Collected Courses of the Hague Academy of International Law* 9, 125.

[46] Ulf Linderfalk, *On the Interpretation of Treaties* (Dordrecht, Springer, 2007) 64.

[47] Ian Sinclair, *The Vienna Convention on the Law of Treaties* (Manchester, Manchester University Press, 1984) 126.

[48] Serge Sur, *L'interprétation en droit international public* (Paris, Pichon Durand-Auzias, 1974) 272.

[49] Waldemar Hummer, 'Problemas juridico-linguisticos de la dicotomia entre el sentido ordinario y el especial de conceptos convencionales segun la Convencion de Viena sobre el Derecho de los Tratados de 1969' (1975) 28 *Revista Española de Derecho Internacional* 97, 108.

We noted above that the defining feature of lexical ambiguity is the existence of two or more different and competing senses. The ordinary and special meaning of a treaty term are manifestly competing senses of that term so, in linguistic terms, VCLT Article 31(4) only ever applies in situations of lexical ambiguity. All treaty terms have an ordinary meaning (or sense), but some also have a special meaning (or sense). For VCLT Article 31(4) to come into play, the treaty term must have at least two different senses: an ordinary one and a special one. This mirrors the common condition for the static and dynamic approaches to the problem of intertemporal linguistics through which the Problem only comes into play where semantic change in a treaty term's produces two different senses of it: an original one and a later-emerging one.

It can accordingly be stated that, while the VCLT's treaty interpretation rules do not address the problem of intertemporal linguistics, they do address an interpretative situation analogous to it. Moreover, they dedicate a separate rule and separate method to solving the difficulty created by competing ordinary and special senses of a treaty term. As will now be seen, the method VCLT Article 31(4) provides for resolving the lexical ambiguity it addresses is broadly consistent with how modern-day linguistics resolves ambiguity. This means that this study's linguistics-inspired method for solving the problem of intertemporal linguistics is not foreign to the field of international law, but in fact tacitly baked into its established rules for treaty interpretation.

IV. INTERPRETERS DISAMBIGUATE BEFORE THEY 'DE-VAGUEFY'

We noted above that the rules of treaty interpretation applied to inconclusiveness created by semantic change generally start working at the latest possible stage of language processing: the point at which vagueness emerges through attempts to apply a term to a concrete factual situation. Indeed, the standard interpretative method used by the law simply jumps straight through a host of linguistic levels to the semantic-pragmatic content, accessing, along the way, an unstructured and unspecific hodgepodge of interpretative rules and doctrines.

In a book chapter on language processing written largely from the cognitive science perspective, Cangelosi distinguishes between four sequential and distinct levels of analysis conducted by the human brain when it interacts with human language.[50] There is, first, the *phonetic* level which associates certain sounds made with specific words. Then comes the *lexical* level which links a word with an internal meaning and (sometimes) an external real-world referent, usually through a shared lexicon. The third analysis is carried out on the *syntactic* level, through which meaning is refined on the basis of word order and

[50] Angelo Cangelosi, 'Language Processing' in Michael A Arbib and James J Bonaiuto (eds), *From Neuron to Cognition via Computational Neuroscience* (Cambridge MA, The MIT Press, 2016) 693.

the use of shared grammatical rules. Finally, there is the *pragmatic* level, which takes into account the social context of communication, usually to determine the precise range of effects that a speaker intends to convey. The ambiguity with which we are concerned exists on the second, lexical level, while the resolution of vagueness that legal interpreters often jump to largely takes place on the fourth, pragmatic level. Just as the human brain processes lexical issues before pragmatic ones, an interpreter should always resolve any ambiguity *before* attempting to resolve any vagueness. As Azar pointed out in a short but remarkable 2007 paper on the nature of legal interpretation:

> Disambiguation, which is choosing between two possible meanings, comes before de-vaguefying because disambiguation, but not de-vaguefying, is crucial for the understanding of the text. De-vaguefying a term by using one approach or another is possible only if the term is understood in a certain, unambiguous way; it cannot replace a process of disambiguation that can be done by paying attention to context.[51]

Remarkably, treaty interpretation itself impliedly accepts that we must first identify which of a treaty term's competing senses we should use (disambiguate), before we determine its precise scope in the light of a fixed factual or legal situation ('de-vaguefy'). VCLT Article 31(4) allows special meaning to operate as a complete exception to the default ordinary meaning rule. To quote the impressively detailed study of Engelen, there is a

> presumption that the parties have that intention which appears from the ordinary meaning of the terms used by them[, but] this presumption is refutable, for the parties may have intended to give to a term a meaning other than its ordinary meaning.[52]

Kolb states simply that '*le sens spécial est une exception au sens ordinaire*',[53] while Mitchell concludes that this provision reflects the simple fact that: 'in some cases, the parties may not have intended that a term have its ordinary meaning'.[54] Clearly, where a special meaning was potentially intended, international adjudicators will determine whether the term was used in an ordinary or special sense before going to the trouble of ascertaining its precise content. In the context of VCLT Article 31(4), therefore, treaty interpreters will disambiguate before they de-vaguefy. As Van Damme points out, it is only logical that 'the special meaning itself might require a substantive amount of interpretation',[55] but this need only be carried out after the special sense of the treaty term is the one that has been determined to be applicable.

[51] Azar (n 16) 137.
[52] Engelen (n 44) 111.
[53] Kolb (n 5) 439.
[54] Andrew D Mitchell, 'The Legal Basis for Using Principles in WTO Disputes' (2007) 10 *Journal of International Economic Law* 795, 812; see also Engelen (n 44) 111.
[55] Isabelle Van Damme, *Treaty Interpretation by the WTO Appellate Body* (Oxford, Oxford University Press, 2009) 351.

Already in 1928, Ehrlich had referred to an example of an international court or tribunal determining, first, which sense of the term to interpret, then endeavouring to unpack it using the textual method that relies on dictionaries:

> The award in the arbitration between Chile and Peru that was handed down in 1871 referred to Bouvier's Law Dictionary for the definition of the term 'liquidation'. However, noting that the verb 'to charge' did not have, according to the context, any technical meaning, it referred to Webster's dictionary for this term.[56]

The *termini technici* rule now expressed in VCLT Article 31(4) thus provides for disambiguation prior to the de-vaguefying more commonly associated with interpretation. It takes a situation where there are several candidate senses (*acceptions*) for a treaty term and decides which of them should be selected. As Kammerhofer has noted, it proceeds on 'the assumption that each word has one meaning, or, at least, one meaning that can be fixed contextually'.[57] It is only then, once the one meaning or sense has been identified, that the term – or more precisely the sense of the term determined to be the one which was used by the parties – should have its vagueness maximally resolved through a process of interpretation focused on de-vaguefying.

This defined two-step process makes sense from a judicial economy perspective. By first determining whether an ordinary or special meaning should be used – and thereby constraining the range of possible semantic contents, this method makes it simpler to identify the precise semantic-pragmatic content of a treaty term. Even where the special sense selected turns out to be vague in the context of the particular case, there is still a considerable saving of complexity, effort and risk for the interpreter who only has to de-vaguefy one, rather than two, senses of a polysemous treaty term. After all, it would be foolish and inefficient to try to work out how a use of the term 'bays' should precisely be defined, before determining whether it is meant to be understood in an ordinary or technical sense. Only once the sense of a treaty term is determined, should an interpreter move to ascertaining the semantic and, eventually (if necessary), semantic-pragmatic content of the term.

The recent interpretative practice of the field's principal judicial organ, the ICJ, also discloses a recognition of the need to resolve ambiguity before resolving vagueness. The *Related Rights* case centred around the interpretation of the expression '*con objetos de comercio*' in the 1858 Treaty of Limits. Costa Rica interpreted it as meaning 'for the purposes of commerce' and, Nicaragua, as meaning 'with articles of trade'.[58] The Court was accordingly presented with a problem of ambiguity arising from the competing senses of '*con objetos de*'.

[56] Ludwik Ehrlich, 'L'interprétation des traités' (1928) 24 *Collected Courses of the Hague Academy of International Law* 1, 108 (present author's translation).

[57] Jörg Kammerhofer, *Uncertainty in International Law: A Kelsenian Perspective* (London, Routledge, 2011) 90.

[58] *Dispute regarding Navigational and Related Rights (Costa Rica v Nicaragua)*, Judgment [2009] ICJ Reports 213, 236 (§ 45).

In the present context, it is most significant that the judgment of the Court recognised this as an ambiguity and resolved that ambiguity as its first interpretative step, finding that it was 'reasonable to infer that the Parties tended to understand "objetos" in its abstract sense'.[59]

It is thus abundantly clear that, where an expression is inconclusive on account of both ambiguity and vagueness, an interpreter should always disambiguate it before de-vaguefying it. Before walking down the long road of determining the precise scope of a treaty term for the purposes of a defined fact situation, an interpreter at a fork-in-the-road needs to know which road to follow. Just as the hearer of an ambiguous utterance about 'banks' will not try to determine what exactly the speaker is saying about 'banks' before determining which kind of bank the speaker is talking about, the interpreter of a treaty term ambiguous as between its ordinary and special – or original and later-emerging – senses must first determine in which sense it is used, and only then determine the term's precise scope. By first engaging in disambiguation, interpreters determine which dictionary sense (lexical variant) they should try to unpack or indeed which dictionary to look at. Yet they only postpone and do not usually manage to avoid the subsequent task of having to unpack the chosen definition or meaning of that lexical variant, given that it almost inevitably turns out to be too vague to be applied to the concrete situation demanded by the case.

The fact that we regularly see treaty interpreters jump straight to the VCLT's techniques for de-vaguefying even in circumstances which present both ambiguity and vagueness does not mean that we should consider resolving vagueness before ambiguity. Indeed, this practice is most likely just a further reflection of how attractive the broad and flexible VCLT rules are to treaty interpreters, combined with the fact that those rules only provide for disambiguation in the relatively rare situation in which there is some evidence of a special meaning. It could also be a consequence of treaty interpreters not recognising certain interpretative issues – like the issue posed by the choice between relevant different original and later-emerging meanings of a treaty term – as issues of lexical ambiguity in the first place. Finally, even some interpreters who recognise that they are faced with an issue of ambiguity might, as Azar suggests,[60] choose to ignore the possibility of resolving that ambiguity and jump straight to methods of resolving vagueness in order to maximise the flexibility of their interpretative enterprise.

Ultimately, interpretative practice that seeks to define the specific boundaries of the term's semantic-pragmatic content before identifying the particular semantic sense in which it is used is either failing to see the problem of intertemporal linguistics or deliberately avoiding it. This study, however, is dedicated to solving this Problem, so must ensure that it is identified and responded to in the most intellectually appropriate manner possible. Since the Problem is a problem of lexical ambiguity, interpreters confronting it should first engage in a process of disambiguation.

[59] ibid 238–40 (§§ 50–56).

[60] Azar (n 16) 124 *et passim*.

8

Disambiguating Original and Later-emerging Senses Using a Temporal Sense-Intention

I. DISAMBIGUATION IS ACHIEVED THROUGH IDENTIFYING THE SENSE-INTENTION

IF THE PROBLEM of intertemporal linguistics is a problem of lexical ambiguity, then the solution to the Problem would appear to reside in how we disambiguate the precise kind of lexical ambiguity it presents.

It is only natural that everyday speakers, linguists and computer programmers alike use different methods to resolve inconclusiveness arising from the very different phenomena of ambiguity and vagueness. Whereas inconclusiveness arising from vagueness usually presents a situation of too little meaning, inconclusiveness arising from ambiguity presents, at least in the first instance, the problem of too much meaning. In order to generate the required precision from the underspecified term, interpretative techniques aimed at resolving vagueness must inherently cast their net wide and their probes deep. The resolution of vagueness creates more precise meaning within the framework set out by the vague term. By contrast, the resolution of ambiguity simply requires discarding some candidate meanings in favour of others. It adjudicates between and selects from the range of available meanings, but does not inquire into their essence nor develop them, so need not be as expansive or comprehensive a process as that which is used to resolve vagueness.

Lexical ambiguity is a very common, almost omnipresent phenomenon. According to one study, 44 per cent of a random sample of English words had more than one dictionary definition, with more commonly used and older words even more likely to have multiple senses.[1] Yet lexical ambiguity has not traditionally attracted much attention because, in everyday speech and comprehension, it can be resolved relatively easily by inferences as to which sense of a word was used.[2]

[1] See Cyma Van Petten, 'Lexical Ambiguity Resolution' (2002) 81 *Psychology Review* 867, 867.

[2] See Marianna Apidianaki, 'Acquisition automatique de sens pour la désambiguïsation et la sélection lexicale en traduction' (Doctorat en linguistique, Université Paris-Diderot – Paris VII, 2008) 7 – tel.archives-ouvertes.fr/tel-00322285.

Laboratory studies of how this is done by human language users have led to various models being proposed including the 'exhaustive access', 'ordered access' and 'selective access' models.[3] They all rely on the same inputs – immediate textual context – and the precise mechanism through which the lexical ambiguity is disambiguated by the human brain was traditionally not important enough to require analysis.

However, the relatively recent and quite rapid development of machine-based natural language processing ('NLP') in the context of search, translation and bot technologies has made lexical ambiguity a problem that now has to be identified, isolated and addressed. The feedback loop between the literature on artificial intelligence, cognitive science and theoretical linguistics has delivered such clarity that we can now reliably distinguish between lexical ambiguity and the other types of the inconclusiveness that, together, are the focal point of the theory and practice of legal interpretation. Most significantly, with the frameworks and methods that have been created around natural language processing, we now have a conceptual roadmap for elaborating different responses for interpreters faced with different types of inconclusiveness.

We have seen that the ambiguity created by the semantic change with which we are concerned in an analysis of the problem of intertemporal linguistics exists on the lexical level alone. In computational linguistics and, as commercial search, translation and bot technologies develop, in computing in general, resolving specifically lexical ambiguity has become so important that a dedicated field of 'Word Sense Disambiguation' ('WSD') has emerged. Word Sense Disambiguation is a part of the sub-field of NLP that deals with reading comprehension by computers, called 'Natural Language Understanding' ('NLU') and considered a hard problem of Artificial Intelligence on account of the great variety and complexity in human language use that undermines attempts to model it. Its task is to select the best sense to attribute to a word appearing in a given context. If a computer is to understand a natural language input accurately, it must determine which of many dictionary senses of the same word is being used.

In the present context, the salient fact is that the various word sense disambiguation methods employed in the different modern-day applications of natural language processing all focus on two key linguistic facts: communicative intention and (immediate) context. As will be seen in chapter 9, the immediate context is regarded by the linguistics literature as the most reliable indicator of the intention used to disambiguate terms, but it is – and always remains – the ascertainment of the communicative intention that is the goal of WSD's inquiry. As pointed out by Kaur and Singh, 'natural language processing involves a set of tasks and phases that evolves from the lexical text analysis to … one in which

[3] Van Petten (n 1) 868.

the author's intentions are shown'.[4] Where there is lexical ambiguity, a hearer of an ambiguous phrase will usually understand the sense intended by the speaker, but a computer may not.[5] As the linguists Haugh and Jaszczolt have noted, '[p]otentially ambiguous utterances result in unambiguous acts of communication thanks to the recognition of the speaker's intentions'.[6]

Word sense disambiguation techniques are thus methods for getting from the objective features of the text to the speaker's intention as to the sense in which a lexically ambiguous term is used. They all assume that there is, to quote Miller, 'a single unambiguous communicative intention underlying every word in the document or speech act under consideration' that needs to be identified.[7] Indeed, the existence of – and need to identify – a single word-sense-intention for every lexically ambiguous word is regarded as so fundamental that it is barely ever mentioned explicitly. Most of the WSD literature focuses instead on finding the best methods for reliably identifying that intention, what this study will refer to simply as the 'sense-intention'.

II. THE SENSE-INTENTION IS VERY DIFFERENT TO OTHER INTERPRETATIVE INTENTIONS

The use of intention to disambiguate is inherently logical from a linguistics or computer science perspective, but, in the treaty interpretation context, the mere mention of intention is fraught with danger. First, what has been called the 'received wisdom … that the general rule of interpretation put paid to the notion of interpreting in accordance with "the intention of the parties"',[8] despite recent efforts to declare it a misconception,[9] continues to undermine efforts to invoke intention as part of a solution to a problem of treaty interpretation. Second, legal arguments referring to intention are plagued by the fact that there are many different types of intention, with practitioners and scholars often being unclear about the precise type of intention they are invoking. In this section, we will see that, so long as one does not rely too heavily on the preparatory work

[4] Jaskiran Kaur and Amardeep Singh, 'A Customized Adaptation of Traditional Lesk Method for Sense Disambiguation of Punjabi Words from Medical Domain' (2015) 3 *International Journal for Research in Applied Science & Engineering Technology* 1045, 1045.

[5] Apidianaki (n 2) 7; Kaur and Singh (n 4) 1045.

[6] Michael Haugh and Kasia M Jaszczolt, 'Speaker Intentions and Intentionality' in Keith Allan and Kasia M Jaszczolt (eds), *The Cambridge Handbook of Pragmatics* (Cambridge, Cambridge University Press, 2012) 17.

[7] Tristan Miller, 'Adjusting Sense Representations for Word Sense Disambiguation and Automatic Pun Interpretation' (Doktorarbeit, Technische Universität Darmstadt, 2016) 75 – tuprints.ulb.tu-darmstadt.de/5400/.

[8] Eirik Bjorge, 'The Vienna Rules, Evolutionary Interpretation, and the Intentions of the Parties' in Andrea Bianchi, Daniel Peat and Matthew Windsor (eds), *Interpretation in International Law* (Oxford, Oxford University Press, 2015) 189.

[9] See especially Eirik Bjorge, *The Evolutionary Interpretation of Treaties* (Oxford, Oxford University Press, 2014).

of a treaty, there is in fact no impediment to leaning on a notion of intention in a treaty interpretation context (section A). We will then distinguish between sense-intention and other types of intention invoked in this context (section B), all the while noting how the sense-intention has already found recognition as part of VCLT Article 31's special meaning rule.

A. International Law does not Reject the Relevance of Party-intention to Treaty Interpretation

Mention of intention in the treaty interpretation context is controversial due to the quite widely-held view that the drafters and negotiators of the VCLT, by rendering recourse to a treaty's preparatory work a mere supplementary means, completely turned their backs on the notion that the parties' intention (or 'party-intention') should play a role in the interpretation of treaties. In entertaining testimony given to the *Wintershall* tribunal as the Claimant's expert on international law, Christoph Schreuer, for example, argued in relation to an alleged absence of any mention of the intention of the parties in VCLT Articles 31 and 32, that '[i]ntention is not a concept that is used by the Vienna Convention on the law of treaties'.[10] When pushed, he admitted that it 'is relevant to the extent that it finds expression in the text', but insisted that his predecessor as Chair of International Law at the University of Vienna, Karl Zemanek, 'used to fail students when they gave the answer that the intention of the parties was significant for the interpretation of treaties'.[11]

In fact, however, the ILC Law of Treaties Study Group and the Vienna Conference sessions that finalised the terms of the VCLT only ever turned their back on heavy use of the preparatory work of a treaty as evidence of party-intention, not on the importance of party-intention itself. Regrettably, references to the intention of the parties in an interpretation context have been equated with heavy reliance on the preparatory work of the relevant treaty since the earliest days of efforts to codify the rules of treaty interpretation. Indeed, when Hersch Lauterpacht, as a rapporteur for the IDI, proposed treating the intention of the parties as '*un élément décisif en matière d'interprétation de traités*',[12] he encountered vehement resistance.[13] Then, when the IDI's next rapporteur on treaty interpretation, Gerald Fitzmaurice, chartered a new path that emphasised the role of the text and downgraded the role of the preparatory work – from the primary source of reference in all interpretative disputes to one of three 'other means of interpretation' to be used where the interpreter considers the use of such means

[10] *Wintershall Aktiengesellschaft v Argentina*, Award (ICSID Tribunal, ARB/04/14, 8 December 2008) 51 (§ 86).

[11] ibid (§ 86).

[12] See Institut de droit international, 'De l'interprétation des traités' (1956) 46 *Annuaire* 318–19.

[13] ibid 320–21.

necessary – he was regarded by many as having acceded to an 'anti-intention' movement in treaty interpretation.[14] In fact, Fitzmaurice was not denying the need to interpret treaties in the light of the parties' intentions, but merely re-ordering the means of inferring those intentions. As he made clear 20 years later as a judge of the European Court of Human Rights in the *National Union of Belgian Police* case:

> [T]he real *raison d'être* of the hallowed rule of the textual interpretation of a treaty lies precisely in the fact that the intentions of the parties are supposed to be expressed or embodied in – or derivable from – the text which they finally draw up, and may not therefore legitimately be sought elsewhere save in special circumstances ...[15]

At the first Vienna Conference session of 1968, McDougal (for the US) railed against the draft interpretation provisions that he considered reflected a 'textual approach to interpretation [that] was impossible to apply' and had, at least according to his reading of its accompanying commentary 'flatly rejected ... common intent as the goal of interpretation'.[16] His proposed amendment, which returned attention to the preparatory work, attracted some qualified support from other delegates,[17] but was also roundly criticised and, on 22 April 1968, was ultimately rejected by 66 votes to eight with 10 abstentions.[18]

What is significant in the present context is that this proposed amendment was not rejected because it insisted on the importance of intention to the interpretation of treaties, but because it favoured interpretation according to a purely subjective intention revealed in materials such as the preparatory work, rather than the more objective intention apparent on the face of the treaty. For example, in one of the most strident criticisms of McDougal's proposal, the Uruguayan delegate, Jiménez de Aréchaga, pointed to the inherent unreliability of a supposed common intention of the parties deduced from the preparatory work.[19] He emphasised the will revealed by the sacred text of a treaty over any less reliable and more subjective evidence of the 'supposed real will of the parties' that, if privileged, 'would float like a cloud over the *terra firma* of a contractual text'.[20] He did not disavow the role of intention, but wholeheartedly rejected the notion that parties 'be allowed freely to invoke their supposed real will' in place of what the treaty says.[21] The Polish delegate, Nahlik, also insisted

[14] ibid 340–47.

[15] *National Union of Belgian Police v Belgium* (Merits), Separate Opinion of Judge Fitzmaurice (European Court of Human Rights (Grand Chamber), 4464/70, 27 October 1975) 29 (§ 9[i]).

[16] UN Conference on the Law of Treaties, 'Official Records, First Session, Vienna' (Vienna, United Nations, 1968) 167 (Thirty-first meeting – 19 April 1968, per McDougal [United States of America], §§ 43 and 39 respectively).

[17] ibid 168–72 (per Makarevich [Ukrainian Soviet Socialist Republic], Thirty-first meeting – 19 April 1968, § 54), (per Dadzié [Ghana], Thirty-first meeting – 19 April 1968, § 70), (per Krispis [Greece], Thirty-second meeting – 20 April 1968, § 9).

[18] ibid 185 (Thirty-third meeting – 22 April 1968, § 75).

[19] ibid 170 (per Jiménez de Aréchaga [Uruguay], Thirty-first meeting – 19 April 1968, § 64).

[20] ibid (per Jiménez de Aréchaga [Uruguay], Thirty-first meeting – 19 April 1968, § 63).

[21] ibid (per Jiménez de Aréchaga [Uruguay], Thirty-first meeting – 19 April 1968, § 63).

upon the importance of parties' intentions while attacking the proposed US amendment, claiming that '[t]here was no proof more direct and more authentic of the intentions of the parties than the text they drew up together to embody those very intentions', the 'most stable and permanent element of a treaty',[22] a point made elegantly by Charles De Visscher who, in his *Théories et réalités en droit international public* published that same year, wrote that:

> The judge is not asked to penetrate the intimate designs of the contracting parties; he is expected to discover by the means at his disposal that part of their intentions that external signs reveal. Now the words freely chosen by the parties are *par excellence* or at least primarily the instrument of this externalization.[23]

As Sinclair put it at the First Session of the Vienna Conference, the Commission 'had simply wished to recognize that the evidentiary value of preparatory work was less than that of the text of the treaty itself'.[24] When, just prior to the Vienna Conference's vote on the US's proposed amendment, Humphrey Waldock was given the floor as an Expert Consultant, he confirmed that it was the role of the preparatory work that had been relegated in importance, not the role of intention.[25]

The move away from an undue focus on the often-concealed subjective intention appearing in the preparatory work makes sense in the international domain, but an overall rejection of the relevance of intention to interpretation does not. From a linguistic perspective, there is also considerable appeal in an approach that attempts to identify the *objective* – really *intersubjective* – intention from material that is readily available to all participants in the discourse. The concept of 'apparent meaning' has linguistic support in the notions of communication proposed by such linguists as Taillard, who understands communication as arising from 'an intention to let my audience know of my intention to inform them of something',[26] and Recanati, for whom there is a communicative intention 'if and only if [an "utterance"] makes an intention of this type manifest'.[27] Poggi defines even the speaker's intention objectively, emphasising the role of so-called 'co-text' and saying:

> The speaker's intention does not coincide with what the speaker has in mind, but with what she demonstrates: in other words, what counts is the intentional action to demonstrate, the expressed or recognizable intention to make salient an object.[28]

[22] ibid 173–74 (per Nahlik [Poland], Thirty-second meeting – 20 April 1968, §§ 22 and 25).

[23] Charles de Visscher, *Theory and Reality in Public International Law (Théories et réalités en droit international public)* (Percy Ellwood Corbett tr, Princeton NJ, Princeton University Press, 1968) 395–96.

[24] Vienna Conference Records, 1968 Session (n 16) 178 (per Sinclair [United Kingdom], Thirty-third meeting – 22 April 1968, § 9).

[25] ibid 184 (per Waldock [Expert Consultant], Thirty-third meeting – 22 April 1968, § 68).

[26] Marie-Odile Taillard, 'Beyond Communicative Intention' (2002) 14 *UCL Working Papers in Linguistics* 189, 190.

[27] François Recanati, 'On Defining Communicative Intentions' (1986) 1 *Mind & Language* 213, 239.

[28] Francesca Poggi, 'The Myth of Literal Meaning in Legal Interpretation' (2013) 1 *Analisi et diritto* 313, 315.

Moreover, a continued focus on identifying the intention, but not a purely subjective one, finds support in the interpretative approaches of not only common-law systems, but also some prominent civil law systems.[29]

The unease elicited in the hearts of many international lawyers by any mention of intention in relation to treaty interpretation harks back to a notion of intention that is overly subjective and unnecessarily connected to reference to a treaty's preparatory work.

We saw in the previous section that the VCLT's only interpretative rule that disambiguates expressly does so by referring to intention. While earlier expressions of the *termini technici* rule tended to invoke a presumption in favour of special meaning for all terms 'which in legal terminology have an accepted connotation' and understood specific evidence of intention as potentially rebutting that presumption,[30] under the formulation of VCLT Article 31(4) the default position is ordinary meaning and special meaning will only be assigned to a treaty term 'if it is established that the parties so intended'.[31] For many, this reliance on party-intention for the purposes of treaty interpretation made VCLT Article 31(4) a vestige of – or, to use Kolb's words, a 'Trojan horse' for – the subjectivist approach to treaty interpretation that the law of treaties codification project was meant to have left behind.[32] In his commentary on VCLT Article 31, Sorel labels Article 31(4) as the 'reintegration of the intention of the parties',[33] with McDougal considering Article 31(4) a 'modest concession'[34] to the subjectivist approach that previously held sway prior to the elaboration of the VCLT and Spiermann concluding that the VCLT's 'objective approach is balanced by Article 31(4)',[35] such authors thereby revealing their view that Article 31(4) allows the spirit of the *école subjectiviste* live on.

VCLT Article 31(4) – and all other rules of treaty interpretation that require some constrained reliance on party-intention – should not, however, be regarded

[29] Under s 157 of the *Bundesgesetzbuch* (German Civil Code), for example, contracts are to be interpreted objectively, the notion of the *Empfängerhorizont* ensuring that the intention feeding into the interpretative process is that which a reasonable addressee of the relevant declaration would understand the intention to be in the circumstances, see Otto Palandt and Gerd Brudermüller, *Palandt Bürgerliches Gesetzbuch: mit Nebengesetzen insbesondere mit Einführungsgesetz* (München, C H Beck, 2017) 124–25 (§ 133, sub-paras 9, 14); Basil Markesinis and others, *The German Law of Contract: A Comparative Treatise* (Oxford, Hart Publishing, 2006) 288.

[30] See, eg Hersch Lauterpacht, *The Development of International Law by the International Court* (New York, Praeger, 1958) 59–60; Harvard Law School and James W Garner, 'Draft Convention on the Law of Treaties' (1935) 29 *Supplement to the American Journal of International Law* 653, 940.

[31] Vienna Convention on the Law of Treaties 1969 (1155 UNTS 331), art 31(4).

[32] Robert Kolb, *Interprétation et création du droit international: Esquisses d'une herméneutique juridique moderne pour le droit international public* (Bruxelles, Bruylant, 2006) 437.

[33] Jean-Marc Sorel, 'Article 31 – Convention de Vienne de 1969' in Olivier Corten and Pierre Klein (eds), *Les conventions de Vienne sur le droit des traités: commentaire article par article*, vol 2 (Bruxelles, Bruylant, 2006) 1324.

[34] Myres S McDougal, 'The International Law Commission's Draft Articles upon Interpretation: Textuality Redivivus' (1967) 61 *The American Journal of International Law* 992, 994.

[35] Ole Spiermann, *International Legal Argument in the Permanent Court of International Justice: The Rise of the International Judiciary* (Cambridge, Cambridge University Press, 2005) 99.

as misnomers that are out of place in a world of treaty interpretation governed by the VCLT rules, because those rules actually allow party-intention to play an important – albeit somewhat covert – role. The concern that VCLT Article 31(4) betrays the spirit of the VCLT rules by appealing to the subjective intentions of the parties is even more misplaced when one considers the narrow notion of party-intention that it appeals to. Here, as in other areas of public international law, practitioners and scholars alike are led astray by a failure to distinguish between structurally and functionally distinct phenomena, on this occasion simply because they all use words derived from the Latin verb '*intendere*'.

Having built its theory on the foundations of linguistics, this book cannot avoid using the word 'intention', because, as explained above, linguistics explicitly appeals to a form of communicative intention used to disambiguate competing senses of terms. We are thus left with trying to avoid the confusion and sensitivities that regularly accompany using the word 'intention' in a treaty interpretation context by being extremely clear about the particular type of intention we are seeking to identify when disambiguating between the original and later-emerging senses of a treaty term.

B. Sense-Intention is Much Narrower and Qualitatively Different to Concrete Intentions Used to Define the Semantic-pragmatic Scope of Treaty Terms

In an era in which interpreters and scholars alike are straying so often from the objectively ascertainable intention of the parties who drafted a treaty, contemporary authors' emphasis on party-intention provides a most timely reminder of what treaty interpretation is really about. However, saying party-intention is at the core of the interpretative process is not enough if it is understood to include almost all types of intention and extend to almost all types of matters.

Party-intention conceived of in a very general sense is in fact anything at all that is concordant with the meaning arrived at through a use of any of the interpretative rules in VCLT Articles 31–33 – or, at the very least, any of those appearing in VCLT Article 31(1). Bjorge's 2014 book on the evolutionary interpretation of treaties notably defines the intention of the parties as 'the result which one reaches if the general rule of interpretation is applied correctly'.[36] Even if Bjorge is right that this is 'the best definition which the ILC has been able to produce',[37] that would still not justify using such a general notion in order to decide whether to use the original or later meaning of a changing treaty term, as Bjorge's monograph often appears to. Since the elements of even the Article 31(1) rule of treaty interpretation are so various and capable

[36] Bjorge (n 9) 63.
[37] ibid.

of pointing in so many different directions in different case situations,[38] insistence on the relevance of a highly diffuse, all-encompassing concept of intention, like insistence on the diverse, general and flexible VCLT rules, provides no interpretative guidance at all. Again, while such a notion of intention will inevitably provide an ex post justification for a static or dynamic approach being taken, it will rarely – if ever – provide a means for determining whether a static or dynamic approach should be taken to the Problem in the first place.

The functional definition of party-intention that neither specifies what type of intention should be identified nor constrains the sources from which it should be ascertained is therefore of scant utility to a study seeking to solve an interpretative problem. In the world of public international law, intention is such a nebulous notion that an extremely wide definition of the intention relevant to treaty interpretation is singularly unhelpful. Without a narrower definition, international lawyers citing the parties' intention in relation to interpretation may be talking about the intention as regards the specific treaty term, of the treaty provision, of the entire treaty or even of the entire regime of which the treaty forms a part. In addition, these many intentions are understood in different respects. In identifying the intention, international lawyers sometimes seek and discern what the parties intended to *say*, but other times they focus on what the parties intended to *do* or even what they intended to *achieve* when they devised a treaty term, treaty provision, treaty or entire regime.

Bjorge's work is itself a case in point. He distinguishes between abstract intentions and concrete intentions, intentions of principle and, quoting the *Iron Rhine* award[39] 'the general idea the parties had in mind'.[40] Bjorge states that his book 'follows Dworkin and Letsas in assuming that abstract intentions must be more important than concrete ones, and that intentions of principle ought to trump intentions of detail',[41] but never explains why this is the appropriate preference in relation to the different types of interpretative activity he considers, including those that address the Problem. In any event, Letsas's approach takes us too far from the interpretation of treaty terms in general (and conveniently for Letsas, towards object and purpose) by understanding abstract intentions to be those dedicated to maximising human rights protections.[42] As demonstrated in section 5.II.B, the pursuit of that one fixed objective does not provide a consistent answer to the problem of intertemporal linguistics.

When one takes all the different permutations of intention into account, one sees that, in treaty interpretation alone, the intention of the parties can mean

[38] See ch 5 above.

[39] *Iron Rhine ('Ijzeren Rijn') Railway between the Kingdom of Belgium and the Kingdom of the Netherlands*, Award (2005) XXVII RIAA/RSA 35.

[40] Bjorge (n 9) 62–63.

[41] ibid 62.

[42] See George Letsas, 'Intentionalism and the Interpretation of the ECHR' in Malgosia Fitzmaurice, Olufemi Elias and Panos Merkouris (eds), *Treaty Interpretation and the Vienna Convention on the Law of Treaties: 30 Years On* (Leiden, Martinus Nijhoff Publishers, 2010) 267–72.

at least 12 different things. This diversity is itself problematic from the perspective of this study's search for some firm guidance on whether a treaty term subject to semantic change should be given its original or later-emerging meaning. Once there are many different forms of intention in play, they can point in different directions, one (or more) suggesting that a treaty term be given its meaning at the time of the treaty's conclusion at the same time that another (or more) suggest that the same term should be given its meaning at the time of the treaty's application. It is therefore abundantly clear that only one specific type of intention can offer the international adjudicator any guidance permitting a firm answer to the Problem.

Fortunately, this study has a sufficiently limited focus for it to avoid having to identify the different types of intention for all the different interpretative situations that might arise in public international law. It is not dedicated to how to interpret treaties generally, but to resolving a species of lexical ambiguity within them, to identifying the particular sense in which a specific treaty term is used. For clarity, this book therefore resorts to the use of a partial neologism and studiously refers to the relevant party-intention as the 'sense-intention', a form of intention readily distinguishable from other notions of intention that are prominent in this area of international law.

It is the sense-intention that linguistics invokes for disambiguating between competing semantic contents of the one term. The sense-intention is focused uniquely on the specific treaty term, rather than the treaty provision, the whole treaty or the relevant legal regime. In addition, it refers uniquely to what the drafters intended to say, not what they intended to do or to achieve. Finally, and perhaps most importantly, it is functionally different in the sense that, instead of determining the precise semantic-pragmatic content of a treaty term, it simply determines which of the competing senses the drafters used when employing the term.

VCLT Article 31(4) also only refers to a sense-intention when it says that '[a] special meaning shall be given to a term if it is established that the parties so intended'.[43] Unfortunately, many international lawyers have somewhat justifiably understood the 'meaning' in Article 31(4) to mean the precise 'semantic-pragmatic content' rather than the mere semantic sense of the expression and therefore the intention invoked by Article 31(4) to be a wider form of intention. The Ghanaian delegation to the Vienna Conference, for example, betrayed such an understanding of what VCLT Article 31(4) means by 'meaning', when it said that it 'failed to see how the special meaning intended by the parties was to be discovered if the use of the preparatory work of the treaty' could not always be resorted to for the purposes of Article 31(4),[44] with the US delegation taking a very similar view.[45]

[43] VCLT, art 31(4).

[44] Vienna Conference Records, 1968 Session (n 16) 171 (per Dadzié [Ghana], Thirty-second meeting – 20 April 1968, § 70).

[45] ibid 168 (per McDougal [United States], Thirty-first meeting – 19 April 1968, § 47).

This is partly the fault of the terms used by VCLT Article 31(4) itself, particularly in English. The ambiguity of the English word 'meaning' and the French word *sens* between what is really word-sense (*acception*) and semantic-pragmatic content (*signification*) cannot have helped early – or even modern-day – interpreters of what became VCLT Article 31(4). This confusion persists today. In 2008, Scott argued that the intention inquiry required by Article 31(4) inherently brought the preparatory work into play, also claiming that the provision 'constitutes an exception in that the *travaux* can legitimately serve as a primary source of interpretation as long as the purpose is the focused one of proving a contended-for special meaning'.[46] In a 2011 *RGDIP* article, Corten went so far as to quote the terms of Article 31(4) before saying 'it is clear from this provision that it is the intention of the parties that constitutes the determining criterion that must guide the entire interpretative process'.[47]

However, VCLT Article 31(4) actually does not reintroduce the notion that the precise parameters of a (vague) treaty term should be determined according to the parties' subjective intentions, first, because it does not require the identification of a subjective intention,[48] and second because it never actually states that the semantic-pragmatic content of the term can be determined by the parties' intentions at all. As Engelen astutely observes, the readings of VCLT Article 31(4) that consider it to authorise the use of *travaux* to determine the meaning of a treaty term are misguided because 'this paragraph does not provide for an alternative, more subjective, process of treaty interpretation'.[49] As he points out,

> the special meaning of a term, just like its ordinary meaning, should be determined by reference to the context as defined in paragraph 2, the object and purpose of the treaty, and the subsequent agreements and practices, which, according to paragraph 3, should also be thrown into the crucible.[50]

Upon closer inspection, the terms of Article 31(4) themselves do not seem to extend as far as most international lawyers think they do. When Article 31(4) says '[a] special meaning shall be given to a term if it is established that the parties so intended', the 'if so intended' construction suggests that the intention is in relation to a process, not a particular meaning. Authors concerned that

46 Craig Scott, 'Diverse Persuasion(s): From Rhetoric to Representation (and Back Again to Rhetoric) in International Human Rights Interpretation' (2008) 4 *Comparative Research in Law & Political Economy Research Paper* 1, 24.

47 Olivier Corten, 'Les techniques reproduites aux articles 31 à 33 des conventions de Vienne: approche objectiviste ou approche volontariste de l'interprétation?' (2011) 115 *Revue génerale de droit international public* 351, 356 (present author's translation).

48 Draft Art 70(3), in: International Law Commission, *Yearbook 1964, vol II* (New York, United Nations, 1965) 52 (Waldock's Third Report); see also Appendix 1; see further Franciscus Antonius Engelen, *Interpretation of Tax Treaties under International Law: A Study of Articles 31, 32, and 33 of the Vienna Convention on the Law of Treaties and Their Application to Tax Treaties* (Amsterdam, International Bureau of Fiscal Documentation, 2004) 150.

49 Engelen (n 48) 164.

50 ibid; see also Isabelle Van Damme, *Treaty Interpretation by the WTO Appellate Body* (Oxford, Oxford University Press, 2009) 350–51.

Article 31(4) reintroduces the subjectivist approach are effectively reading 31(4) as saying that '[a] treaty term shall be given the meaning that it is established *that* the parties intended', but this construction has a different nuance, a difference even more obvious in French. In the final, carefully-reviewed French version of the VCLT text, the gender of the word '*telle*' confirms that it is not the special meaning that is intended, but something more general: '*[u]n terme sera entendu dans un sens particulier s'il est établi que telle était l'intention des parties*'.[51]

A review of the origins of VCLT Article 31(4) confirms this reading. The PCIJ's *Legal Status of Eastern Greenland* judgment of 1933 provides the clearest and best-known judicial statement of the difference between an ordinary and special meaning in the 50-year period that undoubtedly influenced the post-war codification efforts. Norway argued that the treaty did not use the word 'Greenland' in its geographical sense, but in a different sense common at the time.[52] In the primary language of that judgment, French, the Permanent Court interestingly used not just the word '*sens*', but also the more precise '*acception*', saying:

> C'est là un point pour lequel la charge de la preuve incombe à la Norvège. Le sens géographique du terme "Groënland", c'est-à-dire la dénomination qui est généralement employée dans les cartes pour indiquer l'île tout entière, doit être considéré comme *l'acception* usuelle de ce terme. Si l'une des Parties allègue qu'un *sens* inusité ou exceptionnel doit y être attaché, c'est cette Partie qui doit établir le bien-fondé de ce qu'elle avance. De l'avis de la Cour, la Norvège n'a pas réussi à prouver sa thèse.[53]

In English, '*l'acception usuelle*' was translated by the broader 'ordinary meaning', just as '*[l]e sens géographique*' was translated as 'the geographical meaning'.[54] However, in French the word '*acception*' has a much narrower meaning closer to the English 'sense' than the English meaning, while the word '*sens*' is ambiguous between denoting a lexical variant or a semantic-pragmatic content. In the present author's view, the use of the French word '*sens*' together with '*acception*' – and rather than '*signification*', for example – indicates that, for the Permanent Court, Norway's burden of proof lay not on establishing what semantic-pragmatic content was intended when the parties wrote 'Greenland', but merely the sense that the word 'Greenland' was used in. Since the *Eastern Greenland* judgment, the rule in VCLT Article 31(4) has actually only ever required the

[51] Convention de Vienne sur le droit des traités 1969 (1155 UNTS 331), art 31(4) (emphasis added). A reading of art 31(4) which understood it to be demarcating the precise semantic-pragmatic content of a treaty term according to the parties' intention would simply have read '[u]n terme sera entendu dans un sens particulier s'il est établi que *tel* était l'intention des parties'.

[52] *Legal Status of Eastern Greenland*, Judgment [1933] PCIJ Reports Series A/B No 53, 49.

[53] ibid: 'This is a point as to which the burden of proof lies on Norway. The geographical meaning of the word "Greenland", ie the name which is habitually used in the maps to denominate the whole island, must be regarded as the ordinary *meaning* of the word. If it is alleged by one of the Parties that some unusual or exceptional *meaning* is to be attributed to it, it lies on that Party to establish its contention. In the opinion of the Court, Norway has not succeeded in establishing her contention.' (PCIJ's translation) (emphasis added).

[54] ibid.

alleging party to prove that a treaty term was used in a special sense – but not the precise contours of the meaning of that sense of the word.

As our notions from the field of linguistics have shown us, VCLT Article 31(4) does not interpret in the most common sense of resolving vagueness, it simply disambiguates. Moreover, when it resolves the lexical ambiguity between special and ordinary senses of a treaty term, this rule of international law looks at the same type of intention that word-sense-disambiguation algorithms look at when they resolve the lexical ambiguity of homonymous or polysemous terms entered into an online translation tool – what we have called the 'sense-intention'. The sense-intention is thus not only a notion demanded by a consideration of the Problem from the perspective of linguistics, but also a notion that is embedded into the fabric of one of the VCLT's interpretative rules. There is accordingly little reason to disavow the important role that it can play in helping interpreters solve problems of intertemporal linguistics.

III. THE RELEVANT SENSE-INTENTION IN THE INTERTEMPORAL LINGUISTICS CONTEXT IS A '*TEMPORAL* SENSE-INTENTION'

The notion of sense-intention might be particularly narrow compared to the notions of intention generally used in international law, but there are still different types of sense-intention. The sense-intention that disambiguates between the original and later-emerging meaning of a treaty term to help solve the problem of intertemporal linguistics is different in character to, for example, the sense-intention that disambiguates between homonyms typed into an online translation tool and the sense-intention that VCLT Article 31(4) appeals to in order to decide between the ordinary and special meaning of a treaty term.

In simplistic terms, VCLT Article 31(4) requires interpreters to determine what type of dictionary the drafters of a treaty wanted them to use. For example, if a treaty term contained the word 'elasticity', an identification of the sense-intention associated with that word would determine whether the interpreter should start with a dictionary of psychology, physics or economics.[55] In the case of lexical ambiguity between the meaning of a treaty term at the time of the treaty's conclusion and the time of its application, one can think of the interpreter's disambiguation exercise in a similar, but slightly different fashion. Should an interpreter faced, in 2009, with the Spanish term '*comercio*' in a treaty of 1858, look at a Spanish dictionary of the 1850s or of the 2000s? The identification of the sense-intention associated with that treaty term '*comercio*' will determine the selection of one or other dictionary, so the function performed by the sense-intention is the same.

[55] Or, more often, which of a term's specialised senses within the one dictionary definition an interpreter should base his/her interpretation on, see 'elasticity, n.', *OED Online* – www.oed.com/view/Entry/60134.

A difference emerges however from the fact that, whereas both the ordinary and special sense of a treaty term are presumably known to the drafters of a treaty in the VCLT Article 31(4) situation, the drafters of a treaty later producing lexical ambiguity through semantic change will only know the original meaning of the word and indeed cannot know the later-emerging meaning. Both candidate senses of a term that has a technical meaning exist at the time of the treaty's conclusion, so evidence of intention contemporaneous with drafting and the context can determine which particular sense was intended, but this same evidence will not suffice for the type of lexical ambiguity arising where there is a problem of intertemporal linguistics. Whereas VCLT Article 31(4) turns on whether or not there is a specific sense-intention to use a special (or an ordinary) sense of the treaty term, the sense-intention capable of solving the Problem cannot turn on whether there is a specific sense-intention to use the original or later-emerging sense of the treaty term, because the latter sense is not known or capable of being known at the time the relevant communicative intention formed and manifested itself.

This is precisely why some scholars of international law appear to consider that recognition of the parties' intention in this context inherently leads to a static approach to the Problem. If the intention inquired into is a concrete and direct sense-intention – rather than a sense-intention-one-step-removed – and only *Sense A* of a term existed at the time of the treaty's conclusion, then the interpreter will invariably arrive at the conclusion that *Sense A* was selected, because *Sense B* could not have been. We have even seen some international decisions that appear to have fallen into this trap. Indeed, the award of the Tribunal in the *La Bretagne* arbitration of 1986 effectively resolved the Problem by looking at the parties' direct sense-intention:

> Therefore, when the Parties used the term 'Canadian fisheries regulations' they could hardly have *had in mind at that time* regulations covering fish processing on board fishing vessels.
>
> The Tribunal consequently cannot accept Canada's argument on that point, for it must above all bear in mind what the International Court of Justice has called 'the primary necessity of interpreting an instrument in accordance with the intentions of the parties at the time of its conclusion'…[56]

Equally, in the *ICS v Argentina* and *Daimler v Argentina* investment arbitration awards of 2012, the time bound nature of party-intention apparently even led the interpreter directly to an application of the principle of contemporaneity.[57]

[56] *Filleting within the Gulf of St Lawrence between Canada and France ('La Bretagne')*, Award (1986) XIX RIAA/RSA 225, 252 (§ 43, translation from *Dispute Concerning Filleting within the Gulf of St Lawrence ('La Bretagne')* (1986) 82 ILR 590, 624)(emphasis added).

[57] *Daimler Financial Services AG v Argentina* (Jurisdiction), Award (ICSID Tribunal, ARB/05/1, 22 August 2012) 90 (§ 220).

As these international decisions show, using a direct sense-intention such as that evoked by VCLT Article 31(4) in the particular scenario produced by semantic change would embed a static bias into the proposed solution to the Problem. It would effectively close off treaties to all linguistic and legal developments that were not and could not have been foreseen. If we are to remain committed to the notion of a disambiguating sense-intention despite this, we therefore need to make a minor adjustment to the nature of the intention to be sought. Instead of asking directly what is, in this context, the quite pointless question of whether *Sense A* or the then unknown *Sense B* was originally intended, we move to one-level higher in terms of abstraction and ask whether the term was intended to be used in a sense that would be frozen in time or a sense that would move with the times. We are still moving in the frame of lexical ambiguity, but instead of asking whether a term has one meaning or another meaning, we are asking the slightly different question of whether the term has a *fixed* sense or a *mobile* sense.

The words 'fixed' and 'mobile' have been deliberately chosen to mirror the French terms '*fixe*' and '*mobile*' used in relation to the problem of intertemporal linguistics by three Francophone international lawyers who have played a substantial role in the recent development of the case law of the International Court of Justice on this topic. In his individual opinion in the *Gabčíkovo* case, Judge Bedjaoui advocated taking a static approach to the Problem by default and conceptualised it as involving a '*renvoi fixe*' that could be contrasted with a '*renvoi mobile*' which would, in exceptional circumstances justify an interpretation in light of law that had subsequently developed.[58] Twelve years later, in the important *Related Rights* case, Alain Pellet as counsel for Nicaragua, applied these notions of *renvoi fixe* and *renvoi mobile* in a context that purported to directly address the Problem.[59] Finally, Judge Guillaume, an ad hoc judge in that same case, made a declaration in which he explicitly linked '*l'interprétation "contemporaine"*' to '*renvoi fixe*' and '*l'interprétation "évolutive"*' to '*renvoi mobile*'.[60]

Drawing on the above cases' mention of *renvoi* in this precise context, some commentators have acknowledged – albeit often only implicitly – that the possibility of a dynamic approach to the Problem is premised on a subjective intention of the drafters that the terms used change through time. In his 2006 article on treaty interpretation and extraneous legal rules, Duncan French drew on the *Gabčíkovo* opinions to characterise this as an 'inter-temporal *renvoi*',

[58] *Gabčíkovo-Nagymaros Project (Hungary/Slovakia)*, Separate Opinion of Judge Bedjaoui [1997] ICJ Reports 120, 121–22.

[59] *Dispute regarding Navigational and Related Rights (Costa Rica v Nicaragua)*, Verbatim record of public sitting, 5 March 2009 at 10am, 49–50 (per Pellet for Nicaragua).

[60] *Dispute regarding Navigational and Related Rights (Costa Rica v Nicaragua)*, Declaration of Judge ad hoc Guillaume [2009] ICJ Reports 290, 294 (§ 9).

writing: 'at the level of theory at least, inter-temporal *renvoi* is premised upon a subjective understanding of a treaty, that meanings change only when the parties themselves intended their words to alter in light of shifting circumstances'.[61] Of course, the meaning can always change independently of what the drafters intended, but French is commenting on whether or not that change should be recognised within the treaty. He is undoubtedly right that intention plays a key role in this regard.

In the *Gabčíkovo* case, the use of the word '*renvoi*', meaning 'reference', was not misplaced as the case and specific dicta related to whether legal norms outside of the parties' treaty could be incorporated into it.[62] In the *Related Rights* case, however, the prospect of a dynamic approach arose not from a change to the law, but simply from a potential semantic change; there was no question of 'referring out' as there was in the *Gabčíkovo* case.[63] Indeed, it is notable that Judge Guillaume then invoked the more precise terms of the IDI's 1975 Wiesbaden declaration on the intertemporal law that avoided mention of a *renvoi* and spoke instead of a treaty term's '*acception au moment de l'établissement de la disposition ou dans son acception au moment de l'application*'.[64]

The present study accordingly considers that the best way of understanding the sense-intention that allows for ambiguity created by semantic change to be disambiguated is by speaking of whether the parties intended to give the treaty term:

(i) a 'fixed sense' – pursuant to which it would not be affected by any semantic change after the conclusion of the treaty; or
(ii) a 'mobile sense' – pursuant to which it would be affected by such changes.

This obviously remains a 'sense-intention', but is a particular type thereof. For want of more accurate adjectives to distinguish this important, specific type of sense-intention from the many other types of intention, we will call it the 'temporal sense-intention' (or 'TSI'). The TSI is the specific type of party-intention that itself determines whether an interpreter should or should not take account of a semantic change affecting the meaning of a treaty term after the treaty's application, but prior to the time at which it falls to be applied.

[61] Duncan French, 'Treaty Interpretation and the Incorporation of Extraneous Legal Rules' (2006) 55 *International and Comparative Law Quarterly* 281, 296.

[62] *Gabčíkovo-Nagymaros Project (Hungary/Slovakia)*, Judgment [1997] ICJ Reports 7; see further s 6.II.B(ii) above.

[63] *Dispute regarding Navigational and Related Rights (Costa Rica v Nicaragua)*, Judgment [2009] ICJ Reports 213; see further s 6.II.B(iii) above.

[64] In English: 'as understood at the time when the provision was drawn up or as understood at the time of its application' (IDI translation adopted by the ICJ translation) – Institut de droit international, 'Le problème intertemporel en droit international public – Résolution' (Wiesbaden, 1975) 2 (§ 4); *Related Rights*, Guillaume Declaration (n 60) 294 (§ 9).

IV. NOTIONS AKIN TO THE TEMPORAL SENSE-INTENTION EMERGING FROM CASE LAW AND SCHOLARSHIP RELATING TO THE PROBLEM

In the precise area of the sub-field of treaty interpretation addressing the problem of intertemporal linguistics, party-intention has been referred to relatively frequently. Crucially, the most sophisticated references to intention in this context appear to be referring to a type of intention akin to what this book calls the 'temporal sense-intention' or 'TSI'.

In recent years, emphasis on some form of the party-intention in response to the Problem has become more accepted. In a 2005 award on jurisdiction in the *RosInvest v Russia* investment arbitration, the Tribunal referred to a group of cases considered to touch on the Problem and, in an extremely rare attempt to extract a guiding principle from the diverse practice on the issue, said:

> The common thread among the multilateral examples just referred to is that their nature or circumstances provide evidence that the Parties themselves *intended or understood that an evolutionary approach was appropriate to the interpretation* and application of what they had agreed upon, and exactly the same common thread is to be found in the two bilateral cases the Claimant invokes.[65]

Modern-day scholars accept that the dynamic approach in particular finds its basis in the (original) intention of the parties. Corten, for example, has stated that:

> The voluntarist approach is therefore not, by definition, one that remains confined to the subjective intention of the authors of the text at the time of its elaboration. It can perfectly well integrate a dynamic dimension, and we can even consider that this dimension is very much linked to voluntarism. It is precisely because the States intended this, that the treaty must be adapted to historical developments, which the interpreter must demonstrate in practice.[66]

Most notable, however, is Pellet's view, expressed as counsel in the *Related Rights* case, that the problem of intertemporal linguistics (conceived by Pellet as a contest between the theory of *renvoi fixe* and *renvoi mobile*) ultimately just boils down to a question of the intention of the parties:

> Mr President, the question of the effect of the passage of time on the interpretation of treaties has been the subject of an impressive number of scholarly works, endlessly discussing the comparative virtues of 'contemporary' interpretation (or of 'renvoi fixe' (fixed reference)) in comparison to evolutionary interpretation (which is the 'renvoi mobile' (mobile reference)). I agree that this is an intellectually stimulating problem, but I am not sure that it justifies the veritable war of religions being waged by those who support one or the other of these approaches, approaches which

[65] *RosInvestCo UK Ltd v Russia* (Jurisdiction), Award (Stockholm Chamber of Commerce Tribunal, V079/2005, October 2007) 43 (§ 40) (emphasis added).

[66] Corten (n 47) 357 (present author's translation).

> must be combined if a reasonable result is to be achieved. And the basic principle that constitutes the backdrop to this operation has no mystery and seems to me to actually be indisputable; it is the same principle that inspires the law of treaties as a whole: everything comes back to *the intention of the Parties*.[67]

It is not terribly surprising that the notion of party-intention appears as a potential solution to a problem of interpretation. We have seen that intention is a nebulous notion sitting behind interpretative rules which exists in many forms and can therefore be used to justify just about any desired interpretative outcome. Indeed, as the study of Bjorge shows, a particular notion of intention can even justify non-interpretative instances of evolutionary treaty interpretation *qua* progressive adjudication.

What is remarkable for the present study is that, among the few pieces of case law and scholarship touching on the Problem, a certain number refer specifically to a type of intention that closely resembles the temporal sense-intention that this study has derived from its linguistics-inspired analysis of the issue. References to such a type of intention are implied in the quotes above, but more explicit in comments made by esteemed international lawyers ranging from Eduardo Jiménez de Aréchaga and Max Sørensen to Donat Pharand and Hugh Thirlway.

When a part of the Problem first came before the ILC's Law of Treaties Study Group at a meeting to discuss Waldock's draft Article 56(1) ('to be interpreted in the light of the law in force at the time when the treaty was drawn up'), Jiménez de Aréchaga said:

> The intention of the parties should be controlling, and there seemed to be two possibilities so far as that intention was concerned: either they had meant to incorporate in the treaty some legal concepts that would remain unchanged, or, if they had had no such intention, the legal concepts might be subject to change and would then have to be interpreted not only in the context of the instrument, but also within the framework of the entire legal order to which they belonged. The free operation of the will of the parties should not be prevented by crystallizing every concept as it had been at the time when the treaty was drawn up, as proposed in paragraph 1.[68]

At the very next meeting, Tsuruoka also insisted – in relation to the same proposed static rule for legal changes with potential repercussions on a treaty's meaning – that '[i]f the interpretation showed that the parties had wished to follow the evolution of international law, it was international law at the time when the treaty was interpreted which prevailed'.[69]

[67] *Dispute regarding Navigational and Related Rights (Costa Rica v Nicaragua)*, Verbatim record of public sitting, 5 March 2009 at 10am, 49–50 (per Pellet for Nicaragua) (Pellet's emphasis, present author's translation).

[68] International Law Commission, 'Yearbook 1964, vol I' (New York, United Nations, 1965) 34 (per Jiménez de Aréchaga, 728th meeting – 21 May 1964, § 10).

[69] ibid 36–37 (per Tsuruoka, 729th meeting – 22 May 1964, § 24).

Then, after the VCLT had been adopted and in the context of his conceptually very rigorous IDI report touching on changes to the meaning of treaty terms effected by changes to the legal framework, Max Sørensen also came close to speaking of the temporal sense-intention: 'Was it *intended* to consider the rules of law existing at the time the deed was drawn up, or was it *intended* to take into account subsequent developments? The answer depends on the circumstances of the particular case'.[70]

Perhaps most significantly, even the ICJ appears to have alluded to what this book calls the temporal sense-intention on a couple of occasions. It is salient that in the relevant part of its *Aegean Sea* judgment, one of the first major international decisions advocating a dynamic approach to the Problem, the Court made several references to the intention of the parties. In response to Greece's attempts to invoke the *Petroleum Development Ltd v Sheikh of Abu Dhabi* case in support of its static position, the Court found that it needed to 'appreciate the intention of a party to an instrument'.[71] It then spoke of 'a presumption that a person transferring valuable property rights to another *intends only to transfer the rights* which he possesses at that time' and, after characterising the contested expression 'the territorial status of Greece' as a generic term, said that a 'presumption necessarily arises that its meaning was *intended* to follow the evolution of the law and to correspond with the meaning attached to the expression by the law in force at any given time'.[72] The Court found, on the basis of that presumption, that it was 'hardly ... conceivable that [... the expression was] intended to have a fixed content regardless of the subsequent evolution of international law'.[73] The *Aegean Sea* Court's focus on the primacy of the parties' intentions as to the meaning of the term through time is manifest and notable. As Higgins has noted, '[p]resumed intention was ... the basis that the Court relied on in the *Aegean Sea* case to distinguish the finding in the Abu Dhabi arbitration, on which the Greek government relied'.[74]

In a key part of the most recent major international judgment addressing the Problem, the *Related Rights* judgment of 2009, the ICJ also focused on finding whether the parties intended the contested term to have a fixed sense or mobile sense, saying:

> [W]here the parties have used generic terms in a treaty, the parties necessarily having been aware that the meaning of the terms was likely to evolve over time, and where the treaty has been entered into for a very long period or is 'of continuing duration',

[70] Institut de droit international and Max Sørensen, 'Le problème dit du droit intertemporel dans l'ordre international – Rapport provisoire' (12 February 1973) *Annuaire* 1, 45 (present author's translation) (emphasis added).

[71] *Aegean Sea Continental Shelf (Greece v Turkey)*, Judgment [1978] ICJ Reports 3, 32 (§ 77).

[72] ibid (§ 77) (emphasis added).

[73] ibid (§ 77).

[74] Rosalyn Higgins, 'Time and the Law: International Perspectives on an Old Problem' (1997) 46 *International & Comparative Law Quarterly* 501, 518.

> the parties must be presumed, as a general rule, *to have intended* those terms to have an evolving meaning. …
>
> This is so in the present case in respect of the term '*comercio*' as used in Article VI of the 1858 Treaty.[75]

Somewhat ironically, this statement may have been provoked by Pellet who, as counsel for Nicaragua in that case, also invoked a notion similar to the temporal sense-intention in relation to the Problem, saying:

> The question is therefore whether, at the time of the signature of the 1858 treaty, Costa Rica and Nicaragua had intended to freeze the situation prevailing at that time or whether they had conceived it as having to adapt to future developments.[76]

It is notable that scholars of international law are particularly likely to advert to a type of intention akin to the temporal sense-intention when considering the problem of intertemporal linguistics in relation to a specific case. Professor Alain Pellet observed this while acting as counsel in the *Related Rights* case, while Professor Donat Pharand appeared to realise it when formulating his important dissenting opinion in the *La Bretagne* arbitration of 1986:

> It would thus appear from the above that the Parties in 1972 did not intend to give to the term 'pêche' as restrictive a meaning as adopted by the Tribunal. In any event, it would be unreasonable to assume that, in an agreement of an indefinite period such as this, *the Parties intended to freeze the meaning* of 'pêche' as it might have been then understood. Indeed, the Parties expressly provided for new regulations to be adopted by Canada in the context of the law of the sea developments, which were taking place at the time.[77]

While Thirlway's comments on the principle of contemporaneity in his 1992 re-examination of Fitzmaurice's 1957 principles of treaty interpretation seem – in light of the substantial practice relating to this principle between 1957 and 1991 – disappointingly cursory, the decision-based analysis he undertook did appear to move him to observe that the two conflicting positions could be resolved through what is effectively an identification of the temporal sense-intention. For Thirlway, the following qualification on Fitzmaurice's original formulation of the principle of contemporaneity had to be added 'in the light of recent decisions of the Court':

> Provided that, where it can be established that it was the intention of the parties that the meaning or scope of a term or expression used in the treaty should follow

[75] *Related Rights*, Judgment (n 63) 29–30 (§§ 64–67) (emphasis added).

[76] *Dispute regarding Navigational and Related Rights (Costa Rica v Nicaragua)*, Verbatim record of public sitting, 5 March 2009 at 10am, 50 (§ 4, per Pellet for Nicaragua) (present author's translation).

[77] *Filleting within the Gulf of St Lawrence between Canada and France ('La Bretagne')*, Dissenting Opinion of Donat Pharand (1986) XIX RIAA/RSA 266, 275 (§ 31, translation from *Dispute Concerning Filleting within the Gulf of St Lawrence ('La Bretagne')* (1986) 82 ILR 590, 648) (emphasis added).

> the development of the law, the treaty must be interpreted so as to give effect to that intention.[78]

Another scholarly text focusing on the impact of changes in the law, Campbell McLachlan's study of VCLT Article 31(3)(c) also appeared to conclude that whether the term should be given a fixed or mobile sense is the key fact for resolution of the Problem: 'The enquiry is thus into whether the concept is, in the context in which it is used, a mobile one'.[79]

Ultimately, while these pieces of case law and scholarship often do not refer to the temporal sense-intention precisely or in its entirety, they clearly advert to something very similar to it and thus provide considerable authority for using the TSI as the key component of the solution to the problem of intertemporal linguistics.

[78] Hugh Thirlway, 'The Law and Procedure of the International Court of Justice 1960–1989: Part Three' (1992) 62 *British Yearbook of International Law* 1, 57.

[79] Campbell McLachlan, 'The Principle of Systemic Integration and Article 31(3)(c) of the Vienna Convention' (2005) 54 *International and Comparative Law Quarterly* 279, 317 (§ 24).

9

Features of Interpretative Situations that Might Imply a Temporal Sense-Intention

NOW THAT WE have determined the specific type of intention that, once identified, can lead to a resolution of the Problem, we are left with the key issue of how to identify the temporal sense-intention.

I. SENSE-INTENTIONS ARE USUALLY INFERRED FROM CONTEXT

In the world of linguistics, the sense-intentions that disambiguate lexical ambiguity are identified primarily through an analysis of the context in which the term was used. Falkum, for example, notes that the hearer of an instance of lexical ambiguity uses context (in her view of a linguistic or extra-linguistic kind) as the basis for determining what meaning it is reasonable to suppose the speaker to have used.[1] A leading article on Word Sense Disambiguation also cites 'the *context* of the word to be disambiguated' – together with a lexicon – as one of the two major means for 'assign[ing] each occurrence of a word to the appropriate sense'.[2] Since the Lesk Algorithm was developed in 1986, the WSD methods themselves have focused on the immediate textual context of an ambiguous word and, with the development complex synonym-mapping databases such as Princeton University's well-known WordNet[3] and the entry into an era of big data, they can now quite reliably disambiguate polysemous words through that context alone.

The cognitive-science side of linguistics tells us that language users build up their phrases, adding details that make it clearer what they are saying through context, grammatical organisation and a range of pragmatic factors. On the

[1] Ingrid Lossius Falkum, 'The Semantics and Pragmatics of Polysemy: A Relevance-Theoretic Account' (PhD Thesis, University College London, 2011) 78 – discovery.ucl.ac.uk/1139079/1/1139079.pdf.

[2] Nancy Ide and Jean Véronis, 'Word Sense Disambiguation: The State of the Art' (1998) 24 *Computational Linguistics* 2, 3 (emphasis added).

[3] See Princeton University, 'WordNet – A lexical database for English' – wordnet.princeton.edu.

other side of the coin, or really perlocutionary/illocutionary divide, listeners and interpreters draw on the same information and, through progressively uncertain inferences, strip away ambiguity to determine more and more exactly what the speaker means. It has become accepted that the brain can resolve lexical ambiguity – but generally not vagueness – already at the lexical level and without resorting to pragmatic inferences.[4] For Azar, one of the key differences between ambiguity and vagueness is that 'linguistic context' is usually sufficient to resolve ambiguity, but 'provides no clues for the clarification of vague words'.[5] Resolving vagueness is a complex process that frequently requires all possible linguistic and extra-linguistic facts to be taken into account – including those associated with pragmatics such as the speaker's goals and the wider, situational context of the utterance. Resolving lexical ambiguity is, by contrast, a relatively simple process than can be carried out without resorting to pragmatic inferences, by looking at the immediate textual context alone.

The rules of treaty interpretation themselves accept that context usually suffices for identifying the sense-intention capable of disambiguating between competing senses of the one treaty term.

First, on the more general level, there is acceptance of the view that the first point of reference where party-intention needs to be distilled is the textual context. Sur, for example, has noted that 'the intention of the parties … must first be sought in the text taken in its context (as the element that best embodies this intention)',[6] while Kammerhofer claims that each word only has 'one meaning that can be fixed contextually'.[7]

In relation to the resolution of the best-known international law ambiguity between the ordinary and special meaning of a treaty term, adjudicators and scholars overwhelmingly agree that the party-intention referred to in VCLT Article 31(4) – a sense-intention – should usually be determined on the basis of the textual context alone. Already in 1963, Degan had noted that whether a special meaning should be assigned is something to be concluded from the context of the treaty.[8] Then, at the Vienna Conference session of 1968, Humphrey

[4] See, eg Dan Sperber and Deirdre Wilson, *Relevance: Communication and Cognition* 2nd edn (Oxford, Blackwell, 1995) 206–08; Steven L Small, Garrison W Cottrell and Michael K Tanenhaus, 'Preface' in Steven L Small, Garrison W Cottrell and Michael K Tanenhaus (eds), *Lexical Ambiguity Resolution: Perspective from Psycholinguistics, Neuropsychology and Artificial Intelligence* (San Mateo CA, Morgan Kaufmann, 1988) 401–02.

[5] Moshe Azar, 'Transforming Ambiguity into Vagueness in Legal Interpretation' in A Wagner, WG Werner and D Cao (eds), *Interpretation, Law and the Construction of Meaning: Collected Papers on Legal Interpretation in Theory, Adjudication and Political Practice* (Dordrecht, Springer, 2007) 127–28.

[6] Serge Sur, *L'interprétation en droit international public* (Paris, Pichon Durand-Auzias, 1974) 272–73 (present author's translation).

[7] Jörg Kammerhofer, *Uncertainty in International Law: A Kelsenian Perspective* (London, Routledge, 2011) 90.

[8] VD Degan, *L'interpretation des accords en droit international* (The Hague, Martinus Nijhoff, 1963) 88.

Waldock cited the key authority in this area to emphasise that interpreters will and should look first to the context in order to determine the applicable Article 31(4) sense-intention, being reported as stating that:

> [I]n the *Legal Status of Eastern Greenland* case, the Permanent Court of International Justice had considered whether the word "Greenland", used in certain treaties between the parties to the case, meant the whole island, or had been used in the special meaning of Eastern Greenland; that question had been discussed in the Court *by reference to the context* and not to the preparatory work.[9]

Recent scholarship confirms this view. A 2007 article by Mitchell, for example, also highlighted context as the factor determining an intended special sense of a treaty term.[10]

Yet while context will almost always suffice for resolving some types of lexical ambiguity (such as the true homonymy between the different senses of the word 'bank'), it is less useful for disambiguating ambiguity between closer word senses. For some instances of ordinary versus special meaning, such as the ordinary and technical senses of the word 'bay', the context might give some indication, but it will not always provide a conclusive indication of the relevant sense-intention. The type of ambiguity presented by the problem of intertemporal linguistics occurs, as we saw above, at a higher level of abstraction than most ambiguities and is therefore even less likely to be resolved by textual context alone.

Where the sense-intention cannot be reliably inferred from the immediate textual context in which the term is used, one needs to move out to wider textual context, then to non-textual context and eventually to other pragmatic indicia of the relevant communicative intention. Experts on treaty interpretation such as Villiger appreciate this when they suggest that an interpreter who cannot resolve whether a treaty term is used in an ordinary or special sense should focus on the wider form of context set out in VCLT Article 31(2) and any subsequent agreements and subsequent practice regarding the interpretation of the treaty,[11] with Nolte highlighting the role of subsequent conduct in this regard.[12] Other international lawyers consider that the VCLT Article 31(4)

[9] UN Conference on the Law of Treaties, 'Official Records, First Session, Vienna' (Vienna, United Nations, 1968) 184 (per Waldock [Expert Consultant], Thirty-third meeting – 22 April 1968, § 71) (emphasis added).

[10] Andrew D Mitchell, 'The Legal Basis for Using Principles in WTO Disputes' (2007) 10 *Journal of International Economic Law* 795, 805: 'The meaning of a term may be informed by the entire treaty containing that provision, including the text and structure of the treaty, and principles reflected in it. This context may indicate that the parties intended a particular treaty term to have a special meaning, or which of several possible meanings they intended.'

[11] Mark E Villiger, 'The 1969 Vienna Convention on the Law of Treaties: 40 Years After' (2011) 344 *Collected Courses of the Hague Academy of International Law* 9, 306: 'the required intention of the parties to employ a special term will transpire in good faith from one of the authentic means of interpretation in paragraph 2 or subparagraphs 3 (a) and (b)'.

[12] International Law Commission and Georg Nolte, 'Introductory Report for the Study Group on Treaties over Time: Jurisprudence of the International Court of Justice and arbitral tribunals

sense-intention can be inferred, in such cases, from the evidence most regularly associated with party-intention, the preparatory work. In the *Litwa* case, for example, the Polish government argued for a special meaning of the term 'alcoholics' in ECHR Article 5(1)(e) on the basis of the treaty's preparatory work.[13] Certain *travaux* will constitute a form of wider context.

It is critical to note that the interpreter's focus must remain uniquely on identifying the sense-intention. Context merely constitutes the best evidence from which one can infer that sense-intention. Crucially, many of the pragmatic indicia of meaning referred to in VCLT Articles 31 and 32 will barely point to a sense-intention at all. Evidence of what the parties wanted to concretely achieve, for example, will rarely be relevant for inferring the sense-intention because that type of intention stops at the sense in which a party used a term and the treaty's object and purpose will almost invariably be too remote from that very specific word-use. Equally, the relevant rules of international law applicable between the parties might impliedly indicate the sense in which the parties to a treaty used a term, but are much less likely to do so than the context in which the term was used or even evidence exactly contemporaneous with the conclusion of the treaty.

One of the international lawyers sufficiently astute to search for something akin to the temporal sense-intention in an effort to resolve the Problem, Campbell McLachlan, proposed resorting to all of the other interpretative elements listed in VCLT Articles 31 and 32 in order to establish such an intention:

> [C]onsistent with the overall approach adopted by the Vienna Convention, it is submitted that a safe guide to decision on this issue will not be found in the chimera of the imputed intention of the parties alone. Rather, the interpreter must find concrete evidence of the parties' intentions in this regard in the material sources referred to in Articles 31-2, namely: in the terms themselves; the object and purpose of the treaty; the rules of international law; and, where necessary, in the *travaux*.[14]

However, most of these indicia of meaning will generally be too remote from the sense in which a term was used to reveal it. When seeking to identify the sense-intention to disambiguate a treaty term, interpreters must resist the temptation to resort generally to the interpretative indicia set out in VCLT Articles 31 and 32. Many of these indicia of semantic-pragmatic meaning – being dedicated to the resolution of vagueness rather than ambiguity – are ill-suited to the

of ad hoc jurisdiction relating to subsequent agreements and subsequent practice' in Georg Nolte (ed), *Treaties and Subsequent Practice* (Oxford, Oxford University Press, 2013) 177.

[13] *Witold Litwa v Poland*, Judgment (ECtHR, 26629/95, 4 April 2000) 15 (§ 55); see also Magdalena Forowicz, *The Reception of International Law in the European Court of Human Rights* (Oxford, Oxford University Press, 2010) 67–68.

[14] Campbell McLachlan, 'The Principle of Systemic Integration and Article 31(3)(c) of the Vienna Convention' (2005) 54 *International and Comparative Law Quarterly* 279, 317 (§§ 23–24); see also Bruno Simma, 'Consent: Strains in the Treaty System' in Ronald StJ Macdonald and Douglas M Johnston (eds), *The Structure and Process of International Law: Essays in Legal Philosophy, Doctrine, and Theory* (The Hague, Martinus Nijhoff Publishers, 1983) 496.

distinct process of disambiguating through the inference of the sense-intention. Interpreters should instead look uniquely at the evidence that best suggests what that sense-intention was – beginning, of course, with context. Indeed, it is notable that, when McLachlan then states examples of how his equivalent of temporal sense-intention may be determined, he ends up relying on considerations that all fall outside the scope of the VCLT's interpretative rules.[15]

The present author submits that the temporal sense-intention capable of solving problems of intertemporal linguistics is, notwithstanding McLachlan's claim, in fact to be found in the 'imputed intention of the parties alone'. If the imputed intention is understood uniquely as a temporal sense-intention and methodically inferred from different indicia of it, it need not be the 'chimera' that McLachlan apparently fears it would be. More broadly and more importantly, if they wish to solve the problem of intertemporal linguistics appropriately, interpreters must only disambiguate and should accordingly ensure that their focus does not prematurely shift from the task of inferring a sense-intention, including by referring prematurely to VCLT rules designed to help resolve vagueness.

The particular type of sense-intention that interpreters faced with the problem of intertemporal linguistics need to identify simply requires that we cast our net widely enough to capture all features of interpretative situations that are capable of implying a fixed or mobile sense-intention. The sense-intention that WSD algorithms need to identify can generally be inferred from just the immediate textual context. Equally, the sense-intention that disambiguates ordinary and special meaning under VCLT Article 31 can usually be found within the scope of the relevant treaty's text, Van Damme, for example, pointing out after a study of this issue in the context of the WTO Appellate Body's *US – Stainless Steel* report that 'proof of a special meaning must be established on the basis of the text of the treaty, not factors extraneous to the text'.[16] Yet VCLT Article 31(4) effectively applies a default presumption in favour of the ordinary meaning, so it can stop at a constrained range of indicia of the sense-intention without leaving the interpreter unable to make the relevant decision. As will be seen, there is no basis for making an equivalent default presumption in favour of either a fixed or mobile sense-intention, so the risk of a lack of guidance will remain real unless we do our best to identify and isolate any matters capable of indicating a particular temporal sense-intention.

Even if international lawyers only rarely end up engaging directly and rigorously with the Problem, they often invoke specific features of the interpretative situation before them in order to justify taking an apparent position on it. Moreover, as we saw in the last section of the previous chapter, some international

[15] McLachlan (n 14) 319 (§ 24).

[16] Isabelle Van Damme, *Treaty Interpretation by the WTO Appellate Body* (Oxford, Oxford University Press, 2009) 537–38; *United States – Final Anti-Dumping Measures on Stainless Steel from Mexico*, Report [2008] WT/DS344/AB/R 44 (§ 96).

lawyers even refer to such features in relation to an intention that resembles the temporal sense-intention. It is accordingly worthwhile, and in keeping with this study's objective to stay – wherever possible – within the bounds of the discipline of international law, to briefly evaluate the main interpretative features highlighted by international case law and scholarship in support of static and dynamic interpretations. The remainder of this chapter will assess whether any one or more of these interpretative features indeed implies the existence of a particular temporal sense-intention such that identification of those features in particular case will help solve a problem of intertemporal linguistics.

II. 'BY DEFINITION EVOLUTIONARY' AND 'GENERIC' TERMS AS INDICIA OF A MOBILE SENSE-INTENTION

In the June 1971 *Namibia* advisory opinion correctly regarded as sitting at the fountainhead of the modern evolutionary interpretation doctrine, the judges advocating the new interpretative approach stated that the treaty terms being interpreted were 'by definition evolutionary'.[17] Since that time, several international courts and tribunals – and countless authors – have invoked the nature of the treaty term being interpreted to justify the adoption of a dynamic approach to the Problem. The *Namibia* court's focus, in certain parts of its opinion, on the character of the terms being interpreted, rather than the outcome of the interpretative exercise, suggests that it thought there was something inherent in the nature of the terms that enabled it to assign a mobile sense-intention and ultimately arrive at a dynamic approach. Unfortunately, neither the *Namibia* advisory opinion nor any of the many decisions and opinions following it have clarified what makes a treaty term 'by definition evolutionary'.

The related notion of a 'generic term' so popular in the evolutionary treaty interpretation literature suffers from the same defect. It too has not been defined with anywhere near the clarity that would suffice for a practically workable presumption to be developed. In the *Aegean Sea* case, the Court famously stated that:

> Once it is established that the expression 'the territorial status of Greece' *was used in Greece's instrument of accession as a generic term* denoting any matters comprised within the concept of territorial status under general international law, *the presumption necessarily arises that its meaning was intended to follow the evolution of the law* and to correspond with the meaning attached to the expression by the law in force at any given time.[18]

[17] *Legal Consequences for States of the Continued Presence of South Africa in Namibia (South West Africa) notwithstanding Security Council Resolution 276 (1970)*, Advisory Opinion [1971] ICJ Reports 16, 30 (§ 53).

[18] *Aegean Sea Continental Shelf (Greece v Turkey)*, Judgment [1978] ICJ Reports 3, 32 (§ 77) (emphasis added).

This putative link between a feature of the treaty term itself, through a presumption, to a particular temporal sense-intention is exactly what the present chapter is looking for. As Palchetti has said, '[s]ince the use of generic terms creates a presumption in favour of a dynamic interpretation of their meaning, the classification of a term as "generic" is an element which may impact considerably on the outcome of the interpretative process'.[19] Yet, there is a complete lack of any clarity about what makes a treaty term a 'generic term' in this sense, making the alleged presumption effectively unusable.

The word 'generic' was used in relation to terms more than five times in the *Aegean Sea* judgment, but was never explicitly defined, perhaps suggesting that its meaning is borrowed from established ordinary usage or a related field of endeavour. In law, as in chemistry and the biological sciences, 'generic' is generally understood in opposition to 'specific' as a term that describe a class or group of things, rather than the specific things within that group. Indeed, the first judge on the International Court of Justice to use the expression 'generic term', Judge Lauterpacht, used it in this sense in his 1955 *South-West Africa Voting Procedure* Separate Opinion.[20] This very broad understanding of a 'generic term' is consistent with that which emerges from a remarkably brief definition of it in one of the cases to apply it in a temporal interpretation context, the *Related Rights* court saying: 'the term "*comercio*" as used in Article VI of the 1858 Treaty … is a generic term, referring to a class of activity'.[21]

If, to be a 'generic term', a term must simply refer to a class rather than an item and be general rather than specific, it is clear that this is not an adequate basis for implying a particular temporal sense-intention. Whether or not terms will be general often depends upon the context in which they find themselves and how they are used. For example, while wine may be generic in a taxonomic system regarding different types of wine, in another, such as a system for different alcoholic beverages, it will be specific. In the international law context, 'UN bodies' may seem generic and 'the Security Council' may seem specific, but 'the Security Council of the Cold-War era' is more specific again, suggesting that, in certain contexts, 'Security Council' is a generic term.

Moreover, if all terms that describe anything that might be a category are generic terms, then most treaty terms will be generic, because rules and principles are usually phrased in quite general terms. If almost every term used in a treaty is – or can be – a generic term and all generic terms create a presumption that a mobile sense-intention was used, then we are for all intents and purposes in

[19] Paolo Palchetti, 'Interpreting "Generic Terms": Between Respect for the Parties' Original Intention and the Identification of the Ordinary Meaning' in Nerina Boschiero and others (eds), *International Courts and the Development of International Law: Essays in Honour of Tullio Treves* (The Hague, Asser Press, 2013) 94.

[20] *South-West Africa-Voting Procedure*, Separate Opinion of Judge Lauterpacht [1955] ICJ Reports 90, 115–16.

[21] *Dispute regarding Navigational and Related Rights (Costa Rica v Nicaragua)*, Judgment [2009] ICJ Reports 213, 243 (§ 67).

the realm of an almost general presumption in favour of mobile sense-intention and, with it, a dynamic approach to the Problem.

A case-based attempt at defining a 'generic term' extensionally is also doomed to failure. When we compare Higgins' claim that 'the main channel' is not a generic term in the *Kasikili/Sedudu Island* case to other treaty terms that have been considered 'generic terms' in this context, such as 'disputes relating to the territorial status of Greece' (*Aegean Sea*), 'exhaustible natural resources' (*US – Shrimp*) and '*comercio*' (*Related Rights*), we see that the differences between those deemed and not deemed generic terms are likely to be too numerous to reveal the essence of a generic term.

There appears, for example, to be a definite/indefinite distinction that corresponds to non-generic and generic terms respectively but, upon closer inspection, the authentic French text of the apparently generic term 'territorial status' also appears with a definite article: '*les différends ayant trait au statut territorial de la Grèce*'.[22] Moreover, one only needs to look two paragraphs above the reference to 'exhaustible natural resources' in the GATT, to see a term equally likely to be qualified as generic preceded by a definite article: 'the products of prison labour'.[23]

The apparent singular/plural distinction between 'the main channel' and the other treaty terms considered generic can also not be considered significant for identifying generic terms, as it would make no sense to ascribe a fixed sense-intention to 'the main channel' and interpret it statically, while assigning a mobile sense to 'the main channels' and interpreting it dynamically.

Clearly, the many international lawyers stating that generic terms give rise to a dynamic approach therefore understand what it means to be a 'generic term' in a more particular sense. Unfortunately, that apparent sense of 'generic terms' turns out to be, like the notion of 'by definition evolutionary terms', completely circular.

Immediately after declaring the relevant terms of the Covenant of the League of Nations to be 'by definition evolutionary', the judges who penned the *Namibia* advisory opinion did not define what that meant but simply went on to say: '[t]he parties to the Covenant must consequently be deemed to have accepted them as such',[24] plainly revealing some circularity. When Judge Higgins impliedly defined a 'generic term' in her declaration appended to the *Kasikili/Sedudu* judgment, she also did so in a largely circular fashion, saying:

> 2. The term 'the main channel' is not a 'generic term' (cf *Aegean Sea Continental Shelf, I. C. J. Reports 1978*, p. 32, para. 77) – *that is to say, a known legal term, whose content the parties expected would change through time*.[25]

[22] *Aegean Sea*, Judgment (n 18) 21 (§ 48) (emphasis added).
[23] See General Agreement on Tariffs and Trade (1947) 1947 (55 UNTS 187), art XX(e).
[24] *Namibia*, Advisory Opinion (n 17) 31 (§ 53).
[25] *Kasikili/Sedudu Island (Botswana/ Namibia)*, Declaration of Judge Higgins [1999] ICJ Reports 1113, 1113 (§ 2) (emphasis added).

These definitions of 'by definition evolutionary' or 'generic' terms all highlight the fact that, for certain terms, 'the parties [were] necessarily … aware that the meaning of the terms was likely to evolve over time',[26] then build this very awareness back into their definitions. The discerning of a 'party awareness of the term's evolution' may indeed be the source of an inference that the parties were open to that evolution or, in the terms of the *Related Rights* judgment, that the parties 'intended those terms to have an evolving meaning', but there is a clear circularity in saying that this awareness presumption is raised by any term that raises the awareness presumption. Indeed, if the process of inference is to avoid the evidentiary difficulty of inquiring into a subjective state such as awareness (or temporal sense-intention) by presumptively attaching that awareness (or temporal sense-intention) to certain types of terms, then the particular types of terms that raise such a presumption must be able to be identified through their objective features alone.

In this regard, it is important to note that the relevant texts focus not on what type of term the treaty term is, but instead on how it was used. The *Aegean Sea* dictum at the origin of the generic term doctrine did not even speak of the mobile sense-intention presumption being generated by the fact that 'the territorial status of Greece' *was* a generic term, but instead by the fact that the term was '*used as*' a generic term,[27] while the relevant statement from the *Related Rights* judgment also speaks of 'the term "*comercio*" *as used* in Article VI of the 1858 Treaty' being generic.[28] Even some of the most detailed writing on the concept of generic terms in this respect, such as Palchetti's article, 'Interpreting "Generic Terms"', focuses on the consequences that the use of generic terms is said to have, rather than defining their generally-applicable and objectively-ascertainable features.[29]

In sum, the oft-used notions of 'by definition evolutionary' and 'generic' terms are ultimately too imprecise and too circular to be used as indicia of a mobile sense-intention. By effectively defining them as terms that the parties recognised as likely to undergo semantic change after the treaty's conclusion, the case law and scholarship on these types of terms have undermined the possibility of an objective feature of a treaty term implying a particular sense-intention. Yet they have simultaneously left open the possibility that, where there is evidence of such likely-semantic-change-awareness, a mobile sense-intention may be able to be implied – such an implication being neither particularly strong, nor particularly weak. This outcome is summarised schematically in Figure 6 below.

[26] *Related Rights*, Judgment (n 21) 30 (§ 66).
[27] *Kasikili/Sedudu*, Higgins Declaration (n 25) 1113 (§ 2).
[28] *Related Rights*, Judgment (n 21) 30 (§ 67) (emphasis added).
[29] See Palchetti (n 19) 97–105.

Figure 6 TSI Indicator: Terms with semantic-change awareness

Ch 9 §	Feature referred to as source of static or dynamic approach	Feature actually used as basis of inference of sense-intention/ approach	Implies which temporal sense-intention?	Strength of implication
II	'By definition evolutionary' terms	Awareness of likelihood of semantic change	Mobile	Medium
	'Generic' terms			

III. TERMS THAT CONSTITUTE LEGAL CONCEPTS AS INDICIA OF A MOBILE SENSE-INTENTION

Several decisions of international courts and tribunals and scholars of international law have suggested that legal concepts should be interpreted dynamically. Of course, the *Namibia* advisory opinion found directly that concepts embodied in Article 22 of the Covenant of the League of Nations, which therefore had a legal aspect to them, were 'by definition evolutionary'.[30] Equally, Judge Higgins, when purporting to define a generic term but really defining all terms to be presumed to be subject to diachronic semantic change, spoke of 'known *legal* term[s]'.[31] In his short survey of examples of when a term is used as a mobile one for the purposes of the Problem, McLachlan speaks generally of terms 'which carry with [them] an evolving meaning in general international law' and gives examples that clearly qualify as legal concepts, namely the concepts of expropriation and fair and equitable treatment in bilateral investment treaties.[32]

Already back in 1966, Waldock had given examples of legal concepts as among those to which the Fitzmaurice's principle of contemporaneity cannot be applied, saying in his sixth report to the ILC on the Law of Treaties:

> Moreover, as the Special Rapporteur pointed out in his third report, the rule cannot be formulated in the simple form in which it is stated by Sir G Fitzmaurice and by the Court in the *United States Nationals in Morocco* case; for the content of a word, eg 'bay' or 'territorial waters', may change with the evolution of the law if the parties used it in the treaty *as a general concept* and not as a word of fixed content.[33]

Waldock's formulation – 'used [the term] in the treaty as a general concept' – not only represents an oft-ignored precursor to the generic term doctrine laid

[30] *Namibia*, Advisory Opinion (n 17) 31.
[31] *Kasikili/Sedudu*, Higgins Declaration (n 25) 1113 (§ 2) (emphasis added).
[32] McLachlan (n 14) 317 (§ 24).
[33] International Law Commission, *Yearbook 1966, vol II* (New York, United Nations, 1967) 96 (Sixth report on the law of treaties, by Sir Humphrey Waldock, Observations and proposals of the Special Rapporteur, § 7) (emphasis added).

down almost 10 years later in the *Aegean Sea* case, but betrays some of the same circularity that rendered presumptions based on 'by definition evolutionary' or 'generic terms' ill-advised. If a term must be *used as* a legal concept, then the term just *being* a legal concept will not be enough.

The authorities and common sense both attest to the need to make this important qualification. In the earliest international decision we discussed as having a potential bearing on the Problem, the *Puget Sound Agricultural Company* tribunal was called upon to interpret the expression 'belonging to'.[34] The notion of 'belonging' is linked to ownership and sits at the heart of legal systems around the world, so the term must clearly be regarded as a legal concept. Yet, in that case, the parties using the word belonging were not considered to have used it in a mobile sense that followed the legal evolution of the concept of 'belonging'. In the Anglo-American treaty of 1846, the term 'belonging' was determined to have been used in a fixed sense and interpreted using a broadly static approach to the Problem, just as it is likely to be in situations where the same term appears in sovereignty contexts.[35] In other contexts, however, there seems to be no reason why 'belonging' could not be interpreted dynamically. Ultimately, the fact that the treaty term constitutes a legal concept is not itself decisive of the temporal sense-intention, it will depend on the context in which that concept is used.

The relevant case law confirms that it would not be advisable to presume a mobile sense-intention for all treaty terms using legal concepts, irrespective of the type of legal concept and from whence it draws its meaning. Far too many legal concepts have been used in a fixed temporal sense or simply interpreted statically. Consider the word '*Thalweg*' used in Article III of the 1890 Anglo-German Treaty and interpreted in the *Kasikili/Sedudu* case. Despite *Thalweg* already being a known legal term in 1890, the Court indicated that it was interpreting it statically by referring to an IDI text from 1887 to explicate its meaning.[36] While it is not certain, the Court's critical consideration underlying the choice of a static approach for interpreting the treaty term appears to have been that, in 1890, there was no indication that the German word '*Thalweg*' would evolve and take on the quite special meaning it has today.[37] The parties who drafted the 1890 Anglo-German Treaty could therefore not be considered to have been aware of the probability that their treaty term would be subject to

[34] *Claims of the Hudson's Bay and Puget's Sound Agricultural Companies*, Award (1869) I, ch VIII (Moore's) History and digest of the international arbitrations to which the United States has been a party 237; *Affaire des Compagnies de la baie d'Hudson et du détroit de Puget*, Sentence (1869) II RIAA/RSA 498.

[35] See, eg *Sovereignty over Pulau Ligitan and Pulau Sipidan (Indonesia/Malaysia)*, Judgment [2002] ICJ Reports 625, 657–58 (§§ 63–64).

[36] *Kasikili/Sedudu Island (Botswana/ Namibia)*, Judgment [1999] ICJ Reports 1045, 1062 (§ 25).

[37] ibid (§ 25).

semantic change and therefore could not fairly be regarded as using the term with a mobile sense-intention.

Other well-known legal concepts fall into the same category. Within the space of four years, the international legal concept reflected by term 'continental shelf' was interpreted using both the dynamic approach[38] and the static approach.[39] In the first case, between Guinea-Bissau and Senegal, the fact that the term had an inherently dynamic component prevailed over the static implication arising from the territorial aspects of the case, whereas in the latter it did not. The Tribunal noted, first, that the expressions 'territorial sea', 'contiguous zone' and 'continental shelf' already existed as known legal concepts at the time the treaty was concluded. It also pointed out that the parties had themselves specified, in the preamble to their treaty, that they wanted to define their maritime boundary 'taking into account' the first law of the sea conventions, conventions which included these terms.[40]

In other words, the parties were understood as having used the terms in a way that made a *renvoi* out to a legal regime in which the concept was likely to develop. In several cases often regarded as authorities for the dynamic approach, the drafters of the relevant treaty have been deemed to have made such a reference. Already in the PCIJ's *Nationality Decrees* advisory opinion of 1923, an international court had held the issue of what matters were, 'by international law … solely within the domestic jurisdiction of' a State[41] to be a question that 'depend[ed] upon the development of international relations'.[42] Equally in investment disputes addressing the concept of fair and equitable treatment, the clauses using this phrase are habitually understood as referring out to an external and dynamic customary international law standard.[43] We have also seen cases in which the parties to a treaty, while using words describing what is clearly a legal concept, do not refer out to an external treaty regime in which the meaning of that concept could be expected to develop. Indeed, in the oft-neglected *Rights of US Nationals in Morocco* judgment's interpretation of '*liberté économique sans aucune inégalité*' a static approach to the Problem was taken because there was no such external *renvoi*. Indeed, the treaty regime in the context of which this

[38] *Case concerning the delimitation of maritime boundary between Guinea-Bissau and Senegal*, Decision of 31 July 1989 (1989) XX RIAA/RSA 119.

[39] *Maritime Delimitation in the Area between Greenland and Jan Mayen (Denmark v Norway)*, Judgment [1993] ICJ Reports 38.

[40] *Guinea-Bissau/Senegal*, Award (n 38) 152 (§ 85).

[41] Treaty of Peace at Versailles 1919 (225 Consol TS 188; UKTS 4), Covenant of the League of Nations, art 15, para 8.

[42] *Nationality Decrees in Tunis and Morocco*, Advisory Opinion [1923] PCIJ Reports (Series B) No 4, 24.

[43] See, eg *Mondev International Ltd v United States of America*, Award (ICSID(AF) Tribunal constituted under NAFTA Chapter 11, ARB(AF)/99/2, 11 October 2002) 43–44 (§ 125).

concept was most likely to develop was not external to the treaty, but the text being interpreted itself: the Act of Algeciras.[44]

Clearly, it is not just the use of a legal concept, but the use of a legal concept that draws its meaning from outside of the treaty that is capable of evidencing the kind of understanding among the drafters that could indicate that a term should be interpreted dynamically. When using an external legal concept, the parties expressly ensure that, as Oppenheim's textbook points out, 'the interpretation of a treaty's provisions cannot be divorced from developments in the law subsequent to its adoption' such that 'the concepts embodied in a treaty may not be static but evolutionary'.[45] In these particular circumstances, it could be assumed that the parties concluding the treaty were aware of the likelihood of a change in the precise parameters of the concept and they can thus be presumed to have used the terms in a mobile sense.

Where the parties employ known legal concepts, an exceptional situation arises. In such situations, the parties can be deemed to have foreseen, if not the subsequent semantic change in the treaty term itself, then at least the substantial likelihood of that semantic change. The *renvoi* out of the bounds of the treaty is, after all, a deliberate act that in and of itself exhibits an openness on the basis of which a mobile sense-intention can reliably be inferred. As Alan Boyle has noted, '[e]volutionary interpretation is easiest when the treaty in question expressly incorporates current international law'.[46]

It is accordingly safe to conclude that, if the parties employ a term in a treaty, knowing that the same word is a key concept in an external legal regime, this quite strongly implies that they understood and intended the meaning of the term appearing in their treaty to follow any changes in meaning occurring outside of the treaty – a fact summarised by Figure 7.

Figure 7 TSI Indicator: Terms that are legal concepts in external regimes

Ch 9 §	Feature referred to as source of static or dynamic approach	Feature actually used as basis of inference of sense-intention/ approach	Implies which temporal sense-intention?	Strength of implication
III	Terms that are legal concepts	Terms that are legal concepts in a regime external to the treaty	Mobile	Medium-Strong

[44] *Case concerning Rights of Nationals of the United States of America in Morocco (France v United States of America)*, Judgment [1952] ICJ Reports 183–85; see further Julian Wyatt, 'An Original or Modern-Day Meaning for Treaty Terms? The Problem of Intertemporal Linguistics in the Case Law of International Courts and Tribunals' (Doctorat en droit, University of Geneva, 2017) 120–22 – archive-ouverte.unige.ch/unige:102376 (s 3.2.3.5).

[45] Robert Jennings and Arthur Watts (eds), *Oppenheim's International Law*, vol 1, 9th edn (Oxford, Oxford University Press, 2008) 1268–82.

[46] Alan Boyle, 'Reflections on the Treaty as a Law-making Instrument' in Alexander Orakhelashvili and Sarah Williams (eds), *40 Years of the Vienna Convention on the Law of Treaties* (London, British Institute of International and Comparative Law, 2010) 21.

IV. TERMS IN HUMAN RIGHTS TREATIES AS INHERENTLY POSSESSING A MOBILE SENSE-INTENTION

Several international law practitioners and scholars tackling the question of how to interpret treaties through time cite the nature of the treaty – or even the nature of the field of international law in which the treaty operates – as a basis for a static or dynamic interpretation of that treaty's terms.

Human rights treaties are the type of treaty most commonly cited in this regard. There is indeed a widely held view that these treaties should always be interpreted following a dynamic approach. Malgosia Fitzmaurice attributes this to the structural nature of human rights courts, highlighting the Strasbourg Court's autonomy from each State Party's internal order,[47] while several authors link it to the purpose apparently being pursued by such treaties. Arato, for example, very clearly distinguishes between human rights treaties and boundary treaties on this basis, saying: 'In contrast to boundary treaties, the need for human rights treaties to adapt to new circumstances over time is much less controversial, and indeed fairly well established in the practice of international tribunals'.[48] Andenas and Bjorge, for their part, have gone so far as to state that 'one of the principal characteristics of the ECHR is its dynamic evolution',[49] while Bernhardt sought to explain why this is the case, saying:

> The considerations valid for human rights conventions are to a certain extent exceptional. … The internal laws and the opinions in the society in the field of homosexual relations, on the status of unmarried mothers and their children might have changed, and these changes are decisive indicators for the adequacy of an evolutive interpretation of the relevant human rights convention.[50]

The suggestion that something akin to a fixed or mobile sense-intention can be attached to all the terms used by such treaties is surprising. Treaties can be quite diverse instruments with terms used in multifarious ways to fulfil a host of different functions. If the analysis in chapters 7 and 8 is correct and what matters for resolving the problem of intertemporal linguistics is the temporal sense-intention applying to the particular treaty term, then these general claims regarding human rights treaties are highly questionable.

As chapter 3 pointed out, many international human rights lawyers – and many international lawyers generally – confuse the broad form of the

[47] Malgosia Fitzmaurice, 'Dynamic (Evolutive) Interpretation of Treaties, Part I' (2009) *Hague Yearbook of International Law* 101, 152.

[48] Julian Arato, 'Subsequent Practice and Evolutive Interpretation: Techniques of Treaty Interpretation Over Time and Their Diverse Consequences' (2010) 9 *Law & Practice of International Courts and Tribunals* 443, 486.

[49] M Andenas and E Bjorge, 'Juge national et interprétation évolutive de la Convention européenne des droits de l'homme' (2011) 4 *Revue du droit public et de la science politique en France et à l'etranger* 997, 998 (present author's translation).

[50] Rudolf Bernhardt, 'Evolutive Treaty Interpretation, Especially of the European Convention on Human Rights' (1999) 42 *German Yearbook of International Law* 11, 21.

evolutionary interpretation doctrine widely followed by international human rights courts with a dynamic approach to the Problem. While they sometimes overlap, in the field of international human rights law, a predilection for a theory of progressive adjudication is much more readily discerned than a predilection for using the later-emerging meaning of a treaty term irrespective of the practical consequences of doing so. When judges and scholars state that human rights treaties must always be interpreted dynamically, they are not usually saying that their terms must always be given their meaning at the time of the treaty's application instead of their meaning at the time of the treaty's conclusion, but instead the meaning that produces the most modern or progressive outcome.

This reflects a teleological approach emphasising an implied object and purpose pursuant to which the human rights treaty follows and keeps pace with social and legal changes occurring outside the system. However, as pointed out in chapter 5 above, a progressive teleology does not always equate to a dynamic approach to the Problem. Indeed, in certain situations, such as in the case of exceptions, a semantic change may expand the scope of the exception and, if taken account of, thereby limit – rather than enhance – the ability of the treaty to achieve its drafters' apparently progressive objectives. It accordingly becomes clear that, while one may be able to draw the inference that a *teleological intention* runs with all terms in a human rights treaty, one cannot draw the inference that a *temporal sense-intention* runs with all the terms in a human rights treaty.

Yet this does not mean that at least some of the terms of a human rights treaties cannot imply a particular temporal sense-intention. As Bruno Simma pointed out in one of the first international law articles to discuss evolutionary interpretation in any detail, the fact that 'conventions for the protection of human rights' 'oblige the parties to adjust their domestic law and practice to common standards' means that they 'deserve separate considerations' and makes it, for this noted international jurist, 'not [by] mere chance that the discussion of the possibilities and limits of a "dynamic" interpretation was primarily ignited by the practice of the organs of the European Convention on Human Rights'.[51] It is indeed the fact that major substantive provisions of international human rights treaties commit States to the observance of legal and moral standards, standards which can obviously change through time, that makes a dynamic interpretation of those substantive provisions appropriate. States who commit to observing such standards throughout the life of the treaty, as most indisputably do, can be taken to be holding the intention of meeting not just what those standards are understood as requiring at the time of the treaty's conclusion, but also what they may require long after the treaty was concluded. To the extent that the contested terms are included in the expression of these standards, the drafters are impliedly turning their minds to – and welcoming – a probable change in the meaning of such terms.

[51] Simma (n 14) 496–97.

When, in the quote excerpted above, Bernhardt spoke of how international human rights treaties might, through evolutive interpretation, take into account changes in 'the internal laws and the opinions in ... society in the field of homosexual relations, on the status of unmarried mothers and their children' et cetera, he was clearly referring to taking them into account in the interpretation of substantive provisions through which States commit to standards of conduct, often in very morally- or legally-loaded terms. In the 2007 *RosInvest* award on Jurisdiction, an investment tribunal was faced with an argument invoking evolutionary treaty interpretation authorities from the field of international human rights law and rejected it not by noting that it was interpreting a bilateral investment treaty with a different object and purpose, but rather by noting that something akin to a mobile sense-intention could only be presumed in human rights contexts because 'the Contracting Parties [in that type of treaty] must have intended that the principles and concepts which they employed should be understood and applied in the light of developing social attitudes'.[52]

We should therefore choose not to follow international lawyers who consider that all the terms in human rights treaties should be interpreted dynamically, but may at least conclude that a subset of those terms, namely all the substantive terms through which States positively commit themselves to meeting human rights standards on an ongoing basis, raise an inference of a mobile sense-intention and thus point to, all other things being equal, an interpretation that adopts their meaning at the time of the treaty's application.

Those au fait with the case law of the European Court of Human Rights are likely to object at this point, asserting on the basis of the high-profile *Loizidou v Turkey* judgment of 1996, that the dynamic approach was explicitly extended to non-substantive provisions.[53] However, the relevant statement of the ECtHR in that case, like many statements of the living instrument doctrine, infers a progressive teleological intention from the fact of that a human rights treaty is being interpreted, not a temporal sense-intention. The present study accepts that a progressive teleology can attach to all terms of human rights treaties – be they substantive or procedural – but sees no basis for the assertion that a mobile sense-intention arises from anything more than the substantive provisions through which States commit to certain standards of conduct.

The restriction of the scope of the basis of the inference from terms in human rights treaties in general to terms used to commit to human rights standards speaks against much authority, but is clearly necessary. It rests on solid conceptual bases and may illuminate other potential sources from which a temporal sense-intention can be inferred. Indeed, if one were to generalise

[52] *RosInvestCo UK Ltd v Russia* (Jurisdiction), Award (Stockholm Chamber of Commerce Tribunal, V079/2005, October 2007) 42 (§ 39).

[53] *Loizidou v Turkey* (Preliminary Objections), Judgment (European Court of Human Rights (Chamber), 15318/89, 23 March 1995) 21 (§ 71).

from a State committing to a human-rights standard to a State committing to any standards, the indicium would be much more applicable and therefore much more useful.

In the areas of international law where clearly defined words constitute a kind of *renvoi* out of the treaty to another regime using the same term, the parties' openness to future semantic change is quite clear (see subsection III above). However, in the human rights context the main regimes are often the treaties themselves so the treaty drafters cannot signal their mobile sense-intention by using a legal term of art that is likely to undergo change in an external system. They must instead use a social, political or moral term of art and trust that this too will be a signal of a mobile sense-intention. Of course, one cannot be as certain of a *renvoi* to an external moral system as one can be to another regime of international law, but in some extreme cases this intention will be relatively evident. Indeed, when States commit to a prohibition on 'torture' or 'degrading treatment' they cannot but be aware that notions of what constitutes torture and what constitutes degrading treatment are likely to change in the wider social, moral and political universe. By using these specific terms, they can be assumed fairly safely to have welcomed that change and thus to have expressed a mobile sense-intention regarding the meaning of those expressions.

We have accordingly learnt from our analysis of the many claims that terms in human rights treaties always require a dynamic approach to the Problem: (a) that not all of them imply a mobile sense-intention and (b) that those which do are used to commit one or more States to a standard of conduct – both within and outside human rights treaties. The latter fact is presented schematically in Figure 8.

Figure 8 TSI Indicator: Terms committing States to standards of conduct

Ch 9 §	Feature referred to as source of static or dynamic approach	Feature actually used as basis of inference of sense-intention/ approach	Implies which temporal sense-intention?	Strength of implication
IV	Terms in human rights treaties	Terms in clauses committing States to standards of conduct	Mobile	Medium

V. TERMS IN TERRITORIAL TREATIES AS INHERENTLY POSSESSING A FIXED SENSE-INTENTION

If human rights treaties are the archetypal example of treaties that international courts should interpret dynamically, then boundary treaties are the archetypal example of treaties that should be interpreted statically.[54]

[54] Arato, for example, alluded to this exact contrast in his study of a notion related to the problem (Arato [n 48] 486).

Many international lawyers suggest that treaties granting sovereignty and/or delimiting boundaries are inherently fixed through time and therefore exclude the possibility of a dynamic interpretation.[55] Indeed, whereas the principle of contemporaneity is now frequently ignored on the basis that it has been replaced by the dynamic approach, in the context of boundary treaties it is still considered to apply. For example, in 2012, Alvarez-Jiménez wrote:

> According to the principle of contemporaneity, treaty words should be given the meaning they had at the time of the conclusion of the given treaty. This is a principle that, although it always contemplates exceptions, is particularly relevant in the interpretation of boundary treaties, by virtue of a particular principle existing in this domain: the stability of boundaries.[56]

The presumption of a static approach has even been extended beyond territorial treaties to territorial cases, Galindo Pohl stating that in such cases '[t]here is no place … for the interpretative processes which have been used in branches of law undergoing development and reorganisation' and that 'it is wrong to take this updating approach with regard to matters governed by the desire for stability, such as matters of State frontiers'.[57]

As these quotations reveal, the insistence on the static approach in territorial contexts arises from the importance of the *stability of frontiers principle*, a time-honoured and very well-established principle of international law. In the *Temple of Preah Vihear* case, the Court was faced with a claim to rectify the infamous French map to reflect the true watershed line provided for in Article I of the Franco-Siamese boundary treaty of 13 February 1904. It saliently stated:

> In general, when two countries establish a frontier between them, one of the primary objects is to achieve stability and finality. This is impossible if the line so established can, at any moment, and on the basis of a continuously available process, be called in question. … Such a frontier, so far from being stable, would be completely precarious.[58]

The Court's statement that parties designating frontiers between them wish to fix their borders once and for all is logical and considered uncontroversial.

[55] See, eg Eduardo Jiménez de Aréchaga, 'International Law in the Past Third of a Century' (1978) 159 *Collected Courses of the Hague Academy of International Law* 1, 48–49; 'Rejoinder of Nicaragua', *Dispute regarding Navigational and Related Rights (Costa Rica v Nicaragua)* (International Court of Justice, 2008) 155–56 (§ 3.98); *Dispute regarding Navigational and Related Rights (Costa Rica v Nicaragua)*, Verbatim record of public sitting, 5 March 2009 at 10am, 50–51 (§ 5, per Pellet for Nicaragua).

[56] Alberto Alvarez-Jimenez, 'The International Court of Justice's Use of the Vienna Convention in the Interpretation of Boundary Agreements: 2000–10' (2012) 3 *Journal of International Dispute Settlement* 409, 30 (footnote omitted).

[57] *Boundary dispute between Argentina and Chile concerning the frontier line between boundary post 62 and Mount Fitzroy ('Laguna del Desierto')*, Dissenting Opinion of Reynaldo Galindo Pohl (1994) XXII RIAA/RSA 53, 56–57 (part I, §§ 12–13).

[58] *Case concerning the Temple of Preah Vihear (Cambodia v Thailand)* (Merits), Judgment [1962] ICJ Reports 6, 34.

This statement of principle has been confirmed on several occasions, including by the *Aegean Sea* judgment which confirmed that boundary agreements are excluded from the rules pertaining to a fundamental change of circumstances.[59] Of course, the *rebus sic stantibus* doctrine only applies to allow parties to withdraw from or terminate a treaty in the quite exceptional circumstances listed in VCLT Article 62.[60] If the territorial boundaries fixed by treaties are considered so inviolable that they are even exempted from the application of this very exceptionally applicable rule, then they must also be exempted from modification through mere semantic change to the meaning of a treaty term that was used to define them. Even the progressive Edward McWhinney was forced to admit that treaty clauses fixing boundaries have been rendered immune from 'adjusting old legal rules … to meet new societal conditions and also new values in the plural World Community of today'.[61]

The stability of frontiers principle is sometimes expressed as a presumption of party-intention based on the nature of the agreement made. Judge Shahabuddeen, for example, describes it as 'the principle that parties to a boundary agreement are presumed to intend to establish a definite, complete and continuous boundary'.[62] There can be little doubt that this presumed party-intention is wholly inconsistent with a mobile sense-intention in relation to any of the terms used within the clause fixing the boundary. If international courts and tribunals were to acknowledge any semantic change that a term within that clause undergoes, then the meaning of the clause could change, altering the frontier itself. Since States agreeing a frontier cannot have intended moving borders between them, they must be, by incontestable logical deduction, presumed to have fixed the sense of the treaty terms the use to do this.

While a fixed sense-intention follows from the application of the well-established principle of the stability of frontiers, this does not mean that it can be presumed in all territorial treaties or territorial cases. Some terms within territorial treaties that may need to be interpreted as part of a territorial dispute, such as those occurring in a dispute resolution clause, will be largely unrelated to the fixing of stable frontiers. Ultimately, the presumption of a fixed sense-intention arises not from the presence of the contested term in a territorial *treaty*, but instead from the fact that the term helps to *fix a boundary* – the only respect in which a part of a territorial treaty attracts the application of the stability of frontiers principle.

[59] *Aegean Sea*, Judgment (n 18) 36; see also *Territorial Dispute (Libyan Arab Jamahiriya/Chad)*, Judgment [1994] ICJ Reports 6, 37 (§§ 72–73); *Territorial Dispute (Libyan Arab Jamahiriya/Chad)*, Separate Opinion of Judge Shahabuddeen [1994] ICJ Reports 44, 44–50.

[60] Vienna Convention on the Law of Treaties 1969 (1155 UNTS 331), art 62.

[61] Edward McWhinney, 'The Time Dimension in International Law, Historical Relativism and Intertemporal Law' in Jerzy Makarczyk (ed), *Essays in international law in honour of Judge Manfred Lachs/Etudes de droit international en l'honneur du juge Manfred Lachs* (The Hague, Nijhoff, 1984) 198.

[62] *Libya/Chad*, Shahabuddeen Separate Opinion (n 59) 45.

This realisation would have assisted Alvarez-Jiménez when his focus on the interpretation of 'territorial treaties' brought the *Related Rights* judgment's dynamic interpretation of '*comercio*' into play and left him scrambling for a means to distinguish it from the other authorities that interpreted territorial treaties statically.[63] If, instead of speaking of territorial treaties, he had concentrated his inquiry on treaty terms that fix boundaries, he would have had less difficulty explaining the ICJ's desire to use the dynamic approach to interpret '*comercio*' – which was not even used in a treaty clause that fixed a boundary.

However, there is a further important qualification that needs to be made. Some cases analysed by this study have referred to apparently dynamic interpretations of terms such as 'continental shelf', including when those terms are used in clauses delimiting maritime boundaries. How do such interpretations avoid offending the principle of stability of the frontiers? Are these cases wrongly decided? If not, what does it say for the strength of the presumption of a fixed sense-intention outlined on this basis just above?

The most notable of these instances is the *Guinea Bissau/Senegal* arbitrators' finding that the term 'continental shelf', as used in an April 1960 French-Portuguese Agreement by exchange of letters that delimited the relevant boundary, could be interpreted dynamically. The relevant part of the 1960 Agreement provided that:

> As far as the outer limit of the territorial sea, the boundary shall consist of a straight line drawn at 240° .... As regards the contiguous zones and the continental shelf, the delimitation shall be constituted by the prolongation in a straight line, in the same direction, of the boundary of the territorial seas.[64]

Of course, the meaning of the 'continental shelf' had changed between 1960 and 1989, such that it extended further out to sea when the treaty fell to be applied than when the treaty was concluded. In this situation, the Arbitral Tribunal had no hesitation in choosing the meaning of the treaty term at the time of the treaty's application, saying:

> In view of the fact that the 'continental shelf' existed in the international law in force in 1960, and that the definition of the concept of that maritime space then included the dynamic criterion indicated, it may be concluded that the Franco-Portuguese Agreement delimits the continental shelf between the Parties over the whole extent of that maritime space as defined at present.[65]

Prima facie, this indeed seems to violate the principle expounded just above that terms used in a clause defining a boundary carry with them – as a result of

[63] Alvarez-Jimenez (n 56) 31–32.

[64] See *Guinea-Bissau/Senegal*, Award (n 38) 150 (§ 80) (translation from *Guinea-Bissau v Senegal Maritime Delimitation Case 1989* (1989) 83 ILR 1, 43 and *Case concerning the Arbitral Award of 31 July 1989 (Guinea-Bissau v Senegal)*, Judgment [1991] ICJ Reports 53, 57 (§ 12)).

[65] ibid 152 (§ 85) (translation from *Guinea-Bissau v Senegal Maritime Delimitation Case 1989* (1989) 83 ILR 1, 4643).

the stability of frontiers principle – a fixed sense-intention and should thus be interpreted statically. However, as some of the authorities at least impliedly indicate, the stability of frontiers principle only applies *between States*. The *Temple of Preah Vihear* judgment and Judge Shahabuddeen spoke of the principle applying 'when two countries establish a frontier between them'[66] and the Libya-Chad judgment spoke of 'two States [having a] border between them'.[67]

The principle does not, however, apply where the boundary between a State and territory not owned by another State is fixed, such as the high seas and, in this case, what is now called 'the Area'. The logic of this qualification on the stability of frontiers principle is plain to see. States commit to certain and final boundaries between their territories so as to avoid coming into conflict with each other. Indeed, when the *Temple of Preah Vihear* judgment inferred the parties' intention to fix the frontier between them with finality, it did so after observing that the period in the lead-up to the 1904 Boundary Treaty had been characterised by 'trouble and friction' between Siam and France over what territory belonged to each of them.[68] When there is a line between States, any movement inherently encroaches on the territorial rights of one of them and risks a conflagration. When there is instead a line between a State's territory and territory that belongs to no one, there is no such risk – or at least an almost negligible risk – of conflict. In the first case, States have an interest in not allowing the line to move and can therefore be presumed not to allow for any changes to it as a result of changes to the meaning of any word determining it. In the second case, States have no clear interest in not allowing the line to move. Indeed, given that international legal evolution traditionally cedes commonly-held territory to States rather than taking it from them, they might even be willing for the line to move in accordance with future changes to the law and having corollary changes to the meaning of the legal concepts used to define that line in their treaty. In such cases, there is clearly no basis for inferring that the parties held a fixed sense-intention through the stability of frontiers principle, because the basis of that principle does not apply and the parties may even have wanted their border with commonly held territory to move through time.

The *Guinea-Bissau/Senegal* award indirectly reflects this result. The term 'continental shelf' was not used to delimit a boundary between two States, but to determine how far their agreed delimitation extended out onto the seabed. No presumption of a fixed sense-intention arose in relation to the interpretation of this term, so it was open to being interpreted statically or dynamically according to other considerations, with it ultimately being interpreted dynamically for the factual and linguistic reasons set out in subsection III above. However, if there had been an unqualified and hard rule against interpreting terms in treaty clauses defining all frontiers dynamically, this important international decision

[66] *Preah Vihear*, Judgment (n 58) 34; *Libya/Chad*, Shahabuddeen Separate Opinion (n 59) 49.
[67] *Libya/Chad*, Judgment (n 59) 37 (§ 72).
[68] *Preah Vihear*, Judgment (n 58) 33.

would have contravened the presumption. With our intuitively appealing qualification of 'used to determine a frontier between to two States', however, the presumption remains fully intact and strong enough to be presented as such when summarised in Figure 9. Indeed, this presumption is ultimately very valuable for inferring the particular temporal sense-intention and solving the problem of intertemporal linguistics in a number of cases.

Figure 9 TSI Indicator: Terms used to fix boundaries between States

Ch 9 §	Feature referred to as source of static or dynamic approach	Feature actually used as basis of inference of sense-intention/ approach	Implies which temporal sense-intention?	Strength of implication
V	Terms in territorial treaties	Terms used to fix boundaries between States	Fixed	Strong

VI. TERMS IN TREATIES OF FIXED AND CONTINUING DURATIONS AS IMPLYING FIXED AND MOBILE SENSE-INTENTIONS RESPECTIVELY

We have already seen that the fact that the treaty being interpreted was of a 'continuing duration' was considered to support the dynamic approach taken in the *Related Rights* judgment[69] and the putatively dynamic interpretation undertaken by the WTO Appellate Body in the *China – AV Products* dispute.[70] This consideration also played a very prominent role in the *Aegean Sea* judgment where, after declaring a presumption of a mobile sense-intention on the basis of 'the territorial status of Greece' being a generic term, the Court stated:

> This presumption, in the view of the Court, is even more compelling when it is recalled that the 1928 Act was a convention for the pacific settlement of disputes designed to be of the most general kind and *of continuing duration*, for it hardly seems conceivable that in such a convention terms like 'domestic jurisdiction' and 'territorial status' were intended to have a fixed content regardless of the subsequent evolution of international law.[71]

In the *La Bretagne* award of 1986, both the majority and the dissenting opinion of Donat Pharand directly invoked a mobile sense-intention on the basis of the 1972 Canada-France treaty's unlimited duration. De Visscher and Quéneudec reprised the terms of the above-cited section of the *Aegean Sea* judgment,[72]

[69] *Related Rights*, Judgment (n 21) 30 (§ 67).

[70] *China – Publications and Audiovisual Products*, Report (WTO Appellate Body, WT/DS363/AB/R, 21 December 2009) 161 (§ 396).

[71] *Aegean Sea*, Judgment (n 18) 32 (§ 77) (emphasis added).

[72] *Filleting within the Gulf of St Lawrence between Canada and France ('La Bretagne')*, Award (1986) XIX RIAA/RSA 225, 247 (§ 37).

while Pharand, who took a more obviously dynamic approach than the majority, stated the position even more forcefully, saying that: 'it would be unreasonable to assume that, in *an agreement of an indefinite period* such as this, the Parties intended to freeze the meaning of '*pêche*' as it might have been then understood'.[73] This view is well-established across different fields on international law. In the field of international environmental law, Judge Weeramantry stated that, because the 1977 Hungarian-Czech treaty at issue in the *Gabčíkovo* case 'was to operate for decades into the future, it could not operate on the basis of environmental norms as though they were frozen in time when the Treaty was entered into'.[74] In a study of the nature of WTO obligations, Joost Pauwelyn considered the fact that 'most WTO provisions can be said to be of a continuing nature' to 'plead … in favour of interpreting [the WTO] treaty in an evolutionary manner, that is, in line with understandings and law at the time of application'.[75]

Against this weight of authority, this study must apply its conceptual framework to the issue and consider de novo whether the simple fact that a contested term occurs in a treaty of a continuing duration implies a mobile sense-intention and thus, all else being equal, a dynamic approach to a problem of intertemporal linguistics. When one puts the question in this way, considers it in concrete terms and analyses the relevant dicta more closely, cracks start to appear.

Many treaties are intended to apply for perpetuity, but the parties do not always simultaneously intend to leave their terms subject to change. Indeed, territorial treaties are often intended to last forever, yet, as revealed just above, their terms are accompanied by a fixed – not mobile – sense-intention when they occur in clauses fixing boundaries between two or more States. Indeed, the vast majority of treaties are intended to be of a continuing duration. If the simple fact of a treaty being of a continuing duration were sufficient to indicate that its terms carried with them a mobile sense-intention, then even terms in perpetual territorial treaties would have to be interpreted dynamically. This clearly cannot be the case; one cannot build a presumption of a mobile sense-intention from the mere fact that the term appears in a treaty that is for a continuing duration.

It is submitted that, if there is an implication of a temporal sense-intention presumption to be found in the length of a treaty, then it could only exist in the negative form of the presumption generally proposed. A treaty which is not of

[73] *Filleting within the Gulf of St Lawrence between Canada and France ('La Bretagne')*, Dissenting Opinion of Donat Pharand (1986) XIX RIAA/RSA 266, 275 (§ 31, translation from *Dispute Concerning Filleting within the Gulf of St Lawrence ('La Bretagne')* (1986) 82 ILR 590, 648), (emphasis added).

[74] *Gabčíkovo-Nagymaros Project (Hungary/Slovakia)*, Separate Opinion of Vice-President Weeramantry [1997] ICJ Reports 88, 113–14.

[75] Joost Pauwelyn, 'The Nature of WTO Obligations' (2002) 1 *Jean Monnet Working Papers* 1, 34–35.

a long and continuing duration, but is instead of a short and fixed duration, may potentially imply that its terms carry a fixed sense-intention and should be interpreted using the static approach. However, while semantic change may be unlikely in a short period, it may nonetheless have been considered possible and welcomed by the parties concluding their treaty of short duration. For example, a treaty establishing cross-border cooperation over a five-year period to strengthen financial institutions by imposing capital ratios and the like may wish to follow the course of changes to the regulatory concepts concerning capital ratios and the like that it has used. In the *Gabčíkovo-Nagymaros* case, the majority of the Court found that the parties had committed to the internal evolution of their treaty regime without relying on it having a long-term or continuing nature.[76]

Ultimately, despite the broad support for the notion that a treaty of continuing duration implies a dynamic interpretation, the stronger implication is raised by the inverse feature of an interpretative situation – as shown in Figure 10. The fact that a contested term appears in a treaty of short and fixed duration may imply a fixed sense-intention, albeit rebuttably and only quite weakly.

Figure 10 TSI Indicator: Terms in treaties of continuing/fixed duration

Ch 9 §	Feature referred to as source of static or dynamic approach	Feature actually used as basis of inference of sense-intention/ approach	Implies which temporal sense-intention?	Strength of implication
VI	Terms in treaties of continuing duration		Mobile	Weak (if any)
		Terms in treaties of short and fixed duration	Fixed	Weak-medium

VII. TERMS IN CONSTITUTIVE INSTRUMENTS AS IMPLYING A MOBILE SENSE-INTENTION

Along with human rights treaties, the constitutive instruments of international organisations are the most commonly cited substantive type of treaty to supposedly generate a dynamic approach to the Problem.[77] Fitzmaurice had noted as early as 1951 that international lawyers may single out 'constitutions of international organizations such as the United Nations' for 'what might be called creative or dynamic methods of interpretation',[78] while the ILC debates and case

[76] See *Gabčíkovo-Nagymaros Project (Hungary/Slovakia)*, Judgment [1997] ICJ Reports 7, 67 (§ 112); see further s 6.II.B(ii) above.

[77] See, eg Bernhardt (n 50) 21.

[78] Gerald Fitzmaurice, 'The Law and Procedure of the International Court of Justice: Treaty Interpretation and Certain Other Treaty Points' (1951) 28 *British Year Book of International Law* 1, 7–8.

law from the same era reveal several statements pleading for the use of a different interpretative approach for this type of treaty.[79]

Modern-day authorities continue to maintain this position. Recent editions of *Oppenheim's International Law* state that there is 'room for the view that a treaty of a "constitutional" character should be subject to somewhat different rules of interpretation so as to allow for the intrinsic evolutionary nature of a constitution',[80] while the 2007 *RosInvest* award on jurisdiction singled out 'constituent instruments of international organizations' with human rights treaties as 'special cases' in which parties should be assumed to be open to changes in the meaning of 'principles and concepts'.[81] It is, however, Sato who most lucidly links constitutive instruments to a mobile sense-intention:

> [B]ecause constituent instruments are reasonably considered to contain many concepts and provisions of mobile reference, the provisions concerned will, unless the intentions of the parties are proved to be reference to a fixed content upon the examination, be regarded to be based upon a mobile reference and will be so interpreted. To this extent, the evolutionary nature of constituent instruments will be supported by the theory of inter-temporary law and their evolutionary and teleological interpretation will have a legitimacy.[82]

As cogent as they might seem, these claims are nonetheless undermined by the two same defects that undermined the claim that terms in human rights treaties imply a mobile sense-intention.

First, it is simply too broad-brush to imply that all the terms in constitutive instruments must be interpreted dynamically. Several of them do not even appear in clauses that put in place the structural features apparently requiring a dynamic approach. Sato may be right that such treaties may be 'reasonably considered to contain many concepts and provisions of mobile reference', but this means that it is the existence of terms of this character that indicate the mobile sense-intention, not the fact that they appear in treaties of a constitutive character. It is salient in this regard that, in one of the strongest statements of the argument that treaties like the Covenant and the UN Charter should be interpreted dynamically, Sørensen in fact said that 'major contemporary normative conventions *often use* such "evolving concepts"'.[83]

[79] See, eg International Law Commission, 'Yearbook 1964, vol I' (New York, United Nations, 1965) 276–78 (765th meeting – 14 July 1964, § 18 [per de Luna] and § 41 [per Rosenne]); *Legal Consequences for States of the Continued Presence of South Africa in Namibia (South West Africa) notwithstanding Security Council Resolution 276 (1970)*, Separate Opinion of Judge de Castro [1971] ICJ Reports 170, 184.

[80] Jennings and Watts (n 45) 1268–82.

[81] *Rosinvest*, Award (n 52) 42 (§ 39).

[82] Tetsuo Sato, *Evolving Constitutions of International Organizations: A Critical Analysis of the Interpretative Framework of the Constituent Instruments of International Organizations* (The Hague, Kluwer Law International, 1996).

[83] Institut de droit international and Max Sørensen, 'Le problème dit du droit intertemporel dans l'ordre international – Rapport provisoire' (12 February 1973) *Annuaire* 1, 15–16 (§ 20) (emphasis added).

Second, the longstanding consensus that constitutive instruments must be interpreted differently, does not necessarily require interpreting them in a manner which favours the later-emerging meaning of a treaty term over its original meaning, but rather interpreting them in a more flexible and creative manner. This mode of interpretation belonging to the teleological school was the focus of Fitzmaurice's inquiry in the section of his work quoted just above,[84] while the equivalent comments of de Luna placed emphasis not on allowing treaties to follow changes in the meaning of their terms, but on allowing for 'the institutional development of international organizations'[85] and more 'extensive' interpretation than treaties of a contractual type.[86] Even Judge Spender, an ICJ judge who later became so closely associated with a conservative judicial and interpretative philosophy, emphasised a teleological – but not dynamic – approach in the section of his *Certain Expenses* separate opinion apparently calling for a less static approach to interpreting constitutive instruments. In comments which 'greatly impressed' authorities such as Rosenne in relation to this issue,[87] he focused on the need to give the Charter, on account of its very lofty purposes, a 'meaning ... consistent with the purposes sought to be achieved'.[88] A notably more progressive ICJ judge, Judge Lachs, also emphasised the importance of interpreting constitutive (or 'constituent'[89]) instruments teleologically, saying that 'giving certain provisions of the constituent instrument a meaning which was very remote from that envisaged by the parties at the time of signature' was justified if this was to ensure the 'operation of a treaty ... in the light of the realities of international relations'.[90]

However, just because, according to such esteemed international lawyers, the static approach can be trumped by the teleological approach in relation to the Charter, does not mean that, for all constitutive instruments, the static approach should never be used in the first place. These arguments being made in support of extra flexibility and certain teleological approaches to the

[84] Fitzmaurice (n 78) 7–8: '(ii) Teleological method. Certain of the individual Judges, while agreeing with the Court that the intentions of the framers are to be looked for primarily in the treaty itself, go much farther and adopt an avowedly teleological basis of interpretation. (fn 1 – This attitude tends to be taken up principally with reference to the interpretation of the constitutions of international organizations such as the United Nations, where there may well be a special case for the use of what might be called creative or dynamic methods of interpretation.)'.

[85] ILC Yearbook 1964, vol I (n 79) 276 (per de Luna, 765th meeting – 14 July 1964, § 18).

[86] ibid (per de Luna, 765th meeting – 14 July 1964, § 18): 'The rules being drafted should not become a strait-jacket capable of frustrating, for example, the institutional development of international organizations. Obviously, there was a difference between an extensive and a restrictive interpretation of treaties of a contractual type and that of constituent instruments of international organizations.'

[87] ibid 278 (per Rosenne, 765th meeting – 14 July 1964, § 41).

[88] *Certain Expenses of the United Nations (Article 17, paragraph 2, of the Charter)*, Separate Opinion of Judge Sir Percy Spender [1962] ICJ Reports 182, 186–87.

[89] Note that English-language international law texts appear to refer to these instruments interchangeably as either 'constitutive' or 'constituent', with the present author preferring the former for consistency with the expression '*acte/instrument constitutif*' in international law's other main language.

[90] ILC Yearbook 1964, vol I (n 79) 286 (per Lachs, 766th meeting – 15 July 1964, § 46).

interpretation of constitutive instruments are important and may well be valid, but they do not show how being a treaty of this type can yield an inference of a mobile sense-intention in relation to all terms in that type of instrument, nor prompt an adoption of the later-emerging rather than original meaning of those terms.

The constitutional character of a treaty like the UN Charter does not imply that the parties drafting it wanted the meaning of its terms to shift with linguistically and legally prompted semantic changes. Indeed, drafters of domestic constitutions frequently seek to limit the malleability of the terms in an effort to maximise political stability. While a detailed review of the individual terms of constitutive instruments such as the UN Charter falls outside the scope of this study, it is far from clear that its authors intended all the terms they used to move with the times. Their overall objects and purposes might have been clear, but this had no bearing on the temporal sense-intention they attached to the specific terms of their treaty, a sense-intention that cannot be presumed to be mobile simply on account of the treaty being constitutive of an international organisation. There is accordingly no basis for declaring the fact that the term is within a constitutive instrument to be a reliable indicator of it taking a mobile TSI, as set out in Figure 11.

Figure 11 TSI Indicator: Terms in constitutive instruments of IOs

Ch 9 §	Feature referred to as source of static or dynamic approach	Feature actually used as basis of inference of sense-intention/ approach	Implies which temporal sense-intention?	Strength of implication
VII	Terms in constitutive instruments of international organisations		Mobile	Weak (if any)

VIII. TERMS IN CLAUSES ESTABLISHING A SITUATION AND LAYING DOWN A RULE RESPECTIVELY

In the veritable mountain of scholarship published in the wake of the ICJ's 2009 *Related Rights* judgment, an *AFDI* article by Sarah Cassella stands out for its effort to put a rigorous conceptual basis beneath the Court's comments on what kind of circumstances justify the dynamic interpretation of a treaty term.[91] Drawing on Jean Combacau's writings on the difference between rules and

[91] Sarah Cassella, 'Rééquilibrer les effets inéquitables d'une délimitation territoriale : l'arrêt de la Cour internationale de Justice du 13 juillet 2009 dans l'affaire du Différend relatif à des droits de navigation et des droits connexes (Costa Rica c. Nicaragua)' (2009) 55 *Annuaire français de droit international* 253.

situations in the context of the intertemporal law doctrine,[92] Cassella considers that we can safely presume a mobile sense-intention where the parties '*ont entendu poser une règle*' and a fixed sense-intention where the parties '*ont entendu … constituer une situation juridique*'.[93]

It should not escape our attention that the distinction used by Cassella in this context is really just a form of the much older *traité-loi/traité-contrat* distinction so beloved in France and which has also been occasionally applied in relation to evolutionary treaty interpretation.[94] Indeed, already in 1925, *traités-lois* had been linked to the creation of '*règles de droit international*' and *traités-contrats* to the creation of '*situations juridiques particulières entre Etats*'.[95]

On a high level, this *règle* versus *situation* theory is very attractive. It uses the power of the intertemporal law, without being selective or corrupting it, properly applying both of the two limbs of Huber's *Island of Palmas* dictum. It also seems to accord quite well with the few indicia of the temporal sense-intention ultimately yielded from the analysis conducted in this chapter. The legal concepts that we concluded may well indicate a mobile sense-intention, along with the commitment by States to standards of conduct, clearly involve the 'laying down of a rule' (*poser une règle*). Equally, the terms used to fix boundaries between States – to which we ascribed a presumption of a fixed sense-intention – are clearly used as part of 'establishing a legal situation' (*constituer une situation juridique*). It even helps explain the differences between majority and minority opinions on major cases touching on the problem of intertemporal linguistics. Indeed, whereas the *Aegean Sea* majority appeared to understand Greece to be putting a potentially modulating rule in place – and favoured a dynamic approach, Judge de Castro characterised the jurisdictional declaration as creating a fixed legal situation of consent comparable to that created by a claim to territory – and favoured a static approach.[96]

There does seem to be a sufficient correlation between this distinction and the two temporal sense intentions. It seems relatively safe to infer from a term being in a treaty clause establishing a legal situation that it was used with a fixed sense-intention and, from a term is in a treaty clause laying down a rule, that it

[92] Jean Combacau, 'L'écoulement du temps' in Société Française pour le Droit International (ed), *Le droit international et le temps: colloque de Paris (actes du XXXIVe colloque de la Société Française pour le Droit International)* (Paris, Pedone, 2001) 101–02.

[93] Cassella (n 91) 264–65.

[94] See, eg IDI and Sørensen (n 83) 16 (§ 20); Sergio Aly, 'L' "interprétation évolutive" en droit international public' (Mémoire de DEA, Institut universitaire de hautes études internationales, Genève, 1997) 74; Eva Greschek, *Die evolutive Auslegung voelkerrechtlicher Vertraege am Beispiel des GATT* (Frankfurt, Peter Lang, 2012) 31, 67; see also ILC Yearbook 1964, vol I (n 79) 36 (728th meeting – 21 May 1964, § 7, per Verdross).

[95] Paul Duez, 'L'interprétation des traités internationaux' (1925) 32 *Revue générale de droit international public* 429, 430: 'Tantôt il est traité-loi, créant ou enregistrant des règles de droit international; tantôt il est traité-contrat, créant des situations juridiques particulières entre Etats.'

[96] See *Aegean Sea*, Judgment (n 18) 31–33 (§§ 74–79); *Aegean Sea Continental Shelf (Greece v Turkey)*, Dissenting Opinion of Judge de Castro [1978] ICJ Reports 62, 69–71 (§§ 15–18).

was used with a mobile sense-intention. As indicated in Figure 12's schematic summary of this indicator of the TSI, the implication raised by whether a clause states a rule or establishes a situation is even quite strong. However, this does not mean that this subtle distinction between two different types of treaty clause can be used as part of a solution to problems of intertemporal linguistics. Indeed, as will be seen in chapter 10,[97] great difficulty arises when we seek to apply it.

Figure 12 TSI Indicator: Terms in clauses establishing a situation/laying down a rule

<table>
<tr><th>Ch 9 §</th><th>Feature referred to as source of static or dynamic approach</th><th>Feature actually used as basis of inference of sense-intention/approach</th><th>Implies which temporal sense-intention?</th><th>Strength of implication</th></tr>
<tr><td rowspan="2">VIII</td><td>Terms in treaty clauses establishing a legal situation</td><td></td><td>Fixed</td><td rowspan="2">Medium-Strong</td></tr>
<tr><td>Terms in treaty clauses laying down a legal rule</td><td></td><td>Mobile</td></tr>
</table>

IX. IMPLICATIONS OF A TEMPORAL SENSE-INTENTION ARISING FROM THE NUMBER OF PARTIES TO A TREATY

The number of parties to a treaty is only rarely cited as a feature of an interpretative situation affecting whether or not a term should be interpreted statically or dynamically. In 2010, Nolte, as the Special Rapporteur for the ILC's Treaties over Time Study Group went so far as to state broadly that '[t]he ICJ ha[d] recognized the possibility of an evolutive interpretation for multilateral as well as bilateral treaties, and even for unilateral declarations',[98] which would mean that the number of parties is irrelevant to the question addressed by this book.

However, the situation is actually quite nuanced, particularly as regards unilateral declarations. Pure unilateral declarations technically fall outside of the VCLT Article 2(1)(a) definition of treaty, but most of the unilateral declarations with which international courts and tribunals are concerned occur in the context of a bilateral or multilateral treaty. These prominently include declarations or reservations regarding the scope of a State's consent to the jurisdiction of an international court or tribunal (for example, under Article 36(2) of the ICJ Statute) and unilateral commitments to freer trade or services at the WTO.

The practice of international courts and tribunals interpreting such unilateral declarations through time does not disclose a predilection for either the

[97] See s 10.III.A below.
[98] ILC, Treaties over Time, Introductory Report (2010) (n 12) 25.

static or the dynamic approach. When China's unilateral commitments as to trade in certain services were interpreted in the *China – AV Products* dispute, the WTO Appellate Body purported to take a dynamic approach, but never actually did so and, in any event, drew no general conclusions as to the particular temporal sense-intention implied by such an instrument.[99] In the *Aegean Sea* case, Judge de Castro's dissenting opinion characterised a unilateral declaration as to jurisdiction as an instantaneous 'declaration of intention' and argued very fully and clearly that a static approach must inherently be applied to such declarations.[100] Indeed, Judge de Castro appears to take the view that the granting of consent is an instantaneous act establishing a legal situation akin to fixing a boundary between States.

Yet declarations as to jurisdiction are often forward-looking and may take into account – and even welcome – changes to the legal, political and factual framework that impact on the terms they use. They are generally made for situations arising many years into the future, an aspect of a treaty that has been used to justify a dynamic interpretation of a treaty term in many cases. Indeed this is how the same unilateral declaration was understood by the majority of the Court in the *Aegean Sea* case. The judgment even contrasted the permanence of the situation raised by a jurisdictional declaration with that imposed by a grant of rights to exploit natural resources (in the non-treaty *Petroleum Development* case invoked by Greece).[101]

As the *Aegean Sea* majority's and minority's respectively dynamic and static interpretations of the same terms in the same jurisdictional declaration indicate, the fact that a term appears in a unilateral declaration does not imply any particular approach to the Problem, nor indeed the existence of either an inherently fixed or mobile sense-intention. Judge de Castro's argument, while well-made, does not impose itself against the counter-authority of the majority approach in the same case and the intuitive need to allow for unilateral declarations that willingly follow the development of the law.

Support for the view that *bilateral* treaties should be interpreted *statically* and *multilateral* treaties *dynamically* is considerably more widespread. Among scholars who have studied the problem of intertemporal linguistics in some detail, there even appears to be some consensus that a dynamic approach is a phenomenon applying principally – and at least most justifiably – to multilateral treaties. In a section dedicated to the '*[v]ecteurs d'interprétation évolutive*', Aly began by saying that, as regards the type of treaty, one must essentially refer to '*traités-lois multilatéraux et aux traités constitutifs d'organisation internationale*'.[102] Another author of a detailed study on dynamic treaty interpretation, Malgosia Fitzmaurice, has argued that 'a certain dynamism in interpretation is necessary, particularly in relation to multilateral treaties

[99] *China – AV Products*, WTO AB Report (n 70); see further s 6.II.C(ii) above.
[100] *Aegean Sea*, De Castro Dissenting Opinion (n 96) 63, 67–68 (§§ 4, 12).
[101] *Aegean Sea*, Judgment (n 18) 32 (§ 77).
[102] Aly (n 94) 74.

creating international organizations and human rights conventions'.[103] A key supporter of the evolutionary treaty interpretation doctrine, Rudolf Bernhardt, accepted that while '[b]ilateral treaties or treaties with only a few parties should not be excluded from an evolutive interpretation, … [t]he main area in which an evolutive interpretation is indicated is in the field of multilateral treaties'.[104] Multilateral treaties have also been singled out for the taking of a dynamic or evolutionary approach by a recent German study of evolutionary interpretation,[105] and countless other contemporary scholarly works. In the 2012 *Daimler* and *ICS* investment awards, tribunals chaired by Pierre-Marie Dupuy notably came to the same conclusion from the other side, stating that 'the classical rule of interpretation known as the principle of contemporaneity … is particularly pertinent in the case of bilateral treaties'.[106]

For the purposes of this study, what is most significant is that the link between multilateral treaties and dynamic interpretation is not mediated through a finding as to a temporal sense-intention held by the parties in relation to the contested term. There is no argument that a bilateral treaty implies that its terms carry a fixed sense-intention, nor that a multilateral treaty implies that its terms carry a mobile sense-intention. Instead, the link drawn between multilateral treaties and a dynamic approach, almost exclusively by doctrine, is made through reference to *policy*. There may be good reasons to assign a mobile sense-intention to the terms in multilateral treaties – and these will be evaluated in chapter 10 – but, as the summary in Figure 13 shows, there is no basis for inferring the actual existence of a mobile sense-intention for a term simply because it was included in a multilateral treaty.

Figure 13 TSI Indicator: Terms in unilateral, bilateral and multilateral instruments

Ch 9 §	**Feature referred to as source of static or dynamic approach**	**Feature actually used as basis of inference of sense-intention/ approach**	**Implies which temporal sense-intention?**	**Strength of implication**
IX	Terms in unilateral declarations		Fixed	Weak (if any)
	Terms in bilateral treaties		Fixed	Weak (if any), policy-based
	Terms in multilateral treaties		Mobile	

[103] Malgosia Fitzmaurice, 'Dynamic (Evolutive) Interpretation of Treaties and the European Court of Human Rights' in Alexander Orakhelashvili and Sarah Williams (eds), *40 Years of the Vienna Convention on the Law of Treaties* (London, British Institute of International and Comparative Law, 2010) 55.

[104] Bernhardt (n 50) 21, 17.

[105] See Greschek (n 94) 67.

[106] *Daimler Financial Services AG v Argentina* (Jurisdiction), Award (ICSID Tribunal, ARB/05/1, 22 August 2012) 90 (§ 220); see also almost identical terms in *ICS Inspection and Control Services Limited v Argentina* (Jurisdiction), Award (Permanent Court of Arbitration Tribunal, PCA Case No 2010-9, 10 February 2012) 96 (§ 289).

X. CONCLUDING OBSERVATIONS ON THE INTERPRETATIVE FEATURES CITED BY THE CASE LAW AND SCHOLARSHIP

The objective of this chapter was to identify features of interpretative situations from which treaty interpreters might be able to infer the temporal sense-intention capable of solving problems of intertemporal linguistics. Its review of the features commonly highlighted by the international case law and scholarship in support of static and dynamic interpretations yielded mixed results. International lawyers seeking to justify the static and dynamic approaches that they are or advocate taking have often been guilty of overstating their case, arguing that all the terms of certain types of treaties imply a static or a dynamic approach. Through its conceptually more robust focus on the key intermediate question of the temporal sense-intention, this study was able to refine those claims such that features of interpretative situations reliably implying a particular approach were able to emerge. By discerning the implied focus of the relevant authorities on how particular treaty terms are used, rather than the wider treaty framework in which they occur, we have brought to light features of interpretative situations which, if identified, suggest that the relevant treaty term carried with it a fixed or a mobile sense-intention.

The analysis of each of these features revealed that, while some strongly imply a particular sense-intention, others do not actually imply a sense-intention at all. By way of summary, these features of interpretative situations and the extent to which they imply a particular temporal sense-intention are now brought together in one combined table, Figure 14.

Figure 14 TSI Indicators – Summary Table

<table>
<tr><th>Ch 9 §</th><th>Feature referred to as source of static or dynamic approach</th><th>Feature actually used as basis of inference of sense-intention/ approach</th><th>Implies which temporal sense-intention?</th><th>Strength of implication</th></tr>
<tr><td rowspan="2">I</td><td rowspan="2">Context</td><td rowspan="2">Immediate textual context, including express or implied definition of contested treaty term</td><td>Fixed</td><td>Strong</td></tr>
<tr><td>Mobile</td><td>Strong</td></tr>
<tr><td rowspan="2">II</td><td>'By definition evolutionary' terms</td><td rowspan="2">Awareness of likelihood of semantic change</td><td rowspan="2">Mobile</td><td rowspan="2">Medium</td></tr>
<tr><td>'Generic' terms</td></tr>
<tr><td>III</td><td>Terms that are legal concepts</td><td>Terms that are legal concepts in a regime external to the treaty</td><td>Mobile</td><td>Medium-Strong</td></tr>
<tr><td>IV</td><td>Terms in human rights treaties</td><td>Terms committing States to standards of conduct</td><td>Mobile</td><td>Medium</td></tr>
</table>

Ch 9 §	Feature referred to as source of static or dynamic approach	Feature actually used as basis of inference of sense-intention/ approach	Implies which temporal sense-intention?	Strength of implication
V	Terms in territorial treaties	Terms used to fix boundaries between States	Fixed	Strong
VI	Terms in treaties of continuing duration		Mobile	Weak (if any)
		Terms in treaties of short and fixed duration	Fixed	Weak-medium
VII	Terms in constitutive instruments of international organisations		Mobile	Weak (if any)
VIII	Terms establishing a legal situation		Fixed	Medium-Strong
	Terms laying down a legal rule		Mobile	
IX	Terms in unilateral declarations		Fixed	Weak (if any)
	Terms in bilateral treaties		Fixed	Weak (if any), policy-based
	Terms in multilateral treaties		Mobile	

While the limited international case law and scholarship tackling the Problem has quite understandably not revealed an obvious means for inferring the relevant temporal sense-intention, it has fortunately given us the ingredients which we can now – in chapter 10 – carefully combine to produce a workable solution to the problem of intertemporal linguistics.

10

Organising the Features into a Workable Method for Inferring the Temporal Sense-Intention and Solving the Problem

I. CONTEXT INCLUDING DEFINITIONS – THE BEST EVIDENCE OF SENSE-INTENTION

WE SAW AT the start of the last chapter that, in cognitive linguistics, in computational linguistics and in international law itself, immediate spoken or textual context constitutes the best evidence of the sense-intention that disambiguates between the different senses of a term.

The clearest respect in which an element of a treaty's context will help identify the sense-intention is through a *definition*. In the analogous situation of VCLT Article 31(4), definitions are commonly regarded as providing the best evidence of a (sense-)intention to use a special, rather than an ordinary meaning. Gardiner, for example, cites 'a treaty's definition provision' among the most obvious cases of special meaning,[1] while Kammerhofer speaks of a presumption that the ordinary meaning of a treaty term was used unless the parties 'specified a "special meaning", such as *termini technici* by way of a purpose-built definition'.[2] International practice also reveals a heavy reliance on definitions as part of assessments of whether a treaty term is used in an ordinary or special sense. In the *Young Loan* arbitration, for example, counsel told the Tribunal that 'an essential point for your appreciation of the situation – the word "rate of exchange" in the London Agreement has a special meaning, a special meaning which is *defined by* Clause 13'.[3]

[1] Richard K Gardiner, *Treaty Interpretation* (Oxford, Oxford University Press, 2008) 294.

[2] Jörg Kammerhofer, *Uncertainty in International Law: A Kelsenian Perspective* (London, Routledge, 2011) 90.

[3] *Belgium, France, Switzerland, UK and USA v Germany ('Young Loan Arbitration')*, Dissenting Opinion of Robinson, Bathurst and Monguilan (1980) XIX RIAA/RSA 494, 141 (emphasis added).

Where the treaty itself does not contain an express definition of the relevant term, other direct statements of the parties as to their sense-intention may provide a strong and direct indication of what they meant when they used the term. Gardiner encourages reference to interpretative declarations,[4] while Judge Vio Grossi's *Artavia* dissent emphasised the importance of 'the agreements, instruments and practices … intimately connected with the relevant treaty'.[5]

Like the sense-intention that disambiguates ordinary and special senses of a treaty term, the temporal sense-intention that disambiguates fixed and mobile senses of a treaty term is best evidenced by an express statement connected with the treaty *directly* stating the temporal sense that is intended. However, direct express statements as to temporal sense-intention are, at least at the present time, very rare.

Indirect statements of a temporal sense-intention thereby reveal themselves to be the next best evidence of what interpreters need to disambiguate between the original and later-emerging meaning of a treaty term. Just as an express statement through which the parties submit the terms of their agreement to science will manifest their intention to use a treaty term in a special, scientific sense,[6] an express statement through which the parties agree to follow the external development of an area of international law will reveal their intention to use a treaty term from that area of law in a mobile sense. Statements such as 'the continental shelf, as understood at the time of this treaty's signature' and 'the continental shelf pursuant to the meaning international law assigns to that term at the time of the act in question' will indirectly disclose a fixed and mobile sense-intention respectively.

Regrettably, even this type of qualification as to the meaning of a term through time remains extremely rare in current treaty practice. *Implied* forms of definition or qualification that do not speak directly or indirectly of the temporal aspect are more common and will in some cases still leave no doubt as to the parties' temporal sense-intention.

For example, a treaty which defines or qualifies the meaning of a contested term by using a fixed *extension* (set of referents)[7] will generally be sufficient for identifying whether the term should be understood in a fixed or mobile sense. Imagine, for example, that the GATT 1947 had included, after the words 'relating to the conservation of exhaustible natural resources', the words 'namely all types of oil, gas and coal as well as the mineral resources copper, iron ore, lead, nickel, quartz, bauxite and cobalt'. Even if the meaning of 'natural resources' external to the GATT then broadened to include animals including dolphins,

[4] Gardiner (n 1) 294.

[5] *Case of Artavia Murillo et al ('In Vitro Fertilization') v Costa Rica* (Preliminary Objections, Merits, Reparations and Costs), Dissenting Opinion of Judge vio Grossi [2012] Inter-Am Ct HR (Ser C) No 257 15.

[6] See ibid 5.

[7] See s 4.III.C above.

they would not have been able to be brought within the scope of the GATT provision because, by fixing the extensional range of the term, the parties would have revealed a fixed sense-intention for the term 'exhaustible natural resources'.

The temporal sense-intention applying to a treaty term can also be strongly implied by a definition or qualification which defines a treaty term using a constrained range of *intensional* characteristics. To adapt the example used above in relation to an extensional definition, now imagine that the GATT 1947 contained a separate definition which provided that '"exhaustible natural resources" means all non-living, naturally occurring substances that can be bought and sold and are commonly used as part of an economically important industry of a State'. Such a definition of the relevant treaty term would have disclosed a manifestly fixed sense-intention such that semantic changes external to the treaty could not have brought living things that are not commonly bought and sold as part of an economically important industry – such as dolphins or sea turtles – within the scope of the treaty's meaning of 'exhaustible natural resources'.[8]

Definitions, interpretative statements and express and even implied qualifications on the meaning of a particular term rarely feature in the treaties interpreted and applied today. Unlike contract drafters in many legal systems, the drafters of modern-day treaties are not in the habit of defining all the instrument's key terms. Indeed, the practical challenges of treaty-making – particularly multilateral treaty-making – often discourage negotiators from raising such thorny issues as how a key term should be understood, lest the attempt to agree on a definition of that term torpedo a fragile consensus that may have formed around a draft provision. The present author is aware of no treaty which expressly defines a term in a fixed or mobile sense and, for the moment, precious few that define terms with sufficiently clear and fixed intensions or extensions for a temporal sense-intention to arise impliedly from their definitions.

For the purposes of this chapter, such direct evidence is too uncommon to be particularly useful to interpreters trying to identify the temporal sense-intention in order to choose between the original and later-emerging meanings of a treaty term. However, it is absolutely critical to observe that such evidence, if available, will provide the very best evidence of the temporal sense-intention, prevailing over all other factors that might point to an intention to use a term in a fixed or mobile sense. Since some definitions of treaty terms – and some textual contexts

[8] One might be tempted to think that, in this kind of situation, the parties chose to use a special meaning of the term 'exhaustible natural resources' that renders it immune from changes to the ordinary meaning of the term occurring outside the treaty. However, it was not necessarily a special – or non-ordinary – meaning at the time of drafting. It is accordingly more accurate to understand the parties as having chosen to use the ordinary meaning of a treaty term but, by defining it according to fixed features, expressing their intention that its treaty meaning not be subject to the vagaries of potential semantic change.

generally – may be sufficient to determine the temporal sense-intention without further inquiry, an investigation of whether such contextual indications of the TSI exist constitutes the first step in the method for solving the problem of intertemporal linguistics – as shown in Figure 15.

This priority not only follows from what linguistics tells us is at the core of the interpretative task raised by a problem of intertemporal linguistics, but is also essential from a practical perspective. It accords treaty drafters the right to render apparent – through definitions and express qualifications – whether they used a term in a fixed or mobile sense; a practice that is, in light of the many unclear contests between original and later-emerging meaning that have arisen, likely to become more prevalent in future treaties. Indeed, as the below-listed set of inferences and presumptions as to the temporal sense-intention becomes more established, States will have a better idea, already when negotiating a treaty, of whether a fixed or mobile sense-intention is likely to be attributed to their use of particular treaty terms. The possibility of adding a definition or qualification that expresses a temporal sense-intention therefore provides States who want to counter the temporal sense-intention likely to be assigned to a term with an option to ensure that the term is assigned only the temporal-sense intention that they in fact possessed.

Figure 15 Chart for Inferring the Temporal Sense-Intention – Context

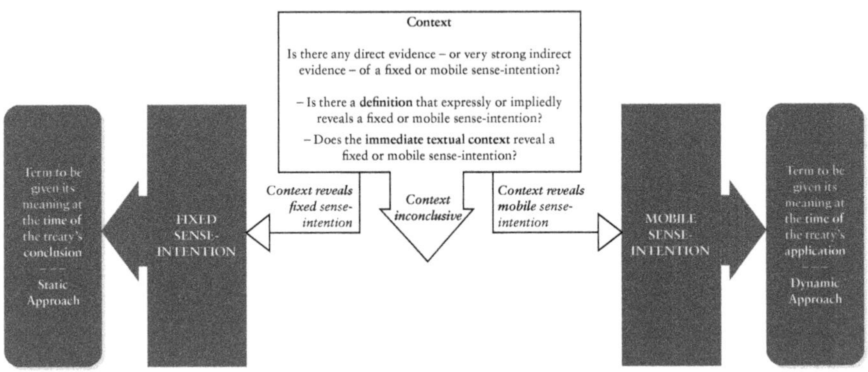

II. WHERE CONTEXT RUNS OUT – USING OTHER INDICIA AND PRESUMPTIONS FOR INFERRING THE TEMPORAL SENSE-INTENTION

A. Private Law Analogies for Inferring Party-intention

Private law analogies show us that there is no need to give up hope where a court or tribunal needs to infer a party-intention that is more abstract than that which can be safely inferred from context. Both the intention constituting the choice of a governing law under private international law and the intention to be legally bound in various systems of contract law provide pointers as to: (i) the other kinds of facts from which such an intention can be inferred; and (ii) how those facts can be used to determine the relevant party-intention.

All major systems of private international law agree that the selection of a governing law to apply to an international commercial contract depends primarily on the parties' intention.[9] Like the temporal sense-intention, however, the somewhat abstract 'governing-law-intention' will often not be stated expressly, so courts are regularly required to infer or presume it.

For its part, the intention to be legally bound is one of the key criteria for the formation of a contract in many systems of law.[10] As the '*Wille*' in the German word '*Rechtsbindungswille*' used for this criterion captures, this is also a question of party-intention. Here also, the parties will rarely state expressly that they intend to be bound. More often than not, a court or tribunal will have to engage in a process of inference in order to determine whether this somewhat abstract intention to be bound existed.[11]

B. Using Indicia and Presumptions

In these and other areas of law, the relevant intention is inferred from that which appears to *indicate* it, the broad category of features that this book will refer to as 'indicia'. The word 'indicium' is preferable to other words commonly used in the legal, linguistic and specifically interpretative contexts,[12] because it refers very generally to that which indicates without presupposing any particular manner of indicating. For civil lawyers the word 'indicium' is likely to evoke the evidentiary notion equivalent to circumstantial evidence in common law jurisdictions, a welcome analogy in light of how items of circumstantial evidence ('*indices*' in French) come in different levels of quality, rely on inference and only ever produce a finding that is less certain than that which is produced by other evidence such as proof ('*preuves*'). Like an *indice* in French law, the indicia of fixed and mobile sense-intentions set out in this chapter may apply to an intention ('*un indice d'une volonté*') and come in various strengths, 'strong indicia' ('*indices puissants*') and 'weak indicia' ('*indices légers*').

[9] The latest attempt at an international harmonisation of these rules, the Hague Principles of Choice of Law, states this expressly and clearly: '1. A contract is governed by the law chosen by the parties.' (Principles on Choice of Law in International Commercial Contracts 2015, art 2).

[10] This notion is key in most common law systems (with the exception of the United States, per the Restatement), German law, French law and the laws of other civil law jurisdictions, see Gregory Klass, 'Intent to Contract' (2009) 95 *Virginia Law Review* 1437, 1437–38.

[11] See, eg Daniel Matthias Klocke, *Erklärungsbewusstsein und Rechtsbindungswille: Willenserklärung und Rechtsgeschäft* (Halle an der Saale, Universitätsverlag Halle-Wittenberg, 2014) 33–36.

[12] It is better to speak of 'indicia' than 'criteria' (which evoke the idea of a standard or requirement), or 'implicatures' (which generally only appear in linguistic contexts) or 'factors' or 'facts', the latter two notions being too broad and, unlike indicia, not defined by their ability to indicate something important.

All the facts from which a governing-law-intention or an intention to be legally bound may be inferred fall within the general category of indicia. Courts may infer the common intention as to which law should govern a contract from a broad range of indicia including which legal system's courts or tribunals the contract selects as the forum for any disputes, whether the contract is in a standard form known to be governed by a certain system of law, an express choice of law made by the same parties in a related transaction, or references to provisions or even concepts of law that are specific to a particular system.[13] In English law and most common law systems of law, whether or not there is an intention to be legally bound is determined through what Klass calls an 'all-things-considered inquiry' into the 'totality of the circumstances',[14] including the type of agreement, the completeness and specificity of its terms and the nature of the parties' relationship.[15]

As indicia, these considerations do not themselves overtly express an intention to use a specific law as a governing law or to bind or not bind, but instead merely indicate, in all the circumstances, the existence of the relevant intention. On the basis of a combination of logic and experience, we infer what the parties intend in a certain sense from something that they do which may be related, yet is different. For example, it may be safe to infer from experience that commercial parties generally want to be legally bound by their promises, whereas family members generally do not. Indeed, the probability of an indicium indicating an intention is something that can even be derived and assessed sociologically and incorporated into the legal process carried out at this level because such indicia ultimately draw their power from how strongly they imply the existence of a particular party-intention.

It is notable in this regard that, in the field of computational linguistics, contemporary word-sense disambiguation algorithms frequently use clear trends of behaviour that emerge from data in order to more reliably estimate – or infer – the sense-intention of a user speaking (or usually typing) in different contexts. For example, a WSD mechanism behind a search engine may presume that a person entering the word 'pizza' late on a Friday night intends to find pizza delivery services open late on a Friday, rather than a recipe for homemade pizza. The unprecedented availability of so-called 'big data' that can disclose trends should lead to safer and safer inferences of this type. A less precise analysis of the same type appears to underlie many of the indicia for party-intention that we have singled out. For example, the now abandoned presumption that parties who chose the courts of a certain country also intended to choose that country's law to govern their contract probably found its greatest favour in a

[13] See Brooke Adele Marshall, 'Reconsidering the Proper Law of the Contract' (2012) 13 *Melbourne Journal of International Law* 505, 14–15; see also Julian Wyatt, 'Chronique de droit international privé australien' (2017) 2 *Journal du droit international (Clunet)* 673, 708–14.

[14] Klass (n 10) 1454.

[15] See Edwin Peel and Guenter H Treitel, *The Law of Contract* (London, Sweet & Maxwell, 2015).

less globalised era when, statistically, there was only very rarely a disjunction between those two intentions.

Public international law also uses indicia in determinations of intention, often referring to them as presumptions or even, somewhat regrettably, as rules. The so-called rules for treaty interpretation set out in VCLT Articles 31(1), 31(2) and 31(3) actually present different indicia, using an unstructured factor-based analysis to ascertain the parties' specific semantic-pragmatic intention, with several different elements of equal value being 'thrown into the crucible'.[16] In his admirable 1928 Hague Course on 'Treaty Interpretation', Ludwik Ehrlich spoke of similar considerations as *présomptions* on the basis of which a treaty could be interpreted, thus linking the party-intention governing treaty interpretation to certain features of particular interpretative situations.[17] This established international legal method means that even if the details of the approach we will use are drawn from private law analogies, the approach itself is not foreign to the field in which we will be applying it.

However, many modern-day public international lawyers worry about using presumptions as to intention. Such criticism is generally based on the view that presumptions, which are vested with greater force and effect than mere indicia, displace other factors that might be important in some cases. Even in the precise context of the problem of intertemporal linguistics, French, for example, expressed some general reservations about the use of presumptions, arguing that 'whilst [they are] undoubtedly a most useful judicial tool', they run the risk of 'contradict[ing] … actual intention'.[18]

Epistemologically, however, a presumption can only speak against an actual sense-intention where that sense-intention is known, and presumptions are precisely at their most useful as a judicial tool when what they have presumed is not – and indeed cannot be – known. Moreover, if an indicium is such a strong indicator of party-intention that it does not matter if it displaces other factors, then there is no need not to use it as a presumption. It is accordingly submitted that fears about the use of presumptions can be overcome if an indicium is only allowed to function as a presumption where it incontestably implies a particular temporal sense-intention.

[16] This expression appears to have been coined by Special Rapporteur Waldock and was used in commentaries accompanying the 1966 draft Law of Treaties articles – International Law Commission, *Yearbook 1966, vol II* (New York, United Nations, 1967) 220, commentary of draft art 28, para 8. The expression has since been quoted or used in the treaty interpretation context by many international lawyers, including: Mark E Villiger, 'Article 31 – General Rule of Interpretation' in Mark E Villiger, *Commentary on the 1969 Vienna Convention on the Law of Treaties* (Leiden, Martinus Nijhoff Publishers, 2009) 436; and Eduardo Jiménez de Aréchaga, 'International Law in the Past Third of a Century' (1978) 159 *Collected Courses of the Hague Academy of International Law* 1, 47.

[17] Ludwik Ehrlich, 'L'interprétation des traités' (1928) 24 *Collected Courses of the Hague Academy of International Law* 1, *passim*.

[18] Duncan French, 'Treaty Interpretation and the Incorporation of Extraneous Legal Rules' (2006) 55 *International and Comparative Law Quarterly* 281, 296–97.

In addition, since much of the benefit of presumptions is associated with an increase in legal certainty, they should only be used where it is clear whether or not they apply. Indeed, in a well-functioning legal system, presumptions elicit a response from parties who know that an applicable presumption would take their agreement in a direction in which they do not want it to go. If, however, the parties negotiating the agreement do not know whether a presumption will apply, they will be less likely to react to its effect and uncertainty will remain. In other words, the lines demarcating the scope of each scenario's application must be clear, not vague. In the words of Zazkis, the set of situations from which any presumption arises must be 'crisp' and not 'fuzzy'.[19] If a presumption is to be used to determine the temporal sense-intention, it is therefore essential that it be expressed in the manner of a crisp dichotomy which leaves no doubt as to whether or not it applies in a particular situation.

If this book is to arrive at an appropriate solution to the problem of intertemporal linguistics, it must accordingly only vest an indicium of a temporal sense-intention with the power of a presumption if (a) that indicium incontestably implies a particular temporal sense-intention and (b) it will clear in all cases whether or not that indicium is present.

This approach accords with the practice of courts and legislators who need to infer party-intention in the private law contexts tendered as analogies above. Whether a matter indicating a party-intention should be regarded as a mere indicium or a presumption depends primarily on an appraisal of the degree to which an intention can be reliably inferred from that matter. Views on this can vary, including through time.

For many years, English law deemed an express intention to decide a dispute in an English forum to raise a presumption that the parties had selected English law to govern that contract.[20] This view was then rejected, such that a choice of forum does not carry with it a definitive indication of the parties' intention as to the governing law, but rather 'constitutes one of the factors to be taken into account' in determining the parties' common intention.[21] It remained a 'weighty indication' of that intention,[22] but, because it was permitted to yield

[19] Rina Zazkis, 'Fuzzy Thinking in Non-fuzzy Situations: Understanding Students' Perspective' (1995) 15 *For the Learning of Mathematics* 39, 39.

[20] *Tzortzis v Monark Line A/B* [1968] 1 WLR 406, accepting the principle derived from the maxim *qui elegit judicem eligit jus* (s/he who chooses the judge, chooses the law).

[21] See, eg *Compagnie Tunisienne de Navigation SA v Compagnie d'Armement Maritime SA* (1970) [1970] All ER 71 (per Lord Morris); see also Ian Brownlie, 'Decisions of British Courts During 1969–1970 involving Questions of Public or Private International Law' (1970) 44 *British Yearbook of International Law* 213, 221. This treatment of a choice of forum as an indicium of intention regarding the choice of governing law is shared by the legislative provisions elaborated in more civil law dominated jurisdictions, see Regulation (EC) No 593/2008 of the European Parliament and of the Council of 17 June 2008 on the law applicable to contractual obligations (Rome I) 2008, recital 12; and Principles on Choice of Law in International Commercial Contracts 45 (§ 4.11).

[22] See Marshall (n 13) 15 (and authorities cited therein).

to other indicia of the relevant intention, it was effectively downgraded from a presumption to a mere indicium of party-intention as to governing law.

Not only have presumptions been downgraded to indicia, but mere indicia have also been upgraded to presumptions. The contract law of Commonwealth countries has, for example, upgraded the indicium of the relationship between the parties to two opposing presumptions of the intention to be legally bound. In commercial situations, the parties are presumed to have intended to be legally bound by any promises they make or obligations they undertake, but in family situations they are presumed not to be bound by such promises and obligations.[23] In this case, the role played by the indicium has perhaps been elevated not so much because of the strength of the implication it raises, but because of the crisp dichotomy and corollary practical benefit it offers in the form of a (rebuttable) presumption.

Many indicia can never become rules or presumptions, because they are only ever capable of raising an inference in concert with the consideration of other indicia. For example, if the parties' contract refers to the notion of a resulting trust, this will not be decisive of whether the parties intended to choose English or Australian law to govern their contract. If, however, all related transactions between the parties selected either English or German law, then the reference to resulting trusts would strongly suggest that the parties intended to apply English law to their contract. Indicia of this type must be assessed together with other indicia, either by being thrown into the crucible with other indicia as to the party-intention (as common law judges are comfortable doing) or by being arranged in a flow-chart style legal disposition to be applied carefully, but more mechanically (as codes in some civil law countries require). Features of an interpretative situation that do not reliably imply any particular party-intention, however, do not even merit being thrown into that crucible, because they are in fact not indicia of the relevant intention at all.

We have accordingly clarified that, to infer a party-intention, we should classify the different features of an interpretative situation according to (a) the strength of any implication that they raise and (b) how easily the presence of that feature can conclusively be identified (their crispness/fuzziness). There are effectively three categories. In the context of our search for a treaty term's temporal sense-intention, a particular feature of an interpretative situation may:

(i) raise a *presumption* as to the existence of a (fixed or mobile) temporal sense-intention;
(ii) constitute a *mere indicium* of a (fixed or mobile) temporal sense-intention to be weighed and balanced with other such indicia; or
(iii) function as *neither a presumption nor an indicium* because it does not reliably imply any particular temporal sense-intention.

[23] See Dena Valente, 'Enforcing Promises: Consideration and Intention in the Law of Contract' (LLB Thesis, University of Otago, 2010) 45 – www.otago.ac.nz/law/research/journals/otago036314.pdf (and authorities cited therein).

When we outlined the different features of interpretative situations cited in support of static and dynamic treaty interpretations in chapter 9, we drew some brief conclusions as to the strength of the implication raised by certain features and finished by summarising these in a table. That analysis revealed that there are effectively three features that are candidates for raising presumptions as to a particular temporal sense-intention, with the remainder either constituting mere indicia or something that interpreters seeking to infer the temporal sense-intention need not concern themselves with at all.

III. PRESUMPTIONS – STRONG AND INDEPENDENT INDICATORS OF A PARTICULAR TEMPORAL SENSE-INTENTION

We will be best-served by starting our search for potential presumptions of the temporal sense-intention with the features of interpretative situations that chapter 9 considered most strongly imply either a fixed or mobile sense-intention. Leaving the textual context and definitions of the contested term to a category of their own as the best and primary evidence of the temporal sense-intention, three different features highlighted by the case law and scholarship present themselves for consideration in this regard:

(i) the medium-strong implication that treaty terms that are legal concepts in a regime external to the treaty carry a mobile sense-intention (section 9.III);
(ii) the strong implication that terms used in treaty clauses fixing boundaries between States carry a fixed sense-intention (section 9.V); and
(iii) the medium-strong implication that, whereas a term in a treaty clause establishing a legal situation carries a fixed sense-intention, a term in a treaty clause laying down a legal rule carries a mobile sense-intention (section 9.VIII).

A. The Situation/Rule Distinction is not Sufficiently Clear to be Used as a Presumption

The third-listed feature of an interpretative situation is exactly the kind of feature that is ill-suited to being used as a presumption of a temporal sense-intention. There is undoubtedly a strong correlation between both (a) using a treaty term to establish a legal situation and a fixed sense-intention and (b) using a treaty term to lay down a legal rule and a mobile sense-intention. However, it will often be very difficult to determine whether the treaty term was used to establish a situation or lay down a rule.

The author who first presented the *situation/règle* distinction in this context, Combacau, himself conceded that the determination of ‘whether the authors intended to lay down a rule or constitute an individual legal situation' is not easy.[24] The *Aegean Sea* case demonstrates this difficulty. Greece's reservation excluding 'disputes relating to the territorial status of Greece' could be seen as both establishing a situation and laying down a rule.[25] Unfortunately, this is not a rare situation. In the case of constitutive instruments of international organisations, many treaty terms will establish situations and rules at the same time. Equally, in many jurisdictional declarations, the same clause might be understood as creating a *situation* in terms of consent for dispute situations in the *past* and laying down a *rule* for dispute situations set to arise in the *future*.

In many real-world situations, this distinction, so alluring on account of its apparent simplicity, suddenly starts to look devilishly complex. The setting down, in the context of a boundary delimitation treaty, of a border on the continental shelf or the granting of fishing rights in relation to certain areas would seem to be regarded as acts through which the parties intended to create a legal situation. Yet, we saw that, in a case such as the *Guinea-Bissau/Senegal* arbitration, the parties concluding the treaty may have intended the situation they established to evolve. This means that, at best, the claimed link between legal situations and fixed sense-intentions must be subject to an important qualifier of whether the situation to be established was intended to itself evolve. This, of course, takes us back closer to the inquiry as to the temporal sense-intention that we started with, rendering a focus on whether a rule is lain down or a situation created – which is itself likely to be fiercely contested – of limited practical utility.

There can be little doubt that the *situation/règle* distinction is a valuable meta-principle for understanding the temporal sense-intention associated with a term and that, where a treaty term can be identified as establishing one or the other, this may indicate a fixed or mobile sense-intention. Combacau and Cassell's distinction may accordingly be used as two *indicia* for the temporal sense-intention to be weighed and balanced with other features of interpretative situations that loosely imply a particular sense-intention.[26] Ultimately, however, this distinction lacks the clarity of application that would allow it to be able to be used as a *presumption* in the plan of attack that international adjudicators should adopt in order to determine whether to interpret a treaty term according to its original or later-emerging meaning.

[24] Jean Combacau, 'L'écoulement du temps' in Société Française pour le Droit International (ed), *Le droit international et le temps : colloque de Paris (actes du XXXIVe colloque de la Société Française pour le Droit International)* (Paris, Pedone, 2001) 101–02 (present author's translation).

[25] See *Aegean Sea Continental Shelf (Greece v Turkey)*, Judgment [1978] ICJ Reports 3, 31–33 (§§ 74–79); *Aegean Sea Continental Shelf (Greece v Turkey)*, Dissenting Opinion of Judge de Castro [1978] ICJ Reports 62, 69–71 (§§ 15–18).

[26] See s 10.IV below.

B. Terms Used to Fix a Boundary between States Create a Presumption of a Fixed Sense-Intention

It is, by contrast, relatively easy to determine whether a contested treaty term was used to establish the particular legal situation of a boundary between two or more States. In light of the importance of boundaries, the narrow range of international courts and tribunals capable of determining them and the structure given to international cases by prayers for relief, it is difficult to see how a dispute could emerge over the preliminary question of whether a treaty term was used in the context of fixing such a boundary (rather than how exactly it should be delimited).[27] The presence or absence of this feature of an interpretative situation will almost invariably be clear; it presents precisely the kind of crisp dichotomy from which presumptions of a particular party-intention can be fashioned.

Moreover, the fact that the contested treaty term appears in a clause fixing a boundary between States raises an implication of a fixed sense-intention that is, for the reasons set out above, very strong. The paramount importance of the stability of frontiers principle in such situations makes it safe to infer that the parties concluding the treaty intended that the boundary would not move, and therefore that the semantic-pragmatic content of the terms used to fix that boundary would not change through time.[28]

This feature thereby meets the criteria for being used as a presumption of the relevant party-intention. The presumption effectively operates to apply a fixed sense-intention to any term used to fix a boundary between States, resulting in a static approach being taken to the interpretation of that term if it presents a problem of intertemporal linguistics. Where the contested term does not fix a boundary between States, the inquiry into the temporal sense-intention to be assigned to it continues.

C. Terms Using Legal Concepts from a Regime Outside the Treaty Create a Presumption of a Mobile Sense-Intention

The final feature that emerged from chapter 9's analysis as presenting an at least quite strong implication of a particular temporal sense-intention, the use of a

[27] Even in the difficult case posed by the 1960 agreement interpreted in the Guinea-Bissau/Senegal arbitration, the term 'continental shelf', despite appearing in a clause fixing a boundary between States, itself only fixed the scope of the agreement's application, not the actual boundary between the States, that honour being reserved to the 'prolongation in a straight line, in the same direction, of the boundary of the territorial seas' – see *Case concerning the delimitation of maritime boundary between Guinea-Bissau and Senegal*, Decision of 31 July 1989 (1989) XX RIAA/RSA 119, 150 (§ 80).

[28] See s 9.V above and references therein.

legal concept from a regime external to the treaty, also meets the criteria for being used as a presumption.

First, it presents a relatively crisp dichotomy because it will generally be easy for any interpreter of a treaty – particularly an international court or tribunal taken to evidence of how the word was used at the time of the treaty's conclusion – to determine whether or not the drafters of the treaty were invoking a legal concept from an external regime. Indeed, in one of the most important international decisions touching on the Problem, the *Guinea-Bissau/Senegal* tribunal gave a mobile meaning to the term 'continental shelf' in the treaty of 1960, which it determined already had a known legal content in the 1958 Geneva Conventions, but refused Senegal's request that it dynamically interpret a clause that Senegal considered referred to the exclusive economic zone – a legal notion that the tribunal determined had only become an accepted part of international law in 1982, well after the conclusion of the treaty being interpreted.[29]

Second, as indicated by the case law addressing the Problem where such terms were at issue, it is relatively safe to infer from the use of a legal concept as a treaty term that, all other things being equal, the parties wanted the meaning of that term to follow its evolution in the external regime impliedly referred to, thereby investing the term with semantic mobility.[30]

We can therefore propose that, where interpreters are faced with relevant semantic change to a treaty term that is a legal concept that had (at the time of the treaty's conclusion) a meaning in a regime outside of the treaty, they should apply a mobile sense-intention to it, leading to a dynamic approach to the problem of intertemporal linguistics.

D. Putting the Two Competing Presumptions in the Right Order

The last-mentioned presumption arising from the use of legal concepts from an external regime obviously points in the opposite direction and produces a diametrically opposed outcome to the first presumption raised by the use of a contested treaty term to fix a boundary between States. It is, moreover, quite possible – even probable – that the two presumptions will be raised by the same treaty term. If we are to build a workable method for solving the Problem, we must therefore place these two competing presumptions in the appropriate order.

[29] *Guinea-Bissau/Senegal*, Award (n 27) 151–52 (§§ 84–85).
[30] See s 9.III above and references therein.

We have already seen that the term 'continental shelf' is used in many treaties and has been interpreted by many international courts and tribunals, including in situations where its semantic content had changed between the time of the relevant treaty's conclusion and the time of its application. We saw, in addition, that international courts and tribunals have sometimes employed a static approach and sometimes a dynamic approach when interpreting the term 'continental shelf'. In the 1989 *Guinea-Bissau/Senegal* award, an illustrious panel of three international lawyers effectively applied a mobile sense-intention to the use of this term,[31] while in the 1993 *Jan Mayen* judgment, the ICJ effectively gave 'continental shelf' a static interpretation.[32]

It appears to the present author that both of our two presumptions applied in the latter case, but not the former. In the *Jan Mayen* situation, Norway's (Jan Mayen's) and Denmark's (Greenland's) continental shelves overlapped,[33] so the judgment's interpretation of 'continental shelf' determined the rights *as between* the parties. In the *Guinea-Bissau/Senegal* case, by contrast, the award's interpretation of 'continental shelf' determined how far the straight line between Guinea-Bissau's and Senegal's respective interests would extend into the high seas,[34] so that term and its interpretation did not determine the rights as between the parties.

Therefore, in the only interpretative situation which presented both features giving rise to the opposed presumptions we have identified, the *Jan Mayen* case, the ICJ gave a clear priority to the presumption that a term fixing a boundary between two or more States carries a fixed sense-intention and should therefore be interpreted using the static approach to the Problem.

While one should be careful not to draw conclusions from a restricted sample of case law, the position implied by the one key difference between these two diametrically opposed decisions can be followed on the basis that it accords with common-sense. In chapter 9, we noted the critical importance of the stability of frontiers principle and characterised the presumption of a fixed sense-intention arising from it as stronger than the presumption of a mobile sense-intention arising from the use of a legal concept. It is not only consistent with the case law, but also inherently logical that, where both apply, the fixing boundaries presumption should be privileged over the legal concept presumption.

[31] *Guinea-Bissau/Senegal*, Award (n 27) 152 (§ 85).

[32] *Maritime Delimitation in the Area between Greenland and Jan Mayen (Denmark v Norway)*, Judgment [1993] ICJ Reports 38, 50–52 (§§ 26–30).

[33] See the map in Nuno Sérgio Marques Antunes, *Estoppel, Acquiescence and Recognition in Territorial and Boundary Dispute Settlement* (Durham, International Boundaries Research Unit, 1999) 28 (Fig 8).

[34] See the map in Masahiro Miyoshi, *The Joint Development of Offshore Oil and Gas in Relation to Maritime Boundary Delimitation* (Durham, International Boundaries Research Unit, 1999) 37 (Fig 13).

The next part of our flowcharted solution to problems of intertemporal linguistics can accordingly be presented as shown in Figure 16.

Figure 16 Chart for Inferring the Temporal Sense-Intention – Presumptions

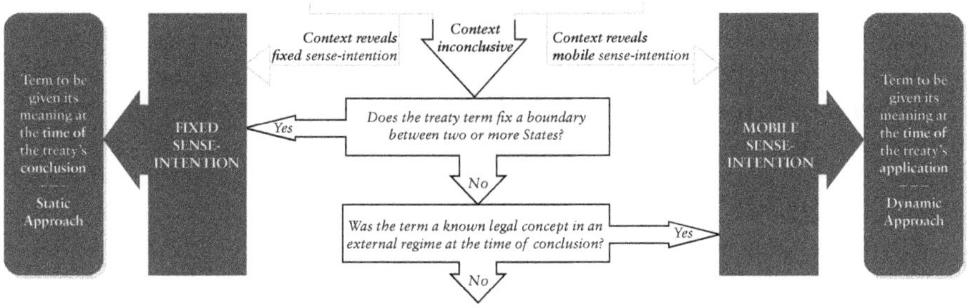

IV. MERE INDICIA – INDICATORS THAT TAKEN TOGETHER MAY CLEARLY IMPLY A FIXED OR MOBILE SENSE-INTENTION

All of the features of interpretative situations that chapter 9 concluded imply – more than only weakly – a particular sense-intention, but which cannot be used to create presumptions, should nonetheless be considered as indicia of the temporal sense-intention. These include:

- the implication of a mobile sense-intention where there is evidence of the parties having been aware that the contested treaty term would be likely to undergo semantic change after the conclusion of the treaty (see section 9.II);
- the implication of a mobile sense-intention where the contested treaty term is used to commit a State to a certain standard of conduct (see section 9.IV);
- the implication of a fixed sense-intention where the contested treaty term appears in a treaty of short and fixed duration (see section 9.VI); and, as initially discussed as a potential presumption above,
- the implication of fixed and mobile sense-intentions respectively where the contested treaty term establishes a legal situation or lays down a legal rule (see section 9.VIII).

Since none of these indicia rise to the level of presumptions, they should not be considered in any order or priority, but simply considered together as part of a general inquiry into whether, on balance, there is a clear implication that the contested treaty term was used with a fixed or mobile sense-intention. In circumstances where the implication raised by all of them is not particularly strong, it would simply not be appropriate to give one or more of them priority over the others.

Moreover, such weighing and balancing, an exercise well-known to international lawyers generally, and even treaty interpreters specifically, ensures that due account can be taken of the differing strengths of the implications that may be presented by the same interpretative feature in different cases. For example, if there is strong direct evidence that the parties concluding the treaty had adverted to the possibility that the meaning of the treaty term they were using would change through time, it would be appropriate, in the absence of strong evidence of any other countervailing indicia, to conclude that the term was used with a mobile sense-intention. In addition, the weighing exercise ensures that if there is an overwhelming prevalence of the features implying, for example, a mobile sense-intention, and no feature implying a fixed sense-intention, then it will be safe to conclude that the parties attached a mobile sense-intention to the contested treaty term.

Finally, treating these features as indicia to be weighed against each other – rather than as presumptions that definitively assign either a fixed or mobile sense-intention – leaves open the possibility of a conclusion that neither temporal sense-intention clearly arises on balance from an assessment of all of the different interpretative features from which one might reliably be inferred. While this may appear to undermine this study's quest for a workable solution to every real-world problem of intertemporal linguistics, it actually helps us find it. Indeed, as will now be seen, much of the strength of the method proposed in these pages can be derived from the relative certainty of the outcome that its application will produce. This certainty is not undermined by a method which only allows mere indicia of the temporal sense-intention to decide between the original and later-emerging meaning where, on balance, they clearly imply a fixed or mobile sense-intention. It would, however, be undermined if even more borderline and therefore less predictable outcomes of that weighing-of-indicia exercise were permitted to decide the matter.

In its schematic form, the proposed method therefore presents these indicia together and unordered in one box representing the weighing exercise, from which three potential outcomes are possible: (i) a fixed sense-intention and static

Figure 17 Chart for Inferring the Temporal Sense-Intention – Mere Indicia

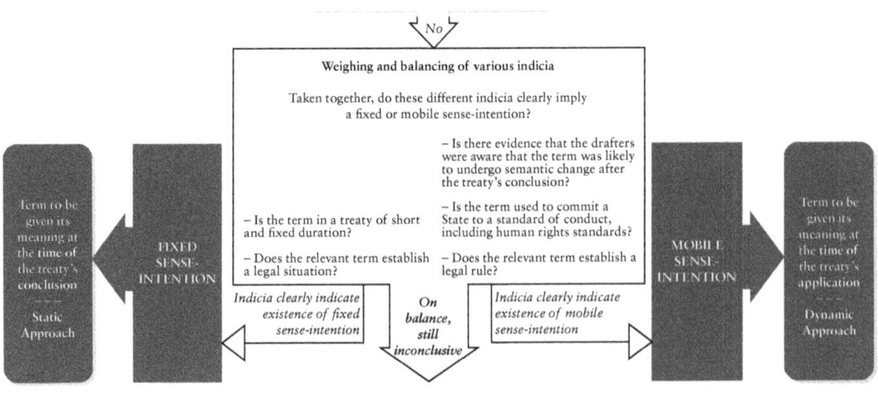

approach to the Problem; (ii) a mobile sense-intention and dynamic approach to the problem; and (iii) an ongoing inconclusiveness as to the temporal sense-intention that leaves the problem to be solved by other considerations – as represented by the three different arrows emerging from the bottom of the central box in Figure 17.

V. TWIN PRESUMPTIONS OF LAST RESORT – USING THE NUMBER OF TREATY PARTIES

There are unfortunately many cases in which an interpretative situation presents a problem of intertemporal linguistics, but none of the features from which a particular temporal sense-intention may be inferred. One can, for example, easily imagine a case in which the contested treaty term is not defined, nor used to fix a boundary, is not a legal concept, nor used to commit a State to a legal standard. It will, in addition, often be difficult to determine whether or not the treaty establishes a legal situation or lays down a legal rule and potentially even whether the treaty can be deemed to be of a short and fixed duration. In such situations, an interpreter will not be able to reliably infer that the parties held a particular temporal sense-intention in relation to the contested treaty term.

A. Imputing Party-intention as a Last Resort

Yet we need not lose hope when reliable evidence of the type of party-intention that we are looking for 'runs out'. As the private law analogies discussed above also reveal, it can be also be appropriate for the law to *assign* the parties an intention in such circumstances. At some point on the scale from proximate and strong indicia of party-intention to features of a situation only very loosely related to that intention, legal reasoning crosses a fuzzy line between logically inferring a tacit party-intention and objectively assigning an intention to the parties that was most likely not even tacit.

However, we should not lose sight of the fact that adjudicators who assign – or *impute* – a particular intention to the parties are doing something very different to adjudicators who *infer* a party-intention. In a different private law context again, Lord Neuberger of the United Kingdom's House of Lords elegantly summed up the difference between an inferred and imputed intention by saying:

> An *inferred intention* is one which is objectively deduced to be the subjective actual intention of the parties, in the light of their actions and statements. An *imputed intention* is one which is attributed to the parties, even though no such actual intention can be deduced from their actions and statements, and even though they had no

> such intention. *Imputation* involves concluding what the parties would have intended, whereas *inference* involves concluding what they did intend.[35]

In the terms used by Landbrecht and Wehowsky in the context of consent in international commercial arbitration, the inferred party-intention is 'actual', whereas the imputed party-intention is 'fictitious'.[36]

It is also critical to note the corollary point that, when inferring intention, an adjudicator acts on the basis of evidence and logical deduction (or induction), whereas an adjudicator imputing intention must generally appeal to policy considerations.

Moreover, it will generally only be appropriate to resort to imputing party-intention, including on policy bases, where it is clear that the particular type of party-intention cannot be reliably inferred. In a contest between the actual intention of the parties and an intention constructed by the adjudicator where none existed at the time, the inferred but actual intention must always prevail. In this regard it is notable that, under the *Rome I* system of European private international law, a presumption as to the governing law can only be used where it is established that the parties neither expressly nor impliedly chose a governing law themselves.[37]

For interpreters searching in vain for features from which they can infer the temporal sense-intention that would help them resolve a problem of intertemporal linguistics, there is an obvious practical benefit in being able to impute a fixed or mobile sense-intention on some other basis. Moreover, because the temporal sense-intention would only be assigned by the interpreter as a last resort, a presumption can still be used without, as French feared, contradicting the actual sense-intention of the parties to the treaty.[38]

However, there still needs to be some basis, even if only a policy basis, for assigning a particular temporal sense-intention to a contested and semantically changing treaty term. Somewhat fortuitously, the analysis in chapter 9 revealed that one of the features of an interpretative situation sometimes cited in support of static or dynamic approaches to the Problem more obviously draws its justificatory force from policy than from inference. Indeed, many of the international lawyers contending that *multilateral treaties* should be interpreted dynamically speak in terms redolent of policy. Bernhardt, for example, characterised this situation as the one where the '*need* of evolutive treaty interpretations' is greatest.[39] Malgosia Fitzmaurice, for her part, not only spoke

[35] *Stack v Dowden* (2007) [2007] UHKL 17 (§ 126) (emphasis added).

[36] Johannes Landbrecht and Andreas Wehowsky, 'Determining the Law Applicable to the Personal Scope of Arbitration Agreements and its "Extension"' (2017) 35 *ASA Bulletin* 837, 841.

[37] Regulation (EC) No 593/2008 of the European Parliament and of the Council of 17 June 2008 on the law applicable to contractual obligations (Rome I), art 4(1).

[38] French (n 18) 296–97, see further above s 10.II.B.

[39] Rudolf Bernhardt, 'Evolutive Treaty Interpretation, Especially of the European Convention on Human Rights' (1999) 42 *German Yearbook of International Law* 11, 17 (emphasis added).

about dynamism being 'necessary' in the interpretation of such treaties, but also explained why, clearly invoking a policy basis when she said that '[i]t is incontrovertible such dynamism in treaty interpretation is *required* in order to account for the practice of States Parties to treaties and the organs of the international organizations'.[40]

B. The Trade-off that Permits Weakly-justified Imputations for Practical Reasons

It is submitted that the argument that multilateral treaties presenting a problem of intertemporal linguistics should be interpreted according to the dynamic approach invokes the same policy basis as that used to argue that large multilateral treaties should be interpreted flexibly and in light of subsequent practice. This has been recently stated explicitly by Nolte,[41] but goes at least as far back as 1964, when de Luna said in an ILC Law of Treaties debate that subsequent practice may even be permitted to 'in effect amend[] the instruments concerned' and that '[n]othing said in the draft articles on interpretation should be capable in any way of preventing that progressive development within international organizations'.[42] The resolution, by subsequent conduct, of the practical problem Article 27 of the UN Charter posed for the operation of the Security Council in the Cold War era provides a well-known and striking example of this accepted phenomenon. It reveals, moreover, that the justification for permitting it lies in the realm of international policy, the underlying concern being to avoid the paralysis of important international regimes. It is but a very small step from this policy-based argument to the policy-based argument related to the Problem and invoked by many authors including Bernhardt and Malgosia Fitzmaurice, pursuant to which the international legal system should not allow large multilateral treaties, such as constitutive instruments and human rights treaties, to fall out-of-step with the legal, political, moral and social realities of the world in which they need to be applied. The argument may often be made in the context of a wider claim more obviously advocating evolutionary interpretation *qua* progressive adjudication, but it nonetheless includes the claim that the authors also intended the language they used to evolve.

[40] Malgosia Fitzmaurice, 'Dynamic (Evolutive) Interpretation of Treaties and the European Court of Human Rights' in Alexander Orakhelashvili and Sarah Williams (eds), *40 Years of the Vienna Convention on the Law of Treaties* (London, British Institute of International and Comparative Law, 2010) 55 (emphasis added).

[41] International Law Commission and Georg Nolte, 'Introductory Report for the Study Group on Treaties over Time: Jurisprudence of the International Court of Justice and arbitral tribunals of ad hoc jurisdiction relating to subsequent agreements and subsequent practice' in Georg Nolte (ed), *Treaties and Subsequent Practice* (Oxford, Oxford University Press, 2013) 183.

[42] International Law Commission, 'Yearbook 1964, vol I' (New York, United Nations, 1965) 285 (per de Luna, 766th meeting – 15 July 1964, § 39).

The argument that multilateral treaties should be interpreted dynamically rests on the same three premises:

(i) that these instruments need to be updated;
(ii) that the parties will not themselves be able to update them (to the extent required or desired); and
(iii) that accepting the subset of changes that impact on the semantic content of a treaty term will usually advance, at least to some extent, the policy objective of ensuring that the treaty is able to remain in-step with modern legal, political, moral and social views.

While some multilateral treaties will be easy enough to amend, as a class of treaty they are on the whole much more difficult to amend – or escape and replace – than bilateral treaties (or, of course, unilateral declarations). As noted by Ginsburg: 'In multilateral settings, … [m]ultiple parties typically do not build easy amendment into the treaty design, and the more parties involved the more difficult any amendments will be to conclude'.[43] In the present author's view, it is the difficulty of amending a treaty that lies at the basis of many calls to interpret treaties more flexibly, more teleologically, in light of subsequent practice, using relevant rules of international law and, of course, more dynamically in the narrower sense of the problem of intertemporal linguistics. The apparent futility of now attempting to amend large multilateral treaties including the United Nations Charter and WTO Agreement has increased pressure on international adjudicators to ensure they move with the times, including by acknowledging changes that are reflected in semantic changes to the terms of treaties. Adjudicators interpreting and applying a unilateral declaration or even a bilateral agreement can usually leave that updating task to the parties if they wish but, where there is no prospect of any party amendment, something effectively constituting an adjudicatory amendment appears more justifiable. There is accordingly a relatively strong policy basis for making multilateral treaties more open to *judicially-sanctioned* – rather than *State-actioned* – development than bilateral treaties and unilateral declarations. In other words, there is a policy basis for imputing a mobile sense-intention to treaty terms within multilateral treaties that are difficult to amend.

The key question then becomes whether such a policy-based imputation of temporal sense-intention can and should be built into our proposed method for solving the problem of intertemporal linguistics. The situations in which sound policy strongly suggests that a mobile sense-intention should be imputed are quite exceptional and difficult to identify. A multilateral treaty regime with many parties may be structured in such a way that it is relatively easy to amend or at least update, with multilateral environmental protection regimes made

[43] Tom Ginsburg, 'Bounded Discretion in International Judicial Lawmaking' (2004) 45 *Virginia Journal of International Law* 631, 661.

up of framework conventions and protocols providing an example – a point adroitly made by Georgopoulos.[44] On the other side of the equation, some bilateral treaties may, on account of geopolitical developments, have become nearly impossible to amend.

Evidently, the number of parties to a treaty does not raise strong enough presumptions to indicate a particular sense-intention in the manner of the fixing boundaries and legal concept presumptions outlined above, or even the different indicia to be considered in the weighing exercise. The number-of-parties imputation is not only policy-based, but relatively weak. This feature of an interpretative situation should therefore only be considered germane to whether the treaty term should be interpreted using a static or dynamic approach where there is no other way of resolving the relevant ambiguity between its original and relevantly different later-emerging meaning. In other words, the number of parties to a treaty should only be used to solve a problem of intertemporal linguistics as a last resort.

We noted above that, in any case, party-intention should only be imputed – rather than inferred – where all else fails and also that there will necessarily be some extra approximation in the reasoning behind a policy-based presumption of last resort. Indeed, when imputing a default intention, the law is effectively using the immense practical benefits of not leaving the matter unresolved to compensate for any weaknesses in the making of such a general presumption.

The so-called rules of treaty interpretation in the VCLT themselves accept such a trade-off when, in the analogous situation of ambiguity between ordinary and special meaning, they impose a default presumption that a treaty term's ordinary meaning be used. In certain situations, such as for quite technical terms or in specialised treaties, there is an artificiality to this default position. However, because it effectively operates only where there is no evidence of a special meaning being intended, there is little risk that it will operate to pervert the terms of the parties' bargain.

In the world of private international law, *Rome I*'s last-resort rule that the 'the contract shall be governed by the law of the country with which it is most closely connected'[45] is similarly broad-brush and logically quite unsatisfactory, yet justified by its immense practical utility.

The presence of such default rules means that courts and tribunals can almost always identify the intention the law needs them to be able to identify and ensures that the interpretation and application of the law is not left paralysed by the difficulty of identifying a party-intention. Moreover, because the parties remain free to contract out of such an imputed choice, presumptions of last

[44] Théodore Georgopoulos, 'Le droit intemporel et les dispositions conventionnelles évolutives: quelle thérapie contre la vieillesse des traités?' (2004) 108 *Revue générale de droit international public* 123, 136.

[45] Regulation (EC) No 593/2008 of the European Parliament and of the Council of 17 June 2008 on the law applicable to contractual obligations (Rome I), art 4.

resort are not overly paternalistic. Indeed, if such presumptions are clearly expressed with a clear scope of application and are widely understood, their recognition will ultimately do more to help than hinder parties negotiating and applying treaties.

C. Minimum Criteria for Presumptions of Last Resort

In terms of the necessary criteria that a last-resort presumption must fulfil, it follows from the practical considerations that justify resorting to such a presumption that it must, *first*, cover the whole range of possible situations. While presumptions that only apply in a small group of cases have limited utility, those that provide a solution in each and every case are extremely useful. In most cases this will be achieved by a general rebuttable presumption or clearly defined alternatives, with one consideration pointing in one direction and another consideration pointing in the other.

Second, where there is more than one presumption built into the frame, it is essential that their bounds do not overlap at all. If there is situation where a treaty term can be both an X and a Y, with an X requiring the presumption of a fixed temporal intention and a Y requiring the presumption of a mobile sense-intention, the existence of an X-and-Y-situation causes the whole last-resort presumption mechanism to break down. This means that what we are looking for in our last-resort presumption is not only the *crispness* that all presumptions require, but also a 'true dichotomy', a pair of notions that are jointly exhaustive of the whole treaty category, but mutually exclusive.[46]

The special and ordinary meaning concepts in VCLT Article 31 provide a good example of a true dichotomy. In the context of a particular treaty term, there is no meaning that is neither special nor ordinary and also no meaning that is both special and ordinary; the two concepts are, it can safely be said, both jointly exhaustive and mutually exclusive. As Kammerhofer has noted, Article 31(4) effectively provides that 'if the drafters of a treaty used a word, they are presumed to have intended its "ordinary" meaning, unless they specified a "special meaning"'.[47]

A default general presumption in favour of the meaning of a treaty term at the time of its application (or alternatively at the time of its conclusion) would also meet these criteria and produce a practical solution to a problem of ambiguity in the same way that VCLT Article 31(4) does. Some even seem to have suggested a default presumption in the context of the Problem. Tsuruoka, for

[46] The word 'dichotomy' can be used in a strict sense pursuant to which 'false dichotomy' is opposed to a 'dichotomy', rather than a subcategory of it. This book uses the expression 'true dichotomy' to emphasise the distinction with false dichotomies and avoid any possible confusion.

[47] Kammerhofer (n 2) 90.

example, appears to nominate the fixed sense of a treaty term as the default sense in all situations of semantic change arising from a change in the law:

> If the interpretation showed that the parties had wished to follow the evolution of international law, it was international law at the time when the treaty was interpreted which prevailed. Otherwise, it was the implied will of the parties at the time when the treaty was concluded that should be applied.[48]

However, as chapter 6 of this study revealed, the post-VCLT authorities on the problem of intertemporal linguistics are simply too mixed to allow for a general presumption of this type. This is especially clear when one reviews the practice of different sub-systems of international law and goes to the effort of determining what position the different adjudicators ultimately took on whether to use a treaty term's original or later-emerging meaning. Moreover, despite the broad statement of the *Iron Rhine* tribunal that the dynamic approach has become entrenched, there is no compelling and authoritative statement that international lawyers as a whole, across all fields of international law, generally favour one approach over the other. Indeed, one post-*Iron Rhine* text even posits the diametrically opposed conclusion, Dörr and Schmalenbach saying in 2012 that 'international judicial practice … on the whole … seems to follow the static approach as a basic rule'.[49] Finally, there would appear to be no sound policy reasons in favour of a generally static or a generally dynamic approach, as there are, for example, in favour of a general preference for ordinary over special meaning.

It would, it is submitted, be far more appropriate to resort to a policy-based presumption of the temporal sense-intention based on the number of parties to a treaty, the weaknesses of that imputation notwithstanding. It is simply necessary that this feature of an interpretative situation can be expressed in a fashion that meets the criteria for last-resort presumptions: it must present a crisp and true dichotomy.

The number of parties to a treaty is inherently quantised, so a clear and non-fuzzy line can be drawn between multilateral treaties (for which the authorities suggest a mobile sense-intention should be presumed) and bilateral treaties (for which authorities including the recent investment awards handed down by Pierre-Marie Dupuy suggest a fixed sense-intention should be presumed). By drawing that line between two and three parties, we are effectively imputing a fixed sense-intention to unilateral declarations. Again, while this does not seem proper from the perspective of making an inference of an actual party-intention, it is certainly not inappropriate either and attracts enough support from the policy considerations associated with ease of amendment to clear the low hurdle

[48] ILC Yearbook 1964, vol I (n 42) 36–37 (per Tsuruoka, 729th meeting – 22 May 1964, § 24).

[49] Oliver Dörr and Kirsten Schmalenbach, 'Article 31. General Rule of Interpretation' in Oliver Dörr and Kirsten Schmalenbach (eds), *Vienna Convention on the Law of Treaties: A Commentary* (Berlin, Springer, 2012) 533 (§ 24).

for last-resort presumptions. After all, most unilateral declarations made in the context of multilateral regimes can be relatively easily withdrawn or modified, reducing the need for them to be brought into line with the evolution of language, law and social values by the third-party interpreter.

The more difficult problem arises with treaties that had two parties at the time of their conclusion, but may subsequently come to have more than two parties. Should such treaties be treated as bilateral or multilateral for the purposes of our last-resort presumption? Does it matter how many parties the treaty had at the time that it fell to be applied or only at the time that it was concluded? It appears to the present author that, even if a temporal sense-intention is imputed rather than applied, it is still taken to exist only at one particular point in time: the moment of the treaty's *conclusion*. Moreover, for forward-looking practical purposes, it is essential that the drafters of a treaty already know, at the time of drafting, whether the default presumption, if it ends up having to apply, will assign a fixed or mobile sense-intention to the treaty's terms. We must accordingly identify, for the purposes of our default presumption, an objective feature of the treaty that is already easily ascertainable at the moment of the treaty's conclusion.

Fortunately, it is well-established that treaties are, at the time of their conclusion, either open or closed, or, more precisely, either fully closed or not fully closed. At the most basic level, treaties are open when they contain a clause allowing for them to be acceded to, closed when they do not, and 'semi-closed' or '*entrouvert*' ('semi-open') when they can be acceded to on certain conditions.[50] A crisp and true dichotomy exists between (i) those which, at the time of their conclusion, can potentially be acceded to by a State which is not a party to it at the time of the treaty's conclusion and (ii) those which cannot be acceded to by any other State under any circumstances (at least not without amendment to the treaty) – the latter being 'fully closed treaties'.

On balance, it seems appropriate, where all else fails, to impute a fixed sense-intention to the terms used in unilateral declarations (even if they are part of a wider treaty regime) and fully closed, bilateral treaties, and to impute a mobile sense-intention to all other treaties. Whether the number of potential parties to the treaty is two or less or three or more is easily and objectively ascertainable at the time that the treaty was concluded and yields an answer for all treaty-making and treaty-making-like acts. It therefore presents a crisp and true dichotomy of two distinct situations that, through valid policy considerations, appropriately allows a particular temporal sense-intention to be assigned where it cannot

[50] See Jean-François Marchi, 'Article 15' in Olivier Corten and Pierre Klein (eds), *The Vienna Conventions on the Law of Treaties: A Commentary* (Oxford, Oxford University Press, 2011) 324–25 (§§ 29–33); Patrick Daillier and others, *Droit international public* 8th edn (Paris, LGDJ, 2009) 192; see also Vincy Fon and Francesco Parisi, 'The Formation of International Treaties' (2007) 3 *Review of Law & Economics* 37, who appear to introduce a further sub-category of treaties that, by allowing accession only upon the approval of the majority of existing signatory States, are neither fully open nor fully closed.

be inferred. These twin presumptions of last resort can be presented diagrammatically as shown in Figure 18.

Figure 18 Chart for Inferring the Temporal Sense-Intention – Twin Presumptions of Last Resort

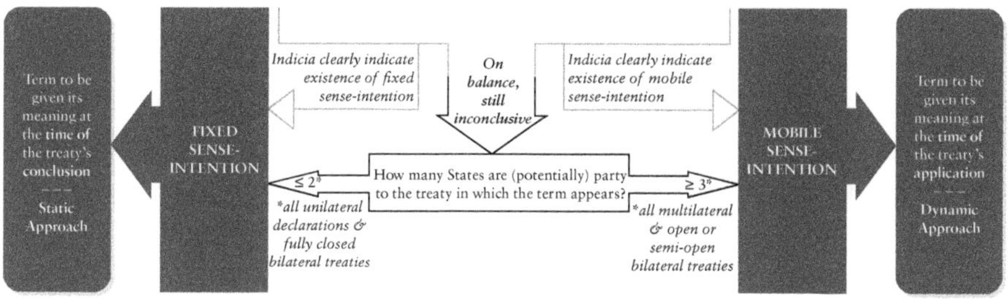

VI. PRACTICAL BENEFITS OF THE PROPOSED METHOD FOR SOLVING THE PROBLEM

With the addition of the twin last-resort presumptions based on the number of potential parties to the treaty in which the contested term appears, this book is able to propose a method for inferring the temporal sense-intention and solving the problem of intemporal linguistics that always results in the selection of either the meaning of the term at the time of the treaty's conclusion or the meaning of the term at the time of the treaty's application. The entire method can be presented most easily as a kind of flow-chart combining all previous steps together, as shown in Figure 19 overleaf.

The practical benefits of such a workable method for appropriately solving the Problem cannot be understated.

From the perspective of interpreters such as adjudicators in international courts and tribunals, this carefully structured sequence of steps for identifying the temporal sense-intention to be assigned to a contested treaty term offers a pathway to a linguistically valid – and legally appropriate – disambiguation of that term. Together with the call to begin the process by disambiguating, the method proposed in this chapter enables treaty interpreters faced with a problem of intertemporal linguistics to avoid the complex and overly flexible rules and principles of treaty interpretation in VCLT Articles 31 and 32 that, being overwhelmingly focused on vagueness, are ill-suited to disambiguating between the competing original and later-emerging senses of a treaty term. Treaty interpreters following the method proposed in these pages need only focus on identifying a specific component of the intention of the parties at the time they concluded the treaty (the temporal sense-intention) and should be able to determine this reliably and appropriately from the features of the interpretative situation before them. Moreover, the relevant court or tribunal could make it clear to the

Figure 19 Chart for Inferring the Temporal Sense-Intention – Complete Method

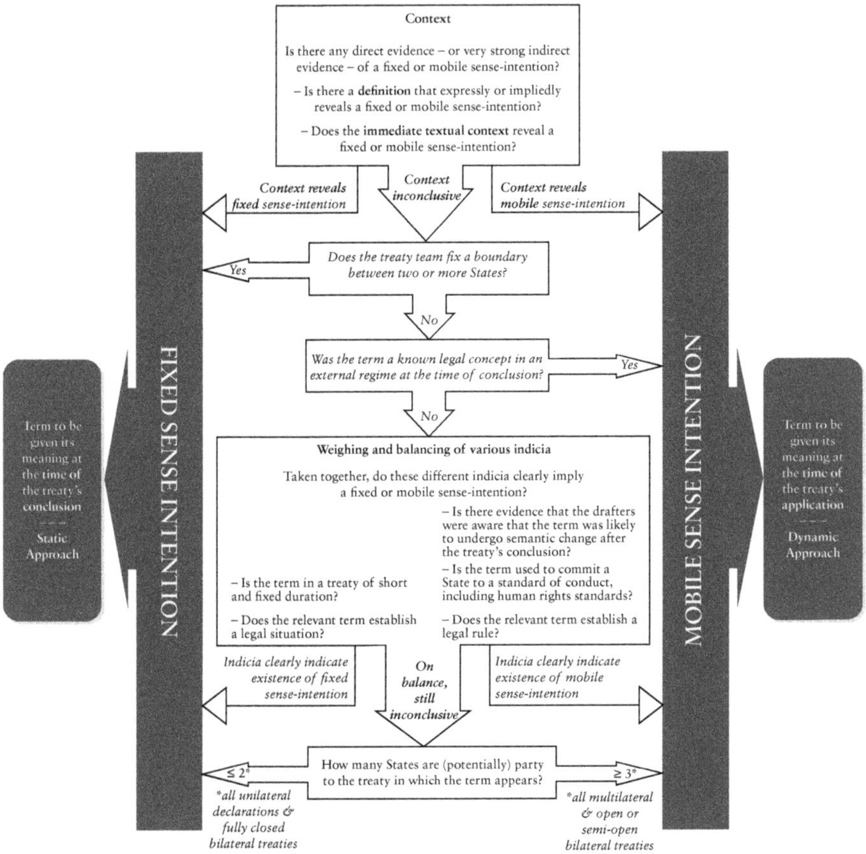

parties that they would follow such a method that always produces a particular result. If they did so, they would then, when applying that method at least to subsequently concluded treaties, only ever do what they warned the States they would do back when those parties had an opportunity to do something about it, thereby rendering themselves immune from the charge that they are denaturing the parties agreement by acknowledging – or refusing to acknowledge – a change to the (semantic) meaning of some of its terms.

From the perspective of the parties to disputes before international courts and tribunals, this proposed method for solving problems of intertemporal linguistics also offers great practical advantages. By ensuring that interpreters do not resort to unstructured and unpredictable applications of interpretative rules that are aimed at the complex task of de-vaguefying treaty terms, they are more likely to receive what all regular litigants generally seek and are entitled to demand: more predictable interpretative outcomes. Indeed, the proposed method ensures that, where a case revolves around the interpretation of a treaty term that has undergone semantic change, its outcome is not left to the vagaries of the wider interpretation process or the values, even whims, of the particular adjudicators.

Part III's proposed method for solving the problem of intertemporal linguistics therefore recommends itself not just because it is consistent with approaches that the most conceptually astute practitioners and scholars of linguistics and international law have taken to such problems, but also because it presents undeniable practical benefits for all the members of the international community most likely to come face-to-face with the Problem.

11

Conclusion

I. SUMMARY

FOR FAR TOO long, the question of whether to give a treaty term its original or later-emerging meaning has been shrouded in conceptual confusion. Attention has instead fallen on two related doctrines – the principle of contemporaneity and evolutionary treaty interpretation – both of which came to be more strongly associated with a distinct debate over whether international courts and tribunals should follow the dictates of legal formalism or instrumentalism. As a result, the very specific issue that Rosenne labelled 'the problem of intertemporal linguistics' half a century ago, has never been specifically addressed, left not only neglected but also unsolved.

Part I of this book sought to refocus attention on the problem of intertemporal linguistics, initially by isolating consideration of it from the related doctrines that have partially obscured it from view, then by using an analytical method to define, as formally and neutrally as possible, the two diametrically opposed approaches that can be taken in response to it.

The conceptual clarity obtained through Part I enabled Part II of the book to cast aside the conventional wisdom surrounding this topic, popular views that developed largely in relation to the structurally and functionally distinct evolutionary treaty interpretation doctrine. It showed that, once our focus is firmly trained on whether the interpreter should assign a treaty term its semantic content at the time of the treaty's conclusion or the time of its application, we must reject both: (i) the view that the VCLT's interpretative rules solve the Problem; and (ii) the view that the post-*Namibia* case law has authoritatively established that a dynamic approach should be applied to any problem of intertemporal linguistics.

Part III was dedicated to formulating a method capable of indicating to interpreters whether they should use the original or relevantly different, later-emerging meaning of a contested treaty term. Recognising that the wide range of international case law and scholarship does not address the Problem with sufficient precision or detail to yield any clear solution to it, Part III turned to related fields of intellectual endeavour in the search for concepts around which the international law material could be re-structured. Leaning most heavily on the field of linguistics so valuable for a study centred on the task of interpretation, it imported and applied the critical distinction between ambiguity and vagueness and determined that the key to solving the Problem lies in the identification of the temporal sense-intention accompanying the contested treaty term. With the help of methods used by cognitive and computational linguistics, as well as areas of private law that infer or impute a party-intention, it then fashioned the various features of interpretative situations that the international case law and scholarship consider relevant to static and dynamic treaty interpretation into a structured, workable and appropriate method for solving the problem of intertemporal linguistics.

II. A PLEA FOR A LESS FLEXIBLE AND MORE LEGALLY CERTAIN SYSTEM OF TREATY INTERPRETATION

By using a quite scientific method, breaking down the interpretative process into functionally distinct constituent parts and drawing conceptual clarity from fields outside of public international law, this book may attract criticism from those accustomed to more classical approaches to the topic of treaty interpretation. In particular, international lawyers who subscribe to the view that 'interpretation is an art, not a science'[1] are likely to consider this book's proposed method for solving the Problem an undue imposition on the enormous flexibility that currently characterises the interpretative process carried out by international courts and tribunals. This view asserts that international courts and tribunals should retain great discretion in their interpretation and application of international law, including the international law that is increasingly found in treaties. It therefore presupposes a particular conception of the appropriate role of the contemporary international adjudicator and, as a corollary, considers the VCLT rules granting international adjudicators such broad interpretative discretion to be completely appropriate. It is notable that the authors of recent books on the temporal aspects of treaty interpretation are careful not

[1] See further, eg Panos Merkouris, 'Interpretation is a Science, is an Art, is a Science' in Malgosia Fitzmaurice, Olufemi Elias and Panos Merkouris (eds), *Treaty Interpretation and the Vienna Convention on the Law of Treaties: 30 Years on* (Leiden, Martinus Nijhoff Publishers, 2010), borrowing from an expression used by the ILC's Law of Treaties commentaries on its 1966 draft articles: International Law Commission, *Yearbook 1966, vol II* (New York, United Nations, 1967) 218, commentary to draft art 28, para 4, and most famously reprised by Sinclair: Ian Sinclair, *The Vienna Convention on the Law of Treaties* (Manchester, Manchester University Press, 1984). See also, eg Alberto Alvarez-Jimenez, 'The International Court of Justice's Use of the Vienna Convention in the Interpretation of Boundary Agreements: 2000–10' (2012) 3 *Journal of International Dispute Settlement* 409, 436; Jan Klabbers, 'On Rationalism in Politics: Interpretation of Treaties and the World Trade Organization' (2005) 74 *Nordic Journal of International Law* 405, 427; Anastasios Gourgourinis, 'The Distinction between Interpretation and Application of Norms in International Adjudication' (2011) 2 *Journal of International Dispute Settlement* 31, 32; Jan Klabbers, 'Virtuous Interpretation' in Malgosia Fitzmaurice, Olufemi Elias and Panos Merkouris (eds), *Treaty Interpretation and the Vienna Convention on the Law of Treaties: 30 Years On* (Leiden, Martinus Nijhoff, 2010) 3.

to undermine and even celebrate both this wide interpretative discretion and the broad, relatively unstructured and therefore very flexible VCLT rules underlying it.[2]

The present author considers that such a broad view of the role of the international adjudicator, while justified in earlier stages of the development of public international law, is no longer appropriate.

Until quite recently, the corpus of international law norms was sparse and patchy, while third-party dispute settlement was a rare, almost exceptional alternative to the political resolution of international disputes. In the years leading up to the 1969 adoption of the VCLT and even beyond that time, international adjudicators remained more focused on developing the still relatively immature international legal system than on predictably and appropriately resolving parties' disputes according to the applicable law. Back when the VCLT was adopted, it was undoubtedly appropriate for its interpretative rules to be cast in broad and flexible terms that would allow international adjudicators to progressively develop international law, including when those adjudicators were interpreting treaties.

However, the last 50 years have seen massive developments, including in fields affecting treaty interpretation. Treaty-making has flourished and third-party international dispute settlement has blossomed. International law now possesses an almost inexhaustible variety of treaties and a range of international dispute settlement bodies that could not even have been dreamt of half a century ago. Third-party international dispute settlement, which was previously focused on helping States alone resolve important geo-political issues, now determines the rights of all sorts of actors, including companies and individuals, frequently in relation to narrow claims under highly specialised treaties. The demands of the parties to international disputes, and therefore the demands on the systems of international dispute settlement and public international law, have changed very markedly. Over the last five decades, the need for the flexibility that allows for the development of international law has substantially decreased, while the need for greater legal certainty has become ever more heightened.

Without a doubt, legal language is, in practice, plagued by substantial uncertainty and legal interpretation – including of treaties – involves considerable complexity. Even a highly developed theory of treaty interpretation therefore needs to afford the interpretative process some flexibility, but it should not leave so much control to such flexible processes that discretion starts to overwhelm the very act of interpretation. There is indeed a real and present risk that, on account of too much flexibility in treaty interpretation, States have started gaining the impression that faithful interpretation of their agreements is being

[2] See, eg Eirik Bjorge, *The Evolutionary Interpretation of Treaties* (Oxford, Oxford University Press, 2014) 188–91; Christian Djeffal, *Static and Evolutive Treaty Interpretation: A Functional Reconstruction* (Cambridge, Cambridge University Press, 2016) 357–58.

ignored in favour of pursuing other objectives. A widespread loss of faith in the interpretative system and, as a corollary, in the process of treaty-making, would have substantial implications for the growth of international cooperation and the strengthening of an international rule of law. Indeed, some State attitudes to the interpretative practices of certain regional courts of human rights already appear to be heading in this dangerous direction, while the increasing bilateralisation of the once highly multilateral trading system has also been exacerbated by such concerns.

In 2019, international law needs a conceptually stronger treaty interpretation system that can cope more easily with the diversity of the modern-day international legal system and meeting the demands of the broad range of actors now depending on international courts and tribunals of one type or another. The time has undoubtedly arrived for fine-tuning the very broad and flexible rules of treaty interpretation and for bringing some greater sophistication to the interpretative process so essential to the development and ongoing appeal of third-party international dispute settlement.

It is only natural that, in a precise area where international law itself has deliberately stayed vague and is characterised by conceptual confusion, efforts to refine its rules must call on the concepts and methods of external, but related fields of intellectual endeavour. Such recourse is particularly worthwhile at a time when the fields related to treaty interpretation, such as legal theory and various sub-fields of linguistics, have recently taken such great strides forward that they now provide a refined conceptual framework with which we can better understand and appropriately develop our own system.

Using teachings from such fields, this book attempts to steer a small part of treaty interpretation away from the very fluid and unpredictable interpretative process that has characterised international adjudication since its inception – a process that was not removed but instead emboldened by the very flexible and compromise-oriented VCLT rules. If one is willing to accept the view that the current international legal system is in greater need of additional certainty than of ongoing flexibility, then the approach and solution to the problem of intertemporal linguistics that is recommended by this book – while far from traditional – should nonetheless constitute a small step towards the necessary development of an important area of contemporary international law.

Appendix – Formal Definitions of Approaches to the Problem

	S1: Static Approach to the Problem	**D1: Dynamic Approach to the Problem**
Common Condition	The meaning of the treaty term at the time of the treaty's conclusion differs from the meaning of the treaty term at the time of the treaty's application. ($x_{\text{t(conclusion)}} \neq x_{\text{t(application)}}$)	
	&	&
Specific Conditions	The interpretation chooses the meaning that the treaty term had at the time of the treaty's conclusion. ($x_{\text{identified}} = x_{\text{t(conclusion)}}$)	The interpretation chooses the meaning that the treaty term had at the time of the treaty's application. ($x_{\text{identified}} = x_{\text{t(application)}}$)

	S2: Static Approach to the Problem	**D2: Dynamic Approach to the Problem**
Common Condition	The semantic-pragmatic content of the treaty term at the time of the treaty's conclusion differs from the semantic-pragmatic content of the treaty term at the time of the treaty's application. ($y_{\text{t(conclusion)}} \neq y_{\text{t(application)}}$)	
	&	&
Specific Conditions	The interpretation chooses the semantic-pragmatic content that the treaty term had at the time of the treaty's conclusion. ($y_{\text{identified}} = y_{\text{t(conclusion)}}$)	The interpretation chooses the semantic-pragmatic content that the treaty term had at the time of the treaty's application. ($y_{\text{identified}} = y_{\text{t(application)}}$)

<table>
<tr><th></th><th>S3: <u>Static</u> Approach to the Problem</th><th>D3: <u>Dynamic</u> Approach to the Problem</th></tr>
<tr><td>Common Condition</td><td colspan="2">The semantic content of the treaty term at the time of the treaty's conclusion differs from the semantic content of the treaty term at the time of the treaty's application.
$(z_{t(conclusion)} \neq z_{t(application)})$</td></tr>
<tr><td></td><td>&</td><td>&</td></tr>
<tr><td>Specific Conditions</td><td>The interpretation identifies a semantic-pragmatic content of the treaty term congruent with the semantic content of the treaty term at the time of the treaty's conclusion.
$(y_{identified} \equiv z_{t(conclusion)})$</td><td>The interpretation identifies a semantic-pragmatic content of the treaty term congruent with the semantic content of the treaty term at the time of the treaty's application.
$(y_{identified} \equiv z_{t(application)})$</td></tr>
<tr><td colspan="3">Where: =: equivalence; ≠: difference; ≡: congruence;
y: semantic-pragmatic content of term; z: semantic content of term</td></tr>
</table>

<table>
<tr><th></th><th>S4: <u>Static</u> Approach to the Problem</th><th>D4: <u>Dynamic</u> Approach to the Problem</th></tr>
<tr><td>Common Condition</td><td colspan="2">The semantic content of the treaty term at the time of the treaty's conclusion relevantly differs from the semantic content of the treaty term at the time of the treaty's application,
$(z_{t(conclusion)} \neq^{*} z_{t(application)})$
meaning that, where these semantic contents take the sets $B_{t(conclusion)}$ and $B_{t(application)}$ respectively, for a relevant C, $(C \in B_{t(conclusion)}$ & $C \notin B_{t(application)})$ OR $(C \notin B_{t(conclusion)}$ & $C \in B_{t(application)})$.</td></tr>
<tr><td></td><td>&</td><td>&</td></tr>
<tr><td>Specific Conditions</td><td>The interpretation identifies a semantic-pragmatic content of the treaty term congruent with the semantic content of the treaty term at the time of the treaty's conclusion.
$(y_{identified} \equiv z_{t(conclusion)})$</td><td>The interpretation identifies a semantic-pragmatic content of the treaty term congruent with the semantic content of the treaty term at the time of the treaty's application.
$(y_{identified} \equiv z_{t(application)})$</td></tr>
<tr><td colspan="3">Where: =: equivalence; ≠: difference; ≡: congruence; ≠*: relevant difference
y: semantic-pragmatic content of term; z: semantic content of term</td></tr>
</table>

Bibliography

Abi-Saab, G, *Cours général de droit international public* (The Hague, Martinus Nijhoff, 1996).

—— 'Fragmentation or Unification: Some Concluding Remarks' (1998) 31 *NYU Journal of International Law and Politics* 919.

A-Khavari, A, 'The Passage of Time in International Environmental Disputes' (2003) 10 *Murdoch University Electronic Journal of Law* 43.

Alvarez-Jimenez, A, 'The International Court of Justice's Use of the Vienna Convention in the Interpretation of Boundary Agreements: 2000–10' (2012) 3 *Journal of International Dispute Settlement* 409.

Aly, S, 'L'"interprétation évolutive" en droit international public' (Mémoire de DEA, Institut universitaire de hautes études internationales, Genève, 1997).

Andenas, M and Bjorge, E, 'Juge national et interprétation évolutive de la Convention européenne des droits de l'homme' (2011) 4 *Revue du droit public et de la science politique en France et à l'etranger* 997.

Antal, L, 'Meaning and its Change' (1964) 2 *Linguistics* 14.

Antunes, NSM, *Estoppel, Acquiescence and Recognition in Territorial and Boundary Dispute Settlement* (Durham, International Boundaries Research Unit, 1999).

Apidianaki, M, 'Acquisition automatique de sens pour la désambiguïsation et la sélection lexicale en traduction' (Doctorat en linguistique, Université Paris-Diderot – Paris VII, 2008).

Arato, J, 'Subsequent Practice and Evolutive Interpretation: Techniques of Treaty Interpretation Over Time and Their Diverse Consequences' (2010) 9 *Law & Practice of International Courts and Tribunals* 443.

Azar, M, 'Transforming Ambiguity into Vagueness in Legal Interpretation' in A Wagner, WG Werner and D Cao (eds), *Interpretation, Law and the Construction of Meaning: Collected Papers on Legal Interpretation in Theory, Adjudication and Political Practice* (Dordrecht, Springer, 2007).

Balkin, JM, 'Framework Originalism and the Living Constitution' (2009) 103 *Northwestern University Law Review* 549.

Barnett, RE, 'Originalism for Nonoriginalists, An' (1999) 45 *Loyola Law Review* 611.

—— 'Interpretation and Construction' (2011) 34 *Harvard Journal of Law and Public Policy* 12.

Beaney, M, 'Analysis' in EN Zalta (ed), *The Stanford Encyclopedia of Philosophy*, Summer 2018 Edition.

Bell, BW, 'Hypnotized by Images of the Past: Dynamic Interpretation and the Flawed Majoritarianism of Statutory Law' (1 November 2002) 2 *Issues in Legal Scholarship*.

Benedek, W, *Die Rechtsordnung des GATT aus völkerrechtlicher Sicht* (Graz, Springer, 1990).

Bernhardt, R, *Die Auslegung völkerrechtlicher Verträge insbesondere in der neueren Rechtsprechung internationaler Gerichte* (Köln, Carl Heymanns Verlag, 1963).

—— 'Homogenität, Kontinuität und Dissonanzen in der Rechtsprechung des Internationalen Gerichtshofs – Eine Fall-Studie zum Südwestafrika/Namibia-Komplex' (1973) 33 *Zeitschrift für ausländisches öffentliches Recht und Völkerrecht* 1.

—— 'Evolutive Treaty Interpretation, Especially of the European Convention on Human Rights' (1999) 42 *German Yearbook of International Law* 11.

Biehler, G, *Procedures in International Law* 1st edn (Berlin, Springer, 2008).

Bjorge, E, *The Evolutionary Interpretation of Treaties* (Oxford, Oxford University Press, 2014).

—— 'The Vienna Rules, Evolutionary Interpretation, and the Intentions of the Parties' in A Bianchi, D Peat and M Windsor (eds), *Interpretation in International Law* (Oxford, Oxford University Press, 2015).

Black, HC, *A Law Dictionary Containing Definitions of the Terms and Phrases of American and English Jurisprudence, Ancient and Modern* 2nd edn (St Paul MN, West Publishing Co, 1910).

Blank, A, *Prinzipien des lexikalischen Bedeutungswandels am Beispiel der romanischen Sprachen* (Tübingen, Niemeyer, 1997).

Bollecker(-Stern), B, 'L'avis consultatif en date du 21 juin 1971 de la Cour internationale de Justice dans l'affaire relative aux conséquences juridiques pour les Etats membres de la présence continue de l'Afrique du Sud en Namibie (Sud-Ouest africain)' (1971) 17 *Annuaire français de droit international* 281.

Bos, M, 'Theory and Practice of Treaty Interpretation (Part I)' (1980) 27 *Netherlands International Law Review* 3.

Böth, K, *Evolutive Auslegung völkerrechtlicher Verträge: Eine Untersuchung zu Voraussetzungen und Grenzen in Anbetracht der Praxis internationaler Streitbeilegungsinstitutionen* (Berlin, Duncker & Humblot, 2013).

Bowett, DW, *United Nations Forces: A Legal Study of United Nations Practice* (London, Stevens, 1964).

Bréal, M, *Essai de sémantique (science des significations)* (Paris, Hachette, 1897).

Brölmann, CM, 'Limits of the Treaty Paradigm' in Matthew Craven and Malgosia Fitzmaurice (eds), *Interrogating the Treaty: Essays in the Contemporary Law of Treaties* (Nijmegen, Wolf Legal Publishers, 2005).

Brown, PM, 'The Interpretation of the General Pact for the Renunciation of War' (1929) 23 *American Journal of International Law* 374.

—— 'The Interpretation of Treaties' (1929) 23 *American Journal of International Law* 819.

Brownlie, I, 'Decisions of British Courts During 1969–1970 involving Questions of Public or Private International Law' (1970) 44 *British Yearbook of International Law* 213.

Buß, T, 'Grenzen der dynamischen Vertragsauslegung im Rahmen der EMRK' (1998) *Die Öffentliche Verwaltung* 323.

Cangelosi, A, 'Language Processing' in MA Arbib and JJ Bonaiuto (eds), *From Neuron to Cognition via Computational Neuroscience* (Cambridge MA, The MIT Press, 2016).

Cannizzaro, E, *The Law of Treaties Beyond the Vienna Convention* (Oxford, Oxford University Press, 2011).

Cantos Gómez, P, *Lexical Ambiguity, Dictionaries and Corpora* (Murcia, Universidad de Murcia, 1996).

Cassella, S, 'Rééquilibrer les effets inéquitables d'une délimitation territoriale : l'arrêt de la Cour internationale de Justice du 13 juillet 2009 dans l'affaire du *Différend relatif à des droits de navigation et des droits connexes (Costa Rica c. Nicaragua)*' (2009) 55 *Annuaire français de droit international* 253.

Chang, Y-T, *The Interpretation of Treaties by Judicial Tribunals* (New York, Columbia University Press, 1933).

Charnovitz, S, 'Exploring the Environmental Exceptions in GATT Article XX' (1991) 25 *Journal of World Trade* 37.

Combacau, J, 'L'écoulement du temps' in Société Française pour le Droit International (ed), *Le droit international et le temps: colloque de Paris (actes du XXXIVe colloque de la Société Française pour le Droit International)* (Paris, Pedone, 2001).

Cook, P and Stevenson, S, 'Automatically Identifying Changes in the Semantic Orientation of Words', Proceedings of the Seventh International Conference on Language Resources and Evaluation ('LREC 2010') (Luxembourg, European language resources distribution agency, 2010).

Corten, O, 'Les techniques reproduites aux articles 31 à 33 des conventions de Vienne: approche objectiviste ou approche volontariste de l'interprétation?' (2011) 115 *Revue génerale de droit international public* 351.

Crystal, D, *A Dictionary of Linguistics and Phonetics* 6th edn (Malden MA, Blackwell Publishers, 2008).

D'Amato, A, 'The Injustice of Dynamic Statutory Interpretations' (1995) 64 *University of Cincinnati Law Review* 911.

Damrosch, LF, 'Concluding Reflections' in LF Damrosch (ed), *Enforcing Restraint: Collective Intervention in Internal Conflicts* (New York, Council on Foreign Relations Press, 1993).

Dawidowicz, M, 'The Effect of the Passage of Time on the Interpretation of Treaties: Some Reflections on Costa Rica v. Nicaragua' (2011) 24 *Leiden Journal of International Law* 201.

Decker, JF, 'Addressing Vagueness, Ambiguity, and Other Uncertainty in American Criminal Laws' (2002) 80 *Denver University Law Review* 241.

Degan, VD, *L'interpretation des accords en droit international* (The Hague, Martinus Nijhoff, 1963).

Dickerson, FR, *The Interpretation and Application of Statutes* (Boston MA, Little Brown, 1975).

Distefano, G, 'L' interprétation évolutive de la norme internationale' (2011) 115 *Revue génerale de droit international public* 373.

Djeffal, C, *Static and Evolutive Treaty Interpretation: A Functional Reconstruction* (Cambridge, Cambridge University Press, 2016).

do Nascimento e Silva, GE, 'Le facteur temps et les traités' (1977) 154 *Collected Courses of the Hague Academy of International Law* 215.

Dörr, O and Schmalenbach, K, 'Article 31. General Rule of Interpretation' in O Dörr and K Schmalenbach (eds), *Vienna Convention on the Law of Treaties: A Commentary* (Berlin, Springer, 2012).

Duez, P, 'L'interprétation des traités internationaux' (1925) 32 *Revue générale de droit international public* 429.

Dugard, J, 'The Opinion on South-West Africa (Namibia): The Teleologists Triumph' (1971) 88 *The South African Law Journal* 460.

—— *The South West Africa Namibia Dispute: Documents and Scholarly Writings on the Controversy Between South Africa and the United Nations* (Berkeley CA, University of California Press, 1973).

Dupuy, P-M, 'Evolutionary Interpretation of Treaties: Between Memory and Prophecy' in E Cannizzaro (ed), *The Law of Treaties Beyond the Vienna Convention* (Oxford, Oxford University Press, 2011).

Dworkin, R, 'The Arduous Virtue of Fidelity: Originalism, Scalia, Tribe, and Nerve' (1996) 65 *Fordham Law Review* 1249.

Ehrlich, E, 'Judicial Freedom of Decision, its Principles and Objects' in E Bruncken (tr), *Science of Legal Method: Select Essays by Various Authors* (Boston MA, Boston Book Company, 1903).

—— 'Freie Rechtsfindung und freie Rechtswissenschaft' (Leipzig, CL Hirschfeld, 1903).

—— *Grundlegung der Soziologie des Rechts* (München, Duncker & Humblot, 1913).

Ehrlich, L, 'L'interprétation des traités' (1928) 24 *Collected Courses of the Hague Academy of International Law* 1.

Endicott, T, 'Interpretation and Indeterminacy: Comments on Andrei Marmor's Philosophy of Law' (2014) 10 *Jerusalem Review of Legal Studies* 46.

Engelen, FA, *Interpretation of Tax Treaties under International Law: A Study of Articles 31, 32, and 33 of the Vienna Convention on the Law of Treaties and Their Application to Tax Treaties* (Amsterdam, International Bureau of Fiscal Documentation, 2004).

Eskridge, WN, 'Dynamic Statutory Interpretation' (1986) 135 *University of Pennsylvania Law Review* 1479.

—— *Dynamic Statutory Interpretation* (Cambridge MA, Harvard University Press, 1994).

Fachiri, AP, 'Interpretation of Treaties' (1929) 23 *American Journal of International Law* 745.

Falkum, IL, 'The Semantics and Pragmatics of Polysemy: A Relevance-Theoretic Account' (PhD Thesis, University College London, 2011).

Farber, DA, 'Statutory Interpretation and Legislative Supremacy' (1989) 78 *The Georgetown Law Journal* 281.

Feldman, AM, 'Evolving Treaty Obligations: A Proposal for Analyzing Subsequent Practice Derived from WTO Dispute Settlement' (2009) 41 *NYU Journal of International Law and Politics* 655.

Fernández de Casadevante y Romani, C, *Sovereignty and Interpretation of International Norms* (Berlin, Springer, 2007).

Fitzmaurice, G, 'The Law and Procedure of the International Court of Justice: Treaty Interpretation and Certain Other Treaty Points' (1951) 28 *British Year Book of International Law* 1.

—— 'The Law and Procedure of the International Court of Justice, 1951–54: General Principles and Sources of Law' (1953) 30 *British Year Book of International Law* 1.

—— 'The Law and Procedure of the International Court of Justice 1951–4: Treaty Interpretation and Other Treaty Points' (1957) 33 *British Year Book of International Law* 203.

Fitzmaurice, M, 'Dynamic (Evolutive) Interpretation of Treaties, Part I' (2009) *Hague Yearbook of International Law* 101.

—— 'Dynamic (Evolutive) Interpretation of Treaties, Part 2' (2010) *Hague Yearbook of International Law* 3.

—— 'Dynamic (Evolutive) Interpretation of Treaties and the European Court of Human Rights' in A Orakhelashvili and S Williams (eds), *40 Years of the Vienna Convention on the Law of Treaties* (London, British Institute of International and Comparative Law, 2010).

Fitzmaurice, M, Elias, O and Merkouris, P (eds), *Treaty Interpretation and the Vienna Convention on the Law of Treaties: 30 Years On* (Leiden, Martinus Nijhoff Publishers, 2010).

Fon, V and Parisi, F, 'The Formation of International Treaties' (2007) 3 *Review of Law & Economics* 37.

Forowicz, M, *The Reception of International Law in the European Court of Human Rights* (Oxford, Oxford University Press, 2010).

Freeman, S, 'Constructivism, Facts, and Moral Justification' in T Christiano and J Christman (eds), *Contemporary Debates in Political Philosophy* (Malden MA, Wiley-Blackwell, 2009).

French, D, 'Treaty Interpretation and the Incorporation of Extraneous Legal Rules' (2006) 55 *International and Comparative Law Quarterly* 281.

Friedmann, WG, 'The Jurisprudential Implications of the South West Africa Case' (1967) 6 *Columbia Journal of Transnational Law* 1.

Frowein, JA, 'Die evolutive Auslegung der EMRK' in T Marauhn (ed), *Recht, Politik und Rechtspolitik in den internationalen Beziehungen* (Tübingen, Mohr Siebeck, 2005).

Garapon, A, 'Les limites à l'interprétation évolutive de la Convention' (2011) 3 *Revista de Estudos Constitucionais, Hermenêutica e Teoria do Direito* 25.

Gardiner, RK, *Treaty Interpretation* (Oxford, Oxford University Press, 2008).

Geeraerts, D, *Diachronic Prototype Semantics: A Contribution to Historical Lexicology* (Oxford, Oxford University Press, 1997).

Gény, F, *Méthode d'interprétation et sources en droit privé positif: essai critique*, vol 2 (Paris, Librairie générale de droit et de jurisprudence (LGDJ), 1919).

Georgopoulos, T, 'Le droit intemporel et les dispositions conventionnelles évolutives: quelle thérapie contre la vieillesse des traités?' (2004) 108 *Revue générale de droit international public* 123.

Gévaudan, P, 'Klassifikation lexikalischer Entwicklungen: Semantische, morphologische und stratische Filiation' (PhD Thesis, Universität Tübingen, 2002).

Ginsburg, T, 'Bounded Discretion in International Judicial Lawmaking' (2004) 45 *Virginia Journal of International Law* 631.

Goldsworthy, J, 'Originalism in Constitutional Interpretation' (1997) 25 *Federal Law Review* 1.

Gourgourinis, A, 'The Distinction between Interpretation and Application of Norms in International Adjudication' (2011) 2 *Journal of International Dispute Settlement* 31.

Greschek, E, *Die evolutive Auslegung voelkerrechtlicher Vertraege am Beispiel des GATT* (Frankfurt, Peter Lang, 2012).

Grotius, H, *The Rights of War and Peace* (Indianapolis IN, Liberty Fund, 2005).

Harvard Law School and Garner, JW, 'Draft Convention on the Law of Treaties' (1935) 29 *Supplement to the American Journal of International Law* 653.

Haugh, M and Jaszczolt, KM, 'Speaker Intentions and Intentionality' in K Allan and KM Jaszczolt (eds), *The Cambridge Handbook of Pragmatics* (Cambridge, Cambridge University Press, 2012).

Heijnsbergen, PV, *International Legal Protection of Wild Fauna and Flora* (Amsterdam, IOS Press, 1997).

Helmersen, ST, 'Evolutive Treaty Interpretation: Legality, Semantics and Distinctions' (2013) 6 *European Journal of Legal Studies* 127.

Hestermeyer, HP and Grotto, AJ, 'Preamble GATT' in P-T Stoll, R Wolfrum and HP Hestermeyer (eds), *WTO – Trade in Goods* (Leiden, Martinus Nijhoff Publishers, 2011).

Higgins, R, 'The International Court and South West Africa: The Implications of the Judgment' (1966) 42 *International Affairs* 573.

—— 'Some Observations on the Inter-Temporal Rule in International Law' in Jerzy Makarczyk (ed), *Theory of International Law at the Threshold of the 21st century: Essays in Honour of Krzysztof Skubiszewski* (The Hague, Kluwer Law International, 1996).

—— 'Ten Years on the UN Human Rights Committee: Some Thoughts Upon Parting' (1996) 6 *European Human Rights Law Review* 570.

—— 'Time and the Law: International Perspectives on an Old Problem' (1997) 46 *International & Comparative Law Quarterly* 501.

Hobbs, JR, 'Granularity', Proceedings of the 9th International Joint Conference on Artificial Intelligence, vol 1 (San Francisco, Morgan Kaufmann Publishers, 1985).

Hockett, CF, 'Review of "The Principles of Semantics" by Stephen Ullmann' (1959) 61 *American Anthropologist* 158.

Hollmann, WB, 'Semantic Change' in J Culpeper et al (eds), *English Language* (London, Macmillan, 2009).

Horace, *The Epistles, Including the Ars Poetica* (WF Masom and AF Watt trs, London, University Tutorial Press, 1905).

Huang, YT and Snedeker, J, 'Semantic Meaning and Pragmatic Interpretation in 5-Year-Olds: Evidence From Real-Time Spoken Language Comprehension' (2009) 45 *Developmental Psychology* 1723.

Hummer, W, 'Problemas juridico-linguisticos de la dicotomia entre el sentido ordinario y el especial de conceptos convencionales segun la Convencion de Viena sobre el Derecho de los Tratados de 1969' (1975) 28 *Revista Española de Derecho Internacional* 97.

Hyde, CC, 'Judge Anzilotti on the Interpretation of Treaties' (1933) 27 *American Journal of International Law* 502.

Hyde, D, 'Sorites Paradox' in EN Zalta (ed), *The Stanford Encyclopedia of Philosophy*, Winter 2014 Edition.

Ide, N and Véronis, J, 'Word Sense Disambiguation: The State of the Art' (1998) 24 *Computational Linguistics* 2.

Institut de droit international, 'Le problème dit du droit intertemporel dans l'ordre international – Délibérations – Première séance plénière: jeudi 7 août 1975 (matin), Annuaire' (1975) *Annuaire* 339.

—— 'Le problème intertemporel en droit international public – Résolution' (Wiesbaden, 1975).

—— 'The Intertemporal Problem in Public International Law – Resolution' (Wiesbaden, 1975).

Institut de droit international and Sørensen, M, 'Le problème dit du droit intertemporel dans l'ordre international – Rapport provisoire' (12 February 1973) *Annuaire* 1.

International Law Commission, 'Yearbook 1962, vol II' (New York, United Nations, 1964).

—— 'Yearbook 1964, vol II' (New York, United Nations, 1965).

—— 'Yearbook 1966, vol I, pt 1' (New York, United Nations, 1967).

—— 'Yearbook 1966, vol I, pt 2' (New York, United Nations, 1967).

—— 'Yearbook 1966, vol II' (New York, United Nations, 1967).

—— 'Yearbook 2001, vol II, pt 2' (New York, United Nations, 2001).

—— 'Report of the work of the sixtieth session', Supplement No 10, A/63/10 (New York, United Nations 2008).

—— 'Report of the work of the sixty-third session', Supplement No 10, A/66/10, (New York, United Nations, 2011).

—— 'Report of the work of the sixty-fourth session', Supplement No 10, A/67/10 (New York, United Nations, 2012).

—— 'Draft conclusions on subsequent agreements and subsequent practice in relation to the interpretation of treaties, with commentaries', A/73/10 (New York, United Nations, 2018).

International Law Commission and Koskenniemi, M, 'Fragmentation of International Law: Difficulties Arising from Diversification and Expansion of international law' A/CN.4/L.682 (Geneva, United Nations, 2006).

International Law Commission, Mansfield, W and McLachlan, C, 'Study on: "The interpretation of treaties in the light of 'any relevant rules of international law applicable in the relations between the parties' (article 31(3)(c) of the Vienna Convention on the Law of Treaties) in the context of general developments in international law and concerns of the international community"', ILC(LVI)/SG/FTL/CRD.3/Rev 2 (United Nations, 2005).

International Law Commission and Nolte, G, 'Annex I Treaties Over Time in Particular: Subsequent Agreement and Practice' in *Yearbook 2008, vol II, pt 2* (New York, United Nations, 2015).

—— 'Introductory Report for the Study Group on Treaties over Time: Jurisprudence of the International Court of Justice and arbitral tribunals of ad hoc jurisdiction relating to subsequent agreements and subsequent practice' in G Nolte (ed), *Treaties and Subsequent Practice* (Oxford, Oxford University Press, 2013).

—— 'First report on subsequent agreements and subsequent practice in relation to treaty interpretation', A/CN.4/660 (Geneva, United Nations, 2013).

Israel, M, 'Saying Less and Meaning Less' in BJ Birner and G Ward (eds), *Drawing the Boundaries of Meaning: Neo-Gricean Studies in Pragmatics and Semantics in Honor of Laurence R Horn* (Amsterdam, John Benjamins Publishing, 2006).

Jackson, JH, 'History of the General Agreement on Tariffs and Trade' in Rüdiger Wolfrum, Peter-Tobias Stoll and Holger Hestermeyer (eds), *WTO – Trade in Goods* (Leiden, Martinus Nijhoff Publishers, 2011).

Jennings, R, 'The Judicial Function and the Rule of Law in International Relations' in *Le droit international à l'heure de sa codification: études en l'honneur de Roberto Ago*, vol III (Milan, Giuffre, 1987).

Jennings, R and Watts, A (eds), *Oppenheim's International Law*, vol 1, 9th edn (Oxford, Oxford University Press, 2008).

Jiménez de Aréchaga, E, 'International Law in the Past Third of a Century' (1978) 159 *Collected Courses of the Hague Academy of International Law* 1.

Johnson Jr, AM and Taylor, RD, 'Revolutionizing Judicial Interpretation of Charitable Trusts: Applying Relational Contracts and Dynamic Interpretation to Cy Pres and America's Cup Litigation' (1989) 74 *Iowa Law Review* 545.

Kadner Graziano, T, *Comparative Contract Law: Cases, Materials and Exercises* (Basingstoke, Palgrave Macmillan, 2009).

Kammerhofer, J, *Uncertainty in International Law: A Kelsenian Perspective* (London, Routledge, 2011).

Kaur, J and Singh, A, 'A Customized Adaptation of Traditional Lesk Method for Sense Disambiguation of Punjabi Words from Medical Domain' (2015) 3 *International Journal for Research in Applied Science & Engineering Technology* 1045.

Kim, NS, 'Evolving Business and Social Norms and Interpretation Rules: The Need for a Dynamic Approach to Contract Disputes' (2005) 84 *Nebraksa Law Review* 506.

Klabbers, J, 'On Rationalism in Politics: Interpretation of Treaties and the World Trade Organization' (2005) 74 *Nordic Journal of International Law* 405.

—— 'Virtuous Interpretation' in M Fitzmaurice, O Elias and P Merkouris (eds), *Treaty Interpretation and the Vienna Convention on the Law of Treaties: 30 Years On* (Leiden, Martinus Nijhoff, 2010).

Klass, G, 'Intent to Contract' (2009) 95 *Virginia Law Review* 1437.

Klocke, DM, *Erklärungsbewusstsein und Rechtsbindungswille: Willenserklärung und Rechtsgeschäft* (Halle an der Saale, Universitätsverlag Halle-Wittenberg, 2014).

Kluck, N, *Der Wert der Vagheit* (Berlin, Walter de Gruyter, 2014).

Kolb, R, *Case Law on Equitable Maritime Delimitation/Jurisprudence sur les délimitations maritimes selon l'équité: Digest and Commentaries/Répertoire et commentaries* (A Perry tr, The Hague, Martinus Nijhoff Publishers, 2003).

—— *Interprétation et création du droit international: Esquisses d'une herméneutique juridique moderne pour le droit international public* (Bruxelles, Bruylant, 2006).

Lachs, M, 'Some Reflections on the Contribution of the International Court of Justice to the Development of International Law' (1983) 10 *Syracuse Journal of International Law and Commerce* 239.

Landbrecht, J and Wehowsky, A, 'Determining the Law Applicable to the Personal Scope of Arbitration Agreements and its "Extension"' (2017) 35 *ASA Bulletin* 837.

Lauterpacht, H, *The Development of International Law by the International Court* (New York, Praeger, 1958).

Lennard, M, 'Navigating by the Stars: Interpreting the WTO Agreements' (2002) 5 *Journal of International Economic Law* 17.

Letsas, G, *A Theory of Interpretation of the European Convention on Human Rights* (Oxford, Oxford Univ Press, 2007).

—— 'Intentionalism and the Interpretation of the ECHR' in M Fitzmaurice, O Elias and P Merkouris (eds), *Treaty Interpretation and the Vienna Convention on the Law of Treaties: 30 Years On* (Leiden, Martinus Nijhoff Publishers, 2010).

—— 'Strasbourg's Interpretive Ethic: Lessons for the International Lawyer' (2010) 21 *European Journal of International Law* 509.

—— 'The ECHR as a Living Instrument: Its Meaning and Legitimacy' in A Føllesdal, B Peters and G Ulfstein (eds), *Constituting Europe: The European Court of Human Rights in a National, European and Global Context* (Cambridge, Cambridge University Press, 2013).

Lieber, F, *Legal and Political Hermeneutics or Principles of Iinterpretation and Construction in Law and Politics with Remarks on Precedents and Authorities* (Boston MA, Charles C Little and James Brown, 1839).

Linderfalk, U, *On the Interpretation of Treaties* (Dordrecht, Springer, 2007).

—— 'Doing the Right Thing for the Right Reason – Why Dynamic or Static Approaches Should be Taken in the Interpretation of Treaties' (2008) 10 *International Community Law Review* 109.

Marchi, J-F, 'Article 15' in O Corten and P Klein (eds), *The Vienna Conventions on the Law of Treaties: A Commentary* (Oxford, Oxford University Press, 2011).

Markesinis, B and others, *The German Law of Contract: A Comparative Treatise* (Oxford, Hart Publishing, 2006).

Marmor, A, *Interpretation and Legal Theory* 2nd edn (Oxford, Hart Publishing, 2005).

Marshall, BA, 'Reconsidering the Proper Law of the Contract' (2012) 13 *Melbourne Journal of International Law* 505.

Martin, A, 'L'interprétation dite évolutive des termes insérés dans des traités intemationaux. Regards sur un arrêt du Tribunal fédéral suisse' in Université de Neuchâtel, Faculté de droit et des sciences économiques (ed), Jacques-Michel Grossen, *Mélanges en l'honneur de Jacques-Michel Grossen* (Bâle, Helbing & Lichtenhahn, 1992).

Martinez Perez, EJ, 'Las interpretactiones evolutivas de los tratados constitutivos de las organizaciones internacionales: El caso de la OMC' in JM de Faramiñan Gilbert (ed), *Globalización y comercio internacional* (Madrid, AEPDIRI, 2003).

McCaig, R, 'The Further Evolution of the Evolutionary Approach to Treaty Interpretation' (2010) 69 *Cambridge Law Journal* 250.

McDougal, MS, 'The International Law Commission's Draft Articles upon Interpretation: Textuality Redivivus' (1967) 61 *The American Journal of International Law* 992.

McLachlan, C, 'The Principle of Systemic Integration and Article 31(3)(c) of the Vienna Convention' (2005) 54 *International and Comparative Law Quarterly* 279.

McWhinney, E, 'The Time Dimension in International Law, Historical Relativism and Intertemporal Law' in J Makarczyk (ed), *Essays in international law in honour of Judge Manfred Lachs / Etudes de droit international en l'honneur du juge Manfred Lachs* (The Hague, Nijhoff, 1984).
Merkouris, P, 'Interpretation is a Science, is an Art, is a Science' in Malgosia Fitzmaurice, Olufemi Elias and Panos Merkouris (eds), *Treaty Interpretation and the Vienna Convention on the Law of Treaties: 30 Years on* (Leiden, Martinus Nijhoff Publishers, 2010).
—— *Article 31(3)(c) VCLT and the Principle of Systemic Integration: Normative Shadows in Plato's Cave* (Leiden, Brill, 2015).
Milanovic, M, 'The ICJ and Evolutionary Treaty Interpretation' (*EJIL Talk!*, 14 July 2009).
Miller, T, 'Adjusting Sense Representations for Word Sense Disambiguation and Automatic Pun Interpretation' (Doktorarbeit, Technische Universität Darmstadt, 2016).
Mitchell, AD, 'The Legal Basis for Using Principles in WTO Disputes' (2007) 10 *Journal of International Economic Law* 795.
Miyoshi, M, *The Joint Development of Offshore Oil and Gas in Relation to Maritime Boundary Delimitation* (Durham, International Boundaries Research Unit, 1999).
Moore, GE, *Principia Ethica* (Cambridge, Cambridge University Press, 1903).
Mowbray, A, 'The Creativity of the European Court of Human Rights' (2005) 5 *Human Rights Law Review* 57.
Orakhelashvili, A and Williams, S (eds), *40 Years of the Vienna Convention on the Law of Treaties* (London, British Institute of International and Comparative Law, 2010).
Palandt, O and Brudermüller, G, *Palandt Bürgerliches Gesetzbuch: mit Nebengesetzen insbesondere mit Einführungsgesetz* (München, CH Beck, 2017).
Palchetti, P, 'Interpreting "Generic Terms": Between Respect for the Parties' Original Intention and the Identification of the Ordinary Meaning' in N Boschiero et al (eds), *International Courts and the Development of International Law: Essays in Honour of Tullio Treves* (The Hague, Asser Press, 2013).
Pauwelyn, J, 'The Nature of WTO Obligations' (2002) 1 *Jean Monnet Working Papers* 1.
—— *Conflict of Norms in Public International Law: How WTO Law Relates to Other Rules of International Law* (Cambridge, Cambridge University Press, 2003).
Payandeh, M, *Internationales Gemeinschaftsrecht* (Heidelberg, Springer, 2010).
Peel, E and Treitel, GH, *The Law of Contract* (London, Sweet & Maxwell, 2015).
Pellet, A, 'Article 38' in A Zimmermann, C Tomuschat and K Oellers-Frahm (eds), *The Statute of the International Court of Justice: A Commentary* (Oxford, Oxford University Press, 2006).
Petersmann, E-U, 'Internationales Recht und Neue Internationale Wirtschaftsordnung' (1978) 18 *Archiv des Völkerrechts* 17.
Phillimore, R, *Commentaries upon International Law*, vol 2 (Philadelphia PN, T & JW Johnson, 1854).
Pinkal, M, *Logic and Lexicon* (G Simmons tr, Dordrecht, Springer Science+Business Media, 1995).
Poscher, R, 'Ambiguity and Vagueness in Legal Interpretation' in PM Tiersma and LM Solan (eds), *The Oxford Handbook of Language and Law* (Oxford, Oxford University Press, 2012).
Pound, R, 'Courts and Legislation' (1913) 7 *American Political Science Review* 361.
Pufendorf, S, *Of the Law of Nature and Nations* (B Kennett tr, London, J Walthoe, R Wilkin, J and J Bonwicke, S Birt, T Ward, and T Osborne, 1729).
Recanati, F, 'On Defining Communicative Intentions' (1986) 1 *Mind & Language* 213.
Reinhold, S, 'Good Faith in International Law' (2013) 2 *UCL Journal of Law and Jurisprudence* 40.
Reuter, P, *Introduction au droit des traités* 3rd edn (Paris, Presses Universitaires de France, 1995).
Rietiker, D, 'The Principle of "Effectiveness" in the Recent Jurisprudence of the European Court of Human Rights: Its Different Dimensions and Its Consistency with Public International Law – No Need for the Concept of Treaty Sui Generis' (2010) 79 *Nordic Journal of International Law* 245.
Roberts, A, 'Power and Persuasion in Investment Treaty Interpretation: The Dual Role of States' (2010) 104 *The American Journal of International Law* 179.

Rosenne, S, 'The Temporal Application of the Vienna Convention on the Law of Treaties' (1970) 4 *Cornell International Law Journal* 1.

Ross, SF, 'The Location and Limits of Dynamic Statutory Interpretation in Modern Judicial Reasoning' (2002) 2 *Issues in Legal Scholarship*.

Rousseau, CE, *Droit international public* (Paris, Sirey, 1970).

Sato, T, 'An Emerging Doctrine of the Interpretative Framework of Constituent Instruments as the Constitutions of International Organizations' (1993) 21 *Hitotsubashi Journal of Law and Politics* 1.

Sato, T, *Evolving Constitutions of International Organizations: A Critical Analysis of the Interpretative Framework of the Constituent Instruments of International Organizations* (The Hague, Kluwer Law International, 1996).

Scalia, A, *A Matter of Interpretation: Federal Courts and the Law* (Princeton NJ, Princeton University Press, 1997).

Schollendorf, K, *Die Auslegung völkerrechtlicher Verträge in der Spruchpraxis des Appellate Body der Welthandelsorganisation (WTO)* (Berlin, Duncker & Humblot, 2005).

Scott, C, 'Diverse Persuasion(s): From Rhetoric to Representation (and Back Again to Rhetoric) in International Human Rights Interpretation' (2008) 4 *Comparative Research in Law & Political Economy Research Paper* 1.

Secretary-General of the United Nations, 'Survey of International Law in Relation to the Work of Codification of the International Law Commission: Preparatory work within the purview of article 18, paragraph 1, of the of the International Law Commission – Memorandum submitted by the Secretary-General', A/CN.4/1/Rev.1 (New York, United Nations, 1949).

Simma, B, 'Consent: Strains in the Treaty System' in Ronald StJ Macdonald and Douglas M Johnston (eds), *The Structure and Process of International Law: Essays in Legal Philosophy, Doctrine, and Theory* (The Hague, Martinus Nijhoff Publishers, 1983).

Sinclair, I, *The Vienna Convention on the Law of Treaties* (Manchester, Manchester University Press, 1984).

Skoczeń, I, 'Minimal Semantics and Legal Interpretation' (2016) 29 *International Journal for the Semiotics of Law* 615.

Small, SL, Cottrell, GW and Tanenhaus, MK, 'Preface' in Steven L Small, Garrison W Cottrell and Michael K Tanenhaus (eds), *Lexical Ambiguity Resolution: Perspective from Psycholinguistics, Neuropsychology and Artificial Intelligence* (San Mateo CA, Morgan Kaufmann, 1988).

Soames, S, *Philosophical Analysis in the Twentieth Century, Volume 1: The Dawn of Analysis* (Princeton NJ, Princeton University Press, 2005).

—— 'Interpreting Legal Texts: What is, and What is Not, Special About the Law' (2009) 1 *Philosophical Essays* 403.

Solan, LM, 'Vagueness and Ambiguity in Legal Interpretation' in VK Bhatia and others (eds), *Vagueness in Normative Texts*, vol 23 (Bern, Peter Lang, 2005).

Solum, L, 'Legal Theory Lexicon: Formalism & Instrumentalism' (*Legal Theory Blog*, 12 August 2012).

—— 'Legal Theory Lexicon: Vagueness & Ambiguity' (*Legal Theory Blog*, 28 June 2015).

Sorel, J-M, 'Article 31 – Convention de Vienne de 1969' in O Corten and P Klein (eds), *Les conventions de Vienne sur le droit des traités: commentaire article par article*, vol 2 (Bruxelles, Bruylant, 2006).

Sperber, D and Wilson, D, *Relevance: Communication and Cognition* 2nd edn (Oxford, Blackwell, 1995).

Spiermann, O, *International Legal Argument in the Permanent Court of International Justice: The Rise of the International Judiciary* (Cambridge, Cambridge University Press, 2005).

Stern, B, 'Interpretation in International Trade Law' in M Fitzmaurice, O Elias and P Merkouris (eds), *Treaty Interpretation and the Vienna Convention on the Law of Treaties: 30 Years On* (Leiden, Martinus Nijhoff Publishers, 2010).

Stern, G, *Meaning and Change of Meaning* (Bloomington IN, Indiana University Press, 1931).

Sur, S, *L'interprétation en droit international public* (Paris, Pichon Durand-Auzias, 1974).

Swartz, N, 'Definitions, Dictionaries, and Meanings' (*Norman Swartz – From My Notebooks*, 8 November 2010).
Taillard, M-O, 'Beyond Communicative Intention' (2002) 14 *UCL Working Papers in Linguistics* 189.
Thirlway, H, 'The Law and Procedure of the International Court of Justice 1960–1989: Part Three' (1992) 62 *British Yearbook of International Law* 1.
Toufayan, M, 'Human Rights Treaty Interpretation: A Postmodern Account of its Claim to "Speciality"' (2005) 2 *NYU Centre for Human Rights and Global Justice Working Paper*.
Toullier, CBM, *Le droit civil français, suivant l'ordre du code*, vol 6 (Paris, Warée, 1823).
Tzevelekos, VP, 'The Use of Article 31(3)(c) of the VCLT in the Case Law of the ECtHR: An Effective Anti-Fragmentation Tool or a Selective Loophole for the Reinforcement of Human Rights Teleology – Between Evolution and Systemic Integration' (2010) 31 *Michigan Journal of International Law* 621.
Ullmann, S, *The Principles of Semantics* (New York, Philosophical Library, 1957).
UN Conference on the Law of Treaties, 'Official Records, First Session, Vienna' (Vienna, United Nations, 1968).
—— 'Official Records, Second Session, Vienna' (Vienna, United Nations, 1969).
Van Alstine, MP, 'Dynamic Treaty Interpretation' (1998) 146 *University of Pennsylvania Law Review* 687.
Van Damme, I, *Treaty Interpretation by the WTO Appellate Body* (Oxford, Oxford University Press, 2009).
Van Petten, C, 'Lexical Ambiguity Resolution' (2002) 81 *Psychology Review* 867.
Vattel E, de, *Le droit des gens, ou principes de la loi naturelle appliqués à la conduite et aux affaires des nations et des souverains*, vol I (Paris, J-P Aillaud, 1835).
Venzke, I, 'The Role of International Courts as Interpreters and Developers of the Law: Working out the Jurisgenerative Practice of Interpretation' (2011) 34 *Loyola of Los Angeles International and Comparative Law Review* 99.
Villiger, ME, 'Article 31 – General Rule of Interpretation' in ME Villiger, *Commentary on the 1969 Vienna Convention on the Law of Treaties* (Leiden, Martinus Nijhoff Publishers, 2009).
—— 'The 1969 Vienna Convention on the Law of Treaties: 40 Years After' (2011) 344 *Collected Courses of the Hague Academy of International Law* 9.
Villiger, ME, 'The Rules on Interpretation: Misgivings, Misunderstandings, Miscarriage? The "Crucible" Intended by the International Law Commission' in E Cannizzaro (ed), *The Law of Treaties Beyond the Vienna Convention* (Oxford, Oxford University Press, 2011).
Viñuales, JE, *Foreign Investment and the Environment in International Law* (Cambridge, Cambridge University Press, 2012).
Visscher, C de, *Problèmes d'interprétation judiciaire en droit international public* (Paris, Pedone, 1963).
—— *Theory and Reality in Public International Law (Théories et réalités en droit international public)* (PE Corbett tr, New Jersey NJ, Princeton University Press, 1968).
von Jhering, R, *Geist des römischen Rechts auf den verschiedenen Stufen seiner Entwicklung*, vol II, 2nd edn (Leipzig, Breitkopf und Härtel, 1869).
Warbrick, C, 'Coherence and the European Court of Human Rights: The Adjudicative Background to the Soering Case' (1990) 11 *Michigan Journal of International Law* 1073.
Wolff, C, *Jus naturae: methodo scientifica pertractatum*, vol 6 (Halle, Renger, 1746).
World Trade Organization, *WTO Analytical Index: Guide to WTO Law and Practice* (Cambridge, Cambridge University Press, 2012).
Wright, Q, 'The Interpretation of Multilateral Treaties' (1929) 23 *American Journal of International Law* 94.
Wyatt, J, 'An Original or Modern-Day Meaning for Treaty Terms? The Problem of Intertemporal Linguistics in the Case Law of International Courts and Tribunals' (Doctorat en droit, University of Geneva, 2017).
—— 'Chronique de droit international privé australien' (2017) 2 *Journal du droit international (Clunet)* 673.

Yasseen, MK, 'L'interprétation des traités d'après la Convention de Vienne sur le droit des traités' (1976) 151 *Collected Courses of the Hague Academy of International Law* 1.

Zarbiev, F, 'Les règles d'interprétation de la Convention de Vienne sur le Droit des Traités: Un outil d'harmonisation en droit international?' in C Chappuis, B Foëx and T Kadner Graziano (eds), *L'harmonisation internationale du droit* (Genève, Schulthess, 2007).

Index

NB–page locators in *italics* refer to information in figures

www.ingramcontent.com/pod-product-compliance
Ingram Content Group UK Ltd.
Pitfield, Milton Keynes, MK11 3LW, UK
UKHW021910150926
475560UK00003B/285

9 781509 929498